DeLong's GUIDE *to*
Bicycles & Bicycling

FRED DeLONG

DeLong's GUIDE TO Bicycles & Bicycling

THE ART & SCIENCE

Chilton Book Company Radnor, Pennsylvania

LIBRARY OF CONGRESS CATALOGING IN PUBLICATION DATA

DeLong, Fred.
    DeLong's Guide to bicycles & bicycling.

    Includes bibliographical references.
    1. Bicycles and tricycles.   2. Cycling.
I. Title.   II. Title: Guide to bicycles & bicycling.
TL410.D44   796.6   74-4133
ISBN 0-8019-5846-1 *hardbound*
ISBN 0-8019-6686-8 *paperback*

All manufacturers' names and model names should be considered
to be registered trademarks.

AMF Wheel Goods, 2.6
Barre Crafters, 18.1
Bendix Div., 7.43, references.
Bicycle Institute of America, 3.33, 7.44
Calspan Laboratories, 12.18, 12.20, 12.49
Cannondale Corp., 15.11, 15.12
Charles Mead, 18.7
Columbia Mfg Co, 2.15, 2.18, 7.1, 9.15
Dale Knapschaefer, 17.3
Dan Henry, 7.54
David Chaney, 13.3
David Siskind, 1.4, 1.5, 1.7, 1.9, 1.10
Ets Huret et ses Fils, 7.90, 7.91, 7.92, 7.95, 7.96, 7.139
Frank Lopez, 4.1, 4.2, 4.3, 6.10
H. Jasik, 7.21
Harris Dynamics, 11.15
Huffy Corp., 2.5
IPD Corp., 7.74
JCI Industries, 18.2, 18.3, 18.6
Klein Company, 3.37
M. Schroth, 4.4, 4.5
Maeda Industrial Corp., 7.93, 7.94, 7.141

Mel Pinto, 2.10, 2.16, 2.17, 2.20
MMM Company, 13.8, 13.9, 13.10, 13.11
Murray Ohio Mfg Co, 2.1
Original Plastic Bike Corp., 3.32
Phil Wood, 7.14, 7.16, 7.36
R.D. Allen, 18.4, 18.5
Raleigh Industries of America, 2.4
Ron Timmerman, 6.22, 6.31, 7.4, 7.9, 7.15, 7.47
Ross Chain Bike Corp., 1.12, 2.7
Schwinn Bicycle Co, 2.2, 2.3, 2.9, 2.19, 2.21, 3.3, 3.4, 3.5, 3.6, 3.7, 3.8, 3.27, 3.34, 4.6, 4.7, 7.45, 7.112, 8.4, 8.7, 12.18, 12.20, 12.48, 12.49, 18.8
Shimano American Corp., 6.34, 7.18, 7.19, 7.23, 7.24, 7.28, 7.37, 7.72, 7.75, 7.79, 7.82, 7.89, 7.97, 7.98, 7.140
Shinichi Toriyama, 11.4, 11.7
Teledyne Corp., 3.35
TOSRVPHOTO, 1.1, 1.3
Touring Cyclist Shop, 15.9, 15.10
Vic Hershfield, 11.8
West Coast Cycle Supply, 2.8
William Vetter, 1.2, 1.6

3   4   5   6   7   8   9   0   5   4   3   2   1   0   9   8

Preface

Bicycling has emerged as the nation's leading participation sport. Even in this highly motorized country, bicycle sales have passed automobile sales. Yet the potential for increased use is only beginning to be realized. Medical authorities plead for a return to regular exercise to improve the health of our citizens. Widespread use of the bicycle as an alternative to the automobile and the use of public transport for travel to work and school would not only alleviate traffic jams and stifling pollution, it would be an ecologist's dream.

The economy of bicycle purchase and use makes it a fine investment. Its speed and versatility make it an efficient choice for short-range personal transportation. As a vacation and leisure time sport, it has no equal. The bicycle becomes a fascinating friend that anticipates your every whim, carries out your every aspiration, and fulfills wants and needs that lie dormant within you. You, in turn, will learn more about yourself and the tremendous undeveloped potential within you that the bicycle can uncover.

Space-age research techniques and equipment are now being tested on an ever-increasing scale throughout the world to determine the best design and methods of construction for suiting the bicycle to its rider. The simple machine that even a child can ride has been a puzzle of components and relationships that were not completely understood despite a century of study. The human engine, it turns out, is perhaps the least understood. Yet bicycle design should make the best use of the power available from this highly variable source of energy. The major purpose of this guide is to let others share this teamwork of man, machine,

and nature. To develop an all-encompassing relationship is our aim.

What is the best saddle height? How far and at what angle should the saddle be placed in relation to the cranks? Where should the handlebar be located—how wide, how high, and how far forward? What is the optimum length of the pedal cranks? At what speeds should the legs turn for best results? Should the body be upright, reclining, or should the rider be on his belly? How are these factors changed as load and speed requirements change?

What bicycle configurations give the best stability, the best maneuverability? How do the brakes work under panic stops, under continuous load such as down a long, steep hill? What is the effect of rain on the braking process? What brake temperatures and pressures are developed?

Where are the weak points in bicycle design? What improved materials can be used? How can weight be minimized without inducing failures at high speeds or from repeated road impact?

How does the tire design affect braking, maneuverability, stability, and life? Should we keep the traditional power transmission system, or should an entirely different system be evolved? Should we use only our legs, or our legs, arms, and body?

Research shows that the answers to these questions are far from cut and dried. Our human engine—its weight and the dimensions of its parts—varies considerably between individuals.

At Calspan Laboratory (formerly Cornell Aeronautical Laboratory), the Schwinn Bicycle Company of Chicago has initiated an extensive research program on bicycle maneuverability, stability, and design. Calspan Laboratory, which has been active in vehicle research for major automobile companies, completed a study in 1970 as a result of a grant from the National Committee on Product Safety. This study was instituted to learn the effects of variations in braking methods on maneuverability and stability. Research for the study resulted in a mathematical model of the bicycle suitable for use in computers. The extended research program, which has been under way for several years, disclosed that the magnitude of many items was not clearly understood during the previous century of bicycle use.

Studies made of roll and yaw momentum and the characteristics of tire resistance under various loads and inflation pressures showed vast differences among brands. Research done in other centers, such as at Delft University, was studied, but the results of this research could not be directly applied. It was first necessary to develop a mathematical model of the cyclist which could be integrated with the model of the bicycle. The effects of speed, rider lean, and steering torque had to be evaluated. These were first studied on full-scale bicycles using mounted rockets. When the rockets were fired, the effect of their side forces was captured by motion picture cameras and data telemetered from sensors on the bicycle.

As the mathematical rider model was developed, its output was checked and modified by comparison with maneuvering on instrumented bicycles by actual riders. The outcome was a computer model of both bicycle and rider which could be displayed on a graphic screen to calculate the position, steer, and roll of the bicycle at fraction of a second intervals. When photographed, this becomes a motion picture of actual performance. Speeds, loads, bicycle dimensions and angles can be varied and the effects on maneuverability and stability determined. The effects of the reciprocating leg mass of the rider, road camber, tire changes, weight of rider, and position of load can also be determined. Applied in actual design, this should result in better and safer bicycles. Designs can also now be checked to determine their properties and if need be modified without the time and expense of building unsuccessful prototypes.

One interesting outcome was a study on the effects on maneuverability and handling of baggage load placement. The poorest results from both the maneuverability and stability standpoint were obtained with the load on the rider's back; the best with it located low and near the rear-wheel center.

Research on other bicycle design problems, including high-speed wheel wobble is being studied at the Calspan Labs, at the University of Michigan, at the Japanese Bicycle Institute, and at several other research centers throughout the world.

DeLong's Guide to Bicycles & Bicycling is a how-to book for both the newcomer and the aficionado.

You will learn about subtle characteristics of bicycle handling that make it respond best to your efforts. You will find the means to enjoy the sport, despite the presence of hordes of motor vehicles on the roads, with confidence and safety. You will experience the pride of accomplishment that accompanies your developing skill and personal fitness.

This book not only tells you what your bicycle is like, but why. You will find it a highly engineered steed with a vibrant heart. You will choose it with care to ride with more ease despite wind and hills and weather. You will find how space-age research is continuing to refine and improve this century-old vehicle. You will learn how to select, care, inspect, and maintain it for best results. Family fun, touring and travel, and competition are described.

This book is dedicated to my wife Pauline, whose lifelong sharing of the joys of cycling as an expert partner in a tandem crew had to be foregone during the preparation of this manuscript (with which she helped); to John (1973 Pennsylvania State Champion) and Doris DeLong, themselves participants in the full sport; and to Dr. Eugene and Helene Gaston of Framingham, Mass., with whom we have shared several exciting tours.

Profound thanks are due to dozens of cycling friends who aided with photos, art, and information. Included in this group are the Bicycle Institute of America and the Bicycle Manufacturer's Association; the Engineering, Sales and Service departments of the Schwinn Bicycle Company; Shimano American Corp; Maeda Industries; Simplex; and Ets. Huret, and Mel Pinto; and cycling friends: Bill Vetter, Chick Mead, Jim Farnsworth, Dave Siskind, Ronald Timmerman, and Frank Lopez. I wish to thank Frank Whitt of London and David Jones of Runcorn, England, Shinichi Toriyama of Tokyo, Japan and David Gordon Wilson of M.I.T. for sharing the results of their investigations and Alan Turner and Pat Westphal of Chilton for their attention to details. To the many other friends who shared their experience, to the officers of the League of American Wheelmen, Dr. Graves and the International Bicycle Touring Society, and The American Youth Hostels, I also extend my heartfelt thanks.

Hatboro, Pennsylvania   FRED DeLong

Contents

CHAPTER I

The Sport of Bicycling

Welcome to the sport of bicyling! You are about to enter a lifetime of fun and companionship that you may never have dreamed possible. New vistas will present themselves for years to come. You and your bicycle will get to know each other intimately. You will also learn more about that fascinating person, yourself.

Astride your willing mount, new adventures and new sights will unfold. Cares will be erased; the feelings of fine health and developing resources which you yourself will earn will make life yours in fuller measure.

While your friend will not desert you, your bicycle may disappear as you ride! As you learn the *art* of bicycling, your bicycle becomes a magic carpet. You will become totally absorbed in your surroundings. Your bicycle, responding to your every wish, will cover hill and dale with a minimum of conscious effort. The breeze will keep you comfortably cool, will caress your hair and skin. Your bicycle is silent, your vision unfettered. The rustle of the leaves, the sound of the wind in the telephone wires, the bark of a distant dog, the "Hello" of a friend or neighbor are yours to enjoy. On a bicycle, you are at the center of your world. Able to sense your position on the road, you are free to look intently at the sights about you. Subtle fragrances announce the presence of things you may not yet have seen. Your bicycle vanishes as you drink in all that is about you.

Weather becomes an experience, not a statistic. Even the wind becomes a strong or silent companion. It may be the soft wind that waves the corn and wheat and tempers the heat. It may be the stiff wind that whistles through the spokes and brings you to a standstill. It may be a helping hand, or a rugged force that never relents. It may be an orchestra conductor, singing through wires like the notes of a cello, increasing in volume and intensity as you climb to a more exposed location. It is yours to sense and enjoy.

AT NIGHT

Riding at night in the silent countryside, the wind diminishes, and your hearing seems more acute. The houses you pass are islands of light in the world of darkness. The city you have left and the towns in the distance are halos of light standing over the horizon. As you proceed in the little puddle of light your generator set provides, you are at the center of a tiny moving world. As you pass a home, its occupants bathed in interior light are your silent friends. The gurgle of the brook you cross announces its refreshing presence. Their shadows transform trees and unoccupied houses into mystic objects. As you pass under wooded cover, the night becomes even more intense. The stars shine upon you; you sense that you are not alone. When the moon rises, your countryside glows in a soft and subdued silver hue. A rabbit scampers out of your silent path, undisturbed by the noise and clatter that a motorcar produces.

ARE YOU A PIONEER?

You may love challenges and adventure. Cycling will give all that you can take. You may work harder than you ever have before. You can see your challenge, plan your attack, and experience defeat or accomplishment. Your bicycle becomes a vibrant, living being, converting your straining effort into bursts of unbelievable speed. You may climb to impossible heights under your own power. You may cover miles—far beyond what you presently believe possible—open-

Fig. 1.1   We're part of the country we travel. *(Courtesy of TOSRVPHOTO)*

ing up new vistas that you had never before really explored. With the proper equipment and the skill and training you will acquire, you can travel the four corners of the earth. You can cross the country or the oceans in hours by air, and then cycling quietly, you can see new lands intimately.

Don't think, however, that you must go far away. Cycling in your city in off-peak hours will give you a new understanding of your home grounds. Even your own neighborhood becomes a more living place as you view it fully on your aftersupper leisurely cruise. Then you may understand why in France the bicycle has for years been affectionately known as "la petite reine" (the little queen). It is a noble yet servile vehicle.

Let it enrich your life!

YOUR GOALS ARE YOUR CHOICE

As you learn more about bicycling, you may wish to sample all its joys: competition, touring, exploration and adventure, and riding to business. Riding alone or with the children and your sweetheart may be your thing. You may wish the pleasant, social cycling events with hundreds of other vivacious companions. Life is not long enough to partake of all cycling's joys. Each has a flavor all its own, and its fun grows as your skill improves. Your time and duties may limit your participation, but you can enjoy the part you play to the fullest at your own pace.

THERE IS NO MAGIC ANSWER

Whenever we give cycling demonstrations at public exhibitions, someone invariably asks, "How can I cycle without exertion?" We're sorry, but it just isn't in the cards. You can buy the lightest bicycle, fit the lowest gears, and stay on the level, but any exercise is work. We can show you how to climb hills with maximum ease, but you still must raise your weight and that of the bicycle to the top with your own power.

Cycling is, however, a pleasant form of exercise. The more you do, the more you will develop, and the more you develop, the greater will be your range and the more intense your enjoyment. At the start, you may come back dog-tired after a short distance. But with even moderate practice, your ability will rapidly increase. Stick it out, and you will be rewarded. You will learn to cycle with much less effort, and you will be stronger and healthier to boot.

The cyclist lives in, becomes a part of, the countryside through which he passes. The road surface underneath his wheels becomes a blur as he accelerates. With the freedom of a bird, he can swoop down an incline and bank around a bend feeling completely integrated with his surroundings. When he climbs, he feels the effort and accomplishment of overcoming the grade. As he breasts the top, he inwardly exults with the knowledge: "I have attained this goal by my own efforts."

You will learn more about your inner reserves of stick-to-itiveness and grit. As you continue to learn and develop, your own sense of worth and well-being will increase. The following pages will help to speed up the process, but the extent of your growth is for you alone to choose.

Fig. 1.2   America the Beautiful. The cyclist is everyone's friend. *(Courtesy of W. Vetter)*

RIDING WITH A CYCLING CLUB

Togetherness is the spirit of bicycling. Byways become fuller and more colorful when explored with your family and friends. The ability to converse with your companions at speed on silently running steeds stimulates companionship. Riding in close formation takes skill and the ability to ride with silky smoothness and unchanging pace, but the rewards are great. Close formation greatly reduces wind resistance and enables the group to obtain high speeds with minimal effort. Each rider experiences the fun of team action, of team accomplishment, far greater than he could attain alone.

The group pictured is one of many that form in the running of a group cycling event, here the Columbus Ohio AYH Tour of the Scioto River Valley, a 210-mile weekend event attended by from two to three thousand participants each year.

WHERE TO CYCLE

On the modern lightweight, geared bicycle, the world is your oyster, but digesting the oyster takes degrees of skill and fitness which you develop in stages. And as each successive stage is reached, you have a new attainable challenge waiting to increase your personal growth.

Long gone are the days when a newcomer to cycling would ask, "But with today's automobile traffic, where can I cycle?" Bicycle lanes are being developed on city streets in most cities. Trails through parks restricted for cycling use not only encourage the new and less confident cyclist, but also allow a relaxing hour or evening of leisurely cycling after a day's work.

As bicycles increase in popularity and motorists come to expect their presence, the problem that was severe when cyclists and unobservant motorists used the same streets will decrease. Even now, there are few areas in cities where alternate lesser-used streets cannot be discovered that lead you to your intended destination with minimum interference and a bit of jogging. Even crowded, traffic-clogged, center city streets are more relaxing when traversed with a maneuverable bicycle that can pick its way through the jams. But except at peak hours when high-speed traffic runs from curb to curb, many of the major wider streets are, with reasonable care and attention, quite practical bicycling routes.

Avoid narrow two-lane roads with constant two-way traffic whenever possible, particularly at night. Gasoline company road maps—made with the dual purpose of eliminating detail to get autos from place

Fig. 1.3   Togetherness. *(Courtesy of TOSRVPHOTO)*

to place in the most direct routes—often simply ignore the road networks suitable for cyclists. These can be located, however, by reference to detailed city street maps, county road maps, and in some urban areas, detailed AAA metropolitan area maps.

As your urge for adventure increases, so does your desire to go farther afield, to reach new horizons, where you will need to know about the ground to be traversed, the heights and steepness of hills and valleys to be encountered. United States Geological Survey maps are available for the entire country, and the 1:62,500 size (about one inch per mile) gives sufficient detail.

Cyclists the country over are contributing greatly to the fund of knowledge available to the trip planner. The League of American Wheelmen, The American Youth Hostels, and The International Bicycle Touring Society are developing increasing numbers of maps and descriptions of suitable cycling routes which are based on the experiences of knowing cyclists who have ridden in all 50 states. In California, the County and State Highway Departments are planning and laying out coordinated bicycling routes throughout the state and beyond with the aid of cycling clubs. Bicycle tour maps for the entire California coast and for related groups of counties are available from the California Department of Transportation's District Information Centers. The District 4 Center is located at 150 Oak St., San Francisco, California 94119. Cycling clubs in many other states are likewise mapping routes throughout their states, through metropolitan areas, and through scenic regions.

Details on the routes themselves concerning the terrain and points of interest are being published in increasing numbers by dozens of publishers; examples are listed in the Appendix. These include guides to such metropolitan areas as New York and San Francisco, extensive guides to Northern and Southern California, and guides to routes throughout all 50 states.

For cyclists who wish to take part in preplanned tours with arrangements for lodging and facilities made in advance, increasing numbers of airlines are providing prearranged package tours in France, Austria, Germany, and England. A series of tours within the United States is being planned by domestic airlines, the League of American Wheelmen, the National Travel Office of American Youth Hostels, and by experienced cyclists and cycling groups. These tours are advertised in bicycling magazines and the League of American Wheelmen's monthly bulletin (see Chapter XIX).

BICYCLE TOURING

Bicycle touring covers a broad spectrum of pleasure, experience, and sometimes pain and fortitude. Until you have toured by bicycle, you are missing a fellowship with the world denied to those who have not taken part.

The tour may be a casual, slow excursion through the byways by yourself. It may be the "randonnée" of France, a journey of many hundreds of miles riding day and night with a group of companions to beat a specified time for the journey. It can be the pre-

Fig. 1.4 Cycling alone. Rural solitude. Yet all nature is one's companion. *(Courtesy of D. Siskind)*

Fig. 1.5   My buddy and I have met the challenge. *(Courtesy of D. Siskind)*

Fig. 1.6   The modern adventurers. English, French, and American IBTS tourists plot their course through Wales.
(Courtesy of W. Vetter)

planned group tour with a pleasant company of varied ability—as done each year by IBTS, AYH—or tours planned by cycling clubs or airlines such as Swissair, Air France, and Pan-Am (see Chapter XIX).

Group touring has an advantage. With a destination in mind, you are not tied to a fixed relationship throughout the day as you are on a preplanned bus, train, or plane excursion. You ride with whom you please throughout the day and join the group in the evening to share experiences. While touring alone can be a great experience, after a week or two, many cyclists find that loneliness appears. It is more fun to tour with a congenial companion or two of equal cycling ability when the trip is extended. In case of trouble or a breakdown on the road, a companion is a tremendous asset. During the day, sharing experiences minute by minute makes the miles go faster and the experiences deeper; shared mealtimes and evenings are more pleasant.

When touring by bicycle, whether in the city or in the countryside, the moderate speed at which you travel allows you to drink in all that is about you and gives you sufficient time to digest it. Your scene moves with sufficient speed to keep the drama going, but if you find something interesting, you can stop to absorb it. You are a part of your moving world—not just a spectator. This is what makes bicycle touring so different.

Preplanning is not only a great part of the fun, but a must for any guarantee of success. Weather can vary from one locality to the next, and a solid week or two of rain or cold will dampen the ardor of all but the true

enthusiast, especially if they are unprepared. Find out what weather is expected in the region you wish to visit and check into the direction and strength of the winds. Riding west in Kansas during the summer, you may face daylong headwinds of great intensity and temperatures into the hundred-and-higher range. Your planned mileage will be more moderate; early morning rising and early afternoon quitting times may be advisable.

Look for roads with little traffic—use county and USGS maps if possible. Winding roads and varied terrain are the most interesting; a new scene continually presents itself around the corner or over the hilltop. A straight, flat road that extends for miles into the distance is not the most enjoyable terrain for a bicycle tour.

Avoid the larger cities if you can. Widespread traffic congestion is not the most pleasant experience. Yet I have had great fun exploring the capitals of foreign countries, such as London and Paris, since there is so much that is "foreign" and different to see that the city becomes a daylong showplace.

Prior to taking part in cycle touring beyond your local bounds, be certain to get into good physical condition. Eat moderately but sufficiently while on the road. If you acclimate yourself by putting in sufficient miles before you start to tour, the trip will be a fun-filled adventure. If you go beyond your ability to combat hills and wind and weather, it can be an experience you may never want to repeat. Be prepared for occasional hardships—and rejoice if they do not appear. But even if they do, you will chuckle over them in years to come.

Fig. 1.7   On to the next night's hostel haven (Wisconsin). *(Courtesy of D. Siskind)*

Bicycle touring *is* pioneering and adventure. Think of it this way, plan, prepare, and take part. You have only one lifetime—not enough to tap the reservoir.

UTILITY CYCLING

There are many reasons favoring bicycling to your place of employment:

Service to self: Health, vigor, living while traveling rather than being transported like a parcel; reliability and convenience; economy.

Service to the community: Reduction of traffic congestion; reduction of air pollution; reduction of noise—the din of traffic and blaring horns.

Service to the nation: Reduction in expenditures needed to accommodate and to park space-consuming motor vehicles on roads and in town; doing your active part to blunt the impact of the impending nationwide energy shortage.

A recent survey indicates that the average passenger vehicle transports 1.3 persons in city traffic. A nose count made on the way to work recently disclosed that from 80 to 86 out of each 100 vehicles that passed me carried only one occupant. What a comparison: my 25 pounds of bicycle transport all of me and my gear; my motorist companions use about 2,500 pounds of vehicle per person to do the same. For each passenger, about 10 glassfuls of gasoline must be burned to transport them a 10-mile trip each way. Imagine the bonfire it would make if 1,000 employees each poured 10 glasses into a receptacle one morning and ignited it in the company parking lot! And if at the same time, the same would be done at adjacent firms! Yet this holocaust is performed every day in bits and pieces all along the streets. We can do our part toward conserving natural resources and fighting pollution if we encourage others to join us on the road.

Another survey a few years ago showed that 60% of commuters drove to and from their places of employment, and 70% of these lived within 11 miles of their work. Just think: 70 out of each 100 commuters—less those who must carry heavy loads of tools or equipment—are within bicycling range of their jobs. The time required, including parking, may differ from bicycling time by only minutes, and sometimes cars take longer!

Cycling to and from work may seem a humdrum way of traveling through city traffic at peak hours, especially when tired after a day's work, but far from

Fig. 1.8   You may sprint for the finish at the end of a race or to the next tree on a spirited touring ride.

being a problem, I find my daily ride of 10 miles to the office a high point of the day. After a hearty breakfast, bundled up to meet the cold in winter or stripped down to enjoy the wind in summer, I'm in a different world once the door closes behind me. The weather becomes part of your day. You don't battle it, like the motorist for the few moments he is separated from his car; you live in it. "Twenty below zero is the chill index today," announces the weather forecaster some winter days. But properly yet lightly clad, and pedaling briskly for the first mile, one warms rapidly. The air is so crisp and refreshing that it feels good just to be in it.

On a bicycle, you are not a sardine in a can; you are an individual. You pass the other workers at their bus stops, youths walking to school, and the same motorists on their way to work. There are the policewomen at the school crossings who flash a welcome smile unknown to the boxed-in motorist. At the slower but steady speeds of bicycling, those whom you pass become familiar friends who often exchange cheery greetings. There is none of the stop and go and stop of auto driving, and the ride to work is more relaxing. When you arrive at the office, the blood is coursing, and you feel wide awake and alert, ready to tackle the worst that comes.

Are you tired after a day's work—too tired to ride home? It may feel like this for the first eighth mile. But then, the rhythmic motion, the fresh air, and the sense that your immediate destiny is under your control act as a booster and a tranquilizer. By the time you reach home, the tensions of the day are gone, battled out and vanquished on the first hill. Instead of flopping fatigued in a chair after a grueling drive in traffic, you feel refreshed.

Now this may not happen immediately. It takes a while to become fit, but the ride becomes easier each day. Winds and rain bring a change of pace and experience.

A traffic jam? So what? We can ride through it, or around it. Snow and slippery streets require extra care and caution, but often you can get up the slippery slopes that tie up miles of traffic, walking if need be the steepest places.

Unfettered by the motorist's prison of glass and steel, the cyclist—he has 360° hearing and 180° visibility—is aware without thinking of everything around him. Since riding doesn't take constant attention, he can muse and think, and the ride goes quickly. He can calculate and plan and reminisce while he rides safely, even in heavy traffic. Fast and dense traffic may require close attention, but even this is only a change of scenery.

As for more practical considerations, you'll need a place at work to change and wash up after the ride, particularly if the pace was fast. As small as it is, you still need someplace to park your bicycle. In a crowded office building, this can be a problem, but a

sympathetic talk with the management will often disclose an out-of-the-way closet or a spot in the basement where the bike can be kept under the stairway on the lowest floor. You can chain your bike to a lamppost at the corner, or where a friendly newsstand operator can keep an eye on the locked bicycle in return for your business.

A change of clothing may be advisable. This can be carried in your saddlebag, or kept in your locker or clothes rack and replaced as needed. If worn only on the job, and not to and from work, clothes stay clean for longer periods.

If you do ride to school or work, try different routes. A change of scenery opens new sights for exploration and makes the ride more adventurous. Try it!

BICYCLE RACING

Bicycle racing is a challenging, demanding, and fascinating sport which teams mind, man, and machine. One of the most grueling of sports, it requires physical prowess, teamwork, the ability to make split-second decisions, precision, and a knowledge of tactics. Only by actually participating can you appreciate split-second reactions to the moves of another rider; the taut spring of dynamic power temporarily unleashed while estimating the reserves of the other competitors; the thrill of precision riding in a pack of cyclists maneuvering at all-out speeds where an extremely slight unprecise move may result in a chain-reaction tumble of two dozen speeding riders; and the searing pain of prolonged maximum effort. If you do not have enough time to train for entry into full-fledged competition, you can feel and observe the color and depth of the Sport of Kings by riding beyond your capabilities at speed with companions during club runs or hill climbs.

Bicycle racing is a sport of movement. There are three major categories: time trialing, track racing, and road racing. There are also hill-climbing events. Cyclocross racing through thicket, stream, fences, and fields is rapidly gaining worldwide popularity. Each has dozens of variations in distance, tactics, and technique; each requires separate skills and training, and each has a separate fascination for those who take part. Whether you are a participant or spectator, if you observe the tactics and study the riders, you will find that your understanding increases your love for the tremendously varied sport of bicycling.

The inbred urge to ride hard and fast may lead you to "time trialing." Riding alone, unassisted by the breezes created behind cars that pass in your direction, the stimulation and the windbreak shelter of other riders, you ride "against the clock." Time trials are generally held over out-and-home courses of 10, 25, 50, and 100 miles and 12 or 24-hour periods. The out-and-home course tends to balance the effects of wind speed and hills, so that various times are compa-

Fig. 1.9   The thrill of competition. *(Courtesy of D. Siskind)*

rable. Times of less than one hour and four hours for the 25 and 100-mile events are common among the better riders. A record distance of over 500 miles has been covered in the 24-hour event.

You are never too old to take part, whether to equal or better a competition record, or to beat your own previous best time. As your age increases, the time for a given distance will also increase. An 80-year-old English cyclist, however, recently set a 165-mile record in a 12-hour event.

Time trialing is a matter of willpower and of rationing your strength so that you finish exhausted from having exerted your maximum output over the entire distance. Your riding pace is smooth with no spurts or sprints. Your schedule, mileage, and watch show your progress or failure throughout the distance.

The road race may be over a "criterium" course, closed off streets in town making a loop course of about a mile in length, with sufficient laps to obtain the required distance, either 10, 25, 50, 100 miles, or 100 or 200 kilometers. The criterium course eliminates the problem of auto traffic. The riders pass each vantage point on the course at two or three-minute intervals, maintaining the excitement and interest of the spectators. "Prime" sprints at intervals throughout the distance further enliven the competition. Slower riders

are eliminated when lapped by the field, maintaining the pace of the event.

The hundreds of hardblown tires hum like a swarm of bumblebees as the pack passes. Any change in tone, intensity, or rhythm signifies that some riders are attempting a "break," where several cyclists team together to escape the main group and gain the lead. The turns or corners, where aggressiveness and skill can gain or lose yards, are a favorite spot for the viewers.

The road race may be held on a rural course, up hill and down, on both wide and narrow roads, sheltered or exposed to the wind, and with the weather good or bad. It may be a "stage" race lasting several days or weeks, such as the "tour de France" which covers several thousand miles of plains and mountains. Tremendous ascents, thrilling descents, time trials, and teamwork occur daily in stages that cover from 100 to 150 miles. During a race, each rider must constantly evaluate not only his condition, but that of his opponents and of his team as well. Who will attack? When should I attack to gain time and distance on the field? Will I be able to maintain the lead, or will the extra effort tire me so that the others can catch and pass me when I have no reserves to call on?

The rider experiences aggressiveness as he attacks and despair as he gives his all on a climb only to be left

Fig. 1.10   The attack is made where yards can be gained. *(Courtesy of D. Siskind)*

behind by stronger riders. There can be fear on the winding, wet, or gravel-strewn descent when caution is thrown to the winds to gain speed and distance. He will feel the torture of cramping muscles and of aching lungs that can't breathe enough air to meet the demands of the moment. He anticipates the sprint at the finish but is elated by being the first to top a hill. Throughout the race, each rider is watching and evaluating not only himself, but also the strategy and the strength of the other competitors.

On the track, the distances are often short. Opponents stand still, balance, and outwait each other to get the most favorable position, then burst for the finish at maximum possible power. If you are behind, you take shelter and then maneuver for the final sprint. At the last instant, you are perhaps inches behind your opponent as he strains to maintain his lead.

The track race may be a team pursuit, in which teams ride together and continually exchange the lead to attain maximum speeds and beat the time or catch the opposing teams in the distance allotted.

The cyclo-cross race is a cross-country event through mud and field, across streams and fences. Off and on the bike, it takes the greatest of skill and endurance to maintain balance under wet and slippery conditions and steep descents. The bike is ridden, carried, or thrown to overcome obstacles.

There are dozens of other events which would take a large book to discuss. Bicycle racing is hard but challenging. If you don't try it, you've missed a big part of the "art" of bicycling.

WINTER WEATHER

With the falling of the leaves, many cycling groups, particularly the racing groups, have in the past hung up their wheels for the "season," as if there were such a thing as a cycling season! Winter—one of the most rewarding times to cycle—is lost, undiscovered. Although it takes a real die-hard adherent, or else an extraventuresome soul, to ride a bicycle, when the snow is deep and blowing, when cars and trucks need tire chains, when streets are filled with icy pools and slush and hills are covered with glare ice, there are cyclists who never miss a day. But even in northern areas, these road conditions are rather rare and far between. Highway road crews are an efficient lot, and most town and country roads are passable within hours or a few days.

Hard-packed snow on the paths and byways has its own particular charm for the cyclist. The soft crunch of the snow under your wheels and the entirely different handling characteristics make your bicycle an old friend in a different cloak. Your closest friends are tested under all sorts of circumstances, and a faithful cycle is no exception.

The change of the seasons comes as a surprise to the town dweller who is locked in a heated house, office, train, or car. Dashing from one to the other, he doesn't discern the gentle changes as they come about and barely notices the falling leaves, the lightening of the skies and the landscape, the steaming of breath on the chilled air, the sound of the wind through the wires and the trees. He is not a part of the refreshing variations in our climate and merely reaches for a heavier overcoat to shiver in as he waits on the corner.

How different it is to take to your bicycle on a wintry day! The warmth of healthful exercise negates the chill of the air. Since the summer heat is gone, an increased riding pace can be maintained without discomfort. The hills in one's path can be attacked with verve. Your bicycle becomes a thing alive as you thrill to its performance under perspiration-free maximum effort. In a lower gear, the cyclist twiddles along at a lower speed while his more rapid leg motion keeps the circulation brisk, the cheeks rosy, the breathing full.

Wintry air is cold and clear. It seems more evident, more discernible. Each breath contains more substance, more power, more "life." It even feels cleaner and purer.

The wintry winds sweep unopposed across the leafless landscape pitting their strength against your own.

Fig. 1.11   Dr. Allan V. Abbott with the bicycle on which he set the world's motor-paced speed record of 138.674 mph in August, 1973.

They are forces with which to reckon, requiring thought and planning to overcome.

The old, familiar routes are reborn in winter. The foliage is gone, and the views it obscured along the roadway are now revealed: the quaint farmhouse across the former cornfield, the valley previously hidden by trees at the hilltop. The winding brook in the glen now lies bare before you, along with its beaver dam. These all add to your admiring and inquisitive view.

Three things are needed to enjoy winter cycling: a flair for adventure, proper clothing, and a light bicycle—preferably one with a fairly wide range of gearing. While I've enjoyed many a winter ride on a single-speed fixed gear bicycle—particularly when accompanied by other riders skilled in the art of "taking pace," that is, riding in a close formation so that the head rider breaks the wind for the others—it is generally advantageous to use a derailleur bicycle with a moderately wide range of gearing. On occasions when the winds are strong and unrelenting, a gear in the high 40s or 50s is a real luxury which enables you to maintain a comfortable pedal speed without fatigue. Speeds are not high, but this is the secret of pleasurable riding against the wind. Combined with hilly country, gears in the low 30s are of real use. With the wind, however, it has often been easy to hold 90 pedal rpm using gears well over 100 (30 mph). Generally, the rule to be considered is: the lower the temperature, the lower the starting-out gear. On a warm day on the level a gear of 70 may be used to start, but when the temperature gets to well below freezing, using gears in the 40s and 50s will start the blood circulating and warm up the body without any cold weather cramp. After a half-mile or so, the gear can be raised a bit, and after a couple of miles, you will find your normal gear comfortable, even on the coldest days.

Clothing worn in cold winter cycling should be light, not bulky, should cover the back below the hips, and should be windproof. Winter clothing is a highly individual matter, and age is a factor. Your feet and hands require special treatment to keep them warm. Younger folks can ride with a minimum of gloves and clothing in weather that would freeze me to an icicle, but for rides in weather down to 20 degrees, an unlined nylon jacket over an office shirt seems enough for me. At temperatures, down to 5 or 10 degrees, I add a flannel shirt. Wool trousers are excellent at these temperatures, provided wind leaks in the front are counteracted with several layers of shorts and, on colder days, thermal or long underwear. Oversize shoes which are light in construction permit the use of two and three layers of long socks—the outer on top of the trouser leg to keep out the wind. Plastic or leather toe clip covers are advantageous, particularly in the wet.

Other cyclists swear by battery-powered socks—with long-life batteries—and layers of clothing with newspaper in between the frontal layers for protection against the wind. Down to 30 degrees, these cyclists require two T-shirts, a sweat shirt, and a turtleneck sweater. The layers permit breathing, and prevent sweating and clamminess, down to 15 or 20 degrees. Add an extra sweat shirt and T-shirt, with more layers as the temperature drops farther. Still others swear by closefitting cycling sweat suits.

A pullover wool cap inside a jacketed hood will warm your arms and head. Bausch and Lomb ski shields allow good visibility while protecting eyes and cheeks from the sting of the wind.

Mittens used by skiers are good protection for the hands. A windproof, unlined mitten with a cuff adds more protection for colder days. It will also keep the wind from going up your sleeves without the restriction caused by elastic at the end of the sleeve.

In spring or fall, or summer at higher elevations, when the weather is raw and dreary, foggy and misty, you may find that cycling can make your day. When there is no wind and the air is cold and damp, a half mile of low-gear pedaling will send a glow of warmth through your body. Through the gloom country traffic seems almost to have ceased to exist. The fog hides the houses, trees, and hilltops, and your world shrinks to a tiny sphere through which you slowly drift. Cattle move about friskily for warmth; ducks and geese call to each other.

The mist obscures the grades ahead—ascents and descents seem tiny—you float as on a magic carpet. Water-soaked trees and bushes emerge from the fog and dissolve behind you—their stature magnified by their reflections on the wet road.

Such days are for intimate companionship with the whole small world through which we move and which moves through us.

POLICE CYCLING PATROLS

Difficulty in patrolling a high-crime area in East Baltimore, Maryland, with foot police and squad cars led to the reintroduction of a bicycle-mounted police detail, the first in a half century. Foot patrols were too slow to get to the scene of a robbery except when by chance they were nearby. Noisy squad cars squeezing through narrow alleys alerted robbers and lacked maneuverability. A bicycle-mounted police patrol, however, possesses speed and maneuverability with silence, takes little room, and can reverse directions in an instant. They can be parked and concealed quickly and don't tie up traffic. Crime rates dropped 50%. Other cities seeing the success of this venture are proceeding with similar cycle patrols.

Figure 1.12 shows the police patrol of Fire Island, New York. Narrow promenades and walks crowded with people are impractical for patrolling with cars, but the bicycle patrol can pick their way rapidly through the crowds to trouble spots, despite wind, rain, or blowing sand.

Fig. 1.12   Police cycle patrols. *(Courtesy of Ross ChainBike Corp.)*

Fig. 1.13   Streamlined enclosures and space-age advances in material selection, sports medicine, and biotechnology permit human-powered speed records of over 50 mph.

CHAPTER II

What Kind of Bicycle Should I Buy?

JUST a few years ago buying a bicycle was a simple task. There were single bar frames, double bar frames, and girls' open frames, all with about the same wheels and tires and a coaster brake. There were racing models, but these were few and far between. Then, in rapid succession, the balloon-tire bike, the three-speed, so-called English lightweight; the high riser, small-wheeled bike; and the ten-speed entered the market. Price ranges were relatively moderate.

Today, there is a vast conglomeration of makes and models from which to choose. Just recently, paging through the advertisements in a bicycle dealers' magazine, I found over 100 makers from all over the United States and 16 other countries. Including purely sidewalk models intended for very young children—which we will not discuss—these makers listed from 5 to 44 models in their catalogs, each with distinct modifications and equipment. Most of these come in several frame sizes. Did you think selecting an automobile was perplexing? We've got it, too!

There is good reason for this. Due to the bicycle boom in the United States, the ages of riders and the types of bicycle usage have greatly broadened. Almost every bicycle manufacturer in every country has sought to become a part of the expanded market by establishing sales representatives and distributors in the United States. Many have quality products, but others have dispatched equipment that is under-designed and sometimes shoddily assembled, using parts and components of limited durability. When covered with a gleaming coat of paint, these factors are not easily discernible. The American Bicycle Industry has evolved a voluntary minimum standard for bicycle construction called BMA/6. Laboratory test-

ing to determine if bicycles meet this standard is available, but many builders do not submit models for test. U.S. Government Consumer Products Safety Commission regulations effective November 1976 covering dry braking, chain guarding, wheel strength and trueness, frame strength, reflectors, exposed protrusions and sharp edges, and handlebar and seat clamping now apply as minimum standards to all except track racing and other special bicycles.

Production methods for bicycle manufacture vary considerably, yet most methods are capable of creating a bicycle satisfactory for limited use. When we demand more than the minimum in safety, durability, finish, stability, and ease of propulsion, however, it pays to look at the bike more closely. Beware of very low-priced imports. These may be hazardously unsafe even for the younger child.

Any bicycle in sound operating condition will move you from one place to another if you work hard enough. However, the bicycle rider who properly conditions himself and uses the proper equipment will find bicycling an exhilarating experience, instead of an exhausting struggle. Some folks reason that the beginner can try any old bicycle to see if he enjoys cycling before investing in a better machine. For an occasional trip to the store, for riding between buildings to classes, or for commuting short distances to school, this can be true. If it is likely to be stolen, or if it must be left out unprotected from the elements and you intend to neglect its maintenance, you're better off trying an old bike. But this reasoning may also prevent the newcomer from ever learning the joys of bicycling. A bike not suited to his needs may discourage him before he can unearth the fun and freedom bicycling

16

provides. It may be possible for you to purchase a used bicycle in good condition with the features you desire, but above all, do not select a bicycle on price alone.

Today, with the tremendous demand for excellent equipment, prices have accelerated to untold heights. Some top-line models cost from six to eight hundred dollars, but unless you are aspiring to world's records or the very finest in touring, these are not for you. You may be paying for the fine handcrafting of shops that produce in very limited quantity, for the artistic hand-filing and painting, and for brand-name, high-priced accessories which actually don't return value in performance in proportion to their prices. Luckily for the buyer, increased bicycle use has made high precision equipment available at moderate cost.

In this chapter we will discuss differences in design and construction so you can compare the features you wish to have and decide what price you can afford. Remember that you can upgrade your equipment by fitting on finer components if your basic frame is sound and suitable in design, or you can trade in for something finer as your needs develop. The bicycle has a tremendous advantage in its longevity. Some of our family bicycles are over 36 years old and still going strong. Over the years, 3-speed derailleurs have been changed to 4, 8, 10, 12 and 15; cranks have been changed to aluminum alloy; and bearings, hubs, and tires have been replaced by more advanced types as the old ones wore out. The basically sound frame remains intact with its new coat of paint. Pedals and brakes are lighter now, and more durable, but the expenses amortized over all these years and thousands of miles are hardly worthy of consideration.

Before we begin tailoring your bicycle to you, let's take a look at the field for a moment. Our two thousand makes and models break down into about 14 categories. We'll forget for the moment the sidewalk bikes, the six-day racers, and the types used for motor pacing, but we'll cover a range of usefulness anyone might enjoy. Then we will list a table of characteristics for you to evaluate and compare which should enable you to choose the proper bicycle for you.

But please note: it takes time and riding experience to really know yourself and your bicycle. This is part of the fun of cycling! You and your pal learn more and more about each other as you ride together. You may like high stability or rapid maneuverability, or some of both. You may like to pedal slowly, or you may prefer greater speed. You may like to take it easy, or you may enjoy the challenge of an all-out effort while climbing hills. You may have that hidden competitive urge that makes you want to beat your companion to the next lamppost. Your size and weight might make comfort of more importance than all-out performance. You may find it necessary to regularly carry bags and parcels—or touring clothing and accessories.

Study yourself and your mount as you ride, not for a day or a month, but for years. It takes time and riding experience to really know yourself and your bicycle. As you grow older together, you may find that your balance of needs shifts. You may find that you need more than one bike to do everything you wish to undertake. When you do, my friend, you have arrived!

COMPARISON OF BICYCLE TYPES

While we have grouped our cycling equipment into 14 categories for guidance, in practice, the bicycle buyer will have to examine his purchase more closely.

The strength and quality of the construction of the bicycle frame, wheels, tires, and other components can vary considerably within each group. Excellent components can be installed on mediocre frames, and component quality can be mixed on the same bicycle. Specifications on bicycles and components are likewise currently in a state of flux.

Bicycle design also varies considerably. Steering stability can vary from extrasnappy to extrastable.

Models identically built by a manufacturer may be marked with five or more separate model and brand names, so that neighboring retail competitors will each have a distinctive brand of equal quality to market. Different prices can be quoted for the several brands to promote marketing.

In the following pages we will give a component comparison rating which may be used as a guide for comparing overall value to the price charged. Photographs of construction and component differences are presented to help you select designs or components more suited for your own needs than were those originally supplied on the bicycle.

Do not be tempted to buy far above your needs. Prices of fine bicycles and components have sharply increased, due to devaluation and the greater demand. Unless you are in a competitive sport where the minutest differences may mean the winning inches at the finish line, medium-priced equipment will get you out and home with ease and satisfaction.

High-riser

The High-riser has a small frame, a short wheelbase, three or five-speed gearing, 20-inch diameter hookbead wheels, a long "banana" saddle with saddle support stays, large-section balloon tires (1.75″ or 2.125″ width), and rubber pedals. It may have a coaster brake and three-speed hub or five-speed derailleur gearing.

This type is used for maneuverability and acrobatic riding under normal to abusive treatment. It is heavy and has a high rolling resistance and high handlebars which do not allow the cooperative use of all muscles. Limit this type to children in the 6–12-year age group.

Cost: $65–$135

Fig. 2.1   The 8-5136 Sporty Hi-Rise Hot Shot by Murray Ohio. *(Courtesy of Murray Ohio Mfg.)*

Middleweight

The middleweight has a moderately erect handlebar position, a double-braced frame, and 24″ or 26″ × 1.75″ tires on hookbead rims. It comes equipped with a single or two-speed coaster brake; there are some three-speed models.

This type is OK for normal riding. It requires riding effort less than that of the high-riser, but too great for distance travel. It has throwaway rubber pedals on one-piece cranks and a spring mattress saddle. Equipped with carriers, it may be used for delivery purposes. It will stand considerable abuse and thus is good for children and for in-plant utility services in factories. It is also good for use on poor road surfaces.

Cost: $60–$105

Lightweight (Ladies' Model—Similar Types in Men's Diamond Frames)

The lightweight has a moderately erect handlebar position. The open type ladies' frame has front and rear caliper brakes and three-speed hub gears. It uses throwaway pedals on one-piece cranks. Tires are 26″ × 1⅜″. It comes equipped with mudguards for wet or

dry weather riding. It uses one-piece cranks or a three-piece crank and axle set with a wedgepin connection.

This type has less rolling resistance. A spring mattress saddle (or an unsprung wider-at-the-rear leather saddle) provides support for the rider sitting in an upright posture, in which most of the weight rests on the saddle. It has been widely used in the past for utilitarian riding, moderate-to-long-distance touring in moderately varying terrains, commuting, and recreation.

With the 1⅜″ tires, it provides sure footing on wet and dry roads. With reasonable care in riding, it will withstand the rough road surfaces found on poorly paved country roads or in city travel.

Cost: $65–$120

Lightweight 5 or 10-speed (Men's Model, Upright Posture)

This type uses 5 or 10-speed derailleur gearing, 27″ × 1¼″ tires on tubular steel rims, front and rear caliper brakes, raised handlebars, and a sprung mattress saddle.

This type has lower rolling resistance than the previous types. Its wider range of 5 or 10-speed gearing permits easier travel in hilly terrain and less effort

Fig. 2.2   The middleweight. *(Courtesy of Schwinn Bicycle Company)*

under hard road surface conditions than the lightweight ladies' model. However, any impact with paving breaks that could cause damage to the rims and tires should be avoided. Due to the erect riding posture, visibility is good in traffic, but hills and wind take more toll than in the types that follow. Rubber pedals permit riding with street shoes if desired.

With wide-range gears this type is well suited for recreational riding on moderate terrain, commuting in the city, shopping, or for moderate distance touring. A comfortable riding position is easy to obtain and visibility and controllability are good.

Cost: $75–$125

Lightweight 10-speed with Dropped Handlebars

This type of machine has had a tremendous surge in popularity. It is commonly called a "racing model," but it should be distinguished from the true racer.

This model has 1″ diameter tubing frames; other makes may use 1⅛″ tubing for the seat and bottom frame tubes. It generally uses one-piece, forged cranks or three-piece, wedge-pin cranks and axle, steel "rat-trap" pedals, 27″ × 1¼″ wheels, and medium-wide-range derailleur gears.

This type may be equipped with a narrow leather saddle or with a mattress-type plastic-covered saddle. It has twin caliper brakes of side or center pull.

The brake levers may be equipped with so-called "safety levers," which permit brake application with the hands either on the lever or on the upper parts of the handlebar.

Due to the lower position of the body, air resistance is reduced, and the weight is more evenly balanced between the wheels. The arms and back muscles can be used in hill climbing.

If properly fitted to the rider's dimensions, this type of bicycle will be quite comfortable, highly maneuverable, and easier to pedal. Higher speeds can thus be maintained. It can be used for general riding for recreation and commuting or for medium and longer-distance touring, including cross country.

If improperly fitted, or with components improperly selected, this type can be uncomfortable. The model shown has a deep drop racing bar. The handlebar stem is short, and the seat is moved forward. The arms and body will be cramped and the back arched. This can lead to fatigue and aching arms, back, and neck. A too low body position may impair visibility.

Some foreign models come already fitted with very narrow, hard, leather saddles designed for high-speed racing on smooth tracks. These cause saddle soreness on rides of any length. The buyer must beware.

Fenders are often missing—resulting in soiled clothing when riding in wet weather.

Cost: $85–$170

The 10-Speed Junior Size has 24″ wheels, 17″ or 18″ frames, and 5½″ cranks.

Cost: $80–$152

10-Speed Club or Sports

At first glance this bicycle differs little from the previous model. However, its frame has stronger, lighter tubing. Selected with greater care, its components—wheels, brakes and saddle—provide easier riding, more positive braking, longer life, and lower friction.

Toe clips and straps are fitted to the pedals. The cranks and axle may be of one-piece or of three-piece, wedge-pin construction. Alloy cranks on squared-shaft-axles appear on some models.

Used with proper care, this type of bicycle is fine for general riding, commuting short and long distances, and traveling in flat or moderately hilly or mountainous country. Easier riding justifies its higher cost. Extra care must be exercised in use, since the lightweight wheels and tires are more easily damaged. The type usually fitted to this bike is 27″ × 1¼″ on straight side rims.

Cost: $160–$250

10-Speed Sports Touring

This type is one step upward in component quality. Specially selected tires reduce road rolling resistance. Stronger but lighter material and the three-piece square axle end, "cotterless construction," make the cranks and axle superior in quality. Frame tubes are made of alloy steel of great strength.

It is lighter than less expensive models, but as strong, and therefore more responsive. Toe clips and straps are fitted to the metal pedals. The pedals them-

SUBURBAN®

Fig. 2.3   The lightweight tourer. (*Courtesy of Schwinn Bicycle Company*)

Fig. 2.4   The lightweight upright tourer—men's diamond frame. *(Courtesy of Raleigh Industries of America)*

Fig. 2.5   The lightweight 10-speed with dropped handlebars. *(Courtesy of the Huffy Corporation)*

Fig. 2.6   The 10-speed club-type sports model. *(Courtesy of AMF Wheel Goods)*

selves are lighter and more weather-resistant. They are adjustable and can be disassembled for cleaning and lubrication. The tires are usually 27″ × 1¼″ on straight side rims, but some models may come with "sew-ups," a tire in which the tube is completely encased in a lightweight casing sewn together and cemented to the lightweight rim.

Cost: $230–$550

Road Racing Bicycle

The true road racing bicycle is a masterpiece of precision. Its components, constructed with great precision from alloy steels and high-strength aluminum forgings, are of the highest caliber. The bearings in the crank hanger and head set, the pedals, and the sprockets are almost free from friction and are resistant to heavy loads and rigid. Frames are light, yet withstand the heavy thrusts of the powerful rider. Wheels are extra light, using "sew-up" or "tubular" tires on rims of extra light construction.

This type of bicycle gives maximum return for the effort expended. It is highly responsive and maneuverable, yet firm and stable in handling.

However, it is delicate and must be ridden accordingly. While capable of very high speeds, this bicycle will not withstand abusive treatment. Its rider must pick his path with care, avoiding rough or jagged surfaces that could damage wheels and tires. Repairs are more expensive than on previous types, although if handled well, component life is longer.

Cost: about $240–$800

Track Racing Bicycle

The track racing bicycle is constructed for maximum performance. Like the road racer, it is built with minimum clearances for greater rigidity. Precision is carried a step further in this racer, which is designed for smooth surfaces and steeply banked tracks.

The front and rear fork ends, fork blades, and rear stays are made of heavy, sectioned material for even greater rigidity and for responsiveness to the explosive power thrusts by the competitive rider. If used on the

Fig. 2.7   The 10-speed tourer. *(Courtesy of Ross Chain Bike Corp.)*

road, it will give good performance, but an over-maneuverable, less shock-absorbing "hard" ride.

Its gearing is "fixed." The pedals continue to turn as long as the bicycle is in motion; it does not coast. This allows the rider to exercise extremely precise control. The frame and steering head angles are steep, with the fork blade offset small; the wheelbase is short. All this gives extreme rigidity and maneuverability.

Cost: $350–$550

The True Touring Bicycle

Luggage carriers are often added to the racing, club, and sports models for use on extended trips; mudguards are also fitted if enough clearance is available. The true touring bicycle, however, is a machine of highest quality, designed with the greatest care.

The components may vary, as may the frame design, according to their owner's plans. For example, tires and rims come in 1¼″, 1⅜″ or 1⅝″ sections; any one of these will be strong, rigid, and durable, yet light in weight and rolling resistance. Tubular "sew-up"

tires may be substituted for good conditions of travel if the bicycle is predesigned to accept them.

The handlebar will most usually be the "Randonneur" which is most suited to touring needs.

Wide-range derailleur gears of 10 or 15-speeds, with a range of from 30 to 90 inches or more, make mountain climbs, even with a load, and rapid descents possible.

Luggage carriers are provided front and rear. These will be rigidly attached to brazed fittings, not clamped on haphazardly as an afterthought. They won't loosen at speed on a rough road.

The frame is designed for absorbing road shock as well as for performance. Steering is designed for stability at speed with load.

Provision is made for the installation of mudguards and electric lighting. In most cases, these are installed at the start.

All components are selected with an eye toward durability and weather tightness, so that long trips can be taken away from a maintenance base. A tire pump and water bottle are provided for.

Fig. 2.8   The road racing bicycle. *(Courtesy of West Coast Cycle Supply)*

Fig. 2.9   The track racing bicycle. *(Courtesy of Schwinn Bicycle Company)*

The easily transported take apart or folding design is becoming increasingly popular.

Cost: about $200–$800 without bags

The frame most widely used on touring bicycles is designed along racing lines. It has a relatively short top tube, closely spaced rear stays, and a rear wheel closely approaching the seat tube—this should be weighed in view of other demands. The racing frame is light and responsive, and with light baggage loads and good roads, it can be quite satisfactory.

For a wider range of terrain, the clearance between fender and toe clip can prevent a fall when maneuvering or climbing at lower speeds. A less steep steering head slope provides good stability and better shock absorption. A longer top tube (see Chapter IV) will permit the use of a shorter handlebar extension. When a handlebar bag is used, it extends the load in front of the steering axis a considerable distance. Combined with a short frame and a correspondingly long extension, its effect on steering and handling can be very deleterious. Likewise, on a bumpy or rough-surfaced road, a short frame with a long extension magnifies the road jar. On a long trip, this will be more tiring.

A bit longer rear stays (44½ cm minimum) provide more clearance and a more comfortable ride while allowing the heels to clear the pannier bag (see Fig. 2.10). Comfort and safety should be weighed against the desire for snappy performance.

Figure 2.11 is another bicycle for long-distance touring on smooth to moderately rough and light-graveled roads. Equipment includes:

Nylon handlebar bag on midsized tubular steel carrier.

Wide tubular platform carrier with pannier bags mounted.

Nylon saddlebag, carrier attached to brazed frame seat stay and eyes.

Hollow aluminum-alloy rims on Phil Wood sealed, precision bearing hubs with 27″ × 1, 1⅛, or 1¼″ nylon tires (also adaptable to 700-25, 700-28, 700-30, 700-32, 700-35, and sew-up tires).

Alloy mudguards, front with sliding fender flap in raised position and built-in generator lighting.

Tire pump and water-bottle carrier with brazed-on mounting.

Mafac Cantilever tandem brakes, rear-brake cable direct routing (200 degree casing arc) with hooded levers.

Aluminum-alloy Randonneur handlebars.

531 chrome-molybdenum braze-welded frame—71 degree head and seat tube angles.

15-speed wide-range gearing (23–116) on TA alloy crank and chainwheel set.

The fully equipped long-range touring and camping bicycle has 650 B-42 mm tires (26″ × 1⅝″), but front forks and rear stays are wide enough to permit the use

Fig. 2.10   The true touring bicycle. (*Courtesy of Mel Pinto*)

Fig. 2.11   The long-distance touring bicycle.

of this wider tire. These tires have relatively thin casings and tread for low rolling resistance. They give better shock absorption, better traction, and more security in mud and rain. With loose gravel, pebbles, rocks, or sand, the larger tire rolls more easily with less tendency to dig in or skid. Tire breaks and rim problems from rough road surfaces are diminished. If good terrain and roads are expected and a lighter load carried, 35 mm or 38 mm (1⅜″ and 1½″) section tires can be fitted for lower friction. Rims are aluminum alloy for lightness.

Alloy mudguards incorporate built-in lighting.

Brakes are Mafac Ref "H" Cantilever with brazed-on mounting and hooded levers.

Handlebars are alloy "Randonneur."

The 15-speed wide-gear range derailleur system uses aluminum-alloy cranks and chainwheels.

Equipment includes front and rear low-center-of-gravity tubular-steel pannier carriers with pannier bags mounted. The low mounting improves stability, lessens the pitchover tendency on steep climbs and descents, and makes the bicycle easier to handle when dismounted.

A saddlebag and handlebar bag can be fitted if desired. The wide front handlebar bag support is made of tubular steel. The proper selection of frame angles and steering geometry provides stable handling even with the extra loading.

Cost: $600–$850

The "Mixte" Frame

Pioneered in France for ladies' use, the "Mixte" frame construction has become increasingly popular with feminine riders. Its top tube extends from the top of the steering head to the rear fork end.

It provides more clearance, making mounting and dismounting easier. It provides a more direct aim for rear-brake-control cables, thus increasing brake effectiveness.

Compared to the more common open-framed construction of ladies' models, it distributes stress more evenly and lowers the values of stress concentration, thus increasing strength and rigidity. The design with the central tube cross section of large (1″) diameter is superior to that with twin small-diameter tubes.

Cost: $150–$550

The Tricycle

While heavier than a bicycle, the tricycle has returned to popularity in some quarters. Maintenance men use them in factories; newcomers to cycling find them easier to ride, since they cannot lose their bal-

Fig. 2.12   A camping and long-range touring bicycle for rough terrain.

Fig. 2.13   Mixte frame, ladies' touring bicycle.

ance; and senior citizens find them advantageous for recreation, shopping, and visiting.

Conversion kits can transform a regular bicycle into a three-wheeler. A differential two-wheel drive is superior and safer in handling than a single-wheel rear drive.

Handling on slopes and turns differs considerably from the two-wheel bicycle and takes considerable practice.

Cost: $150–$250

The Folding or Collapsible Bicycle

For ease of carrying and storing, collapsible bicycles are coming to the fore. These often use smaller wheels—16″, 20″, or 24″—to reduce bulk. Frames may hinge in the center or may be unclamped and completely detached.

Gearshift controls can be rear mounted. While the weight of a collapsible model is invariably greater, its convenience makes this disadvantage worthwhile. Collapsibles can be taken along on trains, planes, buses, in the trunk of a car, or on a boat. At home or in a hotel room, they take up little space, and several may be carried or stored in place of only one conventional cycle.

Cost: $150

Fig. 2.14   Detail of mixte frame construction.

Fig. 2.15   Adult three-speed, take-apart three wheeler. (*Courtesy of Columbia Manufacturing Company*)

Fig. 2.16   The folding bicycle. *(Courtesy of Mel Pinto)*

Fig. 2.17   The folding bicycle collapsed for carrying.
(Courtesy of Mel Pinto)

Tandems

Tandems, bicycles built for two or three, are increasing in popularity—these will be further discussed in Chapter XVI. There are great differences in the costs, safety, and capabilities of tandems.

Three types are shown: a single or 2-speed coaster-brake model (Fig. 2.18), a 5-speed model, both of double ladies' frame construction (Fig. 2-19), and a high-performance lightweight tandem 10-speed for serious use in sports or touring (Figs. 2.20 and 2.21).

Costs are respectively: $190, $220, $500, $1195.

Excellent custom-made touring-tandem costs may reach $900–$1600.

COMPARISON OF BICYCLE COMPONENTS

Searching among many hundreds of makes and models for one to fit your personal riding needs, and your budget, can be quite a task. The guarantee, the maker's integrity, spare parts availability, the dealer's skill and service and his knowledge of the sport are major considerations. Consider these first.

The suitability of the bicycle and its fit to your body and to the demands that you will make on it are the next considerations in obtaining long-term satisfaction.

The bicycle should be easy to ride and should have gearing of a type and range to match the hills and wind and your strength. It should ride comfortably and responsively.

Fig. 2.18   The tandem, with coaster brakes. *(Courtesy of Columbia Manufacturing Company)*

Fig. 2.19   The five-speed Schwinn Deluxe Twinn. *(Courtesy of Schwinn Bicycle Company)*

Fig. 2.20 A 10-speed touring tandem. *(Courtesy of Mel Pinto)*

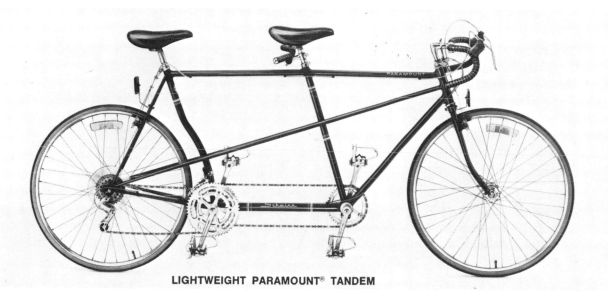

Fig. 2.21 A sports 10-speed tandem. *(Courtesy of Schwinn Bicycle Company)*

It should keep going with minimum attention for a long time.

If your needs change, its construction should permit the easy fitting of components to suit these new conditions. This includes gearing, sprockets, brakes, and handlebars.

The Bicycle Specification Data Sheet at the end of this chapter will give you a rather detailed checklist for comparing components and construction, and the Bicycle Condition Checklist (see Chapter VI) will help you to determine its mechanical condition if the bicycle is being purchased from other than a top-rated dealer. For a rapid comparison, however, compare the frame, the wheels and tires, the hubs and bearings, the saddle, and the accessories.

Frame Tubing

Best: Alloy steels with butted tubing or titanium—Reynolds 531, Columbus, Super Vitus, Isawata or Tange Chrome-Molybdenum use these materials for frame.

Next best: Plain gauge alloy tubing, or Vitus 172 and Durifort butted tubes.

High-tensile carbon steels.

Low-carbon steels with 28 mm or 1⅛″ diameter seat and down tubes (see Chapter V).

Low-carbon steels with main tubes of smaller diameter.

Frame Joining Method

Best: Precision bronze-welded or finely cut and filed lugs joined with silver brazing. Makers build these frames completely in rigid, precision jigs.

Next best: Similar work, but with higher temperature brazing materials. Not jig built.

Full-section lugs, not filed or tapered, die-cast construction.

Resistance-welded with smooth size transition at tube joints.

Arc-welded, butt-welded, butt-brazed, or lapped tube joint with rectangular joint at tubes and head or crank hanger. Don't confuse false press-formed lug contours with separate full reinforcing lugs.

Fork Blades and Chain and Seat Stays

Best: Alloy steel, taper gauge, seamless, with tapering exterior section.

Next best: Alloy steel, straight gauge. Seamed tubing.

High-tensile steel, not alloy. Accurad forge-cast light alloy.

Low-carbon rolled section steel, or forged steel.

Fork Crown

Best: Forged steel or investment cast steel.

Next best: Pressed steel, or plates.

Fork Ends (For superior frame rigidity)

Best: Rear, 7-mm-thick forged or investment cast steel. Front, 5-mm-thick forged or investment cast steel.

Next best: Rear, 5-mm-thick forged steel. Front, 4-mm-thick stamped steel.

⅛-inch-thick stamped steel, fully inserted in tubing of full section.

⅛-inch-thick stamped and formed ends with flattened tubing joint.

Paint

Best: Epoxy finish with proper cleaning and preparation.

Next best: Chip-resistant, multicoat enamel over bonderized, precleaned steel.

Painted without expert cleaning and rust preventive treatment.

Frame and Crank Hanger Bearings and Cranks

Best: Accurately turned and ground, heat-treated bearings with detachable cranks. Campagnolo, Stronglight, Shimano Dura-Ace, or TA are of top quality. Phil Wood sealed precision bearings, threads machined after frame assembly.

Next best: Other makes of detachable cranks, superior quality one or three-piece cranks of alloy steel or Accurad cast light alloy.

Cartridge type preassembled cranksets fit into this category, as do one or three-piece crank sets of low-carbon steel, more feeble cross section, and stamped cups and conical (not radiused) bearing cones.

Wheel Hubs

Best: Sealed precision bearings, or alloy-steel axles with hardened and precision-ground cones, bearing grit seals, angled flanges of light alloy, lightened—Phil Wood, Shimano Dura-Ace, Atom 700, or ACS are examples—With quick release device. Also Campagnolo.

Next best: Precision-machined hubs with heat-treated but not ground cones, and with seals and lightened alloy flanges. Axles of plain carbon steel.

Lesser quality: Plain steel axles, nonangled flanges, inadequate sealing against dirt and grit. Flanges of thinner gauge steel.

Rims

Best: Lightweight aluminum alloy of ample tubular cross section.

Next best: Lightweight alloy solid-rolled section, tubular section steel, well finished.

Lesser quality: Rolled section nontubular steel. Lesser quality plating.

Tires

Best: Silk, nylon, or cotton of thin wall, high-thread count, of high-quality wall and tread stock. The differences must often be measured and are not easily seen. The casing should be flexible yet strong. In wired-ons, Schwinn Le Tour, Wolber Super Sport, Milremo Record, and Michelin Nylon Allege are excellent. Other American makes are being developed. Tubular tires to meet the riding conditions—for racing, training, or touring in silk or lightweight cotton.

Next best: Other types may be less lively, but may be more durable for your particular service. To be avoided, however, are tires with high energy-loss filled compound or reclaim rubber construction.

Pedals

Best: If they suit your purpose, alloy-steel spindle, well-sealed, hardened and ground component racing pedals of forged alloy. Campagnolo, Shimano Dura-Ace, Kyukoto Pro-Ace, Lyotard 65, or Zeus are examples.

Next best: Pedals well sealed with ample-sized adjustable bearings of light steel or alloy.

Lesser quality: Nondismantleable or poorly sealed steel or rubber types.

Handlebars and Handlebar Stem

Best: Lightweight alloy with reinforced center section and forged light alloy or alloy tubular steel stem, of the size and shape to suit you individually.

Next best: Accurad forge-cast light alloy stem with light alloy handlebars, the pattern of the bar and length of the stem in all cases to suit your measurements.

Lesser quality: Mild-seamed steel tubing, plain-cast light alloy or stamped steel handlebar extension.

Saddle and Seat Post

Best: Hand-worked leather of contoured shape, or self-supporting nylon. The best seat post is the light alloy micro-adjusting type—Campagnolo, Simplex, Milremo Nitor, Zeus, and Sakae.

Next best: A more padded saddle with a flexible base may better suit your needs.

A ⅞-inch diameter seat clamp with fine angle adjustment.

Gear Shifters

Best: Shimano Crane, Suntour GT, Campagnolo, Huret Jubilee, or Simplex Competition.

Next best: Other superior models from these companies will be a bit heavier, but will give good performance and may be more durable.

Accessories

Pumps Should have ample capacity and rugged construction, with press-on fitting to the valve, or with a strongly made hose connection. Avoid heavy, flimsy pumps with weak connections that will pull apart when pumping tires hard.

Mudguards Aluminum mudguards with rolled edges and stainless steel mudguards are lightest yet most durable. Get aluminum stays that are bolted to bosses on the frame, not those hooked over the wheel axle.

Lighting Sets These should be voltage regulated with an ample-sized head and taillight and built-in wiring. Avoid wiring which is loosely draped around the frame. Battery lamps are useful for short-distance work and create no drag. Models that meet or exceed the latest (1972) British standards for intensity of illumination are the safest.

Brakes

For children's use, a weather-resistant, reliable coaster brake which is rugged and needs little care and attention is best. Reliable two-speed models are also available from Bendix, NKK, Shimano, Fichtel & Sachs Torpedo.

When used with three-speed gears, an internal expanding brake, such as Torpedo, Shimano Tri-coaster, or Sturmey Archer, provides good service.

For weather-resistance and wet weather efficiency, a Shimano, Wood, or AMF disc brake, or Shimano or Karasawa band brake can be used with derailleurs.

Caliper Brakes

Best: Rugged, strong, well-fitted brakes of forged light alloy, with little play or deflection under heavy braking loads, matched in size to meet the rims properly. Shimano Dura-Ace, Campagnolo, Universal, Weinmann, CLB and Mafac Centerpull, and Altenburger, and GB Centerpull are of high quality. Shimano Tourney centerpull is also in this category.

Lower quality: Aluminum-alloy or steel brakes that are less precisely fitted have obvious play when they are applied and when the wheel is moved back and forth while loaded. This is a sign they are less effective than more durable and expensive models.

This thumbnail sketch of quality features is intended for preliminary comparison. Improved models of other makes are being constantly brought to market, and new materials and methods of construction are being developed. Chapters III–VIII will help you make your own analysis of those items not listed here.

Weight

You may have noted that weight was left until last. Good bearings, low loss tires, and good brakes are more important than is the lightest weight. All things else being equal, the lighter bicycle is the more responsive and will climb hills more easily. But if underdesigned, a light bike can be too flexible to best use your muscular efforts. Look for high quality in the items listed, and save weight where it doesn't decrease performance.

BICYCLE SPECIFICATION DATA SHEET

Brand name

Model name

Bicycle Manufacturer, if known

Model number

Number of speeds
Sprocket sizes, front
Sprocket sizes, rear

Rear hub, make and model
Rear-hub speed ratios

Wheel diameters: Front   Rear

Actual gear range and steps provided

Wheel and tire data:
    Tire, make and model
        Size markings and inflation pressure
        Type of tread   Sidewall,   open,   vulcanized,   color,   reflectorized
        Type of tube valve fitted

    Rims, make and model
        Material
        Rolled section   Extruded   Tubular section
        Pattern of braking surface
        Plating or polish
    Wheel Hubs
        Hub flange, diameter and thickness
        Barrel and flange materials   One-piece   Three-piece
        Type of bearing
        Method of dirt sealing
        Type of attachment: Wrench nut   Wing nut   Quick release   Drop-out prevention
    Number of spokes, length and gauge: Front   Rear
        Spoke material and plating

Frame:
    Frame size at seat tube
    Height of crank center from floor
    Angle to ground: Seat tube   Head tube
    Tube diameters inches: Top tube   Seat tube   Down tube
    Tubing material, make and type identification
    Seamless or welded tubing
    Butted or straight-gauge tubing
    Thickness gauge of tubing
    Type and method of tube joining
        Joint reinforcement   Joining material
    Finish
        Cleaning and rustproofing method
        Type of paint and number of coats
        Chromium plating: locations   and quality

Fork, section (Tubular, solid)
>   Material   Straight gauge or Taper gauge
>   Front fork end stamped or inserted
>   Fork end thickness
>   Offset of fork end from fork centerline
>   Type of fork crown and method of joining
>   Rear fork end stamped or inserted
>   Fork end material: thickness   method of joining

Rear frame chain and seat stays
>   Tubing straight or taper section   Diameter at ends
>   Tubing straight or taper gauge   Gauge of tubing
>   Reinforcements and bridges: stamped, rolled, or tubular?
>   Method of attachment of stays and reinforcements

Steering head bearings:
>   Make and model
>   Construction, cup and cone:
>   Stamped   Turned steel   Turned, heat treated, and ground
>   Number of balls   Ball diameter   Retainer for balls?

Cranks and crank bearings and pedal spindle:
>   One-piece   Three-piece cottered   Three-piece cotterless
>   Make and model   Size and number of balls   Dirt seal method
>   Pedal spindle: Length   Material   Heat treated   Bearings ground?
>   Crank material
>   Crank length, mm
>   Sprocket attaching method
>   Number of sprocket attaching bolts, bolt size, and bolt circle diameter

Front sprocket (chainwheel):
>   Make and model
>   Multiple front sprockets, Permanently joined or separable
>   Material
>   Number, size, and bolt circle diameter of inner sprocket attaching bolts
>   Chainguard: Chain ring   Separate Guard

Rear sprockets (freewheel):
>   Make and model
>   Material   body and cogs
>   Sealed Construction?   Chain derailment ring?
>   Type of removal tool
>   Sprockets removable from outside?   Screw-on or slip-on

Chain:
>   Make and model
>   Width and pitch   Continuous or connecting link

Pedals:

    Make and model

    Type bearing, ball   sleeve

    Material, treads   barrel   axle

    Ball Races turned   turned and ground?

    Bearing dirt seals

    Toe clips and straps supplied?

Derailleur, rear   Make and model

Gearshift control location   Type

Derailleur or gear shift mechanism, front   Make and model

Seat post:

    Make and type

    Top open or closed

    Material   Seat post clamping method in frame

    Diameter   Length   Seat clamp diameter

    Microadjustable

Saddle:

    Make and model

    Length and width

    Top material

    Base, rigid   Flexible   Coil spring frame   Mattress springs

    Frame, two wire   four wire   Flat steel or aluminum

    Seat clamp   Serrated   Microadjustable

Handlebar extension:

    Make

    Plunger diameter and length   Extension length

    Material: Pressed steel   Welded steel   Cast alloy   Forged alloy

    Type expander for clamping: Conical wedge   Split wedge   External clamp

Handlebar:

    Upright   Flat   Dropped pattern

    Width   Rise or drop   Forward or backward "throw"

    Bar diameter   Center diameter

    Material of construction

Brakes:

    Front, make and model   Material

    Rear, make and model   Material

    Type: Center-pull caliper   Side-pull caliper   Side-pull symmetric caliper

        Automotive Internal expanding   Hub shell or metallic shoe

        Disc

Action: Cable and casing

    Hydraulic

    Reverse pedal actuated

Brake Pads: Length and width

Wear adjusting means

Shoe position adjustment means

Cable diameter and number strands

Fixed pads or self-energizing

Type material and pattern

Brake levers:

    Make and model

    Pattern

    Safety lever equipped?

Material

Location of lever when fully applied

Accessories Supplied:

    Mudguards

        Make   Material

        Method and location of attachment means   Rigidity of mounting

    Reflectors

        Rear   Front   Side   Note diameters

    Lighting

        Front lamp, make and model   Diameter   Bulb size

        Rear lamp, make and model   Diameter   Bulb size

        Battery or generator?   Make and model and capacity

        Where mounted   Wiring concealed or exposed?

    Carriers

        Make and model   Front   Rear

        Type construction

        Method of mounting

        Carrier dimensions   Load clamping provision provided

    Water bottle and carrier

        Make   Model   Capacity

        Location and method of attachment

    Tire Pump

        Make and Model   Method of attachment

        Length and diameter   Location

    Other accessories

Weight of complete bicycle less accessories

Weight of complete bicycle and accessories

WHAT MAKE SHOULD I SELECT? WHERE SHOULD I BUY?

Bicycles are available at many locations, for example the department store, the discount house, the auto store, the bicycle shop, and the ski shop. By shopping around, you may obtain suitable equipment at lower costs in some shops than in others. But other factors must be taken into account for your greatest satisfaction.

A bicycle is a piece of finely tuned athletic equipment. It must fit you—all of you, not only your legs—for safety and best performance. Unless you are a skilled bicycle mechanic who can fine-tune the mechanical parts, you need the services of an expert bicycle assembler—even if the bike comes almost assembled in its factory carton. Most American-built bicycles now come with a well-written assembly and care instruction manual packed in the carton. Detailed assembly and repair manuals published for the guidance of retail establishments and customers are available. Some firms, such as Schwinn Company, have established Factory and Field Training Schools for bicycle craftsmen which enable them to properly select and fit the bicycle to a customer's needs, to repair it when needed, and to keep dealer and serviceman aware of new developments in the field. This gives you a greater assurance that your beginning and recurring needs will be met.

Warranties are another matter to consider. Some manufacturers' dealers provide a free service and adjustment policy after a month of use, by which time any discrepancies, such as cable stretch and initial wear in, can be corrected. On the bicycle itself, warranties vary greatly. There is no written United States warranty on many foreign bicycles. Your protection is in the integrity of the distributor and the dealer from whom you purchase. It is always best to get a make whose builder stands behind his product for a lifetime.

Spare parts and repair service is a factor in your evaluation. Some foreign makes have internal parts and accessories made to foreign standards, and while these are excellent in the country of manufacture, replacements are not readily available here. The importer may not have a repair parts stocking service. Even the dealer may not realize this, and you may not discover it until the bike needs repair, perhaps in a remote region. Parts that look alike may vary greatly in durability and accuracy. When two suppliers' rear axles were tested by one bicycle manufacturer, he found that one was 60% stronger than the other. Repairmen report that this same manufacturer's cranks are almost twice as resistant to bending from impact as others. Tests made by this firm on tires of the same size and appearance showed variations from one manufacturer to the next by as much as two to one in rolling resistance and durability, and this despite the bicycle builder's rigid specifications. This firm's severe quality control section takes nothing for granted, and naturally, prices for their models are a bit higher. The buyer, however, does not have the facilities to perform such tests before making a purchase; his laboratory is the open road.

A good bicycle mechanic may be able to make initial adjustments and fit you properly in from 45 minutes to one hour; you might need the best part of an entire morning to do it yourself. Unless you are an expert, the extra cost to have the job done properly is a worthwhile investment. Your own work may be improper, creating the possibility of an accident. I've known the owner-adjusted bike to suffer chain derailment on the road, resulting in the injury of the rider on his first trip.

In our section on maintenance and repair (Chapter VI) a detailed checklist is included for you to use in inspecting your purchase.

What Type Shall I Select?

As you look at our 14 classifications and review their general uses, remember that, at minor expense, a well-equipped dealer can vary a specification to better meet your particular need by exchanging factory-furnished components. See particularly our discussions on pedals, rims, tires, saddles, handlebars, brakes and fitting, gearing, and carriers (Chapter VII).

As we stated earlier, a careful analysis of your actual requirements is important. As you ride, you may learn some things about yourself of which you were initially unaware.

Consider the road surfaces upon which you will ride. If they are relatively smooth and free of glass, cobbles, gratings, and potholes, you can use a lighter rim and tire to get an easier ride. Do you expect much rain, mud, or slippery streets? Are you nimble and careful? Poorer road surfaces and bad weather make heavier rims and larger tires preferable, but the careful, nimble cyclist using lightweight rims and tires may negotiate rough and slippery roads successfully. Nimble or not, for mud and wet, you should fit mudguards.

If you expect to ride with and against the wind for more than moderate distances, a three-speed gear will ease your riding. In inclement weather, the three-speed hub, perhaps with a coaster brake included, will take you back and forth with maximum safety and minimum maintenance problems. Two and three-speed hub gears may be adequate for moderate hills.

Will your riding be mostly short duration trips in the city, at moderate speed? A flat or moderate-rise handlebar may suit you just fine. Rubber pedals allow the use of street shoes. You will be comfortable in business clothing with this type.

A wide-range 5 or 10-speed gearing with dropped pattern handlebars is more adaptable to speed and maneuverability; longer trips against varying winds; and long, steep hills. Your air resistance will be less, and your hill climbing easier, in the dropped bar riding position. For general all-around use, the 10-speed is the most versatile. It is also more delicate and requires more care and maintenance, but once you learn to handle and shift it effectively, it will do almost anything you wish.

For real sports riding, and most certainly for competition, the road racing bicycle has hordes of adherents. Its superior performance flattens hills and cuts opposing winds. Equipped with lightweight luggage carriers, it is extensively used for touring on good roads.

For out-and-out speed and performance on smooth roads and banked tracks, the conditioned rider in moderate terrain can enjoy the spirit and precision of a fixed-gear track racing bicycle.

For the rider who likes to explore and travel long distances in all terrain, who is self-sufficient and able to meet all conditions of wind, grade, and weather, the true touring bicycle with its wide-range 10 or 15-speed gearing will be a faithful and long-remembered companion.

For a casual jaunt around the neighborhood or the seashore, a tandem is twice the fun. It helps to train the inexperienced rider, simplifies riding together in traffic, and enables a stronger rider to assist one less capable. Gearing extends its capabilities. If designed as a racing or as a true touring machine, it can serve as an able mount in all terrain.

Consider your budget when you select your bicycle, but consider your needs even more. A wisely chosen, adequate but not extravagant bicycle will give you years of high return. The riding ease of a fine bicycle equipped with tires of low rolling resistance, a responsive frame, and good bearings must be experienced to be believed. It is difficult to be put into logical form, but it can be felt. Weight alone is not a criterion, although it is a factor. Effectiveness in power transmission can be measured. By doubling the power required at a given speed, the length of time that the power can be expended, and thus the distance covered at that speed, will be reduced to 10 percent or less. A slight difference in performance can thus have appreciable results in fun and accomplishment.

How About a Used Bicycle?

You may be able to make a saving if you purchase a used bicycle, but find out first why the owner wishes to sell. Is he upgrading his equipment; has he bought a new machine and so no longer needs the one to be sold? Is he no longer able to make use of the equipment, or is his storage space overcrowded? Is the former owner deceased? Is the bicycle the property of the owner, or is it possibly stolen merchandise? If in question, determine its source. You are contributing to crime and possibly to the loss of your own bicycle if you do not determine this and take the necessary action.

In Chapter VI there are checklists for a detailed step by step examination of the bicycle to determine its condition. Make the riding test, if you are permitted. Worn sprocket teeth can be seen, compare the teeth with new ones if you are in doubt. Pull the chain away from the front sprocket at about the center of its length of contact with the sprocket. If it can be lifted ⅛ inch (or 3 mm), or if the bottoms of the teeth show space, there is excess wear. Determine the cost of replacing parts shown to be defective in your examination. Thus you can judge if the price asked is fair.

Finding Spare Parts

Bicycles on the American market are made in the United States and imported from two dozen foreign countries. With several hundred makes involved, a lack of international standards complicates the problem of finding spare parts. For instance, English standards for cycle threads are: ⅛-inch diameter bolts, 40 tpi; ⁵⁄₃₂–³⁄₁₆, 32 tpi; ⁷⁄₃₂–¾, 26 tpi. The Italian standard ⁹⁄₁₆ × 20 tpi is made to different tolerances than the English ⁹⁄₁₆ × 20 tpi and is therefore a bit tighter fitting. In addition, purchased components can further swell the spare parts problem since they may be also of many makes. Unfortunately, some importers are interested in the initial sale and do not stock spare parts, leaving it up to the dealer's conscience. Indeed, many importers to whom I have spoken do not know what dimension standards nor what materials of frame construction are used. Visits to several foreign plants disclosed two different dimensional standards exported to the United States on the same brand. American manufacturers who use foreign components make certain that spare parts are available for their customers.

Chains are a bright spot in the picture. One-eighth-inch width × ½-inch pitch is the worldwide standard for single-speed and three-speed bicycles; ³⁄₃₂-inch width × ½-inch pitch without connecting link is standard for derailleur models. Chain length, however, will vary on different models.

Handlebar stems come in 0.813-inch diameter (American); 22 mm, or 0.866-inch (French); or 22.2 mm, 0.875-inch (English); the latter is also used on many other foreign imports, as well as on some American models. Don't guess; use calipers. The differences are small but important.

Handlebars vary in size of tubing and the diameter at which the bar is attached to the handlebar stem (see Table 4.1).

Pedal threads are: American, ½-inch diameter × 20 threads per inch, and English, ⁹⁄₁₆-inch diameter × 20 threads per inch. The Continental European equivalent is 14 x 1.25 -mm thread pitch, or 20.3 threads per inch, but ⁹⁄₁₆ x 20 is also fitted.

Cottered crank axles of three-piece construction may be 0.625-inch diameter, English standard, or 16-mm (0.630-inch) diameter, continental size.

Crank hanger cups may be pressed-in, American type with one-piece cranks; English standard, 1.370-inch × 24 tpi; French standard 35-mm diameter × 1-

mm pitch (25.4 threads per inch); or Italian, 36-mm diameter × 24 tpi. None are interchangeable. Japanese manufacturers usually use the English standard. Most American one-piece cranks are threaded 24 tpi, although Schwinn uses 28.

Crank Hanger Widths affect the axle length and axle bearing spacing to be used; 68 mm and 70 mm are the most common. Axle lengths also vary to suit single, double or triple-chainwheels. Bearing spacing varies slightly among different makes of three-piece cranks.

Fork Stem threading can be American, 1-inch diameter × 24 tpi; English, 1-inch diameter × 24 tpi; or continental, 25 mm × 1-mm pitch (0.98-inch × 25.4 tpi). English Raleigh forks, however, have used 26 tpi instead of 24.

The head bearing cups also vary depending on head tube gauge and diameter. Continental standard is 30.2 mm inside diameter with a 26.5-mm seating diameter on the fork. English head cup seating diameter is about 1.178-inch, if 20-gauge head tubing is used, or 1.194-inch with 22-gauge tubing. American standard bicycle cups are 1 $\frac{9}{32}$-inch approximate cup seating dimension.

Front axles to American and English standards are $\frac{5}{16}$-inch diameter, with 24 and 26 tpi respectively. The continental standard is 8-mm in diameter × 1 mm or 25.4 tpi.

Rear axles are $\frac{3}{8}$-inch in diameter × 24 tpi, or continental, 9.5 mm in diameter × 1 mm, or 25.4 tpi. The hollow axles used with quick-release hubs are larger, having a 10-mm diameter front and rear.

Freewheel threads of English and Japanese standard are 1.370-inch × 24 tpi. French or continental freewheels are metric threaded, 34.7 × 1-mm pitch, and are not interchangeable.

Front Sprocket mountings of the detachable type are usually three or five-bolt mounting. The five-pin, 50.4-mm bolt circle is interchangeable English and continental. Larger diameter three and five-bolt mounting diameters vary considerably in English, French, Italian, and Japanese types. To be certain, obtain the same make and model.

Frame tubing diameter in most lightweight bicycles is 1 ⅛-inch diameter for the seat and down tubes and 1-inch diameter for the top tube. Many American bicycles use a 1-inch diameter throughout. Continental size is 28 mm and 26 mm respectively. While this must be considered if tubes must be replaced in a damaged frame, the seat post and head fittings and accessory clamp sizes also vary. This is further discussed in the section on saddles and seat posts (see Chapter 7).

Front and rear hub widths vary. There are inch and metric one, three, four, five, or six-speed rear hubs. The front and rear fork end widths should match the hub to be used. Japanese dimension standards conform generally to the English in most, but not all cases. European builders may use continental or English dimensions.

In 1973, to overcome worldwide discrepancies in design and a lack of standardization of bicycles and their components, the International Organization for Standardization (ISO)—of which the American National Standards Institute (ANSI) is a member—initiated a task group, #TC/149, Cycles. This group is charged to develop a standard terminology, standard testing methods, dimensional standardization of components and performance standards. The United States became a voting member of this Committee in 1974. Present Italian 55° threading and English Whitworth 55° threading will be replaced by ISO 60° threading. See Figs. 7.6, 7.12, and Table 9.2 for some other proposed ISO standards.

However, even when worldwide standardization is agreed upon, millions of bicycles with nonstandard parts will still remain in service, and replacement parts will still be made and supplied for many years.

CHAPTER III

Comparison of Bicycle Tubing and Frame Construction

THE frame may be termed the "heart" of the bicycle. The material of which a bike is constructed determines its capacity and virility and vitally affects the weight, the strength, the endurance to road impacts and loading, and the responsiveness to the effort of its rider. The material used also contributes in good measure to the cost of building the frame; improved materials not only are more expensive, but their use requires extra manufacturing care.

Except in the higher grade bicycles, which use name brands of tubing having known strengths and qualities, it is usually quite difficult for the buyer to ascertain the type of steel used, its thickness, and its quality. The base material used in bicycles of widely varying cost may be comparable in chemical composition, but the cleanliness of the material and the operations taken in the fabrication of the tube can vary widely. Methods of joining tubes vary considerably, with a wide variation in strength and endurance resulting in frames of similar appearance. Metallurgical examination of the material in the painted bicycle frame is out of the question for the purchaser. Yet internal scratches in the tubing, nonmetallic inclusions in the steel itself remaining from defective steel manufacture, and quality control in the joining of the frame structure can lead to brittleness and failures under riding stresses. The breaking apart at sea of complete ships during colder weather (below 60°F) has been attributed to these identical factors.

Thinner gauges of tubing of uncertain strength may be used by unscrupulous manufacturers to obtain a light frame weight. Decals of unknown tube names resembling decals used on frames built with superior tubing have been used on some imports. Caveat emptor is good advice in this competitive market.

COMPARISON OF TUBING PROPERTIES

Many types of tubing are used in bicycle construction. The major types of steel tubing include electric welded, electric welded and cold drawn over a mandrel, straight-gauge carbon steel, straight-gauge alloy steel, butted carbon steel, and butted alloy steel. Each of these types is made in several chemical compositions. In addition, stainless steels, aluminum alloys, titanium and titanium alloys are in use. Table 3.1 compares the composition and strengths of representative types.

Each type is made in a number of thicknesses. The thickness selected takes into account the tubing strength, the frame manufacturing method, and the demands to be made on the bicycle in service.

New processes of high-frequency electric welding, using currents of 150,000 to 400,000 cycles per second have now been developed which permit high-speed electric welding of very thin gauges of carbon steel, alloy steels, and other metals. Their use may further develop the materials available for bicycle frames.

The makers of low-cost bicycles obtain maximum production at a minimum cost for tube manufacture and frame assembly by using tubing made of extra-low-carbon steel. A series of rollers contours the type 1010 strip steel stock until it forms a tube. The edges are then continuously flash-welded as the tube proceeds, using heavy electric current. The low-carbon content permits ease of welding without embrittlement, but the tube is relatively thick-walled (1.1 to 1.8 mm), correspondingly heavy, and only moderate in strength. As a final

Table 3.1

BICYCLE TUBING CHARACTERISTICS

Type of Tubing (Steel Unless Noted)	Chemical Composition %								Strength				Remarks Strengths in Kg/mm²
	C	Mn	Cr	Mo	V	Si	Ni	P,S°	Ultimate psi	Ultimate Kg/mm²	Yield psi	Yield Kg/mm²	
Electric Welded Low Carbon	.08/.15							.050	45,000	31	25,000	17	
Electric Welded, Carbon	0.15	0.6							45,000	31	25,000	17	
Electric Welded High Carbon	0.30								56,000	39	34,000	17	
Electric Welded, Cold Drawn	0.20	0.6						.060	56,000	39	25,000	17	After Brazing: Ultimate, 31; Yield, 17
Electric Welded, Cold Drawn, Tempered	0.20	0.6						.060	62,000	43	54,000	38	After Brazing: Ultimate, 31; Yield, 17
Cold Drawn, Seamless, "B" Quality	0.15							.050	63,000	44	54,000	38	
Cold Drawn, Seamless, Durifort A35	0.03/0.08	0.50						.010	70,000	49			
Cold Drawn, Seamless, "A" Quality	0.30	0.3/0.9				0.35			58,000	41	36,000	25	
Cold Drawn, Seamless, "A" Tempered	0.30	0.3/0.9				0.35			78,000	55	60,000	42	
Reynolds 531	0.30	1.75		0.30				.050	125,000	88	112,000	79	After Brazing: Ultimate, 79; Yield, 67
Reynolds 753									168,000	117	134,000	93	Low Temp Braze
Chrome-Molybdenum	0.30		1.0	0.30				.010	125,000	88	112,000	79	After Brazing: Ultimate, 79; Yield, 67
Chrome-Molybdenum (Columbus) Vitus 172	0.20	0.68	1.0	0.25		0.23		.010	125,000	88	112,000	79	After Brazing: Ultimate, 79; Yield, 67
Super Vitus 971 XC-38	0.34	0.78				0.34		.001	120,000	85	106,000	75	type 150 V6
Gautier Troussel A.H.R.	.12/18	0.8/1.1	1.25/1.50	0.8/1.0	0.2/0.3	<0.2			126,000	90	106,000	75	
									155,000	110	115,000	80	Higher Strength—Cold Work
Stainless Steel (Crescent)	0.05 max	1.3	18.5	—	—	0.6	9.5	.300	110,000	78	70,000	49	
B.338 Titanium 99% Pure									70,000	49	42,000	34	
Titanium Alloy									90,000	63	80,000	56	

Notes:

Strengths of cold drawn and alloy steel tubing are not directly comparable. Tensile strengths generally increase with more cold work to thinner gauges. Heat treatment can vary actual strength and brittleness considerably.

Strength of cold-worked tubes after brazing may be reduced to that of the tube prior to drawing or tapering. Brazing alloys commonly used have melting points of 1800°F (980°C); 1560°F (850°C); 1350°F (730°C); and (silver alloy) 1150°F (620°C). High-temperature brazing can reduce strengths of 531 and Cr-Mo steel to 70,000 psi (49 kg/mm²) ultimate strength and 50,000 psi (35 kg/mm²) yield strength.

The use of columbium or other trace elements in small quantities permits high-tensile strengths of 80,000 psi with low-carbon steel. The brazing temperatures have less effect on strength with low-carbon steels.

°Phosphorus and sulfur appear in equal amounts. Value shown is for each element separately, not both elements combined. All values maximum.

operation, the tubes are cut to the desired length while still in motion. Labor costs are at a minimum.

This heavy wall tubing is either arc or flash-welded at the frame joints, or brazed directly into the crank hanger shell and head tubes with high-temperature electric or gas blowtorch heating, using a plug or ring of brazing material. In another method, socketed tube joints called lugs are used. The frames may be dip-brazed in molten brass, or blowtorch brazed, using brass pellets preinserted in the joints.

The heavy wall of the tubing resists concentrations of stress that occur at the butt joints at the frame tubes and steering head tubes and at the joining of the frame and rear triangle tubes and the crank hanger. Tubing from 1.6 mm to 1.8 mm thick is used with the unreinforced butt joints; 1.2 to 1.4-mm tubing is commonly used with the reinforcing lug construction.

Low-carbon steels, being relatively soft and weak, bend more easily under impact. If carefully reheated without overheating, bends can often be straightened.

The search for stronger and lighter tubing has led to the use of higher-carbon steels (in the range of from 0.15 to 0.30% carbon). As the carbon content increases, the strength of the steel also increases, and thinner cross sections can be used.

Thinner sections make the frame lighter and more responsive and dissipate road shocks along the tubing. The bicycle is livelier and more comfortable. Thin tubes with softer and weaker tubing may bend or break at the joints, especially if a curb or bump is struck.

JOINING METHODS

The use of higher-carbon tubing requires more care and less overheating at the joints. High temperatures and rapid chilling cause the extra carbon to form harder, more brittle areas in the steel, which may result in joint or tube failure under impact.

The strength of most steels can be increased by cold-working during tube manufacture. The tubing is pulled with great force over mandrels, or its diameter reduced by rolling or impact. However, high brazing temperatures reduce the strength at the joints (where it is most needed) to the values of the unworked tubing.

Malleable iron castings, or pressed and bulged steel stampings made to the proper diameters and angles needed to receive the tube ends (lugs) are usually used in the medium-carbon steel tube frames to align the tubes and reinforce the joints. Tubes should be accurately cut at the ends for maximum strength. Joints in medium-carbon steel can also be bronze-welded. In this method, very carefully mitered tube ends are required so that all adjoining surfaces meet. Then the brazing alloy is applied using an oxygen-gas torch to build a reinforcing fillet at the joint. While the brazing alloy is weaker in strength than steel, the extra thickness of the concave fillet provides ample strength and

distributes stresses. Some constructors braze a reinforcing steel sleeve into the interior at the joint to distribute shock stresses better and further reduce the chance of brittle fracture.

Steel alloys increase strength and permit further lightening of the tubing, and therefore of the frame. One commonly used alloy is SAE 4130 chrome-molybdenum, with 0.30% carbon. Another long successful and very popular tubing, made by Reynolds Division of Tube Industries in England under the trade name of 531, contains 1.75% manganese, which makes the steel tougher and stronger and less brittle, despite its higher hardness and strength. High-grade alloy bicycle tubing starts with excellent control of the steel making process to reduce the size and amount of nonmetallic inclusions and with careful control of alloy content, carbon, and unwanted impurities such as sulfur and phosphorus. Ateliers de la Rive, in France, makers of Durifort, Vitus, and Super-Vitus tubing, after careful chemical and metallurgical analysis of the base alloys, trim the tube ends after each step for impurity removal, and control their processes to make certain that small grain size is attained and that residual crystals of ferrite in the alloy are not retained. Fatigue, they have found, propagates along the lines of least resistance, or along the crystals of ferrite. Fatigue cracks are also born at the ends of nonmetallic inclusions.

These high-grade bicycle tubing steels after fabrication and cold work are given a heat treatment conducted in a carefully controlled furnace atmosphere. Gautier Trousell of Longueville, France makes a tubing called A.H.R. (Acier Haut Resistance), of high-alloy content, including vanadium, which develops great strength. Other well-known tubing makers include Columbus of Italy, Tange, Isawata, Day and Day of Japan, all chrome-molybdenum, Falck of Italy, and Mansmann of Germany.

All of these tubes are seamless, made from a hot pierced billet which is drawn to the required diameter through a series of dies. Most are also available in butted form. Butted tubing is rolled over a mandrel with reduced size ends so that the ends are thicker than the center section. The mandrel is removed by passing the tube through inclined rollers (see Fig. 3.1).

Since frame stresses are concentrated at the joints, and since brazing temperatures cause the steel at the joints to lose some of the strength gained through cold work and heat treatment, a lighter wall thickness in the center allows tube weight to be reduced without a loss in strength. Filing and polishing of the brazed joints for appearance will not result in lost strength.

Table 3.2 gives the available sizes and thicknesses of some popular high-grade tubes. The tubing selected should correspond with the use the rider demands. The lighter gauges are used for time trials, pursuit rac-

Table 3.2

TUBE THICKNESS GUIDE

CARBON STEEL

Tube	EWLC Straight Gauge	EWLC Hvy Duty	EWC Butted	EWC	EWC	EWHC EWCD	CDS "B" Quality Straight Gauge		CDS "A" Quality Straight Gauge		CDS "A" Quality Butted	
Top Tube	1.63 (1 in. dia.)	1.83 (1 in. dia.)	—	1.4	1.25	1.0/0.8	1.02	0.91	1.02	0.91	1.22/0.91	1.02/0.71
Seat Tube	1.63 (1 in. dia.)	1.83 (1 in. dia.)		1.4	1.25	1.0/0.8	1.02	0.91	1.02	0.91	1.22/0.91	1.02/0.71
Down Tube	1.63 (1 in. dia.)	1.83 (1 in. dia.)	1.5	1.4	1.25	1.0/0.8	1.02	0.91	1.02	0.91	1.22/0.91	1.02/0.71
Chainstays	1.63 (¾ in. dia.)	1.63 (¾ in. dia.)		1.5								
Seat Stays	1.63 (⅝ in. dia.)	1.63 (⅝ in. dia.)										
Fork Blade	1.83	2.37	2.0									
Head Tube							1.42		1.22		1.22/0.91	
Steerer	2.1/0.83	2.1/0.83					1.63/1.3	1.63/1.3	1.63/1.3	1.63/1.3	1.63/1.3	1.63/1.3
Notes	1	1	2	3	3	4	4	4	4	4	5	5

ALLOY STEEL

Tube	Isuvata Straight Gauge #026	Chrome-Moly Butted 024	022	019	017	Isuvata Extralight 015 Alpha	Chrome-Moly Straight Gauge	Durifort Butted	Vitus 172	Vitus 971	Tange Champion Chrome-Moly #1	#2	#3	Reynolds 753 Butted	531 SL
Top Tube	1.0	1.0/0.7	0.9/0.6	0.8/0.5	0.8/0.5	0.6/0.3	1.02	1.1/0.75	1.1/0.75	0.9/0.6	1.0/0.7	0.9/0.6	0.9/0.6	0.71/0.376	0.71/0.56
Seat Tube	1.0	1.0/0.7	0.9/0.6	0.8/0.5	0.7/0.4	0.6/0.3	1.02	1.1/0.75	1.1/0.75	0.9/0.6	0.9/0.6	0.9/0.6	0.9/0.6	0.71/0.376	0.71/0.56
Down Tube	1.0	1.0/0.7	0.9/0.6	0.8/0.5	0.7/0.4	0.6/0.3	1.02	1.1/0.75	1.1/0.75	0.9/0.6	1.1/0.8	0.9/0.6	1.0/0.7	0.71/0.457	0.81/0.56
Chainstays	0.8	0.8	0.8	0.8	0.8	0.6	1.42	1.0	1.0	0.8	0.9	0.9	0.9	0.51	0.61
Seat Stays	0.8	0.8	0.8	0.6	0.6	0.4	1.22	1.5	1.2	0.8	0.8	0.8	0.8	0.46	0.56
Fork Blade	1.2	1.2	1.0	1.0/0.8	1.0/0.8			1.0	1.0	1.2	1.2	1.2	1.2	0.91/0.56	1.02/0.56
Head Tube	1.0	1.0	1.0	1.0		1.0				1.0	1.0	1.0	1.0	0.91	0.91
Steerer	2.3/1.6	2.3/1.6	2.0/1.6	2.0/1.6	2.0/1.6			2.5/1.6°	2.5/1.6°	2.5/1.6°	2.3/1.55	2.3/1.55°	2.3/1.55†	1.42	2.34/1.63
Notes	6,9	7	8	10	11	11		7	8	8	7	8	7		11,13
Set lb	5.73	5.35	4.9	4.35	3.85	3.3									3.75
Weight g	2610	2430	2220	1970	1740	1500									1800

NOTE All thicknesses in mm

1. For American high production bicycles
2. For single-tube folding bicycles
3. For moderate-cost adult bicycles
4. For improved-quality adult bicycles
5. For lightweight bicycles
6. For medium-quality lightweight bicycles
7. For road racing bicycles, heavy touring
8. For small frames, club riding
9. For sprinting, 6-day racing
10. For pursuit racing
11. For hour record breaking on track
12. For hill climbing, criterium, general touring
13. Reynolds Seat Stay taper: 13 to 9.5, 14 to 10, 16 to 11 mm
    Chainstay taper: 22.2 or 20 to 13, 12, 11, or 9.5 mm
    Fork taper: 29 × 16, 22.2, or 22 to 13, 12, 11, or 9.5 mm
14. Columbus Seat Stay taper: 14 to 10.5 mm
    Chainstay taper: 22.2 to 12 mm
    Fork taper: 28 × 19 to 12 mm
15. For time trials on road

° Tandem steerers also available in 3.0 and 3.6 mm thickness at base.
† Estimate.

ALLOY STEEL—continued

Tube	Reynolds 531 Straight Gauge	Reynolds 531 Straight Gauge	Reynolds 531 Butted Tandem	Reynolds 531 Butted Club	Reynolds 531 Butted Sprint	Reynolds 531 Butted	Reynolds 531 Butted	Columbus Chrome-Moly PS	Columbus Chrome-Moly PL	Columbus Chrome-Moly SP	Columbus Chrome-Moly SL	Columbus Rekord	Columbus Prototype
Top Tube	0.91	0.71	1.02/0.71 (30 mm diam)	0.81/0.56	1.02/0.71	1.02/0.71	0.81/0.56	1.02/0.71	0.61	1.02/0.71	0.91/0.61	0.50	0.7/0.5
Seat Tube	0.91	0.71	1.02/0.71 (1¼ in. dia.)	0.81/0.56	1.02/0.71	0.81/0.56	0.81/0.56	1.02/0.71	0.61	1.02/0.71	0.91/0.61	0.50	0.7/0.5
Down Tube	0.91	0.71	1.02/0.71 (32 mm dia.)	0.91/0.61	1.02/0.71	0.81/0.56	0.91/0.61	1.02/0.71	0.61	1.02/0.71	0.91/0.61	0.50	0.8/0.5
Chainstays	0.81	0.81	0.81	0.71	0.81	0.81		1.02 (24 mm dia.)	0.71 (22 mm dia.)	1.02	0.71	0.50	0.7
Seat Stays	0.91 or 0.71	0.71	0.81	0.71	0.91	0.91		0.91	0.71	0.91	0.71	0.50	0.5
Fork Blade	1.22	1.22	1.63/0.91 (1⅜ in. dia.)	1.22/0.81	1.42/0.91	1.22/0.81	1.22/0.91	1.02 (16 mm dia.)	0.91 (14 mm dia.)	1.22	0.91	0.90	0.9
Head Tube	0.91	0.71		0.71	0.71 or 0.91	0.71	0.91 or 0.71	0.91	0.71	0.71	0.91	0.80	0.8
Steerer	1.63/1.3	1.63/1.3	1.63/1.3 (1⅛ in. dia. Bottom Tube Oval 2″ × 0.937″)	2.3/1.6	2.3/1.6		2.34/1.63	2.34/1.63	2.34/1.63	2.34/1.63	2.34/1.63	2.5/1.65	
Notes	6,13	6,13	7,13	8,13	9,13	10,13	12,13	9,14	10,14	7,14	12,14	11,15	14
Set Weight lb						5.30	4.63	5.37	4.03	5.24	4.55		3.56
Set Weight g						2400	2100	2435	1830	2375	2065		1615

Table 3.2B

TUBE WALL THICKNESS

Thickness mm	Inches	B.S.W. Gauge
2.337	0.092	13
2.032	0.080	14
1.829	0.072	15
1.626	0.064	16
1.422	0.056	17
1.219	0.048	18
1.016	0.040	19
0.914	0.036	20
0.813	0.032	21
0.711	0.028	22
0.610	0.024	23
0.559	0.022	24
0.508	0.020	25
0.457	0.018	26
0.417	0.016	27
0.376	0.0148	28

ing, or record breaking on nearly flat surfaces, or for lightly built riders who do not carry heavy loads. For example, Eddy Merckx used a frame built with Reynolds tubing of 0.71/0.376 mm gauge butted tubing to set the world's hour record in 1972.

The straight-gauge tubes are more rigid than the butted and give a harsher ride. The heavier gauges provide more resistance to pedaling thrusts, for carrying heavier loads, and for use on large frames for taller riders. Medium thick tubes are employed for hill climbing, criterium racing and general touring. Too great a frame flexibility from extralight tubing would reduce stability and waste energy through frame deflection under road shocks and pedaling forces.

Ultimate tensile strength measures the stress required to break the tube. Yield strength is a measure of the stress in the steel at which permanent stretch or bending commences. A high yield strength means that the frame will resist bending or misalignment to a greater degree. Elongation is a measure of brittleness. High elongation will relieve localized stress by stretching rather than breaking. High-temperature brazing reduces ultimate and yield strengths of heat-treated alloy tubing and carbon steel tubing, and reduces elongation as well.

With these high-strength, higher-alloy tubes, manufacturing processes must be much more precise. Joints must be carefully fitted and aligned; the diameters of the tube ends and the inside diameters of the lugs should be carefully polished and matched in size. A close, precise fit is required, with the tube ends mitered to avoid gaps. A fit too tight or too loose in the joint will greatly reduce joint strength, and the fits are measured in thousandths of an inch. If the tube and lug angles do not match precisely, the tube or lug must be machined or bent. This is sometimes done by cold

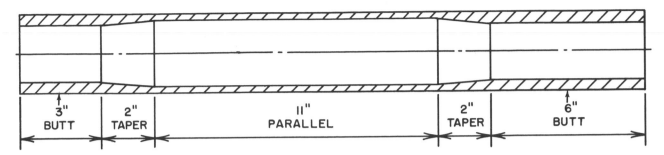

Fig. 3.1   Butted tubing—thicker at the ends than in the body.

bending, or by heating the assembled lug red hot with a torch and hammering it to conformity. Heat forming can produce surface oxidation, decreasing both tube and joint strength.

It can thus be seen that extra costs are incurred in all phases of tubing manufacture and assembly of the frame when high-strength steels are used. When the tubes are thinner, loss of the inherent strength at the tube surface is far more critical than with heavier tubes. The controlled atmosphere or vacuum used in heat treating of the tube during manufacture prevents surface decarburization and loss of strength. The craftsman must use a neutral-flame atmosphere when brazing for the same reason. Unfortunately, the care taken by the frame builder is invisible after the frame has been assembled and painted. Degraded steel grain structure and surface condition is not detectable. Even a well-known "name" builder may employ less-skilled assemblers. Only the most conscientious builders demand perfection.

The brazing temperature, the time required to complete a joint, and the rate of cooling of the joint after brazing, and the area of the tube subjected to heat must be carefully controlled. Overheating causes brass from the brazing to enter the pores of the tubing, causing inclusions in the grain of the steel which make the tubing brittle. With low-alloy tubing, a submerged dip into molten brazing alloy, or the use of a large blowtorch, speeds the brazing process. High-alloy tubing requires a craftsman who heats the lug and tube precisely to the minimum temperatures required for bonding with an atmosphere-controlled small flame torch, and who then keeps the joints away from chilling air currents or the rapid chill caused by setting the frame on the floor after joining. Too rapid a cooling rate induces residual stresses and brittleness from hard spots in the steel.

In very high-grade frames, such as the Schwinn Paramount, the Jack Taylor, and some other precision-built bicycles, the use of higher-cost silver brazing materials in place of the usual brazing material (1050°F to 1200°F vs. 1560°F to 1800°F) combats strength reduction. Since lower temperatures are used, the temper of the steel is retained. With less heat input, the expansion of the joints and tubes is lessened, and smaller residual stresses remain in the frame after brazing. Likewise there is less chance of brittleness from excessive cooling rates.

The sequence of joint brazing is important in avoiding stresses from expansion and contraction. The least critical joints are brazed last so that internal cooling stresses are kept away from the bottom bracket and lower head tube junctions.

Expert craftsmen, such as Singer (Csuka) and Follis, in France, carefully build up fillets in crank-hanger and steering head areas to increase the strength and rigidity of these areas to above that of factory-supplied steel or cast lugs and brackets.

TUBING WEIGHT

Compared to high-production methods, the production of hand-brazed, high-alloy frames is a more tedious, precise job of craftsmanship and handling. This increases costs but results in a lighter, stronger, more-responsive, safer frame which is less likely to fail unexpectedly.

The advantage of using stronger, highly stressed material is shown in Figure 3.2, which gives the results of fatigue testing several bicycle tubing materials. Note that the heavier-gauge, lower-strength materials are subjected to lower intensities of stress reversal than those to which the lighter gauge, high-carbon and the chrome-molybdenum tubes are stressed. Yet the higher-strength materials provide longer life in spite of the greater punishment!

Note the .050 inch thick low-carbon steel fails at 200,000 cycles of 24,000 psi reversing stress. The .044 inch thick, 12% lighter, higher-tensile tubing is stressed to 26,200 psi by the same load, yet it will withstand 1,600,000 cycles. The chrome-molybdenum, only .038 inch thick and 22% lighter in weight, is stressed to 30,500 psi by our assumed load, yet its life well exceeds 10,000,000 cycles of stress!

Table 3.3 shows the comparative differences of weight and resulting rigidity in bending and twist of available dimensions of bicycle tubing. Table 3.4 compares strengths of various tubing materials.

Examples (using Tables 3.2 to 3.4)

(1) One-inch diameter, mild-steel tubing of 1-mm

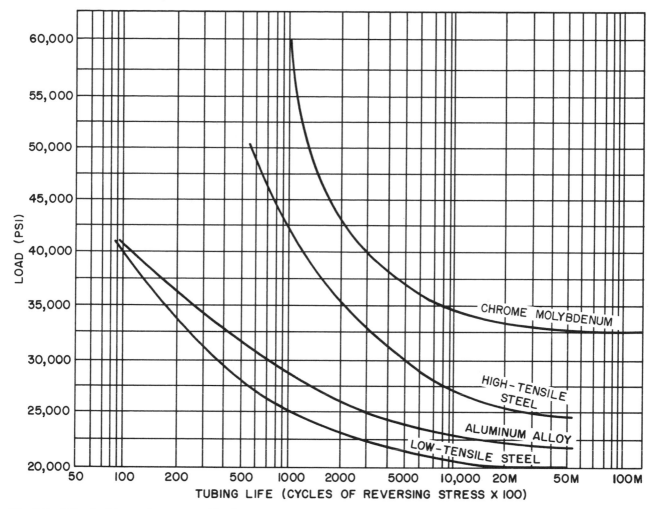

Fig. 3.2   Life of tubing under repeated loading.

Table 3.3

EFFECT OF TUBE DIAMETER AND THICKNESS ON TUBING WEIGHT AND RIGIDITY IN BENDING AND TWISTING

1⅛″ TUBING (28.6 MM)

Tubing Gauge (mm)	0.3	0.5	0.6	0.7	0.8	0.9	1.0	1.1	1.2	1.6
Weight ratio (fraction of 290 g.)	0.43	0.70	0.85	1.00	1.14	1.28	1.40	1.54	1.68	2.28
Bending rigidity ratio	0.45	0.72	0.80	1.00	1.12	1.25	1.38	1.50	1.62	2.20
Torsional rigidity ratio	0.44	0.71	0.85	1.00	1.12	1.24	1.37	1.52	1.62	2.20

1″ TUBING (25.4 MM)

	0.3	0.5	0.6	0.7	0.8	0.9	1.0	1.1	1.2	1.6
Weight ratio (% of 290 g)	0.38	0.62	0.75	0.88	0.99	1.12	1.24	1.36	1.48	1.98
Bending rigidity ratio	0.34	0.50	0.60	0.69	0.78	0.88	0.97	1.05	1.12	1.52
Torsional rigidity ratio	0.32	0.56	0.67	0.77	0.88	0.99	1.10	1.18	1.26	1.72

1¼″ TUBING (31.9 MM)

	0.3	0.5	0.6	0.7	0.8	0.9	1.0	1.1	1.2	1.6
Weight ratio (fraction of 290 g)			0.95	1.10	1.26	1.40	1.56			
Bending rigidity ratio			1.20	1.38	1.56	1.74	1.94			
Torsional rigidity ratio			1.18	1.24	1.40	1.55	1.73			

Notes: Based on 60-cm (23⅝-in.) length of steel straight gauge, 1⅛-in. tubing; 290 grams (0.64 lb) = 100%.
For aluminum alloy tubing use: weight 34% of steel;   For titanium tubing use weight 58% of steel;
  torsional and bending rigidity 34% of steel.   torsional and bending rigidity 55% of steel.

(0.040″) wall thickness weighs about 24% more than 1⅛-inch diameter alloy tubing of 0.7 mm wall (1.24 vs 1.00).

Its rigidity against bending is almost equal (0.97 vs 1.00).

Its resistance to twist is just slightly better (1.10 vs 1.00).

If we use a tensile strength for mild steel of 50,000 psi, for alloy steel of 98,000 psi, despite the 24% greater weight, the tensile strength of the heavier tube is only 63% as great $(1.24 \times \frac{50,000)}{98,000}$. Breakage can occur at lower impact loads than the lighter alloy tube can withstand. If the mild steel tube is stressed under severe riding conditions to 25,000 psi, its fatigue life would be about 100M cycles (Fig. 3.2). The lighter-weight alloy tube, however, even though stressed to 32,200 psi, would have a life exceeding 10,000M cycles of stress.

(2) One and a quarter inch diameter, mild-steel tubing of 0.6-mm gauge weighs 95% as much as 1⅛-inch diameter tubing of 0.7 mm gauge. However, its bending rigidity will be 20% greater (1.20 vs 1.00), and its resistance to twisting loads will be 18% greater (1.18 vs 1.00).

(3) A titanium frame of 1.1-mm gauge tubing is slightly lighter in weight than an alloy steel frame of 0.7-mm gauge tubing of equal diameters ($\frac{1.1}{0.7} \times 0.58 = 91\%$). But its rigidity to bending and twist will be only 86% ($\frac{1.1}{0.7} \times .55$) as great as that of the steel frame.

There are great differences in the strengths of materials used for bicycle frames, but stronger is not necessarily better. For example, aircraft-quality, chrome-molybdenum steel in the as-drawn condition has a minimum tensile strength of 95,000 psi. This material can be improved by heat treatment to tensile strengths of 125,000, 150,000 or 175,000 psi minimum, but reducing wall thicknesses to take advantage of these extreme strengths involves tubings so thin that denting is possible during normal handling. Also, the reduction in strength by lack of extreme care in brazing the frame could result in an unpredictable actual frame durability and could make reheating the entire frame necessary after welding. As a result, the lower strengths of this tubing are generally specified.

The use of cast aluminum alloys for the front fork is another recent development resulting in a reduction in cost. These alloys have a strength of from 32,000 to 36,000 psi, depending on heat treatment. The higher strengths, however, become increasingly brittle. The increased rigidity of steel and its higher strength make the alloy steel fork blade lighter at equal strengths. However, production cost is less with the alloys.

An investigation by Viglioni and Worden of the Naval Air Engineering Center has shown that in very high-strength materials slight internal flaws, inclusions, and discontinuities lead to brittle fractures at far less than the maximum tensile strengths. For chrome-molybdenum, with a possible strength under ultimate heat treatment as high as 240,000 psi, only about 60% of this strength can be attained. One very high-strength titanium alloy is dependable at only 26% of its ultimate strength, while various aluminum alloys showed a range of from 34% to 74%. Widely used for high-grade alloy cranks, 7075-T 6 has a 58% ultimate-stress ratio. This may explain field difficulties caused by the breakage of newly introduced types of high-strength steel tubing.

FORK BLADES

The fork blade and rear stays have a measurable effect on strength and comfort. A carefully engineered offset steers easily and aids in shock absorption. The cross-sectional diameter is often tapered for the same effect. When a tube is tapered, the walls thicken. The maximum stress on the fork, however, is at the top. A liner can be installed at the top, but a better method is to manufacture a taper gauge fork blade.

The Reynolds Company in England, who developed the butted tube, also developed the butted fork tube with tapered gauge. This provides a thicker section at the top, where it is needed, and a thinner gauge for resilience at the lower end, all at a minimum of weight. The tubing is seamless and of maximum integ-

Table 3.4

STRENGTH COMPARISONS OF TUBING MATERIALS

Tubing Material	Tensile Strength (psi)	Fatigue Limit (psi)
0.10% Carbon Mild Steel	45–55,000	18,500
0.15% C, 1.15% Manganese High-Tensile Steel	70–78,000	21,200
Chrome-Molybdenum Steel (can be heat treated to 180,000)	98–114,000	25,500
753 Manganese-Molybdenum Steel	178,000	
"531" Manganese-Molybdenum Steel	100–112,000	
Titanium	38–100,000	
Carbon Fiber-Reinforced Plastic	100–300,000	
Aluminum Alloys	45–55,000	

rity. Naturally, this is more costly than the use of a straight gauge tube or a rolled section tube with press-flattened ends to receive the wheel, but its performance is superior.

Peugeot in France uses a different method, a rolled section fork blade which is brazed at the joint on the rear side.

Similar construction differences can occur on the rear chain and seat stays. A lighter, more-resilient, yet sufficiently rigid frame demands this extra care.

TECHNIQUES OF FRAME CONSTRUCTION

Figures 3.3–3.6 show details of a brazing jig used to build a superior quality handmade bicycle. Note the

Fig. 3.3   Aligning and brazing jig for a custom-built, lugged bicycle frame.
(Courtesy of Schwinn Bicycle Company)

Fig. 3.4   Chain stays and rear fork ends aligned for spacing and squareness.
(Courtesy of Schwinn Bicycle Company)

massive steel plate onto which close-fitting clamps are fitted. These clamps rigidly and accurately align the frame tubes, head tube, bracket shell, chain, seat stays, and bridges during the brazing of lugs.

Figures 3.7–3.9 show the internally lined construction of this accurately built, bronze-welded bicycle frame and the fine workmanship of the finished product.

Production processes of lug frame construction utilize pressed and coined or pin-fitted joints of lugs and tubing, followed by fluxing and dip brazing into a molten bath of brazing alloy.

Other frames are made by electric flash welding of tube ends to bulged extensions of the head tube and bottom bracket shells.

Many domestic bicycles are made by drilling tube-sized holes into the bottom bracket shell and head tubes and inserting the tubes into the shells (see Fig. 3.10). Adding a ring of bronzing material, the assembly is heated by hydrogen or by electrical current until the brazing ring melts and joins the parts. These methods are rapid and useful for low-cost, high-production runs, but a poorly fused joint which has been improperly cleaned can crack under severe stress. Good qual-

Fig. 3.5   Alignment jig for fork assembly.
(Courtesy of Schwinn Bicycle Company)

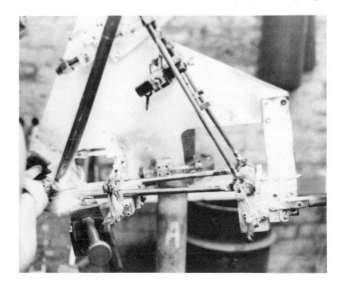

Fig. 3.6   Jig-aligned, bronze-welding frame assembly.
(Courtesy of Schwinn Bicycle Company)

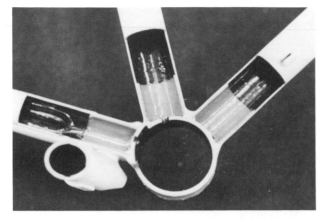

Fig. 3.7   Bronze-welded frame with internal reinforcement at tube ends.
(Courtesy of Schwinn Bicycle Company)

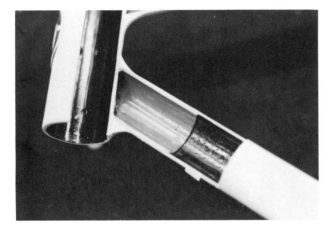

Fig. 3.8   Bronze-welded, internally lugged steering head.
(Courtesy of Schwinn Bicycle Company)

Fig. 3.9   Neat, clean appearance of precisely made, bronze-welded racing frame.

Fig. 3.10   Tubes penetrate crank hanger shell and are brazed at point of entry.

Fig. 3.11   Neatly brazed joints.

ity control, however, results in heavier-weight frames with ample strength (see Fig. 3.11).

An alternate method is to butt-braze the mitred tubes to the solid, undrilled shell exterior.

Figure 3.12 shows the bottom bridge on the chain stays made of an open joint rolled-steel stamping, insecurely joined at the ends. Compare this with the ample tubular bridge with lapped ends securely brazed in Figure 3.13.

Figure 3.14 shows a lapped, tube-brazed joint without internal reinforcement. Figure 3.15 shows a steel-lugged, dip-brazed joint of a popular make. Note that the fit of the lug and tubing is poor, and that there is a considerable gap of unbrazed area. Compare this with the high quality, finely fitted tube joints in Figure 3.16. Figure 3.17 shows a tube failure in a poorly brazed, lugged joint.

The pieces used to join the several frame tubes in lugged construction come in many styles and (see Fig. 3.18) are made of steel, stampings, cast malleable iron, or in years past, of forged construction. The reliefs and cutouts spread out the area where a change in section occurs, and this spread gives less concentration of stress than at the end of a square-cut lug. The cutouts save a bit of weight and produce a more pleasing appearance. On hand-built bicycles, the edges of the lugs are filed down to make a neater-appearing joint and are usually outlined with a contrasting color of paint. While this does not add to the strength or reliability, it is the "artist's touch." It adds both to the cost and to the pride of maker and owner alike.

The fork ends front and rear which support the wheels are an important contribution to frame effectiveness. It is at these points that all the forces of road impact, turning, driving, and braking are applied. If these are not rigid, undue flexibility results. Stability may suffer, and the rider's energy is wasted. Several constructions are in common use, the simplest of which is merely squashing the ends of the fork tubing or stays flat, and stamping out a slot or opening for the wheel axle (see Figs. 3.19 and 3.20).

A second method stamps out the fork end separately. The tube ends are placed over projections on the stamping. The tubing is flattened and coined into the fork end, and then the joint is spot welded or brazed. In other constructions the fork ends are flash welded to the fork end.

The stamped fork end with bosses or braze to permit the stay to extend at full section into the fork end provides additional front and rear end rigidity (see Figs. 3.21 and 3.22). Rigidity depends upon the robustness of the end section. Research conducted some

Fig. 3.13   Substantial, reinforced bridge piece, lightened crank hanger with internal sealing shell.

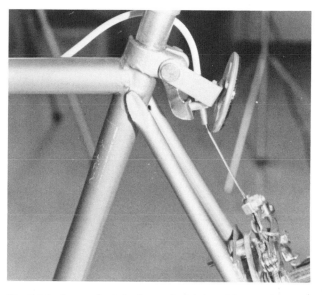

Fig. 3.14   Lapped, tube-brazed joint with no internal reinforcement.

Fig. 3.12   Rolled section bridge piece incompletely joined.

Fig. 3.15   Poorly fitted, lugged, dip-brazed joints.

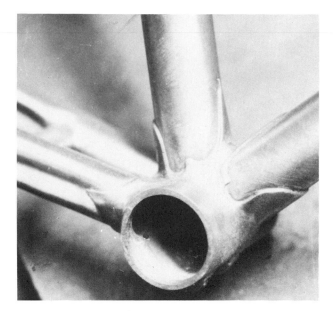

Fig. 3.16   Excellent lug filing, fitting, and brazing.

Fig. 3.17   Tube failure in a brazed lug joint.

years ago by the French Bicycle Manufacturers Association resulted in their recommending a minimum rear-fork-end thickness of 4 mm, which is equivalent to about 5/32 inch. Many bicycles now on the United States market do not meet this standard, but use ⅛-inch stampings. This has resulted in the bending or misalignment of fork ends and in the lower tang of the rear fork end spreading when the axle nut is tightened (see Figs. 3.23 and 3.24). A 5 mm, or 3/16-inch rear fork end is available on medium-high-grade bicycles. The higher grade racing and touring bicycles use a forged-steel rear fork end of 7 mm, or over ¼ inch, thickness (see Fig. 3.26). These are made in several patterns: rear opening for track bicycles, a straight dropout (vertical) for derailleur bicycles, or a forward dropout (see Fig. 3.26). The forward dropout type permits some wheel adjustment if the wheel is out of true or the frame out of line. The straight dropout simplifies wheel removal and will not permit the wheel to pull over in the event of a heavy pull with nuts or quick release insufficiently tightened.

There is a difference of opinion in the trade concerning the merits of stamped steel versus cast lugs and bottom brackets. Cast lugs must be properly bored to accurately match the tube outside diameter and angle for the best fit for brazing. A stamped steel lug that is poorly made will fit poorly (see Fig. 3.15), particularly if lug angles and frame angles do not match. However well-made steel lugs are accurately sized, and less brittle than cast iron lugs. They can be adjusted with heat to match the exact frame angles. If stress relieved to alleviate drawing stresses, they should provide a superior joint.

Cast bottom brackets have a tapered shape and longer chainstay sockets than pressed steel brackets, providing additional rigidity at this hard-worked location. In selecting a bicycle for breaking the world's

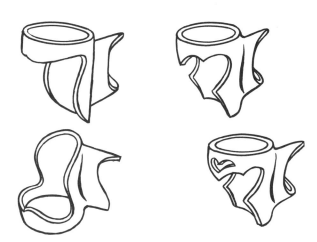

Fig. 3.18   Stock lug cutouts. Investment cast steel (right) provides the full tube precise support.

Fig. 3.19   Flattened tube, stamped-out fork end of below-minimum rigidity.

Fig. 3.20   A flattened tube fork end out of square places a bending stress on the fork end and axle when the wheel nut is tightened.

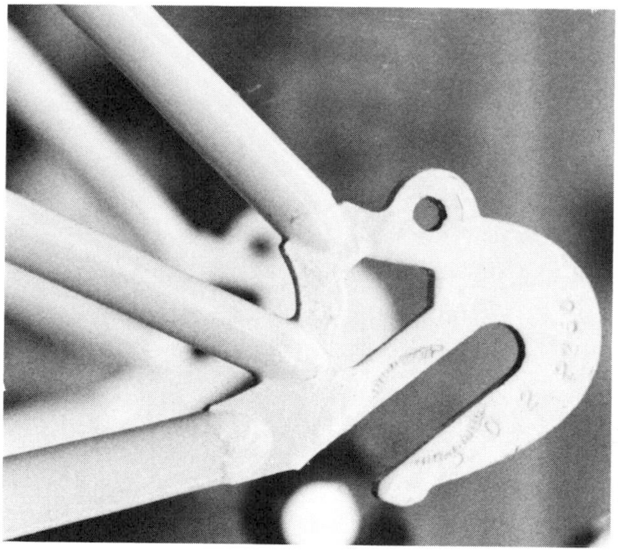

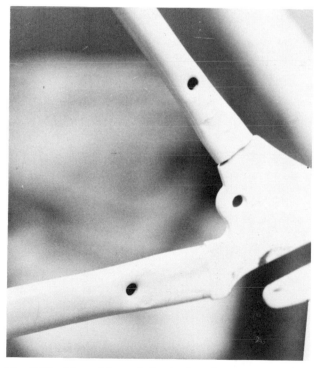

Fig. 3.22   Stamped fork end with full section tube joined.

Fig. 3.23   Pierced large holes in the chain stay can lead water and grit into the crank bearings.

Fig. 3.21   Separate stamped fork end.

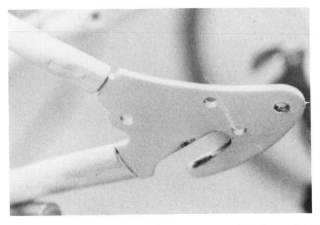

Fig. 3.24   Fork end misfitted into seat stay. Check parallel and alignment of rear axle slots in fork ends.

Fig. 3.25   Rigid, full-section front fork end.

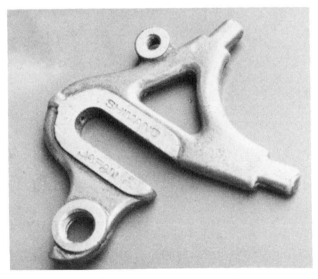

Fig. 3.26   Seven-mm, forged fork end used for maximum strength. Made by Campagnolo, Huret, Simplex, Shimano, and Zeus.

hour record, Eddy Merckx used steel lugs for each joint except the bottom bracket. This was cast, very precisely bored, the ends faced, and pilot tool threaded to receive precisely machined and ground bearing cups.

Some specialty builders use steel lugs and bottom brackets, but reinforce the intersecting surfaces at the head tube and bottom bracket with fillets of weld or braze to increase joint rigidity (see Fig. 3.16).

Due to the superior craftsmanship required to make an excellent bronze-welded frame the bronze-welded frame is less prevalent than in years past. Where the rider demands special frame angle combinations not available with standard lugs, craftsmen will provide this construction. Top-of-the-line specialty builders, such as Jack Taylor, Hurlow, Bob Jackson, René Herse, Alex Singer, Follis, and Urago provide these constructions on request (see Fig. 3.28). Brazed-on fittings for brake cable ends, pump pegs, luggage carriers, and derailleur shift levers are considered a must by the experienced cycle tourist. These provide solid anchorage for the accessories and generator sets, and there is less chance of these items working loose and causing an accident. Likewise, there are fewer clamps projecting to scratch the rider when handling the bicycle while dismounted. Brazed-on brakes are quite rigid.

The racing fraternity generally uses clamped on rather than brazed on accessories. This may be a carry-over from the period when low-temperature silver brazing, precise metallurgical control in alloy tubing manufacture, and careful flame atmosphere and temperature and cooling rate controls were not practiced when brazing, since tube failures sometimes occurred where attachments were brazed onto the frame and the fork.

Tube and bearing alignment must be accurate for the best performance. The illustrations of custom frame building (see Figs. 3.3–3.6) show how this accuracy is obtained. Some misalignment is possible after brazing due to cooling and heating stresses. The frame alignment of the highest grade bicycles is checked from surface plates with precise gauges after brazing and corrected if necessary. Steering head and bottom bracket bearing seats and threads are rectified by the use of piloted facing and cutting tools (see Fig. 3.29).

The Bridgestone Cycle Industry Company of Japan has patented and is producing in high quantities a die-cast frame. Tubes of low-strength or high-strength steel, aluminum or other alloys with a groove rolled near the ends are placed in a jig, which is in turn placed in a large die-casting machine. The bottom bracket, and the head and seat lugs are cast around the tube ends simultaneously at the rate of a frame every 38 seconds. Laboratory and field tests show excellent strength and durability. These frames are being imported for assembly into American-built bicycles. Expensive tooling precludes the use of this process on custom made-to-measure bicycles (see Fig. 3.30).

When using thin-walled tubing, the fatigue strength of the joints should be relative to that of the tubing itself to obtain the highest overall strength-weight efficiency. Filing down the lug ends and relieving the pattern to avoid abrupt changes in thickness reduce stress concentration. However, this is often carried to ridiculous extremes. Long, extended lug patterns that require a longer time for brazing and the application of more heat do not help mechanically. Extremely fancy cutout patterns that take a great deal of time and hand work look very pretty and add a great deal of cost without adding utility. If you wish this for owner's pride, by all means buy it, but don't buy it for its usefulness.

Fit-in-brazed or butt-brazed joints affect strength. The peak strength is attained with a fit clearance of about 0.0015 inches, which provides 130,000 psi in strength. An increase or decrease of 0.0015 inches can reduce the joint strength by 25%, although this may still be ample. An increase to 0.018-inch clearances can reduce the strength of the brazed joint by 50%. Yet I have seen lugged frames in which a calling card could be inserted between tube and lug!

With bronze-welded frame joints, even though its tensile strength is less than the high-alloy tube, the greater ductility of the joining material reduces stress concentration at the joint. Its concave fillet also affords a more gradual change in the section area of the joint which is again conducive to stress dispersal. Nickel-bronze welding, however, is not sufficiently ductile and is not to be recommended for cycle frames.

Fig. 3.28   A bronze-welded frame can be built with any desired tube angles.

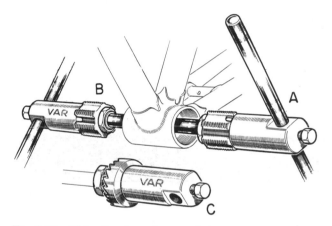

Fig. 3.29   This pilot thread tap and the crank hanger facing tool assure accurate bearing alignment after brazing and frame alignment.

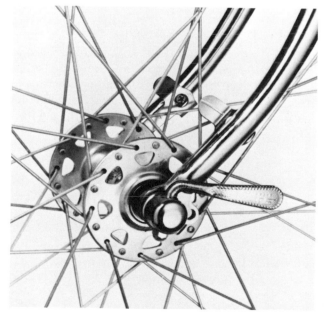

Fig. 3.27   One means of quick-release positive front wheel retention used by United States builders.
(Courtesy of Schwinn Bicycle Company)

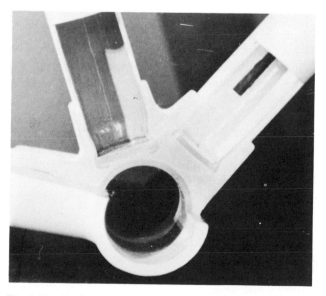

Fig. 3.30   Bridgestone AMF die-cast frame construction.

Arc-welded frame construction is sometimes seen in cheaper machines. Unless the entire frame is stress relieved, which is unlikely because of cost and distortion, arc welding produces a very short but highly concentrated heat-affected zone in which tube strength is greatly deteriorated. Combined with a convex fillet, whose "notch" effect increases stress concentration, fatigue failure and tensile stress failure can be anticipated unless the frame receives post-treatment.

TITANIUM FRAMES

Titanium frames are an exception. These are vacuum welded under extremely precise control. While some models follow conventional design of steel frames, and use almost pure titanium, the Linair division of Teledyne Corporation has overcome the stiffness disadvantage of this metal by using larger than standard tube diameters. The advantage of this was shown earlier in this chapter. In addition, higher-strength titanium alloys with tensile strengths of up to 100,000 psi maximum are used.

STAINLESS STEEL FRAMES

The Crescent-Monark Company of Sweden has introduced frames built of stainless steel. Similar to type 304, these frames are rustless, strong, and light. The Crescent-Monark bikes are brazed, but Bridgestone has employed this tubing in models joined by their die-cast construction.

PLASTIC FRAMES

A more radical departure from conventional bicycle construction was the plastic bicycle (see Fig. 3.32), made by the Original Plastic Bike, Inc., Garden City, New York. While several models of plastic bicycle frames have been made over a period of years in the United States and overseas, this model went all the way! Weight of the complete bicycle is given at 17 pounds. The frame is made from glass-filled Lexan polycarbonate plastic. One, three, and five-speed rear sprockets, double front sprockets, wheel hubs, chain, and handlebars are made of this extrastrong material. Impact strength is high—the same material is used for crash helmets. Its fatigue limit is about 8,000 psi, one-fourth of that for chrome-molybdenum steel. Its stiffness is about one-tenth that of steel, and its weight about one-fifth that of steel. Parts are made of heavier sections on this account, and the frame exhibits considerable flexibility under load.

This material is used without lubrication even in the bearings and plastic brakes. It is unaffected by acids, water, or alkali. Due to the larger frame member sections, the appearance is unconventional, but the bicycle should be useful as an all-weather machine that requires minimum servicing.

Fig. 3.31   Dip-brazed, well-made joint between tube and lugged crank hanger. But holes punched on the bottom tube conduct dirt and water from wheel spray directly into the bearings.

FILAMENT-WOUND, REINFORCED PLASTIC FRAMES

Space-age materials and techniques have great promise in improving bicycle design. Filament-wound, reinforced plastic structures are made by impregnating fiberglass, graphite, boron, or other materials with epoxy or polyester resins. The composite material is light in weight, high in strength, and does not corrode in ordinary atmospheres. It can be pigmented to almost any desired color. Compared to metal frames, the filament-wound structure can be designed for the proper combination of strength and flexibility in different locations of the part. By changing the winding pattern, a tube can have great torsional resistance to pedaling strains and good side rigidity to avoid frame deflection and "whip" and still possess vertical resilience to absorb road shock. Changing the reinforcing pattern at points of greater stress gives the tubing additional strength with little gain in weight.

One interesting property possessed by the reinforced plastics is the dampening of shock. These materials can be made with a lower natural frequency of

Fig. 3.32   A bicycle constructed of Lexan plastic. (*Courtesy of the Original Plastic Bike Corporation*)

vibration than is possible with steels, so hitting a bump is less damaging to the structure, and also to the rider.

Carbon fiber reinforcement shows great promise, but costs are quite high. The graphite fibers presently cost from $20 to $70 per pound. They are very strong—from 200,000 to 300,000 psi—and their stiffness is phenomenal. Engineers use a term called "modulus of elasticity," designated as "E," to express the stiffness of steel. For the layman, this merely represents the amount of stretch or bend of a given structure under a given load. The value exhibited by steel is 30 million; titanium is 16 million; aluminum 10 mil-

lion—but it is 1/3 the weight of steel. Carbon fiber has a stiffness modulus of an incredible 55 million. It is several times stronger than many fine steels, yet its weight is less than 1/5 that of steel. For critical parts in aircraft and spacecraft, a reinforcing strip of graphite-epoxy composite on the surface of a high-strength steel beam greatly increases its strength and stiffness at an acceptable cost increase.

An "E" glass fiber may have a tensile strength of 450,000 psi by itself, a stiffness factor of 10.7 million, and a weight 1/3 that of steel. Its cost, however, is only about 35¢ per pound. As an 80% filler in a fila-

Fig. 3.33   BMA/6 frame loading test being applied to a bicycle at the U.S. Testing Laboratory.
(Courtesy of Bicycle Institute of America)

ment-wound composite material, it can possess a tensile strength of 100,000 psi, a weight less than ¼ that of steel, and a stiffness value of from 3 to 6 million. Different winding patterns and glass contents result in actual values greater or less than those given; a conservative value of 80,000 psi can be counted on, with a weight only ¼ that of steel!

As we saw in our discussion of steel tubing stiffness, increasing the diameter of steel tubing from 1 inch to 1¼ inches increases the bending stiffness by 60% with no increase in weight. By increasing the glass composite tubing diameter, higher strength, equal or greater thickness, and lighter weight can be obtained at moderate costs. With an increased diameter and a small percentage of carbon fiber included, an even greater stiffness can be obtained at a moderate cost increase.

For example, a 1½-inch diameter composite tube with a 60% thicker tubing wall weighs 46% less than a 1⅛-inch tube of Reynolds 531 steel tubing, yet possesses equal stiffness. This tubing will not dent—under impact it bends in, but it pops out again after the force is released. Vibration dampening properties and the potential for custom tailoring wall thickness and strength properties to the actual required values along the tube, will result in a more comfortable ride. Improvements in lug design and joining methods will make their use practical under mass production.

If the frame loading is kept below 30% of ultimate strength, the fatigue life of these materials appears to be almost infinite. This limit is rarely reached, even in a racing frame under grueling conditions. Above these values, microcrazing of the resin bonds between layers and filaments may occur. Moisture can then be absorbed, which eventually weakens the bond.

A unique property of the filament-wound composite is that the material does not yield or stretch up to the point of failure. When failure does occur, the side of a tube may buckle, but it does not come apart or shatter. Thus, composite materials provide an additional safety factor.

ALUMINUM FRAMES

Successful aluminum-alloy frames were developed

in France many years ago. The Caminargent frame was assembled with clamped joints, and the whole bicycle weighed 14 pounds. The Barrat all-welded frame was a work of art made by a master craftsman. Recently, Cegedur-Pechiney, French aluminum supplier, has reintroduced a similar design. Built of Duralinox 5083 alloy, the front and rear fork ends and tubing are welded. The lugs are fabricated and are of extra length. The tubes are joined by Analdite adhesive bonding, as are the fork blades and fork crown and stay bridges. The frame and fork weighs 1,805 grams (4 lb) using 1.5-mm thick tubing.

The low rigidity of aluminum has led Harlan Meyer of Hi-E Engineering in the United States to develop a frame with larger diameter 2024 T-2 Aluminum alloy, joined to aluminum lugs by riveting in aircraft fashion. Another American firm has used 6061 T-6 alloy tubing of high strength but in oversize diameters and heavy wall section; it is extremely stiff, yet light.

ADHESIVE JOINING

The rapidly growing success of the use of industrial adhesives for joining highly stressed parts of automobiles and aircraft has led to their trial in joining the lugs

Fig. 3.34   Tinius Olsen testing machine at Schwinn laboratory measures frame and component strength and deflection at all loads to failure. Output is continually plotted during test.
(Courtesy of Schwinn Bicycle Company)

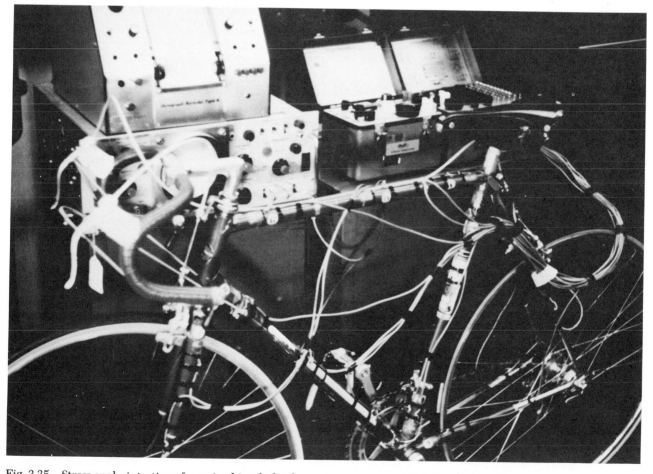

Fig. 3.35   Stress analysis testing of a racing bicycle for design improvement at Teledyne, Linair Division.
(Courtesy of Teledyne Corporation)

Fig. 3.36   Frame alignment gauging table. Gauges check accuracy of head and seat tube alignment and rear fork end width and alignment, while supported at the crank hanger.

and tubes of bicycles. Steel tubing and aluminum tubing have been assembled in this manner. Joint fit tolerances are more precise, so the cost is higher. Water tightness and corrosion in the joints pose production and durability problems. The tubing metal is not heat-deteriorated by adhesive bonding; it retains full strength.

WEIGHT COMPARISON

Titanium frames and forks have been built with weights of 1,700 grams and 1,900 grams for a road racing model.

Titanium is also used in the fabrication of fork ends, seat posts, pedals, handlebar stems, crank hanger and head bearing cups, and crank axles for use in less strenuous racing events.

Steel tubing frames using 0.5-mm tubing weigh about 2,550 grams (5.65 lb), while in 0.3-mm ultralight tubing, a weight of 2,200 grams (4.85 lb) is estimated for 58-cm sizes.

The high cost and comparative rigidity must be considered by the purchaser when frame weights are compared.

Fig. 3.37   The Klein 6061 T-6 aluminum alloy frame, which is welded and heat treated and uses a larger tube diameter, combines low weight and excellent rigidity.   *(Courtesy of Klein Company)*

CHAPTER IV

Fitting the Bicycle—
Your Riding Position

Y ou and your bicycle are a matched team. Your bicycle must be carefully fitted to *your* dimensions for the most enjoyment and best results. Not only your legs, but the lengths of your arms, body, and feet must be considered (see Fig. 4.1). While cyclists may average out to a set of proportions, it is a rare individual who actually fits the average. For example, one of my friends and I are of equal height. Yet if I sit on his bike, I cannot reach the pedals, and his handlebars are too close. On mine, his legs are cramped, and his arms are outstretched.

Look about you. You will see folks short and tall. Now compare those of equal height. Note the height of the hips, the distance of the hands from the hips, and the length of the neck and head. Each will vary considerably. Now place these riders on bicycles. Have them lean forward with the back at a comfortable 45° angle. The person with longer legs will need a higher seat position to straighten his leg with his foot on the pedal. He can straddle a higher frame. Those with a longer body and arm length will need a handlebar position lower and further extended (see Fig. 4.2).

Figure 4.3 gives the dimensions of the bicycle, its saddle and seat post, handlebar and extension, cranks and frame tube dimensions that can be selected to suit each individual rider (see Chapter V for a custom-built frame).

FRAME HEIGHT

We will discuss refinements of these factors in Chapter XI, "Spacecraft with a Human Engine." For preliminary selection, the rider should be able to comfortably straddle the frame with his feet flat on the ground. Too high a frame is dangerous, even for a growing youth. One set of widely used rules of thumb gives the frame height as 12¾ inches less than the out-side height of the head of the femur, or about 9 inches less than the inside leg length, of the cyclist, both measured with the cyclist in stocking feet.

There is some room for variation in this rule. My "formula height" based on the head of femur measurement, gives a 60½-cm (23¾-inch) frame. But for a touring machine, it's sometimes helpful to pull to the edge of the road without dismounting to consult the map, and a slightly lower frame height makes it possible to straddle the bike with the right foot resting on the depressed road shoulder. With a high bottom bracket height, a smaller frame height is desirable. The frame should be high enough so that the handlebar extension is sufficiently inserted in the frame when the bars are placed at the desired height. A sloped top tube accomplishes both ends and provides a stiffer frame.

If the frame is too tall and the rider has long arms and likes a streamlined riding position, he may not be able to lower the handlebar stem sufficiently. In this event, a down-sloped extension, or a deeper-drop bar can be used.

The seat should be raised, or lowered, and its position on the saddleclip altered until the knee is directly over the pedal with the crank at 45° above center. In stocking feet, with the heel on the pedal at its lowest point, the leg should be just straight. You may wish at this time to use the 109% of leg length saddle height described in "The Human Engine." Foot length, body weight, and saddle flexibility should be taken into account, as should the thickness of the soles of the riding shoes used. Expert racers set their saddles to a millimeter! (See p. 195)

Position of the saddle longitudinally is measured from the saddle back to the centerline of the crank hanger by dropping a plumb line from each to the floor. One al-

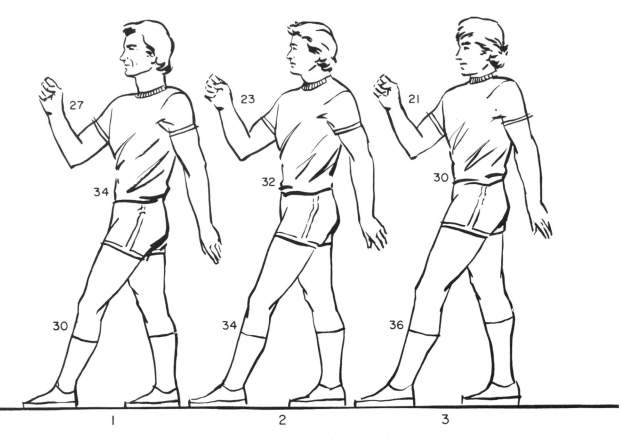

Fig. 4.1   Three riders of the same height with varying leg, arm, body, and neck measurements.

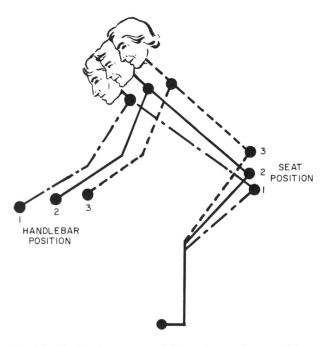

Fig. 4.2   Each rider requires different bar and seat positions.

ternative is measuring from the saddle nose, although this is subject to stretch in length after being put in service. The position of the saddle depends upon the style and intensity of riding to be done. For leisurely riding, a position further behind the crank hanger is selected, perhaps 2½ or 3 inches from saddle nose to hanger center. For speed work and sprints, a position closer to the hanger (knee above crank set at 90°) should be selected first and refined as the rider gains experience.

BODY POSITION

We have grown used to seeing bicyclists sitting in an erect position, as in a chair or motorcar. High-rise children's bicycles accentuate this to an absurd degree with their handlebars raised to shoulder height. This puts the weight close to the back wheel and permits acrobatics. Pulling the handlebar back and lifting the front wheel off the ground may be fun, but it is hardly safe or efficient transportation.

Middleweight and three-speed lightweight bicycles have handlebars of intermediate height, as do racing bicycles used for cyclo-cross events. This position is comfortable for city or moderate-distance riding under easy conditions; the head is erect, and visibility is good.

The road racer uses dropped handlebars from four to five inches below the saddle top level. Sprinters or riders on short-distance speed events may use deep-drop bars, with the grips as much as eight inches be-

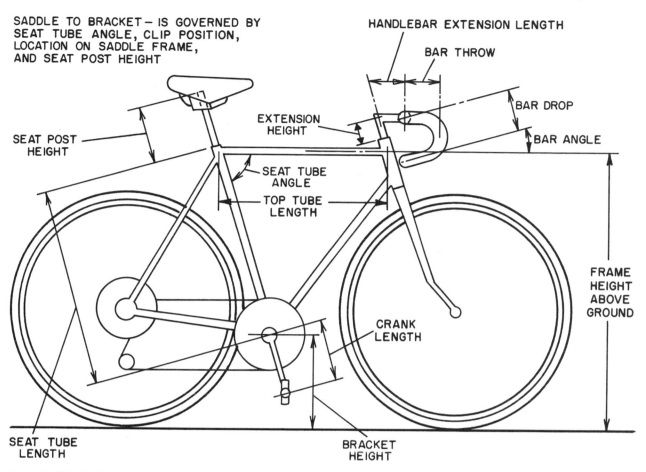

SADDLE TO BRACKET — IS GOVERNED BY
SEAT TUBE ANGLE, CLIP POSITION,
LOCATION ON SADDLE FRAME,
AND SEAT POST HEIGHT

HANDLEBAR EXTENSION LENGTH

BAR THROW

EXTENSION
HEIGHT

BAR DROP

BAR ANGLE

SEAT POST
HEIGHT

SEAT TUBE
ANGLE

TOP TUBE
LENGTH

FRAME
HEIGHT
ABOVE
GROUND

CRANK
LENGTH

SEAT TUBE
LENGTH

BRACKET
HEIGHT

Fig. 4.3   Bicycle dimensions affecting riding position.

low the top of the bar and the bar top itself well below the saddle top. These positions minimize air resistance and enable the arm to pull nearly parallel to the leg thrust for maximum output power.

THE FORWARD LEANING RIDING POSITION

Intermediate between these is a variety of forward leaning positions favored by most experienced non-competitive riders. An examination of our body structure explains why this is so.

We know that our spinal column is a series of vertebrae separated from each other by discs. These discs, in turn, consist of a ring of fibrous cartilage attached to the vertebrae, each of which in turn contains a disc core under tension that acts as an elastic cushion.

When the back is bent, the core displaces and provides additional thickness. In continuous upright sitting or standing, particularly as body weight is increased with age or overeating, the rear part of the disc becomes pinched, while the ligaments in the front which support the spine become stretched. If the body is not bent forth from the waist for considerable periods, the fibrous ring degenerates. Pinching, tiredness, and pain result, and in time the disc can become ossified.

Flexing the trunk forward from the waist with the

back kept straight and not hunched extends the spinal column. You can measure this yourself on a friend with a tape measure. Starting at the base of the spine, with the body upright, measure to the seventh vertebra. Then repeat in the bent-over position. You may find an extension of two inches compared to the erect position.

In this leaning forward position, the body weight is partially supported on the arms. The pressure on the discs diminishes. Relief is first felt on the rear portion, and then the ligaments in front of the spine are relieved. The vertebral muscles, the contraction of which gives lumbago, are further relaxed.

Physicians of the *Societe d'Etudes Medicales du Cyclisme* tell us that in this leaning forward position, the parts of the spine which habitually suffer are in a position which resists degeneration. In one method used to treat back problems, the patient leans over and tugs at an object on the ground. Leaning forward while riding accomplishes the same end. Then too, the deep breathing from cycling exercise enlarges the chest cavity for easier breathing. So from a medical standpoint, doctors agree that our leaning forward position is more healthful. It need not be as accentuated as that of the racer; a horizontal back angle from 45° to 50° is the most comfortable and has its advantages.

Fig. 4.4   With your heel on the pedal, raise the saddle until your leg is straight. *(Courtesy of M. Schroth)*

Fig. 4.6   Upright riding position. *(Courtesy of Schwinn Bicycle Company)*

Fig. 4.5   With the crank at 45° and ball of foot on pedal, place the seat so that your knee joint is above pedal center. For faster riding, do the same with the crank set at 90°.   *(Courtesy of M. Schroth)*

Fig. 4.7   Racing position. *(Courtesy of Schwinn Bicycle Company)*

When the handlebar position is such that the arms are naturally flexed and partially supporting the body weight, the arms act as natural shock absorbers and deaden the shocks from road bumps and undulations. Furthermore, weight supported on the arms need not be supported on the saddle. This relieves pressure and impact on that constantly loaded and delicate area.

By pulling with the arms in opposition to the leg thrust, you can apply additional force when climbing a hill or pressing into the wind. You may be surprised to note, when climbing, that the back muscles support this overhung weight and transfer it to the pedals. As the hill steepens, the weight on your hands decreases and finally becomes an upward pull instead of a downward pressure; thus, your weight and arm muscles actually help you to climb! You may be able to climb without getting out of the saddle to put all your weight on the pedals.

Properly distributed, a larger proportion of your weight is on the front wheel. Crouching over the bars, the cyclist naturally absorbs much of the force of a bump with his arms, and by lifting a part of his lower body weight from the saddle on his toes, the bicycle as a whole can rock beneath him as they pass over a bump. The additional weight on the front also gives better steering control and reduces the chance that the front wheel will slide or bounce upward clear of the ground.

Wind resistance is the cyclist's major antagonist. On a level road, above about eight miles per hour, it is the major resistance to be overcome, and in the leaning forward position, wind resistance may be reduced as much as 40%. Thus, the cyclist can maintain higher speeds with the same effort and make longer trips with no additional energy.

FITTING THE DROPPED HANDLEBAR

Since with dropped bars the arms carry part of the weight, fitting this position is more critical, and there is less tolerance for error than with more erect postures. The common fitting errors are usually due to a mismatch of frame, handlebar, and handlebar extension to the rider's dimensions. After all, a mass-produced bicycle cannot be factory tailored to its eventual buyer without on the spot fitting.

Watch for these errors:

(1) Bars too low; due to too short a handlebar extension height. The stem must be placed deeply enough in the head fitting to avoid breakage in service. On American bicycles, this minimum depth is engraved on the extension. On bikes not so marked, at least 2½ inches is required. If the frame is too small or the extension too low, obtain a higher extension. Otherwise, breathing will be restricted, vision reduced, and weight on the bars will be excessive and fatiguing.

(2) Arms too extended or stretched. A handlebar "throw" that is too long, too long a frame, or a saddle located too far back will overextend the arms. This leads to poor control, numbness of the hands on longer trips, and an inability to coordinate the muscles to best advantage.

(3) Arms too close to the body. A frame or handlebar extension too short, a saddle too far forward, or a bar with too short a "throw" will force the arms too close to the body. This results in poor steering control, wrist ache, rapid fatigue, and in extreme cases even bumping the knees and elbows on turns.

(4) Head held too high. This gives a real "pain in the neck." When a rider first starts to use dropped bars, there is a tendency to try to hold the head in an erect position. Compared to a standing or erect posture, this is similar to craning your neck to look at an airplane overhead. It uses muscles not regularly needed. Inclining the head and looking upward with the eyes requires muscles to support the overhung head weight. However, the rider soon builds up these muscles. The tilted-forward head gives a little better eyebrow shadow in the sun.

As shown in Figure 4.8, as the back is inclined farther forward, the position of the hands must move farther forward and down. In a racing position, for a given distance of bar drop, the shoulders move forward less than when leaning forward from a more erect posture. The handlebar drop and throw proportions used should depend upon the expected range of riding positions that the rider will use.

HANDLEBAR SELECTION AND HAND POSITION

Handlebars come in a multitude of shapes: flat and of medium width; raised in elevation as they come to the rear; excessively raised, as in the small-frame, high-riser bicycle; or wide-sweeping. They may also bend forward and down, with a variety of "throw" (maximum dimension forward of the point of attachment to the extension, "drop" (distance from the point of attachment to the centerline of the lower grips), and width.

Generally, we recognize three categories: (1) the center of the grips is nearer the rider's body than is the point at the center of the steering column; (2) the grips are well forward of the steering column center; or (3) the grips are in line with the center.

When turning with Type 1, the hand on the side of the direction of turn moves in toward the body resulting in a sluggish action and some awkwardness as the hand moves closer to the body. When turning right, both hands move to the left. The Confort and the Trials Sport with a short extension illustrate Type 1.

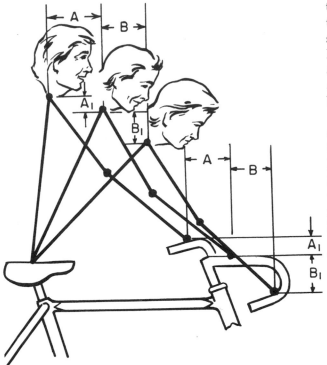

Fig. 4.8   As the body is inclined forward, the hand position moves forward and farther down.

When turning right with the forward throw, Type 2, both hands move outward to the right, although the right moves outward less than the left. When riding easily or braking, the arms, being thrust forward, tend to stabilize the steering. But pulling hard moves the bar more off center, and so most dropped bar bends have sensitive steering.

Type 3, illustrated by the Trials Sport with a longer extension, gives almost equal forward and rear hand motion with little lateral movement. Compared to Types 1 and 2, there is no body sway produced when turning the bars.

Type 1 bars must be wider to avoid hitting the body or knees. Generally, a bar of shoulder width is best. This gives ample room for breathing (a fault of a narrow bar used for close-in racing) and an in-line pull on the grips which reduces the tendency to sway when pulling hard. A wider bar induces a bit more air resistance.

The hand grips should be almost in line with the bicycle center line or splayed outward very slightly to give the most natural hand and arm position. The overall width of a bar with splayed grips must be wider, a definite disadvantage when riding in close quarters and when handling or parking.

A center section perpendicular to the bicycle center line and having ample width for the hands gives a comfortable alternate riding position. The forward throw should turn sharply forward, almost at right angles, to provide a comfortable hand position at the tops.

The bottom of the bar should be nearly parallel to the top section, within 10° or 15°, to give a bar with the most comfort in all positions. A bar such as the one shown in Figure 4.13 is severely limited in this respect. For sprint racing, where distances are relatively short and a very deep drop is needed to reduce air resistance, a steeply sloped top can be used (see the Pista bends in Fig. 4.9).

My longtime favorite is the Randonneur, which combines these features with a slight upsweep from the center which better fits the shape of the hands. Its 16-inch width gives good breathing and control, with space for a handlebar bag in between. A narrower width cramps the hands against the bag. With equal forward throw and drop, the Randonneur suits the 45° back angle riding position admirably.

Table 4.1 lists dimensions of some popular handlebar shapes. It should be noted, however, that the same name bar made by a different manufacturer may differ in dimensions. Be sure to measure before purchasing. Figure 4.9 depicts some common shapes and some handlebar stem differences.

Handlebar stem length of extension can be varied to fit the individual rider's measurements, his saddle fore-and-aft position, and the frame top tube length. The height of the handlebar stem used must permit the expansion slot that grips the inside of the fork tube to be seated several inches inside the tube. Preferably, the clamping should be done below the threaded section of the fork tube, otherwise this may fail while riding at speed and leave the rider without any means of control. A severe crash is almost assured. For production reasons, extra top head race threading is sometimes provided, the tube being cut at shorter heights for short frames. When used in a higher frame, clamping may be in the threaded area.

RIDING POSITION—HANDLEBAR LOCATION

One often sees the rule: to determine your handlebar's location and proper extension, place your elbow against the tip of the saddle and extend your hand toward the front; your handlebar should be located at the tips of your fingers.

While this rule works for some lucky people, it is oversimplified. For greatest comfort and effectiveness, an experienced cyclist will want to set his handlebars at an accuracy of as little as ½ centimeter. Yet handlebars come with forward bends that vary several inches. The saddle itself, when adjusted for proper top tension, can elongate considerably with use. The stated rule does not take into account the angle and length of the upper body, the length of the upper arms, or even the length of the fingers (see Fig. 4.1). A much sounder method uses the entire body and arm as a gauge as shown in Figures 4.15–4.18.

After the saddle height and forward position have been set as previously described, have someone sup-

Table 4.1

SOME HANDLEBAR SHAPES AVAILABLE

TRACK RACING BARS
Deep drops for high speed with relaxed top position for breathing

Maker	Model	Width		Reach		Drop	
		inches	mm	inches	mm	inches	mm
AVA	Pelissier	15 3/4	400	4 1/2	115	6 1/4	160
Belleri	Bel-25	15	380	5 1/8	130	6 3/4	170
Cinelli	Pista 14	15	380	5 7/8	150	7	178
Cinelli	Madison 18	14 1/2	368	4 1/2	114	6 3/4	171
GB	Ventoux	16	406	4	102	6	154
Phillipe	Piste	15	380	5 7/8	150	7	178
Phillipe	Americaine	14 7/8	375	5 1/8	130	7 7/8	200
Titan	Poste	15	380	3 3/16	81	6 1/2	163
TTT	Bevilaqua	14 1/2	370	4 7/8	125	8 1/4	210
TTT	Franco Belga	15 3/4	400	4 7/8	125	6 3/4	170

ROAD RACING BARS
More moderate drop, and shorter reach. Wider bars permit better breathing

Maker	Model	Width		Reach		Drop	
AVA	Criterium	15 3/4	400	4 1/8	104	5 3/4	145
Belleri	Competition 1015	16 1/8 & 17 1/4	410 or 438	5 5/16	135	5 1/2	140
Cinelli	Giro d'Italia	15	380	4 3/4	121	5 1/2	140
Cinelli	Campione	15	380	3 1/2	90	6 1/4	160
GB	Tourmalet	16	406	4	102	5 1/2	140
GB	Olympic	15	380	4 3/4	121	5 1/2	140
GB	Maes	15	380	3 1/2	89	5 1/2	138
Milremo	Franco Belge	14 1/4	363	5 5/16	135	5 1/2	140
Phillipe	Professional	15 1/8	390	4	100	5 3/4	145
TTT	Franco Belga	16 1/2	420	4 7/8	125	6 3/4	170
Wald	#877 American	14	356	4 7/8	124	5 7/8	149
	#853 English	14	356	4 7/8	124	5 7/8	149

TOURING BARS

Maker	Model	Width		Reach		Drop	
Wald	#895 Raked Pattern American	21	533	2 1/4	57	Raised 3	76
	#851 English	21	533	2 1/4	57	Raised 3	76
GB	Touring (good for ladies)	15 1/2	393	4	102	4	102
GB	Capo Berta	15 3/8	390	3 3/4	95	5 1/2	140
GB	All rounder (flat)	21	533	1 3/4	44	1 3/8	35
GB	Comfort (raised or drop)	19 1/2	495	3	76	1 1/2	38
Milremo	Randonneur	16	406	4 1/2	114	4 1/2	114
Pivo	Cyclotouriste	16	406	4 1/2	114	4 1/2	114
Phillipe	Randonneur	16	406	4 1/2	114	4 1/2	114
	Flat	20		2 1/2	60	0	0
Sakae Ringyo	Randonneur	15	380	4 3/8	110	4 3/4	110
Titan	Serci	15 3/4	400	4 3/8	110	4 3/4	120

Notes: Many large bicycle manufacturers make their own handlebars from welded steel tubing. Dimensions may vary from those listed above. Superior lightweight alloy handlebars use AG 3 or AG 5 tempered aluminum alloy for extra strength.

HANDLEBAR DIAMETERS

	Grips		Center	
American	7/8 in	22.2 mm	1 in	25.4 mm
Japanese-English	7/8 in	22.2 mm	15/16 in	23.8 mm
English	15/16 in	23.8 mm	1 in	25.4 mm
French		23.5 mm		25 mm
Titan (Belgian)		23.5 mm		27 mm

HANDLEBAR STEM DIAMETERS

American	0.813 in	20.7 mm
English	7/8 in	22.23 mm
French		22 mm

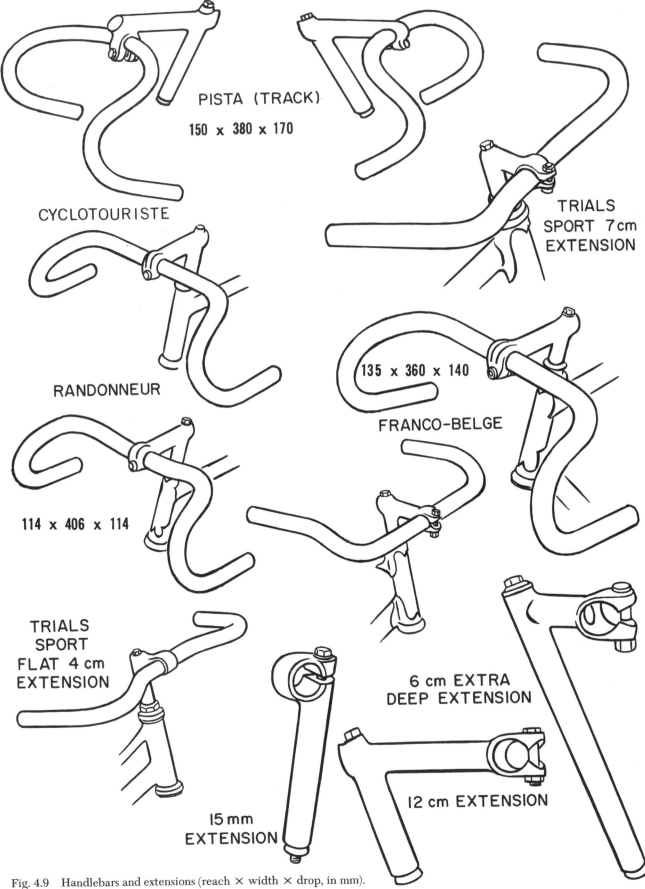

PISTA (TRACK)

150 x 380 x 170

CYCLOTOURISTE

TRIALS
SPORT 7 cm
EXTENSION

RANDONNEUR

135 x 360 x 140

FRANCO-BELGE

114 x 406 x 114

TRIALS
SPORT
FLAT 4 cm
EXTENSION

6 cm EXTRA
DEEP EXTENSION

15 mm
EXTENSION

12 cm EXTENSION

Fig. 4.9   Handlebars and extensions (reach × width × drop, in mm).

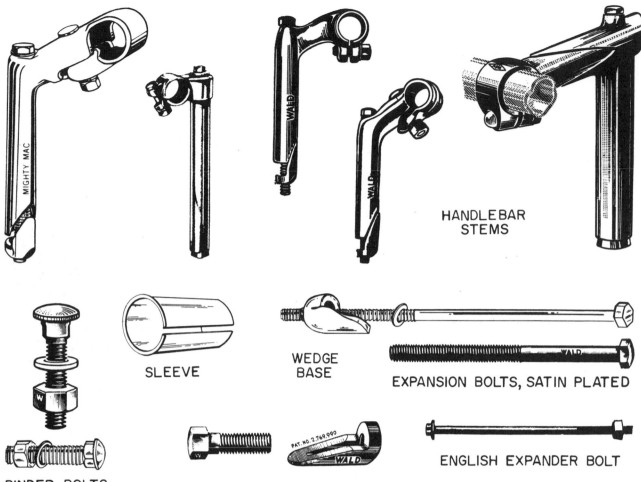

HANDLEBAR
STEMS

MIGHTY MAC

WALD

WALD

SLEEVE

WEDGE
BASE

EXPANSION BOLTS, SATIN PLATED

PAT. NO. 2,769,990

WALD

ENGLISH EXPANDER BOLT

BINDER BOLTS

Fig. 4.10 Handlebar extensions and wedge bolts.

Fig. 4.11 Randonneur bar showing the up-sweep from center.

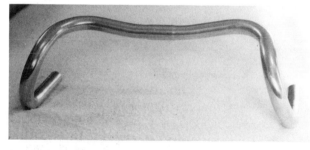

Fig. 4.12 "Touring" upright bar.

Fig. 4.13 Deep drop bar, 40°-out-of-parallel top section. This bar is not suited for road work. Bottom grip and brake levers should be positioned from 10° to 15° counterclockwise.

Fig. 4.14   Square section bar, top and bottom nearly parallel, brake levers properly positioned.

Fig. 4.15   Hold the handlebar on the top with your opposite arm naturally bent.

Fig. 4.16   Rotate your bent arm from the shoulder—without stretching it—toward the upper bar position.

Fig. 4.17   Hold the lower bar position with your opposite arm naturally bent.

Fig. 4.18   Rotate that arm from the shoulder toward the lever grip; gauge its natural position in relation to the other grip.

port the bicycle as you sit upon it. Move about until your position on the saddle feels best. Then, grasping the top of the handlebar with one hand, drop the other arm to the side and let it hang loosely (Fig. 4.15).

Rotate your relaxed arm from the shoulder toward the handlebar top without stretching, and compare the position where your hand would naturally come to the actual bar location (Fig. 4.16).

Repeat the process with the hand on the lower riding position (Figs. 4.17 and 4.18). You can then select a handlebar extension of the length that will bring your handlebar to the most natural location for *your* measurements.

Figure 4.19 shows the result in action. Note that in this touring position, with the back at a 45° angle, the arms are at a natural position with a slight bend. The back is straight, not arched. The handlebar height is that which provides the proper position of the back. For riders of differing proportions of back, leg, and arm length, the relative heights of the saddle and the handlebar top will vary. The rule "make your bar top equal in height to the saddle top" fits only one set of rider proportions; it may not fit you.

The angle of the bottom of the handlebar with respect to the ground is very important for comfort, particularly in a long trip. Start with an angle in the 10° to 15° slope. Ride it a while to see if it feels right. When testing this, you may wish to ride with the bar short of fully tightened, on little-traveled roads. Then you can stop and, without dismounting, adjust the bar angle and try again and again until you get it right. I find that a degree or two makes a good deal of difference in comfort. When you are satisfied, tighten the stem on the bar. The same can be done with the handlebar height to get your perfect fit. You may also wish to purchase an adjustable length extension so you can experiment with the forward location of the bars.

Brake levers should be placed, on a dropped bar, at a point a bit above the horizontal, parallel to your bottom grip.

The modern, dropped "square-shaped" handlebar provides four or five different positions for the hands (see Figs. 4.20–4.23), allowing variations of hand, arm, and back positions that relieve monotony and fatigue. The top center position gives the most upright back position. It increases wind resistance and puts more weight on the seat; both of these are advantageous on steep downgrades. This position is best for looking around at scenery.

Position two, at the forward bend, is well suited for diversified terrain. The rider being farther out, his control of the bicycle is improved.

Position three, on the hoods, stretches the body. It can be used for climbing or for a change. If this position is used quite often, your handlebar extension may be too short.

Fig. 4.19   Relaxed touring position.

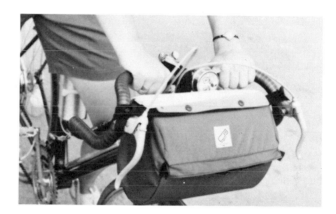

Fig. 4.20   Top of bar center hand position.

Fig. 4.21   Hands at the upper forward bend.

Fig. 4.22   Alternate position on the brake lever hoods.

Fig. 4.23   "On the Hooks" bottom position.

Position four, at the return bottom bend, lowers air resistance, gives good control on fast downhill runs, and provides ready access to the brakes. This is your power position for speed and climbing. The neck is bent more sharply up in this position.

A fifth position can be obtained on the flats of the bottom section of the bar which varies arm position and hand angle.

More variety can be had while touring by combining positions one or two on one hand with four or five on the other. This twists the body and puts a different pressure on the seat, which can be relieving.

The position of auxiliary, or "safety" brake levers which can be operated from positions one and two should be closely checked. The preferred lever position bottoms against the bar, if lever and bar throw match each other. But make certain that the brakes are properly adjusted, or these will bottom before sufficient braking force is available. Synchron brake safety levers have an angle adjustment feature which permits the best relationship to be set.

A safety lever used with a bar of greater "throw" will pull up in front of the bar center section, where it is difficult to apply pressure.

Guidonnet levers fit at the bar center and extend under the bar center. Brakes cannot be applied as well when on the "drops," but some riders prefer these. Make certain that the position of your brake levers permits proper brake operation without interfering with your choice of riding positions.

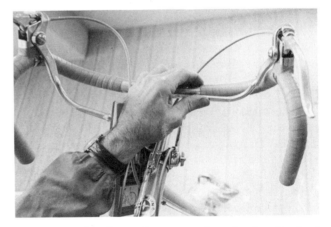

Fig. 4.24   Safety levers bottom against the bar for best pull. Note: brake lever hoods are set too high.

CHAPTER V

The Custom Frame

TYPES OF FRAMES

So you would like the ultimate—a bicycle built specifically for you. Like a well-fitted suit of clothes, nothing can beat it. Yet like a poorly tailored set—or if you grow out of its fitting—it can be inferior to an off-the-shelf model. Likewise, you can become accustomed to a design, so that though it may not be the ultimate, you still find it quite satisfactory. As previously mentioned, learn more about yourself—your type of riding, your aspirations, and the range of your riding conditions. Don't demand the impossible. The best bike for hill climbing may not be best for the descent. The snappy design may be fatiguing on less smooth road surfaces.

If your feet are long, front wheel to toe clearance may be a factor; in a touring mount, your feet may hit the rear panniers if the stays are too short. Don't slavishly copy someone else's frame angles—they may not suit your build. Your choice of fork offset may give you too snappy or perhaps too sluggish steering unless you determine your needs.

Type A (see fig. 5.1) is the classic diamond frame. This is the most common and well-proven frame. The top tube is usually horizontal—this "looks right," although a slightly sloping top tube may give better rigidity and off-the-saddle ground clearance.

Type B uses an extra brace. It gives greater impact strength against head-on blows, but the brace adds weight and gives a bumpier ride.

Type C is the "cantilever" frame. It is flexible and absorbs shocks, but it is also heavier and wastes energy due to frame deflections under pedalling loads.

Type D has a large central member. This design is often used for portable and for folding bicycles, because it is easier to store when space is cramped.

Type E is the juvenile, high-riser frame that uses a high seat and handlebar on a small frame. It is a high-volume seller for roughly treated children's bikes.

Type F is a splayed tube, open frame ladies' model. It is easier to mount and dismount, especially with skirts. It is stronger than the similar Type G parallel tubes.

Type H is the "Italian style" ladies' model. The top tube is bent at its junction with the seat tube to reduce bending stresses.

Type I is the loop or "berceau" design. This design gives a maximum of clearance for mounting and results in minimum strength and pedalling ease.

Type J is the "mixte" frame, in which the tubes run from the top of the steering head directly to the rear fork end. Of the open-frame models, it gives the best stress distribution and strength. One even better variation uses a standard diameter tube from the steering head to the point of central stay attachment for superior rigidity and greater pedaling ease.

Types K–O are tandem-frame constructions. In addition to these models, there are types with both front and rear of open-frame design and types with a series of curved tubes and stays that add to the already lesser rigidity of the extralong frame of the tandem. Type K is an open frame of minimum weight. Surprisingly, if the tubes are of ample diameter, it rides well. Type L adds a central tube that ends at the rear seat tube; this adds some weight, but little strength or rigidity. Type M continues this stay to the rear wheel fork ends. This adds considerably to the longitudinal rigidity needed. If twin tubes are used, there should be bridges be-

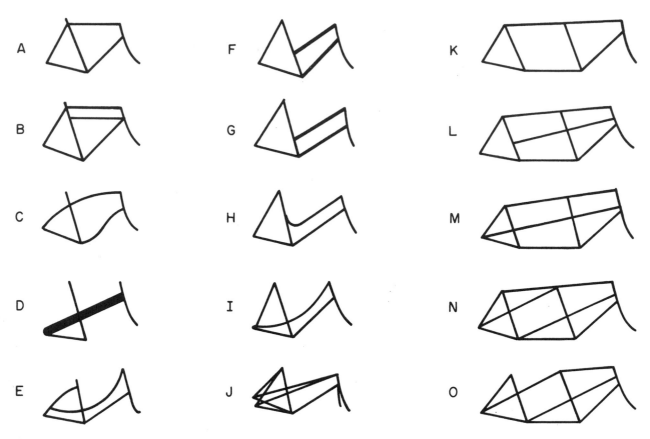

Fig. 5.1   Typical bicycle frame designs.

tween them at intervals to prevent flexing. Type N uses two sets of extra stays, providing extra bracing to the bottom rear crank hanger and the rear fork ends. If the stays are bridged, this gives a quite rigid frame. Type O is similar, but with the rear top tube omitted. Making the upper rear slanted stays of small section allows a torsional deflection from the rear rider's weight that can be readily seen when the front rider holds the stationary tandem upright. However, when the tubes are of ample size and gauge, as in the Schwinn Paramount, this deflection is resisted.

It is necessary to know the names and dimensions of the various parts when discussing frames (see Fig. 5.2). All of these items should be considered when you make the full-scale layout for your custom frame.

FRAME DIMENSIONS

The distance O (horizontally from the center of the crank hanger to the seat lug) determines the angle of steepness of the seat tube, and extended to the saddle top, it determines the saddle position. Riding cadence and riding style dictate the actual distance needed. A saddle is placed more to the rear for a brisk, easy cadence and more to the front as the pedal force increases. A rider who ankles well will have a more rearward position than one who "digs" at the pedals. His saddle will be placed higher than that of a rider

who uses the heel-down-at-the-bottom and push-forward-at-the-top pedaling action. If a rider ankles well and has a long foot, his saddle will be even higher and farther to the rear.

The proper crank length must be selected (see Chapter XI, "The Human Engine"). Cranks are available in lengths of from 162.5 to 180 mm. Some rules of thumb are: $\frac{1}{10}$ your height; 32% or 36% of the knee to ankle plus the ankle to ball of foot measurements (32% at 22 inches to 36% at 18 inches); and ½ the femur length. This gives you a wide range of choices. However, whatever length you select will have a threefold effect. A longer crank will decrease the saddle height. But to get sufficient clearance to avoid hitting the pedals when turning corners, the longer crank will require a higher placement of the crank hanger. Front wheel clearance must be increased from crank hanger to front wheel axle. Racing bicycles most commonly use a distance of 600 mm with 170-mm cranks. Since the wheel is moved relatively slightly at speed in racing, this distance is maintained. But a touring or city machine, which may use mudguards and may require wider sweeps of the bars while maneuvering or climbing, should have a clearance with 170-mm cranks and 27-inch wheels of at least 615 or 620 mm. Longer cranks require additional space. With 26-inch or smaller wheels, this minimum clearance can be reduced.

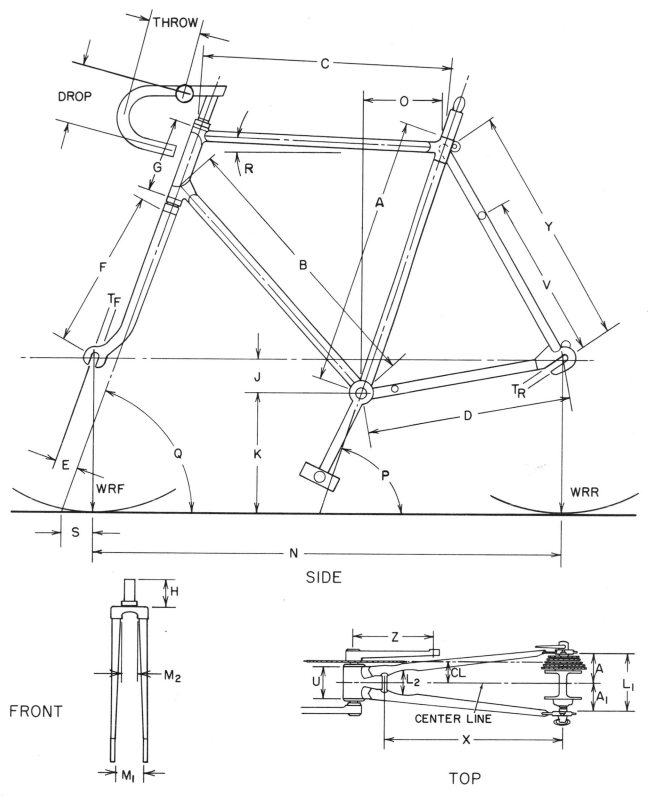

Fig. 5.2 Bicycle specification dimensions.

Rear stay length, D, is determined by wheel size, mudguard clearance, and heel clearance between your heel and your baggage. In no case should it be so small that the wheel cannot be removed without deflating the tire. Comfort versus performance will dictate the compromise. The shorter stay is more responsive, but it gives a choppier ride. With too short a rear stay, the front wheel will lift on a hard pull. The chainline, CL, is normally about 1⅝ inches, or from 41 to 42 mm. However, with a six-speed freewheel, a chainline of 44 mm is preferable. A tandem hub used with an internal expanding brake and 650-42 mm tires should have a chainline of about 49 or 50 mm (about $1^{15}/_{16}$ inches).

Dimensions L and M depend on the hub selected for the bicycle and on the freewheel selection. The frame's dimensions should allow the wheel to fit neatly into it. A fit that is neither too tight nor too loose facilitates wheel insertion and removal. While the front and rear fork ends can be forced open or pulled together with the axle nuts or quick release, this is less than satisfactory. The fork blades or chain stays spreading unevenly results in an inaccurate rear chainline or in the wheels being out of center. Fork ends properly aligned will be rendered out of line, or skewed, when forced into a different point.

Four-speed, five-speed, five-speed with an outer protector ring to avoid chain override, and six-speed freewheels require progressively wider clearances between fork ends. A five-speed cog requires a 1.28-inch freewheel space—even more if mudguard bolt clearance is desired. An outer protector requires 1.34 inches of freewheel space, while a six-speed cog requires 1.40 inches.

Typical hub width dimensions between fork ends are as follows:

Front: 93 mm (3.66 inches); 96 mm (3.78 inches); 100 mm (3.94 inches)—standard on racing bicycles. Even wider front hubs are used on some tandems to improve wheel rigidity (108 mm).

Rear: 102 mm (4.02 inches)—juvenile; 111 mm (4.40 inches)—single-speed rear hub.
108 mm (4.25 inches)—Fichtel and Sachs Torpedo #415 three-speed hub.
114 mm (4.48 inches)—three-speed hubs and coaster brakes.
116 mm (4.57 inches)—Torpedo #515 three-speed hub and coaster brake.
117 mm (4.60 inches); 118 mm (4.65 inches) Sturmey three-speed coaster brake.
120 mm (4.72 inches)—standard for five-speed bicycles; Japanese makers use 121 mm (4.75 inches).
124 mm (4.90 inches)—recommended when top protector is used; 125 mm or 127.6 mm (4.92 inches or 5.00 inches)—required for six-speed cogs.

Tandem rear hubs with internal expanding hub brakes vary from 130 mm to 135 and 140 mm in width between the fork ends (5.12, 5.31, and 5.51″ respectively), and from 127 to 140 mm for disc brakes.

If the wheels are to be interchanged, it is obvious that hub width over the locknuts and chainline and wheel centering must be matched.

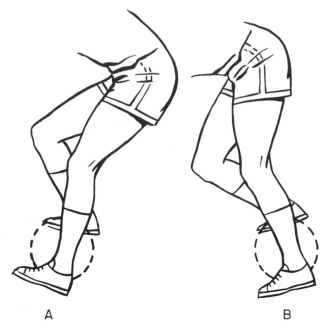

A   B

Fig. 5.3 Saddle position. A, For faster pedal cadence, the saddle is placed more to the rear. B, at higher forces and "digging in," the saddle is moved forward.

THE RACING FRAME

To reduce manufacturing details and complications in stocking lugs of many angles and tubes of many lengths, manufacturers are promoting the standardization of noncustom-built racing frames. This will provide bicycles with good handling qualities which fit riders of average proportions. Capital letters in Table 5.1 refer to Figure 5.2, Bicycle Specification Dimensions, and dimensions are in millimeters, except as shown in inches.

Bracket Height, K, equals 270 mm (10⅝ inches).

From front-wheel center to bottom-bracket center equals 600 mm (23⅝ inches).

Table 5.1

PROPOSED STANDARDS FOR RACING FRAMES

Seat Tube A	Top Tube C	Head Tube G	Chain Stays D
500 (19⅝ inches)	520	85	430
510 (20 inches)	520	95	430
520 (20⅜ inches)	540	92	430
530 (20¾ inches)	540	100	430
540 (21¼ inches)	540	110	430
550 (21⅝ inches)	550	115	430
560 (22 inches)	560	125	430
570 (22½ inches)	570	130	430
580 (22⅞ inches)	580	140	430
590 (23¼ inches)	580	150	430
600 (23⅝ inches)	590	160	435
610 (24 inches)	590	170	435
620 (24⅜ inches)	590	180	435

As the frame becomes taller, the seat tube angle becomes a bit less steeply inclined and the steering head a bit steeper. The smaller frame will have a steeper seat tube and a shallower head tube angle. In the center of the range, from 540 to 580 mm, the frame is "square," that is, the seat and top tube dimensions are equal. Frames shorter than 540 mm have proportionately longer top tubes; frames taller than 580 mm have proportionately shorter top tubes.

These dimensions provide a frame with enough clearance for an "average" foot which is maneuverable and yet reasonably rigid. The tall rider may need an extralong handlebar extension.

Frames used by some of the 1973 stars in the Tour de France varied from these standards. The chain stay lengths were as short as 415 and 425 mm; the top tubes were a bit shorter than those listed, and handlebar extensions were extended to make up the difference. The seat tube angles as used by Merckx in his 590-mm frame ranged close to the usual 73° for road racing work.

THE TOURING BICYCLE

The touring bicycle has other requirements. Traveling into areas where the roads are muddy or soft or covered with snow requires more ample clearance for mud and mudguards. Pannier clearance will be wanted. Front and rear carriers should be thoroughly and securely fixed, which indicates brazed-on fittings. Less steep frame angles allow sufficient caster for steady steering without the fatiguing, choppy ride characteristic of a racing mount. Provisions for keeping the luggage low aid stability and handling. The gearing range will be wider, which makes a longer chain stay an advantage, particularly if triple chainwheels are used. This likewise gives more clearance between tire and stay—a big help if a spoke on the freewheel side breaks in the middle of the boondocks (see Fig. 5.2).

Provisions for lighting and for carrying a water bottle demand brazed-on mounts, if at all possible. Pumps are now available that need no mounting pegs. (Handlebars, extensions, saddles, and pedals are discussed in Chapter VII.)

TRACK BICYCLES

The bicycle for sprints and track events is in a class of its own. These use a smaller, close-built frame for the extreme stiffness necessary to withstand maximum short-term power thrusts. Seat and chain stays are of extralarge section. Clearances are close for maximum rigidity. The tubing gauge will often be heavier than that for road use. Fork blades are short and extra stout. Frame angles are steep—head angles may be as steep as 75°—with a correspondingly short offset of the fork to get maximum maneuverability.

Rear and front fork ends are extra thick to resist deflection under extreme loads. Rear fork ends are rear opening, instead of front. Retainers prevent wheel pullover, and track, instead of quick-release, nuts are used to attach the wheels. Minimum loss of power through frame deflection is a prime objective.

STEERING STABILITY AND HANDLING

Stability and maneuverability are interrelated factors. Choosing between them is a compromise, and as a discerning cyclist, you can decide upon your personal needs when selecting your design. Many factors are involved, including frame flexibility; frame and wheelbase length; the location and height of loads; and the road surface being traveled, its texture, its sideward slope or camber, direction and strength of the wind. Speed, weight and size of wheel and tire, and indeed even the characteristics of the tire itself have a bearing.

Three major factors within the designer's control, however, are the wheel diameter, the steepness of the angle of the steering head, and the offset of the fork. As speed increases, the gyroscopic effect of the rapidly spinning wheel tends to keep the bicycle upright. In the event we lean to one side, this gyroscopic effect turns the front wheel in the proper direction to bring us back into equilibrium. We all recognize that above a certain minimum speed it is easier to keep our balance. Figure 5.4 shows a bicycle on which a second free-rotating front wheel has been mounted. By spinning this extra wheel forward or backward, the gyroscopic effect can be increased or cancelled. If the front wheel is deflected by a stone, the gyroscopic couple works to our disadvantage. Luckily, other factors intervene to help us.

"Trail" (Fig. 5.2, the dimension S) indicates the distance at which the front wheel contact point trails the

Fig. 5.4   Bicycle fitted with a second front wheel.

intersection of the steering axis with the ground. You can see that the amount of this trail will increase as wheel diameter increases and will decrease as the fork offset, E, and the steering head angle, Q, increase.

As the handlebars are turned from the center position, the steering head drops. With the weight that is applied to the steering head, this causes a torque which turns the handlebars. As the angle of lean of the frame is increased, this torque becomes stronger, although the amount the handlebars will turn from center lessens. You can try this experiment. Hold your bicycle upright. Unless perfectly vertical, the handlebars will tend to turn right or left. Now lean the bike bit by bit to one side in increasing amounts. You will find that the handlebars turn more quickly as you increase the lean, but the amount that they turn from the center decreases as the frame is leaned more steeply.

Dr. David Jones, of Runcorn, England, discovered this effect and wrote a computer program to calculate this stabilizing tendency. The stabilizing effect was related to wheel diameter, steering head angle, and trail. Relative values of this effect show the strength of the stabilizing force. A zero value has no effect, a positive value is unstable, and negative values have an increasing tendency to maintain direction.

Many years ago, cycle engineers developed a simple formula that related steering head angle, wheel diameter, and calculated fork offset (E) to give satisfactory steering. The formula is: offset $= r \tan \dfrac{(90° - Q)}{2}$, where Q is the steering head angle, and r is the steering wheel radius.

The graph in Figure 5.6, calculated from Dr. Jones' computer study, shows his stability index for 27-inch wheels, with steering head angles of from 68° to 76°, and for fork offsets from 40 to 120 mm. Note that the "Davison" fork offsets, calculated from the formula above, are also shown. For a range of 68°–75°, these range in the stability range of −4 to −5.2.

Figure 5.5 compares the variable offset front fork on the author's experimental bicycle with a standard fork end. On the experimental model, stability can be adjusted to suit the need.

WHAT STABILITY DO I WANT?

Too much stability makes a bicycle sluggish to handle. It wants to keep on going straight, even if you want to miss a stone or a pothole. On the other hand, if you ride in gravel or snow, the front wheel contacts material ahead of the steering axis, and this tends to throw the wheel out of center to a dangerous extent. If you want to maneuver at low speeds, an extrastable bicycle will make this more difficult.

On high-speed runs, extra stability keeps your bicycle on course so that a stone or bump is less likely to throw you. For no-hands riding at moderate speeds, a

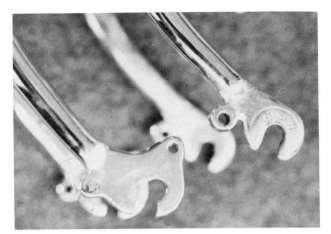

Fig. 5.5   The adjustable offset front fork end used on the author's XP experimental bicycle compared to a standard forged fork end.

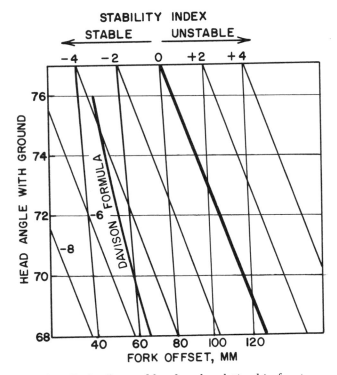

Fig. 5.6   Fork offset and head angle relationship for steering stability with 27-inch and 700-mm wheels. For other wheel diameters, multiply offset by $\dfrac{\text{wheel diameter (mm)}}{700}$.

medium degree of stability makes your bicycle easiest to handle. It's your decision which you prefer. If your riding is mostly at high speeds, often with luggage or on gravel roads, use a high stability index. If you prefer hair-trigger steering for rapid maneuvering, even though the bicycle will require more precise handling, increase either the steepness of the steering head, the amount of fork offset, or both. This will give a lower stability index.

Remember that though hard-blown tires, a short

wheelbase, and snappy steering may make the ride seem easier at first, a softer acting frame and larger section tires reduce the constant day long jarring, saddle soreness, hand and wrist ache. Decreasing the steering head angle and increasing fork offset just enough to maintain the stability index you desire, affords improved shock absorption.

Figure 5.7 gives one rider's evaluation of the handling characteristics of his bicycle. Mechanical trail was modified by modifying the fork offset and the effect of this noted under different road surfaces and speeds. As you ride evaluate your bicycle's performance. You may find that a change in its design would suit you better.

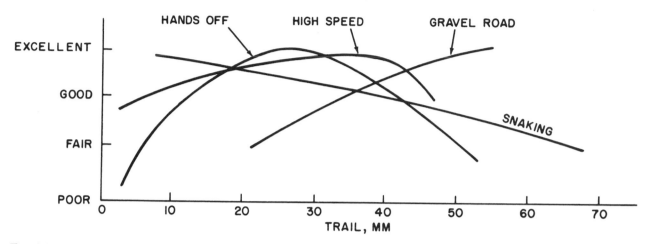

Fig. 5.7 Bicycle stability and handling characteristics.

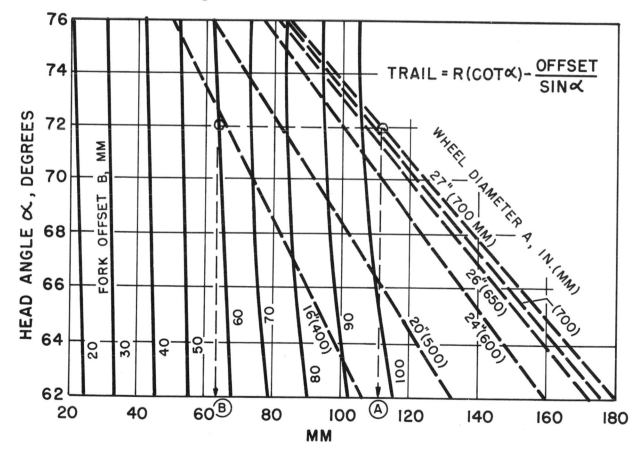

$$TRAIL = R(COT\alpha) - \frac{OFFSET}{SIN\alpha}$$

Fig. 5.8 Calculation of Trail. From Wheel Diameter and Head Angle, find R [Cot α] = A. From Fork Offset and Head Angle, find $\frac{Offset}{Sin \alpha}$ = B. Subtract B from A.

Example: 72° head angle, 27″ wheel diameter, 60 mm offset, A = 110.5 mm, B = 63.1 mm. Trail = 47.4 mm.

CHAPTER VI

Bicycle Inspection and Repairs

Compared to the automobilist the bicycle owner is indeed fortunate. For years automobile designers have buried the parts of a car in sheaths of steel at depths that make it nearly impossible to find and service them. On the bicycle on the other hand, with the exception of the internal parts of three-speed hubs and coaster brakes, practically all of the parts are visible, and their functions are relatively simple. With a little thought and reflection, the cause and cure for most problems can be thought out even by someone with limited mechanical training. You can see or feel wear on parts, and most failures that occur could have been anticipated by feel, sound, or observation during normal riding.

Since many failures that occur on the road happen far from home or repair facilities, it will pay you in both time and money to become your own minor repairs bike mechanic. As an aid to understanding, we will examine the various parts to see how they are made and how they function.

Detailed internal repairs and adjustments, frame repairs, precision wheel building and truing, and altering or modifying components are jobs for first-class mechanics. Some manufacturers run servicing schools to teach the finer points. There are a number of excellent texts, some running as large as five hundred pages, available for further study. The Schwinn Service Manual is an example. Several others with less equipment coverage and less detail are also available. See Bicycling Magazine advertisements.

If you buy your new bicycle in a store that is amply staffed with A one mechanics, your bicycle should be properly assembled, aligned, and adjusted when you receive it. Unfortunately, many bicycle retail outlets do not have personnel trained to prepare the more sophisticated bicycles now in great demand. Likewise, due to the worldwide bicycle explosion, there are at times shortages of skilled workmen and of parts in factories both domestic and foreign. This results in equipment that is not 100% perfect reaching the dealers' shelves. On top of this, equipment is being supplied from unknown suppliers with limited quality control. Figure 6.1 lists a few of the imperfections noted in brand-new merchandise. This list is not all-inclusive, but will give you some points to check to make certain that your equipment is up to the standards you expect.

Once you have taken possession of your bicycle, you should examine it regularly with an eagle eye to make certain that all is well. You can do this in less time than it takes to tell about it. Before and after each ride, and at rest stops when on a long trip, you will be well advised to make a "preventive maintenance inspection," particularly if your speeds have been high, the road surfaces rough, or if you have had or anticipate high-speed maneuvering or braking.

As You Ride

As you ride, keep alert for rattles, squeaks, or rubbing noises. Note the "feel" of your bicycle and all its controls. Slight, easily detected changes signify items that are departing from perfection long before these become unsafe or prone to failure (see checklist, Fig. 6.1).

Look for excess play or slack in brake, derailleur, or three-speed operating cables. Note if gear shifting lacks precision, is not positive, or is slow at the extremes of the ranges. There may be a tendency to overshift.

A steady thumping or bumpy feeling either front or rear indicates that a wheel is out of round. A wavering

Cyclist's While-Riding Evaluation Checklist

	OK	Investigate
Rattles, squeaks, or rubbing noises? Where?	[ ]	[ ]
Wheels bumpy or wobbly?	[ ]	[ ]
Wheels firm or squishy?	[ ]	[ ]
Tires firm or low in pressure?	[ ]	[ ]
Steering steady, hands off, or erratic?	[ ]	[ ]
Reserve brake lever motion left, panic stop?	[ ]	[ ]
Levers and cable housing tight, no loose motion?	[ ]	[ ]
Brake action smooth, no grabby spots?	[ ]	[ ]
Brakes drag after release?	[ ]	[ ]
Brakes squeal or shudder when used?	[ ]	[ ]
Braking power OK?	[ ]	[ ]
Pedals rim true and square? Solid?	[ ]	[ ]
Shake, knock, or grind in bottom bracket?	[ ]	[ ]
Gears shift full range? Slow shift? Overshift?	[ ]	[ ]
Front sprockets, wave or shake?	[ ]	[ ]
Full power in all gears, no skip or slip?	[ ]	[ ]
Gears stay in position set, or shift by self?	[ ]	[ ]
Rubbing chain, front or rear? Which gear?	[ ]	[ ]
Saddle angle OK?	[ ]	[ ]
Saddle height OK? High or low?	[ ]	[ ]
Saddle tight under bumps?	[ ]	[ ]
Saddle comfortable?	[ ]	[ ]
Handlebars tight under hard pull?	[ ]	[ ]
Toe clip size OK? Short or long?	[ ]	[ ]
Carriers load or equipment solid, no shake?	[ ]	[ ]
Headlight and taillight operating? Bright?	[ ]	[ ]
Headlight focus OK for speed used?	[ ]	[ ]
Bike accelerates and coasts easily?	[ ]	[ ]

Fig. 6.1   Cyclist's While Riding Evaluation

feeling may indicate that wheels are loose in bearing fit or have a side-to-side wobble.

Is your steering erratic? Is there a tendency to veer to one side or the other if you relax your hold on the bars? Do the steering bearings feel bumpy as you turn? Do they bind? Loose bearings give a less-than-solid feeling.

When you apply your brakes, do they feel smooth and powerful, or does it require more than normal brake pressure to bring you to a stop? Under hard brake application, your feet should not travel so far back (in coaster brakes) that you are not in a position to apply needed pressure. In a hard stop with hand brakes, is there still ample clearance left between the brake lever and the handlebar? Is the lever so far out that it is difficult to reach? Is the lever attached tightly to the bar, or can you detect play between the bar and the mounting clamp? Once this play develops, it can lead to failure in a very few miles.

If when applying hand brakes you feel tight spots as the wheels revolve, this may indicate that the wheel rims are out of gauge or dented or out of true from side to side or out of round. Do your brakes judder, squeal, or vibrate? Do the brakes return completely upon release, or do they drag on one side?

How about the action of your pedals? They should feel true and solid. Does one foot seem to rock as the pedals turn around, or feel tilted? This can indicate a bent crank or pedal spindle, a loosening pedal (once loose, it can strip its threads or become lost in a short time) or loose pedal bearings.

Does the drive feel easy, yet "solid?" Look down at your front sprockets as they rotate. If they waver back and forth as they turn, they may be bent. Is there any motion that you can see and feel which might be caused by loose bearings?

Is your chain drive smooth under power, or does it appear to skip, to jump teeth, particularly in high gear? This could indicate a tight link in the chain, a stretched chain, or bent, worn, or malformed sprocket teeth either front or rear. Can you hear the chain rubbing on the derailleur cage as you travel? Can this be quieted by adjusting the lever position? If you can stop the noise, does it soon return? Does the derailleur shift without the levers being touched? This indicates that the levers are not sufficiently tightened and are moving under spring pressure.

As you pull on your handlebars and as you turn, do you note any tendency for them to twist out of center with the front wheel or to change the angle of the grips? Does your saddle feel "solid?" When you hit a bump, does it shift height or angle, or rotate a bit out of parallel with the frame? You may have to tighten it; you may have a stripped clamp. If your saddle is not solid, you can lose control at a critical juncture. Is your saddle comfortable? Does it chafe? Do you feel you are "sitting in a bucket?" Is the saddle top firm, or has it gotten loose, sway-backed, or deformed from being wet? Does it feel too high or low? You may have changed to shoes with a different sole thickness! Is the saddle's angle correct, or would it be more comfortable if the angle of its top with the ground were inclined more toward front or rear?

As you make a turn, do the wheels feel solid or squashy (indicating loosening spokes) or wavering or bumpy as described before? These can develop during a ride even if everything was perfect when you started.

The expert cyclist trains himself to immediately notice these departures from mechanical excellence as a matter of course. It is that part of "getting the feel" of your bicycle which makes you partners. The expert notes if his bicycle has its usual ease of movement, or if it is sluggish with tire, or chain and bearing friction problems. His acquired "sixth sense" always assures him of a safe, easy riding mount worthy of his full confidence. He can evaluate any slight imperfection. Some call for an immediate stop and repair; some can be left until there is ample time. Learn to be observant! You will find it makes cycling more stimulating and more fun.

YOUR PM INSPECTION

Before each day's ride, you should be sure that your bicycle is A-OK. If you develop a routine, this can be done in a matter of minutes. Combined with your on-the-saddle feel, you will always know your bike's condition. Before any extended trip, be more thorough; it may be a long walk home if you slip up. On a long trip, use your rest stops not only to check for faults indicated while riding, but also for checking tire condition. It may take miles for a piece of glass to puncture a tube after it is first imbedded.

Let's list these checks in the order: tires, rims, steering, brakes, and drive. Cleaning and lubricating are done as you make your PM (Preventive Maintenance, or Prior to Movement) inspection, or as part of routine overhaul (see Fig. 6.2).

TIRES

Spin each wheel slowly, checking each point on the tread for evenness of wear. Look for cuts or imbedded particles. A cut may be a surface indication of an imbedded piece of glass that will puncture your tube as you ride. Dig these out if you find them. Is the tread true and centered? Are there suspicious bulges or worn spots in the tread? These can indicate fabric failure underneath. Check the sidewalls on each side—especially just above the rim—for cuts, fabric breaks, or bulges.

On a clincher tire, there is usually a small, raised line in the rubber which runs around the tire close to the rim. The spacing between this and the rim should be even. Irregular spacing can indicate that the rim is dented or that the tire is not fully seated. If it is not properly seated, air pressure between the rim and the tire bead may blow the tire off the rim or puncture it. Is the valve fully seated, and perpendicular, or is it skewed sideward or out of line with the spokes (this may predict a failure)?

If the tread is not centered on tubular or sew-up tires, the tire was improperly mounted or not properly centered. It is always good practice with sew-up tires to reduce the tire pressure and squeeze them with your thumbs to feel whether the tire is thoroughly and continually cemented to the rim. If you can roll the base of the tire away from the rim at any point, recement it and allow the cement to harden before starting on your trip. If this is impractical, ride with extreme care; a poorly cemented tire can roll off the rim on a turn and either locking your wheels, throw you over the bars, or giving you no traction, spill you at high speed. Braking on a poorly cemented tire can cause it to roll off the rim. Braking and accelerating forces pulling it back and forth may tear out the valve.

BICYCLE CONDITION INSPECTION

No	Item	Fix	Rep	OK		Fix	Rep	OK	
1	Tires: Front	[ ]	[ ]	[ ]	Rear same	[ ]	[ ]	[ ]	1A
	Inflation pressure	[ ]	[ ]	[ ]		[ ]	[ ]	[ ]	
	Uneven wear, bulges	[ ]	[ ]	[ ]		[ ]	[ ]	[ ]	
	Cuts, imbedded material	[ ]	[ ]	[ ]		[ ]	[ ]	[ ]	
	Fabric breaks	[ ]	[ ]	[ ]		[ ]	[ ]	[ ]	
	Seating cementing	[ ]	[ ]	[ ]		[ ]	[ ]	[ ]	
	Valve straight	[ ]	[ ]	[ ]		[ ]	[ ]	[ ]	
2	Rims: Front	[ ]	[ ]	[ ]	Rear same	[ ]	[ ]	[ ]	2A
	Side wobble	[ ]	[ ]	[ ]		[ ]	[ ]	[ ]	
	Hop	[ ]	[ ]	[ ]		[ ]	[ ]	[ ]	
	Dents or bulges	[ ]	[ ]	[ ]		[ ]	[ ]	[ ]	
3	Spokes: Front	[ ]	[ ]	[ ]	Rear same	[ ]	[ ]	[ ]	3A
	Length	[ ]	[ ]	[ ]		[ ]	[ ]	[ ]	
	Loose, uneven tension	[ ]	[ ]	[ ]		[ ]	[ ]	[ ]	
	Missing or broken	[ ]	[ ]	[ ]		[ ]	[ ]	[ ]	
4	Wheel bearings: Front	[ ]	[ ]	[ ]	Rear same	[ ]	[ ]	[ ]	4A
	Adjustment	[ ]	[ ]	[ ]		[ ]	[ ]	[ ]	
	Tight or rough spots	[ ]	[ ]	[ ]		[ ]	[ ]	[ ]	
	Freedom of rotation	[ ]	[ ]	[ ]		[ ]	[ ]	[ ]	
5	Hub axle and fork end: Front	[ ]	[ ]	[ ]	Rear same	[ ]	[ ]	[ ]	5A
	Axle bent	[ ]	[ ]	[ ]		[ ]	[ ]	[ ]	
	Ends out of parallel	[ ]	[ ]	[ ]		[ ]	[ ]	[ ]	
6	Steering:	[ ]	[ ]	[ ]	Stem tight	[ ]	[ ]	[ ]	6A
	Loose	[ ]	[ ]	[ ]	Bars tight in extension	[ ]	[ ]	[ ]	
	Tight	[ ]	[ ]	[ ]	Grips or tape OK	[ ]	[ ]	[ ]	
	Brinelled	[ ]	[ ]	[ ]	Bar bent	[ ]	[ ]	[ ]	
7	Brakes: Front	[ ]	[ ]	[ ]	Rear same	[ ]	[ ]	[ ]	7A
	Reserve motion available	[ ]	[ ]	[ ]		[ ]	[ ]	[ ]	
	Broken strands or cable	[ ]	[ ]	[ ]		[ ]	[ ]	[ ]	
	Kinked casing	[ ]	[ ]	[ ]		[ ]	[ ]	[ ]	
	Loose lever or casing	[ ]	[ ]	[ ]		[ ]	[ ]	[ ]	
	Blocks centered on rim	[ ]	[ ]	[ ]		[ ]	[ ]	[ ]	
	Condition of block	[ ]	[ ]	[ ]		[ ]	[ ]	[ ]	
	Closed end to front	[ ]	[ ]	[ ]		[ ]	[ ]	[ ]	
	Toe in	[ ]	[ ]	[ ]		[ ]	[ ]	[ ]	
	Clearance, released	[ ]	[ ]	[ ]		[ ]	[ ]	[ ]	
	Return action solid, equal	[ ]	[ ]	[ ]		[ ]	[ ]	[ ]	
	Binding parts	[ ]	[ ]	[ ]		[ ]	[ ]	[ ]	
	Play or loose parts	[ ]	[ ]	[ ]		[ ]	[ ]	[ ]	
	Cable movement free	[ ]	[ ]	[ ]		[ ]	[ ]	[ ]	
	Mounting bolts tight	[ ]	[ ]	[ ]		[ ]	[ ]	[ ]	
	Pedal motion not excessive	[ ]	[ ]	[ ]		[ ]	[ ]	[ ]	
	Torque arm secure	[ ]	[ ]	[ ]		[ ]	[ ]	[ ]	
8	Pedals: Left	[ ]	[ ]	[ ]	Right same	[ ]	[ ]	[ ]	8A
	Tight on to crank	[ ]	[ ]	[ ]		[ ]	[ ]	[ ]	
	Bearing fit or play	[ ]	[ ]	[ ]		[ ]	[ ]	[ ]	
	Not bent	[ ]	[ ]	[ ]		[ ]	[ ]	[ ]	
	Treads complete	[ ]	[ ]	[ ]		[ ]	[ ]	[ ]	
	Toe clips tight, condition	[ ]	[ ]	[ ]		[ ]	[ ]	[ ]	
	Toe strap condition	[ ]	[ ]	[ ]		[ ]	[ ]	[ ]	

No	Item	Fix	Rep	OK		Fix	Rep	OK	
9	Crank: Left	[ ]	[ ]	[ ]	Right same	[ ]	[ ]	[ ]	9A
	Fit OK, bolts or pins tight	[ ]	[ ]	[ ]		[ ]	[ ]	[ ]	
	Bent or twisted	[ ]	[ ]	[ ]		[ ]	[ ]	[ ]	
10	Crank Axle:	[ ]	[ ]	[ ]		[ ]	[ ]	[ ]	10A
	Bearings loose	[ ]	[ ]	[ ]	Bearings tight or rough	[ ]	[ ]	[ ]	
	Axle bent—left	[ ]	[ ]	[ ]	Axle bent—right	[ ]	[ ]	[ ]	
11	Sprockets: Front	[ ]	[ ]	[ ]	Rear	[ ]	[ ]	[ ]	11A
	Bolted tightly to crank	[ ]	[ ]	[ ]	Screwed on tightly	[ ]	[ ]	[ ]	
	No shake if not bolted	[ ]	[ ]	[ ]	Retaining ring or nut tight	[ ]	[ ]	[ ]	
	Inner and outer attached OK	[ ]	[ ]	[ ]	Screwed even spacing	[ ]	[ ]	[ ]	
	Properly and evenly spaced	[ ]	[ ]	[ ]		[ ]	[ ]	[ ]	
	Sprocket bent outer	[ ]	[ ]	[ ]	Rear bent (wavy), which?	[ ]	[ ]	[ ]	
	Sprocket bent inner	[ ]	[ ]	[ ]		[ ]	[ ]	[ ]	
	Sprocket teeth bent	[ ]	[ ]	[ ]	Same, which?	[ ]	[ ]	[ ]	
	Sprocket teeth worn	[ ]	[ ]	[ ]	Same, which?	[ ]	[ ]	[ ]	
	Sprocket teeth chipped	[ ]	[ ]	[ ]	Same, which?	[ ]	[ ]	[ ]	
12	Chain	[ ]	[ ]	[ ]	Free wheel	[ ]	[ ]	[ ]	13
	Condition and lubrication	[ ]	[ ]	[ ]	Engages solidly	[ ]	[ ]	[ ]	
	Stretched or worn	[ ]	[ ]	[ ]	Side wobble	[ ]	[ ]	[ ]	
	Tight links	[ ]	[ ]	[ ]	Radial hop (eccentric)	[ ]	[ ]	[ ]	
	Chain length adjustment	[ ]	[ ]	[ ]	Chain length largest sprockets	[ ]	[ ]	[ ]	
14	Gear shifter: Front	[ ]	[ ]	[ ]	Rear same	[ ]	[ ]	[ ]	14A
	Cable adjustment	[ ]	[ ]	[ ]		[ ]	[ ]	[ ]	
	Cage parallel	[ ]	[ ]	[ ]		[ ]	[ ]	[ ]	
	Cage height 1/16 to 1/4	[ ]	[ ]	[ ]	(Rear cage clearance low gear)	[ ]	[ ]	[ ]	
	Cage travel low gear	[ ]	[ ]	[ ]		[ ]	[ ]	[ ]	
	Cage travel high gear	[ ]	[ ]	[ ]		[ ]	[ ]	[ ]	
	Shift lever tension	[ ]	[ ]	[ ]		[ ]	[ ]	[ ]	
	Cable condition and freedom	[ ]	[ ]	[ ]		[ ]	[ ]	[ ]	
15	Hub gear cable	[ ]	[ ]	[ ]	Hub gear control lever	[ ]	[ ]	[ ]	15
	Proper adjustment	[ ]	[ ]	[ ]	Lever mounting and play OK	[ ]	[ ]	[ ]	
	Hub gear shifts positively	[ ]	[ ]	[ ]	Gear drives positively on each gear	[ ]	[ ]	[ ]	
16	Mudguards: Front	[ ]	[ ]	[ ]	Rear same	[ ]	[ ]	[ ]	16A
	Intact, uncracked	[ ]	[ ]	[ ]		[ ]	[ ]	[ ]	
	Mounting stays and bolts	[ ]	[ ]	[ ]		[ ]	[ ]	[ ]	
17	Carrier: Front	[ ]	[ ]	[ ]	Rear same	[ ]	[ ]	[ ]	17A
	Intact, securely attached	[ ]	[ ]	[ ]		[ ]	[ ]	[ ]	
18	Fork alignment: Front	[ ]	[ ]	[ ]	Fork alignment: Rear	[ ]	[ ]	[ ]	18A
	Offset proper, equal	[ ]	[ ]	[ ]	Chainline-rear and bracket	[ ]	[ ]	[ ]	
	Central with column	[ ]	[ ]	[ ]	Seat and head tube parallel	[ ]	[ ]	[ ]	
	Column not bent	[ ]	[ ]	[ ]	Wheels parallel vertically	[ ]	[ ]	[ ]	19
20	No frame members bent	[ ]	[ ]	[ ]	Wheels in line	[ ]	[ ]	[ ]	21
22	No cracked tubes	[ ]	[ ]	[ ]	No cracks or unfilled joints	[ ]	[ ]	[ ]	23
24	All parts clean	[ ]	[ ]	[ ]	All parts lubricated	[ ]	[ ]	[ ]	
25	Lighting set: Front	[ ]	[ ]	[ ]	Rear same	[ ]	[ ]	[ ]	25A
	Mounting secure	[ ]	[ ]	[ ]		[ ]	[ ]	[ ]	
	Wiring tight, insulation OK	[ ]	[ ]	[ ]		[ ]	[ ]	[ ]	
	Bulbs operable	[ ]	[ ]	[ ]		[ ]	[ ]	[ ]	
	Generator batteries OK	[ ]	[ ]	[ ]	Generator aligned	[ ]	[ ]	[ ]	
26	Condition of paint	[ ]	[ ]	[ ]	Condition of chrome	[ ]	[ ]	[ ]	26A

Fig. 6.2   Bicycle Condition Inspection

Fig. 6.3 Inspect rims and tires and spokes for wear, cuts, fabric breaks, seating, dents, and loose or uneven spoke tension.

RIMS

As you spin the wheel slowly, note any bumps or dents in the rim, particularly on its outer circumference. Look for side-to-side motion where the wheel goes through the brake blocks. Changes in clearance between the brake block and the rim mean the wheel is laterally out of true. When you find a point that moves over toward a brake block, check both sides. You may find a bulge in both directions, caused by bottoming against the rim when hitting a paving break, which will give uneven braking. In slippery weather, the brakes grabbing the rim can initiate a skid, particularly if you are making a turn.

As you rotate the rim, also check for up and down "hops." The rim will appear to travel up and down in relation to the block. This causes a bumpy ride. Do the brake blocks make contact with the center of the rim side? If a bump or hop is too severe, the brake blocks may rub against the tire sidewalls at the bottom of the hop. At the top of the out-of-round spot, under hard brake pressure, the brake block can be pulled into the spokes.

If your rims have either side-to-side wavers, or hops, wheel truing is needed. Check each spoke by "twanging" it as you rotate the wheel to see if any are loose or extra tight (they should twang like overtaut bow strings). You may find that almost all of the spokes are too loose: spoke nipples sometimes unscrew under riding pressure. Check to see if any spokes are broken. Spoke tension should be firm. You should not be able to move a spoke back and forth at its center except with appreciable effort. On a trip tightening or loosen-

ing offending spokes, or replacing a broken spoke, may enable you to complete the trip. Final truing can be done when equipment and time are available. If too far out of true, the rim may have buckled and will require major surgery. Unless you have the skill, it is best to go to a good bicycle shop. A new wheel may be less expensive than a field rebuild.

Check for bearing adjustment. Take the rim between your fingers and press it gently from side to side. With normal cup and cone hub bearings, there should be just a barely perceptible play at this point. Excessive play may indicate the need for bearing adjustment. Lift the wheel, raise the tire valve to the top, and release it. The weight of the valve should rotate the wheel downward. If properly adjusted, the wheel should swing back and forth a half dozen or more times before it stops. A proper bearing fit indicates that the cones are good and true. If you note a tight spot, however, check for a bent axle. Also, there may be dirt in the bearings or a damaged, worn-out cone. Disassembly for inspection and cleaning is then required. If the fit is either loose or tight, the cones and locknuts should be adjusted or the axle replaced. After adjustment, this test can be repeated before the wheel is reinstalled.

Some high-grade hubs in today's better bicycles are made with sealed ball bearings. These have almost no perceptible side play when they are fitted. They will roll easily as previously described.

You have already investigated the possibility of a bent axle by sight. Now look at the fork ends to determine if they are true and parallel. If there is any discrepancy, remove the wheel by loosening the quick release or axle nuts. Then, holding the wheel, turn the axle by hand, holding a pencil tip against the outer end. If as you rotate the axle it moves in relation to your pencil point, the axle is bent and should be straightened or replaced.

An out-of-parallel fork end can bend the axle when the nuts are tightened. Out-of-parallel ends also place a very heavy bending stress on the axle which can lead to premature failure. Cones are cramped against the balls, and this too leads to premature failures. Straightening the fork ends and the axle should be done as soon as possible. Disassembly to inspect the cones for damage is recommended.

Now that you are certain that the hub is true and that the spokes and rim are reasonably accurate, place the wheel in its fork slots and tighten the axle nuts or quick release. Make certain that the front wheel is centered in the fork. If it isn't, loosen the front axle and readjust it. (If this is not easily done, the wheel may be off center, and may require retruing, even if it has no hop or wobble.)

The fork blades may be bent to one side or bent forward unevenly. We will cover this in more detail later (Fig. 6.32 gives measurements for wheel centering). Check both front and rear wheels in the same manner.

STEERING

Steering head bearings can be quickly checked. Loose steering head bearings can lead to erratic steering, and the impact from bumps in normal road riding can cause the balls in the bearing to dent the upper and lower bearing races. The steering head sticks in these dents, called brinelling, as the handlebars are turned and may settle in a spot a little off center. This makes it difficult to maintain a straight line and can cause oversteering or understeering with a possible loss of control at critical times. At high speeds this may contribute to wheel wobble. The front wheel may oscillate from side to side in an uncontrolled manner. While other factors contribute to wheel wobble, this unsafe condition should be corrected.

To check for head bearing fit, turn the handlebars from side to side. If the bearings are out of line due to a bent fork crown or too tight adjustment, it will feel tight. A bumpy condition as you turn from side to side indicates brinelling. Now grasp the handlebar stem with one hand and the top of the front wheel with the other, allowing both wheels to support the bicycle weight. Move your hands alternately toward each other and away from each other. If the steering is loose, you will notice a definite shake which can be easily felt as well as seen. If the head bearings are not adjusted as soon as this is found, brinelling of the bearings can occur.

The correction of brinelled races entails the disassembly and replacement of frame and fork races. If, after the wheels have been trued and the fit and freedom of head bearings adjusted, the bicycle still will not permit hands-off handling at moderate speeds, the frame alignment must be checked.

BRAKES

Press the brake levers toward the handlebars. While holding them down, look into the gap at the top of the brake lever. Make certain that the brake cable end is firmly seated and has sufficient support so that it will not pull through. Check the condition of the cable itself. Any sign of broken strands is an indication that

failure is imminent. Failure may happen at a time when you need them most urgently. If you find one or two broken strands, replace the cable as soon as possible. If you find more than this, replace the cable before riding further.

Fig. 6.5   Detecting head bearing fit. Alternately press hands together and pull them apart—no shake should be felt.

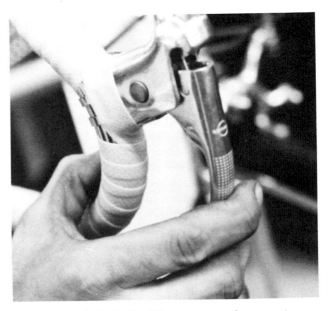

Fig. 6.6   With the brake fully on, reserve lever motion remains. Inspect for broken cable strands.

Fig. 6.4   Brinelled lower steering head bearings give erratic steering.

Now press each brake lever down hard. The brake levers should stop with considerable reserve clearance between the lever and the handlebar, no less than ¾ inch under full braking pressure. If this clearance does not exist, you may be able to reestablish adequate clearance by screwing out on the cable adjusting barrel—if your bike has one—and retightening the locknut. The need to do this indicates cable stretch or brake block wear.

Fig. 6.7   Ample reserve, but lever within rider's finger reach.

Fig. 6.8   Too short a brake reach. Even with the brake shoe at the lower limit of its adjustment, the brake block rubs the tire.

Check your brake blocks to see that there is ample rubber. The blocks should be centered on the rim side. If heavily worn, replacement is needed. Make certain that the closed end of the brake block holder is to the front.

Check the clearance betweeen the rim and the brake shoes. Clearances should be equal and should preferably be kept to from ¹⁄₁₆ to ⅛ inch with the lever released. More clearance may be temporarily needed if the wheel is out of true, but the two defective conditions should be corrected as soon as possible.

If the proper clearance cannot be obtained by barrel adjustment—leaving ample adjustment reserve for additional wear while on the road—the point of cable attachment must be adjusted.

There should be no sharp bends or kinks in the brake cable housing. The cut ends of the housing must be smooth; they should not cut into the cable. This condition causes cable binding and failure to release, requires extra effort when braking, and allows for the chance of cable wear and failure. Check the cable at each point where it enters a housing for broken strands.

Kinks may be bent back into alignment. Close and release the brakes once more. The brake shoes should swing back evenly away from the rim on each side. If they do not clear equally on each side, you may have to loosen and realign the brake mounting or correct faulty brake springs either by replacement or by bending them with punch and hammer. Or, if there is excess friction in the brake cable housing or lever, these can be cleaned and lubricated.

Note whether the brake shoes are evenly "toed-in" at the front on each side. Under forward pull, the toe-

Fig. 6.9   Brake shoe with proper fit, open end of brake shoe to the rear.

in compensates for the normal deflection of the brake arm under load. Check also to see if the brake parts are rubbing against each other. The arms of the brake may have been bent. In some side-pull brakes, when the handlebars are turned fully in one direction, an extending tab may be bent from striking the frame.

Some brakes are constructed of very thin material that bends under severe braking loads. Brake mounting bolts that are not tight will cause any brake to shift as it is applied. Therefore check these mounting bolts to see that they are snug. If the mounting hole for the brake mounting bolt is too large, it will allow the entire brake to rotate as it is carried along by the rim. On some of the thin section brakes, bent tabs limit this rotation. Unfortunately, since this happens under braking stress, these tabs create friction which reduces the brake application pressure. Check these points of bearing for excessive rubbing.

If hub or coaster brakes are fitted, make certain that the torque arm is securely fastened to the frame and the nut and bolt of the supporting clip well tightened. Operate the brake by hand, turning the pedals backward on foot-operated coaster brakes. With motion started just over the horizontal, the brake should be fully applied with about 20° of motion. Motion should not be so great that the rider would not be able to apply foot pressure because the crank is too vertical.

Several disc brakes are now being manufactured (AMF, Wood, and Shimano). If a disc brake is fitted, the rear wheel should be raised and rotated. The disc must run true without rubbing on the pads. The pads themselves should be inspected for ample lining material.

Internal expanding hub and coaster brakes cannot be examined without dismantling. Clearance can be set by cable adjustment. Shoe wear can be detected by a scraping sound when they are in operation.

In general, check all brake parts for wear, binding, and excessive play by operating each part by hand. Check the condition of center-pull bridge cables, and check all mounting and pivot bolts for tightness. Your brakes are your lifeline to safety. Do not shortchange yourself in this inspection—it can save your life.

CRANKS AND DRIVE AND PEDALS*

Grasp the opposing cranks by the pedals. One at a time, wiggle the pedal end up and down and in and out to see if there is excessive play in the pedal bearings. Look at the threaded end to see if the pedal is fully tightened into the crank. Try it with a wrench to make sure. Wiggle the entire pedal up and down to make sure there is no play at the thread. With the crank upright, look at the pedal both horizontally and

*In October, 1973 the International Standards Organization project on bicycle parts standardization team changed the nomenclature of pedal crank axle to the more accurate—spindle.

vertically to see if it has been bent up or down, forward or back. If it is, check the crank itself more closely. It may be bent in or out, or it may be twisted.

Now, holding the cranks at the pedal end, push and pull them from side to side. If you feel a shake, notice whether this is from loose bearings (the whole crank set will move back and forth together), or whether the motion is partially or all in the crank itself at the axle end. Now place the cranks horizontally and press them both down hard at the same time. Then turn them easily for 180° and press them down again, hard. If you feel any give, they may be loose on the axle, or the attachment bolts or wedge pins may be loose. On the one-piece crank sets used on many American bicycles, only the bearing fit test is needed.

Turn each pedal on its shaft to detect any signs of sticking or binding. Check each toe clip to be certain that it is not cracked or bent and that the attaching bolts are tight. Check the toe straps. Are they cut? Is the release end in good condition? Is the release located at the right point (at the pedal top on the outside)?

Now turn the entire crank assembly backward to feel for tightness or bind. Listen for grinding noises. If the pedals or bottom bracket are improperly fitted, loose, tight, or binding, they will have to be dismantled for lubrication or replacement.

Occasionally, an axle bent from hitting a curb or falling will need to be replaced. You can note this as you rotate the crankset.

If the front sprocket is attached to the crank by bolts, or if the inner sprockets are bolted to the outer sprockets, check all these carefully for tightness. They will work progressively looser while riding, and losing an entire sprocket set on a ride is a grueling experience.

Fig. 6.10 Detecting bearing play in the crank hanger.

SPROCKETS AND CHAIN

Rotate the chainwheel (front sprocket) backward, or if the bike is supported off its wheels, in either direction. Removing the chain makes inspection easier. Using a pencil braced against a frame tube, or sighting against the front derailleur cage, check each chainwheel for side to side wobble as it is turned. Check each tooth for grooving or wear on the face that drives the chain. Look also for chipping at the top of each tooth, and see if it is bent toward the inside or outside. Check the inside of the chainwheel for excessive side wear from shifting, and check for side wear on the teeth from running in misaligned sprocket combinations.

With the chain back on, hold back on the rear wheel and put pressure on the pedals. Note the position of the chain on the teeth. If the teeth are worn excessively, or if the chain is worn and stretched, you will note that the chain rides high on the teeth, rather than lying in the bottom of the tooth spaces. The rear sprockets can be checked at the same time. These may be bent, hooked (worn), or broken. Failure in any of these items demands replacement. The chain and sprockets should be replaced together. Satisfaction rarely results when only one is changed.

Now, rotate the cranks. Note the condition of the chain. Is it dirty or rusty? Then it needs cleaning and lubrication. As the cranks are rotated, observe the chain as it rounds the rear sprockets or derailleur jockey pulleys. (This can be done with the bicycle upside down.) At any point where the chain doesn't immediately straighten out there is a tight link that must be loosened. This may be done quickly by bending the chain from side to side at this point.

FREEWHEEL

Spin the rear wheel to see that it will roll without driving the chain. (Some sealed freewheels will, however, do this to a slight extent.) Try the engagement of the freewheel by pushing on the pedals. If it won't drive the rear wheel, a pawl or pawl spring may be stuck or broken. Sometimes this can be cleared by pouring in kerosene and spinning the unit. (If this works you are lucky.) If not, the freewheel must either be replaced or dismantled and cleaned and its worn parts replaced. Parts are hard to obtain in some cases. I have seen freewheels dismantled successfully at the roadside far from home. However, the procedure is delicate and not recommended for the novice. Remember that the outer ball retaining race usually has a left-hand thread.

CHAIN ADJUSTMENT

If you have a single, two or three-speed rear hub (or a five-speed Sturmey-Archer hub), your chain must be neither loose nor tight. Rotate the chainwheel several times until you find the tightest spot—indicated by least motion when you grasp the chain at the middle of its span and move it up and down. There should be about ¼ inch of up and down play at the tight spot. If the play is less or greater, the rear wheel should be moved forward or back. A great difference between the tight and loose spots means that the sprockets are out of round or the chain unevenly stretched. Push and pull the chain from side to side; push it together and pull it apart at the loose spot. Excessive play in the chain can be felt.

The chain fit on a derailleur bicycle can be tried by placing the chain on the large front sprocket and working the rear gearshift lever slowly while turning the crank, until the chain climbs on top of the teeth of the largest rear cog. Stop before it seats itself in the teeth. At this point, the rear derailleur jockey arm should be near the limit of its forward travel—with almost no more take-up available—but not tight. Unless the rear and front sprocket range is small in number, the chain should be shortened if there is considerable extra travel available. Two links at a time must be removed; make certain that the chain is loose enough to permit this.

DERAILLEUR OR HUB GEAR ADJUSTMENT

Side-to-side wobble of the front sprocket noted in the drive test should be investigated and corrected. It may be caused by loose bolts, by a bent crank, or by bent chainwheels. Improper spacers between chainwheels is another cause. Corrections are made with the judicious use of a hammer and a block of wood. Rear freewheels often have wobble and hop when rotated. Unless it is really bad it can often be tolerated—except for racing, which requires precision high-speed shifts. Bent sprocket teeth, however, must be straightened and worn or hooked cogs replaced, both on derailleur freewheels and on single-sprocket hub gears.

Automatic two-speed hubs (Bendix) have no external adjustment. Three-speed hub gears should be adjusted with the gearshift lever at the #2 or "normal" position. Adjust the screw barrel on the operating cable so that the indicator lever reads "N" on the Shimano hub, or so that the indicator spindle is flush with the axle end (seen through the hole in the right axle nut) on Sturmey-Archer hubs. Once this adjustment has been corrected, place the shift lever in each step successively, back up the pedals, and then apply forward pressure. The gears should engage solidly with no slippage in any gear. If they don't, and the addition of light oil to the hub does not correct the condition, dismantling is required for repair.

Check the derailleur operation, after you have first corrected hub and crank axle bearing maladjustment, sprocket wave, worn teeth, and wheels out of line. Frame alignment may be needed (this will be discussed later). You should also have corrected chain tension or wear.

Hang the bicycle with the sprockets at shoulder height so that the action of the derailleurs can be inspected while in operation at close range. Turn the cranks slowly, working the gearshift levers one at a time. First operate the front lever. Inspect its cable in the untensioned lever position. Are there any broken strands? Is the cable excessively loose? If so it should be adjusted to a length just short of snug. Then while turning, shift it to high and release the lever. Does the lever stay in position? If not, it must be tightened.

Was the shift accomplished readily without hesitation? Did the chain overshift to the outside? Check the position of the cage relative to the sprocket. Its outer lower edge should be from $\frac{1}{16}$ inch minimum to $\frac{1}{4}$ inch maximum above the tips of the teeth (see Fig. 7-135). The cage sides must be parallel to the sprockets. The outward travel must be limited to avoid chain overshift. The inner nose of the shifting cage can be bent slightly toward the outside to assist in the shifting.

Now shift to the smaller sprocket position. The chain should fall smoothly to the small inside sprocket without lodging in between the sprockets (this indicates either bent sprockets or improper sprocket spacing washers, which must be corrected).

If the gears will not shift in either direction, the motion-limiting adjustment screws (see Fig. 7.92—parts 520) can be adjusted to increase motion in the desired direction. If the gears overshift, screw in the adjusting screw to limit the cage motion. On some derailleurs, the actual cage position can be changed on its actuating shaft by loosening a set screw and sliding the cage in and out. The Simplex LJ 323 is one such type.

Now try the rear derailleur. Press the rear shift lever to high-gear position (chain on the outside sprocket). Again check the cable tension and adjust it if needed. Pull the lever to low gear (inside sprocket position) while slowly turning the pedals. The chain should progress smoothly onto the large rear cog without overshifting. As with the front derailleur, adjusting screws increase or limit the travel as needed. However, before these are used, sight the derailleur from behind to see if the jockey arms are parallel with the sprockets. The derailleur may have been bent by impact. If so it can be straightened parallel with care. The fork ends might be bent (we checked this previously), or the derailleur attachment hanger may be bent. Be careful *not* to pull on the cage. You may bend it completely out of adjustment.

With large range rear freewheels, the upper jockey cage must be mounted low enough to permit the chain to climb onto the rear large sprocket without the jockey pulley rubbing on the cage. Try this with the front gear changer in both the high and low positions. With some changers, the rear cage will interfere when the front changer is in the low-gear position.

On both front and rear changers, the cable should be checked for freedom of travel in its sheathing and for broken strands or raveled ends.

Mudguards and Carriers

Check these for splits and cracks. They should be complete. Mounting bolts and stays and their mountings should be well tightened and unbent. Carriers should be securely attached at the stays to prevent the clamps from slipping with vibration.

Keeping Out Dirt and Moisture

The Bicycle Inspection Checklist is useful as a guide when making regular condition inspections of your bicycle, and it can also be used to inspect your purchase if you buy a new or a used bicycle. The internal examination of components for wear is a separate subject which requires dismantling the assemblies to determine their actual condition and the state of cleanliness or lubrication. This should be done on a regular basis whose interval depends on how far and how hard you ride, exposure to rain, grit, water, and bad road surfaces. Care in sealing bearings, seat pillars, and other points of entry of foreign material pays big dividends.

Wheel bearings with sealed ball bearings are now being made by several manufacturers, Phil Wood of California being an example. Wood also makes a sealed crank hanger bearing unit. Campagnolo makes a plastic sleeve that fits inside of the crank hanger between the bearing cups and keeps any rain and dirt which enters the seat tube from falling into the bearing races. Complete bottom bracket units that include a slip-in shell are made by Tange and SR in Japan. These units come completely assembled, lubricated, and adjusted, so that dirt does not enter through assembly and handling. Factory labor cost is decreased; however, due to the extra shell, weight is a bit higher.

A very simple, if not an elegant, method will seal the point of dirt and water entry that exists where the crank axle enters the bottom bracket cup and where the wheel cones enter the wheel hub. After applying a grease film to the exterior of the adjusted and lubricated axle or cone, wrap three or four turns of cotton twill tape around these points, tie them tightly with a square knot, and trim the ends. The friction this causes is minimal, but the dirt and moisture protection it provides is very helpful. With this extra protection, these parts can do without servicing for a year and more. On one occasion, I had to ride in water hub deep. Upon dismantling the bearings several weeks later, I found them to be in good condition. Only the chain, the freewheel, and the pedals required work. A sealed freewheel such as that made by Maeda and Maillard might have eliminated that problem, while pedals with improved sealing, such as Zeus, Kyukoto, or Campagnolo, would have minimized the pedal problem.

Chain and seat stays and fork blades usually have small holes in their sides to relieve internal pressure when brazing the frame and to release cleaning acids and speed neutralization when chrome-plating the fork ends. Very often, frame tubes and stays are pierced to allow items to be mounted on the tubes. Some custom builders run brake cables or lighting set wiring through the frame tubes. The point where the seat pillar enters the seat tube and the slot in the seat tube where it is split to permit clamping can both admit water and road grit.

None of these points are usually sealed. In rain, particularly if running without mudguards, grit and water is led through all of these points into the crank bearings. Front and rear fork ends on some bicycles are spot welded to the stays, and any small joint that is not waterproof permits leaks. I have seen frames of several well-known makes whose brazing was incomplete. In one case, upon dismantling the crank hanger, outside light could be seen when examining the joints from the inside.

Keeping the bearings clean and dry should take first order in the cyclist's preventive maintenance program. Under the tremendous pressures that exist between a hard steel ball and the cup or cone on which it rolls, tiny specks of grit act like rocks on a roadway. They are ground into the bearing surface, cause increased friction, and greatly reduce the life of both lubricant and bearing. Search out points of entry, and apply silicone rubber adhesives, which have excellent adhesion, long life, and flexibility, to each point.

When you dismantle parts for cleaning, thoroughly clean the interiors of hubs and bracket shells. Remove the seat pin and brush down the seat tube to clean out grit and rust. Tilt and tap the frame so that any foreign material in the chain stays and tubes can fall into the crank hanger. Then thoroughly clean this, including the threads. Scrupulously clean all the parts; don't wash them in dirty kerosene or wipe them with dirty rags. Examine under a bright light, and preferably with a magnifying glass, all surfaces on which the balls roll. Imminent failure is indicated by grooving or tiny pits or flaking of the surface. Once this starts, pieces of hardened steel continue to flake out and act as rocks in the bearing path (this is fatigue failure). The life of the part is at an end; replace it. Uneven paths where the balls roll indicate misalignment, bent axles, or misaligned fork ends. Determine which it is.

When dismantling any ball bearing assembly—whether it be head set, pedals, bottom bracket (crank hanger), wheel hubs, derailleur jockey pulleys, or freewheels—proceed with caution. Some assemblies contain the bearing balls in pressed steel retainers. Foreign makes often use loose balls which will fall out and bounce away into unknown hiding places. After you have loosened the assembly slightly, peer inside to see if the balls are loose or held in cages. If they are loose, prepare your defense. Count them before you

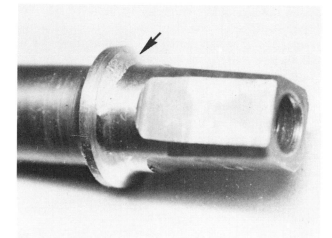

Fig. 6.11   Fatigued bottom bracket axle ball track.

Fig. 6.12   Fatigue failure of wheel bearing cone.

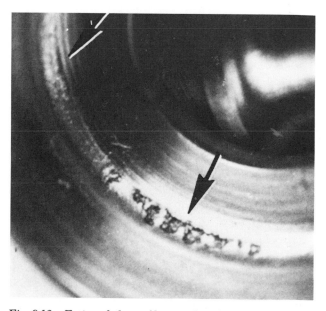

Fig. 6.13   Fatigue failure of bottom bracket cup ball track.

loosen the assembly enough for them to fall out. Put paper or rags on the floor about you to stop the bounce if you do slip up. Have something available to put them in. Use a strong magnet to attract them if you have one. Usually the number of balls is the same on each side, but I have seen new units with unequal quantities placed in them at the factory. After disassembly you should place half the balls in the bearing cup and seat the cone into them. Between the first and last ball, there should be a slight gap not big enough for one additional ball. You can thus determine if one is missing.

Never mix ball sizes. Balls come in $\frac{1}{32}$-inch increments, so compare them closely.

Roll the hub and crank hanger axles on a flat surface—a smooth table top or a piece of glass will suffice. You will be easily able to detect bending from the way it rolls.

Keep your grease scrupulously clean. Clean your hands before using it and keep the lid on when it is not in use. Ball bearing factories use double-filtered grease dispensed from sealed containers in air-conditioned rooms with filtered air.

CUP AND CONE BEARING ADJUSTMENT

The steering head, crank hanger, front and rear wheel bearings, and adjustable pedal bearings of bicycles are generally made in "cup and cone" construction with steel balls separating the parts. Bicycles are not generally constructed with the extreme precision and rigidity required for rigid high-precision bearings. Furthermore, the heavily loaded structure built of lightweight tubing can distort during frame assembly. Under road loads these parts can deflect. Bumps and handling can mar the extra precision built in by machining after frame assembly.

The cup and cone bearing will withstand a limited amount of misalignment and will accept both vertical and side loads from either direction. A large curvature radius of cone or cup reduces load carrying capacity and life, but accommodates inaccuracies along the extended ball path. One of the members, either cone or cup, is generally attached by screw threads. Turning this part will advance it on the threads until all the clearance between cup, cone, and balls is taken up.

Screwing the cone in too tightly will cause a high rolling friction and reduce the self-aligning capacity. Both of these combined will reduce bearing life. For this reason, bearings are adjusted to be just perceptibly loose. If this exact fit cannot be easily attained—if there is a feeling of roughness and dismantling shows a worn-out bearing—note the location of the worn-out point. You may be able to complete a trip by determining the direction of the forces on the bearing and then rotating the wheel axle, hanger cup, or steering member to a less worn position. On one occasion, this enabled the use of a tandem front wheel to complete a weeklong tour in an area where no parts were available.

A locking nut prevents the bearing from turning on the shaft after it has been adjusted. The nut is tightened against the bearing cone, or cup, and friction prevents the bearing parts from further movement. Many mechanics wonder why a perfectly set adjustment will become too tight if the locknuts are secured—even though the cup or cone has not turned on its thread—or remain loose when the locknut is tightened if made intentionally loose.

Figure 6.14 explains this. Some play exists, either between the axle and cone or between the frame thread and cup thread, to permit ease of assembly. Since the threads are triangular in shape, any clearance between the threads will permit motion both up and down and in and out. Thus, when first tightening to get the initial fit, the cup or cone will be pressed outward the amount of the clearance in the threads. When the locknut is tightened, however, it presses the parts inward by the amount of clearance in the threads and makes the bearing fit tighter.

Now if the threads were perfectly uniform and the axles perfectly straight, and if threads and bearing surfaces were concentric, it would be easy to determine just how much extra looseness to initially provide. But parts vary, so the fit is a matter of feel and readjustment.

The amount of extra bearing load that can be applied rather staggers the imagination. The front wheel running load on smooth streets, which may be from about 60 to 100 pounds, is split between the bearings. Hanger and rear wheel bearing loads on a steep hill climb may reach 600 pounds or more and ⅓ of this or less on the level. If our axle has 24 threads per inch and we tighten the cone with a 4-pound force on a 4-inch wrench an extra ¼ turn, the cone would turn in less than $\frac{10}{1000}$ of an inch. Even if half the force on the wrench were needed to overcome the friction of the cone threads on the axle, an end load of almost 1,200 pounds would result. But since the bearing surfaces are at an angle, this effect is multiplied. An actual load between the balls and the bearing surfaces of well over 2,000 pounds can result! This continuous, high preloading will result in extra friction and much-reduced bearing life. Doubling the load on the bearing reduces its life span to ⅛ its normal value! So, a little extra time spent in adjusting cones and bearings returns handsome dividends.

LUBRICATION

There is a lot of nonsense espoused about lubricants for bicycles. Bicycle bearings operate at slow speeds—the wheels turn 375 rpm at 30 mph, the cranks and pedals perhaps from 60 to 120 rpm. The normal electric motor runs all day at 1,760 rpm; jet engines operate at 10,000 or better. Heavier viscosities promote longer bearing life at low speeds.

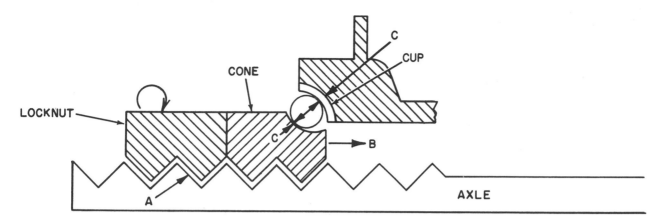

Fig. 6.14 Tightening the locknut against the threads at A pushes the cone in direction B, and this cramps the rolling parts at C.

Fig. 6.15 Replacement cones must match. Note differences in radius, angle, and dimension of ball track.

Fig. 6.16 Uneven ball track on wheel bearing cone due to bent axle or fork end.

Fig. 6.17 This mismatched cone wore out after only a few miles of service.

At normal temperatures, the friction variation between light and medium weight oils or greases is microscopic under bearing loads. The ability of the lubricant to stay put, to seal dirt and moisture out of the bearing is paramount. If you are going to try to break the world's hour record, clean your bearings and use light spindle oil (SAE 5). The difference will be undetectable under load; you would need high-precision apparatus to detect it. Don't be fooled by the difference when spinning the wheel at no load!

In normal service, sealing ability and water resist-

ance are far more important. Bearing life and service life may be more important to you. As the weather gets very cold, from 30° down to zero, the use of a lighter grease or oil will be beneficial, since the oil in the grease thickens considerably when cold. If you race in winter, this is worth consideration.

Normally, a good #2 lithium-base grease is satisfactory for cycle bearings. It is water resistant and smooth. Micron-sized moly-disulfide grease with a lithium base is OK. For cold temperatures, some fluorosilicone greases are made by Dow-Corning and

General Electric Co., Silicone Products Division, Waterford, New York. Humble Oil Co. Beacon P-290 or 325 low-temperature aircraft greases are good for cold, but bleed at normal temperatures. I've had the same with the silicones. They are expensive, a pound would do the whole club for a year. Finden Formula cycle oil is a nonfluid oil that stays put and has moderate friction, but little sealing ability.

Three-speed hubs should be regularly lubricated with light mineral oil. Household or sewing machine oil is OK. Don't use heavy oil, or a vegetable-base oil like 3-in-1. These will gum up the small internal moving parts. Sturmey-Archer recommends SAE 20 oil for their hubs.

An excellent long-service grease with a synthetic base, water compatibility, and extra inhibitors for long life is marketed by Phil Wood, Inc., of Los Gatos, California.

General Electric G-322 L Silicone grease is excellent for aluminum-alloy sprockets. It is a lightweight, water-resistant material that doesn't seem to pick up as much dirt as some other materials and doesn't gum up badly. The Schwinn silicone spray and other equivalent makes are useful on pedal threads, seat clamp and handlebar stem bolts, and brake lever parts before assembly. I use the G-322 L on the pedal threads of alloy cranks to facilitate removal at the airport.

The molylube or lithium-based greases are useful to grease brake and derailleur control cables.

Penetrating greaseless lubricants such as WD-40 and Belray 6-in-1 Molylube are useful to lubricate brake and derailleur linkages.

Lubrication frequency depends on the weather and on how well your bearings are sealed. Unprotected parts, including jockey pulleys, should be lubricated after every rain. Unsealed hubs and bottom bracket must be lubricated at from three to six months, but if sealed, they are good for a year or two.

POWER TRANSMISSION EFFECTIVENESS

The Chain Drive

Russian research indicates that a forwardly inclined, oval foot-travel pattern improves muscular efficiency (see Figs. 11.11–11.14). Pivoted levers and linkages which produce an up-and-down foot action similar to stair climbing have also been tried. When combined with a variable pivot point, as suggested by Professor Wilson of M.I.T., these allow an infinitely variable gearing system. Harris Dynamics has recently built a bicycle of this design (see Fig. 11.15).

Enclosed bevel gears and a shaft drive through the chain stay were used by Columbia at the turn of the century. But experiments on drive efficiency reported in the *Sibley Journal*, an engineering journal of that period, indicate that the transmission of power from the pedals to the driving wheel is accomplished most efficiently by a chain-and-sprocket drive. To this day,

the chain drive when properly maintained is hard to beat for lightness, flexibility, and efficiency.

While the simple and rugged block chain and the one-inch pitch roller chain are still in use for some track and sprint racing, the 1 × ³⁄₁₆-inch roller chain has disappeared from general bicycle use. The ½-inch (12.7-mm) pitch chain has become almost universal throughout the world. Sprocket tooth width has been standardized at ⅛ inch (3.17 mm) for single-speed, two, three, four, and five-speed internally geared or coaster brake hubs. Some older derailleurs with the ⅛-inch pitch chain are still in use.

Current model 4, 5, 6, 10, 12, 15, and 18-speed derailleurs are standardized for the use of ½ × ³⁄₃₂-inch (2.38-mm) width chains. Many front and rear derailleur gear shifting mechanisms in use today, however, will accommodate both chain widths.

Thus in an emergency it may be practical to substitute a ⅛-inch width chain. (Do not use the extra width connecting link provided.) Derailleur chain is joined by pressing in a pin to assure a constant width that will not foul or catch the shifting cages.

How a Chain Is Built

A roller chain is constructed of a series of very accurately sized and fitted parts. Two adjacent links, an inner and an outer, constitute a set. Depending on the center distance between the sprockets, the sprocket sizes used, and the type of shifting mechanism installed, a complete drive chain will normally contain between 100 and 118 links.

The inner link has two side plates which are spaced to fit the sprocket tooth width and joined at each end with a press-fitted hollow bushing. Before assembly, a hollow steel roller is slipped over the bushing.

An outer link joins two inner links. It also has a pair of side plates. Two accurately sized, hardened steel pins are pressed into the accurately sized holes at each end of an outer link plate. These pins are thousandths of an inch smaller in diameter than the inner link bushing into which they fit. When the inner links are slipped over each pin, the second side plate may be assembled. Thus we have the start of a chain (see Fig. 6.18). A chain of 114 links will thus consist of 570 separate parts.

Friction and Wear

In a chain of 114 links, there are 342 points (excluding the side plates) that wear when in service. Turn the pedals of your bicycle and carefully examine the chain as it engages the sprockets. The teeth of the driving sprocket exert a very considerable force on the chain as pressure is applied to the pedals. The inner link roller rides on the flank of the sprocket tooth as it engages and may rotate slightly against the outside of the inner link bushing.

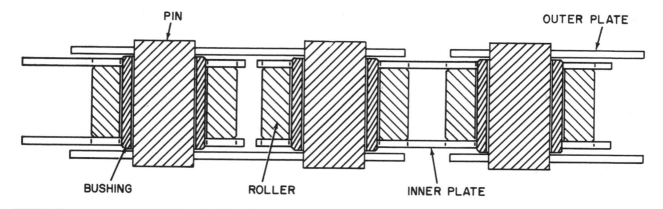

PIN

OUTER PLATE

BUSHING   ROLLER   INNER PLATE

Fig. 6.18   Parts of a roller chain.

Fig. 6.19   A tight-fitted link causes chain jumping and problems with gear shifting.

The two adjacent links at the beginning and end of the chain's path around the sprocket rotate in respect to each other under the full applied force. When the inner link is pulled against the topmost rear sprocket tooth, the next outer link is free to rotate and drop downward to conform to the shape of the sprocket, but when the next outer link transmits power, the full chain tension presses the bushing against the outer link pin. Thus, the succeeding inner link is not free to rotate and must be forced down. The friction between the pin and bushing resists this force and causes wear on the pin and bushing. A similar condition occurs at the front sprocket.

Note also that if the front and rear sprockets are not perfectly in line with each other or are not parallel, the bushing and pin will not pull squarely against each other. When pulling at an angle, there will be a concentration of pressure at the end of the pin and bushing. Even if these points are lubricated, the lubricant will be squeezed away to more lightly loaded areas. Thus more friction and greater wear will occur than if sprockets were in a line. Also, the side of the inner link plate will rub on the side of the sprocket tooth.

Lubrication

Oil placed on the outside of the outer link plates performs no useful function. It attracts dirt and grit and soils hands and clothing. Lubricant on the inside of the inner link plates reduces wear and friction

against the side of the sprocket teeth if the chain is misaligned. However, it also attracts road grit, and the consequent grinding increases wear.

Lubricant between the mating ends of inner and outer links can reduce friction if wear and sprocket misalignment permit these to touch under load. Lubricant between roller and bushing may help as the chain engages the sprocket tooth. This is particularly true if the sprocket teeth are not accurately formed. However, caked dirt and road grit can hinder engagement.

The points where lubrication is most necessary are the heavily loaded surfaces of the outer link pin and the inner link bushings. Yet lubricant must enter these via the constricted space between the inner and outer plates at the ends of pins and bushings. Loads are heavy, speeds are slow, so a high-film-strength lubricant is needed. Low viscosity penetrating oils may reach the pins, but these have a short life; a fortified oil is needed. Successful pin and bushing surface treatments have been devised and utilized on motorcycle chains but not (at this time) on bicycles.

A chain thoroughly cleaned with solvent or kerosene can be placed in a bath of hot oil and allowed to cool. The oil will penetrate into every crevice, but it should be cleaned, link by link, from surfaces where it is not needed. A hypodermic oiler permits the application of oil to a chain in service and applies oil only to each side of each inner link end, where it can reach the bushing. Both methods are tedious, but either will pay off in a minimum accumulation of dirt and grit. The oil bath gear case used on some utility bicycles is heavy and impractical for derailleur bicycles, but it gives the longest life and greatest drive efficiency.

Chain Drive Efficiency Factors

Flooded oil bath lubrication reduces chain drive friction to from ½ to 1%, that is, from 99 to 99.5% of the power supplied will reach the driving wheel.

When the number of sprocket teeth is increased, the chain load and the angle of link motion under load decreases in proportion. Wear and frame distortion under load will also decrease even though drive efficiency may not improve.

A driven sprocket tooth perpendicular to the drive chain is at its greatest diameter. In between successive teeth, the chain pulls at a slightly smaller radius; thus, the speed of the driven sprocket will vary (this is called "chordal action"). For a sprocket of 20 teeth; the variation in speed is 1.2%; for 16 teeth, it is 1.9%. If the number of teeth is decreased to 13 or to 7, the speed variations will be respectively 3% and 11%. Thus a noticeably rough drive can ensue. Further, reducing the number of driven sprocket teeth increases the angle of link movement and the tendency of alternate links not to drop into place. Therefore, teeth may jump on the rear sprocket when under load.

Tooth-form accuracy improves efficiency. Manufacturing shortcuts on less expensive sprockets often result in lower drive efficiency, eccentricity, wobble, and shorter life.

Chain Life and Wear*

As the chain pins and bushings wear, each link of the chain becomes a bit longer. It must then ride a bit farther out on the sprocket teeth. Likewise, if a new chain is used on worn sprockets, it may not properly mesh until some chain wear occurs. As chain wear progresses, the mismatch will accumulate until the chain jumps teeth under load. This will occur when the percentage of stretch equals 200 over the number of teeth.

For a 50-tooth sprocket, this equals 4% wear. Since the depth of case hardening may be only 3%, such an amount of wear is beyond tolerable limits. Indeed, for good drive efficiency, chain company engineers recommend a wear limit of 1%. Thus 24 links of ½-inch pitch chain under load should not measure over 12⅛ inches, for best efficiency, nor over 12⅜ inches before being replaced. The lower limit is advised for derail-

leur chains. A chain which is too flexible as a result of wear may result in chain whip, derailment, or poor shifting action.

Wear rates with a bicycle chain load of from 60 to 300 pounds, operating at a rear sprocket speed of from 150 to 300 rpm, and with sprocket size ranges of from

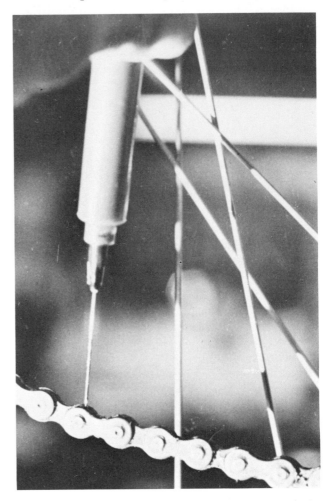

Fig. 6.20   A disposable hypodermic places oil only at the spot where it is needed.

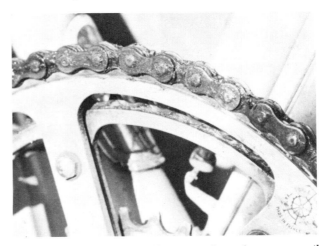

Fig. 6.21   Accumulation of grime and grit from excess oil on the chain.

*Research on chain life by engineers Stephanoff and Aufderheide of the Link-Belt Co. originally published in *Product Engineering*, February 1970, p. 102, is used with their permission in this section.

1:1 to 4:1, are as follows: if only the initial lubricant supplied with the chain is provided, the 3% wear limit may be reached in 1500 miles of use; if oiled and cleaned after each eight hours of use (100–150 miles), the chain life can be extended to ten times that amount; and oilbath lubrication increases the unlubricated chain life from twenty to forty times. Poor lubrication and rusty surfaces increase chain friction from as much as ten to twenty times. Thus 10% or more of the rider's effort can be lost in transmission. Clearly, regular, careful chain cleaning and lubrication pay handsome dividends in chain life and ease of riding.

A plastic-sealed chain which retains initial lubrication has been developed by Sedis of France.

TOOLS FOR BICYCLE REPAIR

A large supply of tools is not required for minor bicycle repairs. Those needed depend on the type of bicycle you buy. For all bikes, some tools commonly found in the home workshop are necessary: a 6-inch adjustable (commonly known as a Crescent) wrench (with thin jaws if you can find it); a ¼-inch tip screwdriver and a ⅛-inch tip screwdriver; a small ball peen hammer; a pair of slip joint pliers (a vise grip pliers is also very useful); wire clippers; a 6-inch half round file; and a punch. Many foreign-made bicycles use metric-sized components, but it doesn't matter with a good adjustable wrench if the nuts are metric, English, or American.

Certain special tools can only be obtained through better bicycle stores. Whatever your bike, you will need a spoke nipple wrench (be sure it fits your nipple sizes). A Mafac #48 or 49 tool kit (see Fig. 6.23) and a flat, punched-steel, all-purpose bicycle wrench are both useful. Ten-speed bikes also require a chain rivet removal tool (small size preferable); a freewheel remover (there are many types—get one that fits *your*

freewheel); a cotterless crank removal tool set (if your bike has cotterless cranks); a Campagnolo T wrench—combination Allen and 8-mm socket wrench. Whatever you do get, spending a few dimes more for good quality will pay in ease of working, knuckles that aren't skinned, and fewer rounded-off nuts.

There are numerous other special bike tools that come in handy for simplifying work on brakes and removing crank wedge pins: cone and pedal wrenches; wheel truing stands; wheel centering gauges; cable clippers; a pin wrench, or 22–28-mm cup open end wrenches; "third hand" and "fourth hand" brake tools, if you want to delve deeper.

A portable tool set that has proved ample in tens of thousands of miles bicycle touring is shown in Figure 6.27. It consists of a 6-inch, thin Crescent wrench, a Mafac 49 tool kit, a chain tool, a small pliers, a ⅛-inch screwdriver, a cotterless crank socket wrench, plus a spare chain link and a spare rear brake and a spare derailleur cable. Every one of these tools has been used, including the freewheel remover, often in remote locations far from shops. There have been almost no occasions where this tool set has been inadequate.

If any amount of night riding is anticipated, a spare set of bulbs is also necessary. The Mafac kit has no rubber solution for tire patching; rubber solution is recommended. A small piece of gummed tire fabric or a dressed down section of an old lightweight tire to act as a "boot" in case of a tire blowout or stone bruise completes the kit. Naturally, a good, well-made tire pump is needed if you are going to ride far from the home base. Tires have a habit of failing as far away as possible from an open filling station. If your tires use Presta valves, be sure to carry an adapter for Schrader connections.

Check your derailleurs for adjustment screws. Your ⅛-inch screwdriver will work on most, even if they have Phillips heads.

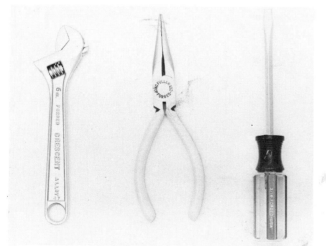

Fig. 6.22   A 6-inch Crescent adjustable wrench, pliers, and screwdriver.

(Courtesy of R. Timmerman)

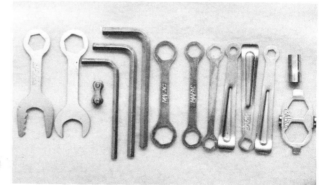

Fig. 6.23   Contents of Mafac kit (less tire patches): wheel-bearing cone wrench, pedal wrench, spare chain link, metric allen wrenches (for stem, derailleur, and seat bolt), three metric box wrenches, three tire irons (with smaller metric box wrench openings), socket wrench (for brake lever nut), spoke wrench, a screwdriver, and a seat bolt tool.

Fig. 6.24   Nine types of rear freewheel removers.

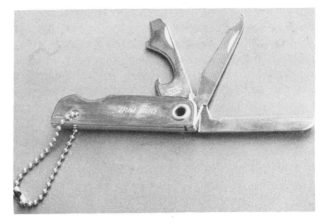

Fig. 6.25   Barbett   Trim-Trio   knife-screwdriver-bottle-opener-file also has hooked point to dig out derailleur or brake cable end fittings.

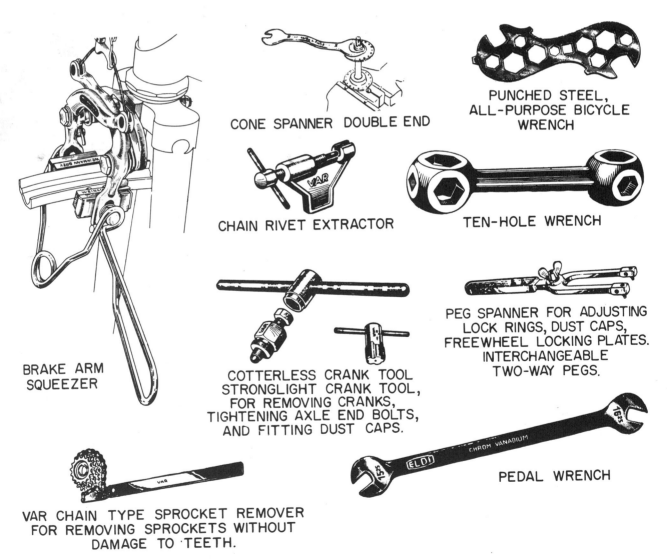

BRAKE ARM
SQUEEZER

CONE SPANNER DOUBLE END

CHAIN RIVET EXTRACTOR

COTTERLESS CRANK TOOL
STRONGLIGHT CRANK TOOL,
FOR REMOVING CRANKS,
TIGHTENING AXLE END BOLTS,
AND FITTING DUST CAPS.

PUNCHED STEEL,
ALL-PURPOSE BICYCLE
WRENCH

TEN-HOLE WRENCH

PEG SPANNER FOR ADJUSTING
LOCK RINGS, DUST CAPS,
FREEWHEEL LOCKING PLATES.
INTERCHANGEABLE
TWO-WAY PEGS.

PEDAL WRENCH

VAR CHAIN TYPE SPROCKET REMOVER
FOR REMOVING SPROCKETS WITHOUT
DAMAGE TO TEETH.

Fig. 6.26   Additional handy workshop tools.

Before a long trip, diligently check all the parts of your bicycle. Dismantle it for internal examination and lubrication. Then ride for from fifty to one hundred miles after reassembly to shake down all adjustments and work out cable stretch. *Never* take a new bicycle on a long trip before a shakedown period unless you are certain of your mechanical inspection and adjustment prowess.

Study the detailed parts breakdowns to see the relationships between the various parts. However, dismantling a three-speed hub involves a lot of tiny parts and takes some mechanical knowledge to reassemble. If you plan to do this, get a service manual that explains the details and the pitfalls which can confront the inexperienced mechanic.

The same is true, but to a lesser extent, of dismantling rear derailleurs, coaster brakes, and two-speed automatic brakes and shifting mechanisms.

FRAME ALIGNMENT

One of the main virtues of a finely constructed bicycle is its excellent alignment. Competition cyclists demand alignment as precise as that on finely tuned racing cars, precision machinery, or aircraft for perfect steering with a minimum of friction and wear. The alignment of the wheels both vertically and horizontally must be correct. Alignment of the drive members reduces friction, loss of chains on bumps, and wear on the sprockets.

Misalignment in the wheels, the frame, the rims and tires may stem from many factors. You may be able to detect misalignment by sighting from a distance behind the bicycle and noting the angularity of the chain or the parallelism of the wheels. But it is best to utilize a systematic procedure (see Fig. 6.28).

Start with the wheels. Check for a bent axle with the wheel removed. If it is bent, replace it. Check the cone adjustment, and readjust it if needed.

Check the rims for truth, side wobble, and hop. Avoid twisting the spokes when truing. Align the nipples if they are improperly angled from the rim.

Check the wheel for proper centering and dish (see Chapter 9, Wheel Building, and Fig. 6.32).

Make a fork end test gauge out of a straight axle. Clamp it in the fork ends and sight on it horizontally and vertically. If the ends do not meet or are improperly spaced, the fork ends need realignment or straightening.

Run a taut string from the left rear fork end around the bottom of the steering head and back to the right rear fork end (Fig. 6.31). Measure to each side of the seat tube. Both measurements should be equal if the steering head is not twisted and the chain stays are not off center line. Run the taut line to the top of the head as a check.

With the wheels properly inserted and centered, a

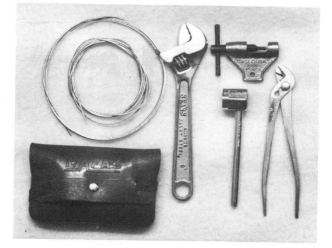

Fig. 6.27   On the road tool kit: Mafac #49 tool and tire patch kit, rear brake cable, rear derailleur cable, 6-inch adjustable wrench, chain tool, cotterless crank bolt wrench, and arc-joint pliers.

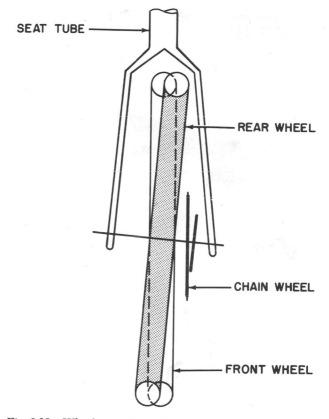

Fig. 6.28   Wheels out of parallel vertically.

straightedge extended along the rear wheel to the front wheel should touch at all four points. (Fig. 6.32). If it doesn't, measure the amount the fourth point is out (Fig. 6.33). If the offset is greater than one cm, determine where the trouble lies—frame twist, chain stays or fork blades not centralized, and correct it.

Measure the chain line both front and rear and their relationship as shown in Figures 6.34 and 6.35. This

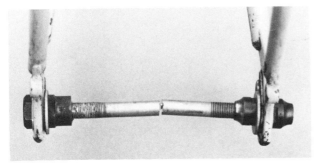

Fig. 6.29   Split axle shows fork ends out of parallel toward the front (top view).

will determine if your drive is true and will aid in analyzing faults found above.

REFINISHING YOUR BICYCLE

The finish on a well-made production bicycle requires great care in processing. The steel is thoroughly cleaned of rust and then dipped or sprayed with a phosphate solution to passivate the surface and render it rust-resistant (Bonderizing is one trade name for this procedure). The frame is then electrostatically sprayed with a paint selected for durability and baked at a high temperature

Fig. 6.30   Split axle shows fork ends out of parallel vertically, fork end too widely spaced (rear view).

Fig. 6.31   Run a taut line from the rear hubs around the bottom and then up around the top of the steering head. Measure distances to the seat tube on both sides for equality.
(Courtesy of R. Timmerman)

Fig. 6.32   Run a straightedge along the front and rear wheels on both sides. Two points on the rear and one on the front must touch.

for hardness and adhesion. Dip coating is also used. The result is a finish that will not peel or flake, and which will resist the spread of rust if scratched. Epoxy finishes provide a very hard, chip-resistant finish and are coming to the fore for even better protection.

Poorly prepared finishes provided on some lower-priced imports bypass some of these important steps. They can and do chip and rust after short periods of service. A "peel" test, using a strip of Scotch or masking tape pressed onto the finish and then pulled off will test adhesion.

If your finish has become shabby, an auto repair and paint shop can redo it. Get the end of a batch of paint after a car is finished—you may save money.

Ordinary aerosol sprays that are not baked on do not give the best results. Dr. William Pritiken of Illinois uses a procedure he finds excellent, using two-part epoxy paints of great hardness and strength. The Sherwin-Williams paint stores and Sears Roebuck both market durable epoxy paints. The Sherwin-Williams paint is called Tile-Clad. Colors-for-Cars, Compton, California, produces highly colorful two-part epoxy finishes. Du Pont Imron two-part mix is also noted for its durability.

All of the old paint must be removed by paint remover, brushing, and scraping, until the frame is perfectly free of the former finish. Wash off the paint remover with water, then clean the frame with xylene.

Naval jelly or phosphoric acid metal cleaners are then used to clean the frame, followed again with a water wash and xylene wipe to dry and remove fingerprints.

Sherwin-Williams recommends a primer for best results, but some other makers feel it unnecessary. Enough two-part mix is made for one coat. From two to three coats are brushed on 24 hours apart. An auto cleaner wax is then used to get a shiny finish.

Fig. 6.33 Measure the offset distance at the front wheel to determine the error in wheel tracking.

Fig. 6.35 A straightedge run from the front sprocket to the rear, accounting for tooth offset from sprocket face, indicates alignment of front and rear sprockets and equality of chain line.

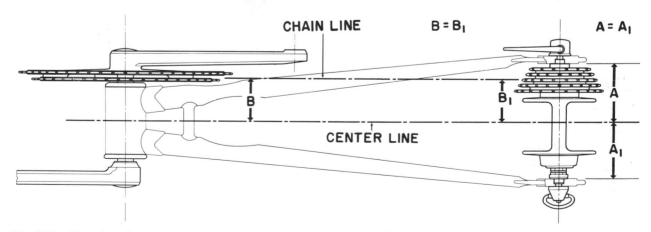

Fig. 6.34 Chain line distances B and B_1 at the center of the front and rear sprockets should be equal.

(Courtesy of Shimano American Corporation)

CHAPTER VII

The Parts of Your Bicycle

NAMES OF PARTS

INTO the well-constructed frame of your purchase are fitted or attached literally hundreds of component parts. The exploded view (Fig. 7.1) identifies the manner in which these parts are ordered for replacement.

Some British parts names have entered the field and are now used interchangeably. For instance, Part 5R, the handlebar stem, is sometimes called an "extension" or a "gooseneck." Part 8R, the crank hanger set, is sometimes referred to as a bottom bracket assembly. Part 9AR, which fits onto it, may be a "Chainwheel," instead of a sprocket. Instead of being a "Rear Cog assembly," Part 16AR becomes a "freewheel." We will use these terms interchangeably.

CRANK HANGER ASSEMBLIES

There are three main types of construction: the one-piece, the three-piece "cottered," (an English term for the wedgepin that joins the crank to the axle), and the "cotterless" type, which uses a square-ended axle with the cranks secured by a bolt or nut threaded to the axle at each end.

One-Piece Crank Hangers

In the one-piece assembly, a forged-steel crank is fitted through the crank hanger (made large enough in diameter to permit it; see Fig. 7.2). Stamped steel cups are pressed into the hanger shell. Bearing cones are threaded onto the crank axle. The right cone screws onto a threaded part of the crank with right-hand threads, and serves to hold the front sprocket in position. A driving projection which is a forged part of the right crank transmits power to the sprocket. This can

be seen in Figure 7.4. Ball bearings in steel retainers are inserted over the axle during assembly. The left cone is screwed into position, its locking nut and washer tightened. The left side parts have left-hand threads that turn counterclockwise to tighten.

Variations in quality and precision of manufacture exist. Some makes are flimsier in crank cross section. The bearing cones are truly conical in shape. Other makes use cranks of stouter section. The cones are contoured to correspond to the radius of the bearing balls. This provides a more solid bearing seat that deflects less under load. The bearing can support a greater load due to its closer conformity. Thus both bearing life and the period between adjustments are lengthened. Schwinn derailleur bikes use heat-treated cranks for additional strength. Due to the large bearing required to permit the insertion of the crank, the one-piece crank is durable, easily serviced and adjusted, and inexpensive. When well made, it is easy rolling. The crank length is fixed, and its weight is a bit greater than the types to be discussed later, but its long, successful use merits serious consideration of its advantages.

Cottered Crank Hangers

Figures 7.5 and 7.6 show the three-piece cottered crankset most common on foreign bicycles and used on some American bicycles as well. Machined and hardened steel cups with threaded exteriors screw into threads machined into the crank hanger. A separate axle of the proper length to give the desired sprocket position has radiused bearing surfaces machined on its exterior. The axle ends are turned to about a ⅝-inch diameter, and a flat area machined across each end of the axle receives the "cotters" or wedgepins which

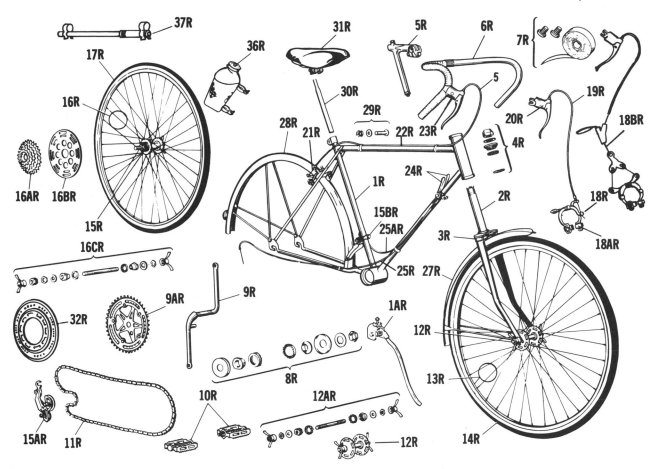

Fig. 7.1 Basic parts—racers. *(Courtesy of Columbia Manufacturing Company)*

1R   Frame
1AR Kickstand
2R   Front fork
3R   Fork cap
4R   Head Steering Set, bearings, cones, etc.
5R   Fork-handlebar stem, racing type
6R   Handlebar, Maes drop type
7R   Handlebar tape with end plugs
8R   Crank hanger set, bearings, cones, etc.
9R   Crank only (one-piece type)
9AR Sprocket, double for 10-speed
10R Pedals, rattrap all metal (left and right, pairs only)
11R Chain for derailleur
12R Front hub, flange type, complete with parts
12AR Front hub set, bearings, cones, axle etc. w/o hub shell
13R Front wheel complete w/o tire
14R Front tire and tube only
15R Rear hub complete with cogs & spoke protector but w/o shifter
15AR 10-speed derailleur shifting mechanism at hub
15BR 10-speed derailleur shifting mechanism front
16R Rear wheel complete with cogs & spoke protector but w/o shifter or cable
16AR Cog assembly only
16BR Spoke protector only
16CR Rear hub set, parts w/o hub shell
17R Rear tire and tube only
18R Front caliper brake arm assembly, side-pull type
18AR Caliper brake shoes. (Pairs same front and rear)
18BR Front caliper brake assembly, center-pull type
19R Front caliper brake cable
20R Front hooded caliper brake lever assembly
21R Rear caliper brake arm assembly
22R Rear caliper brake cable
23R Rear hooded caliper brake hand lever assembly

24R 10-speed control levers (2 in unit with clamp)
25R 10-speed shift cable to rear
25AR 10-speed shift cable to front
27R Front fender and braces
28R Rear fender and braces
29R Seat Post Binder Bolt Set
30R Seat post
31R Saddle, racing suspension type
32R Chain guard, circular
36R Sip bottle, plastic, with clamps
37R Tire pump with clamps

Fig. 7.2 American one-piece crankset disassembled.

Fig. 7.3   American one-piece crankset assembled.

Fig. 7.4   Dual front sprocket with adapter for use with
one-piece crank and cyclo-cross ring.
(Courtesy of R. Timmerman)

Fig. 7.5   Three-piece cottered crank assembly.

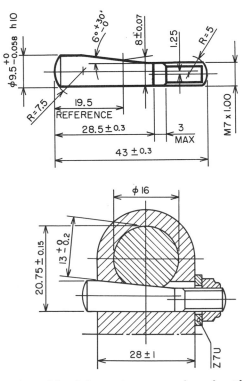

Fig. 7.6   Assembly of three-piece cottered crank with proposed ISO dimensions (mm).

hold the crank in position laterally and transmit the
rider's pedal pressure by bearing on the machined flat
surface of the axle. Due to the leverage from the
greater pedal radius being applied to the axle-driving
flat radius, forces on the cotter can be severe. On a
tandem, it is quite easy to actually shear the cotter pin
in two. Under heavy pedal pressure, the cotter may be
indented and become loose, but careful filing and fitting of the cotter during its mounting reduces the
chance of failure under heavy pulling.

Disassembly of the pressed-in cotter is best done
with a cotter removing tool which has ample leverage.
Hammering the end of the cotter without supporting
the opposite side of the crank can damage both the
cotter and the bottom bracket bearings.

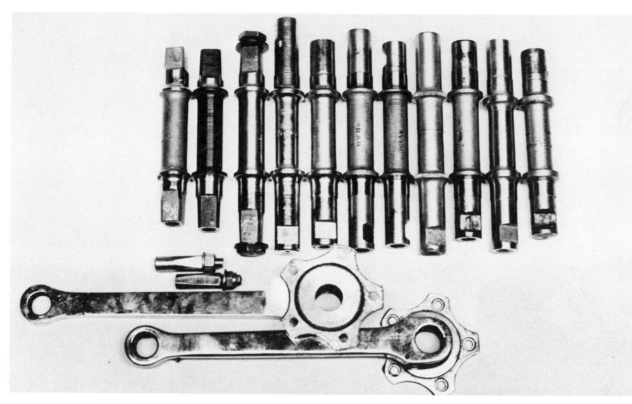

Fig. 7.7   Cotterless (left three) and cottered crank axles with varying bearing spacing and axle lengths to suit crank hanger width and chain line variables. A five-bolt, 50.4-mm cottered crank is shown with English and French cotters.

One advantage of the three-piece crank design is its easily changed crank length. Also, altering the chain-line permits the use of double or triple sprockets by changing the length of axle used.

In some types, the front sprocket is spun permanently onto the right crank and is not removable. In other types, the sprocket is bolted to the crank arm; three or five bolts are normally used. The small diameter, five-bolt system shown in Figure 7.11 with a 50.4-mm bolt circle diameter is common in Europe and England. The three-bolt attachment, standard bolt circle diameter is 116.4 mm in France for steel chainwheels. Other English and Japanese three-bolt mounting sprockets have different bolt diameters, threading, and bolt circle dimensions.

Cotterless Crank Hangers

A third type of crank mounting is known as the cotterless type. The crank axle is made with squared and tapered ends. The cranks have a square taper hole to match. These are made in high-strength aluminum alloy of Accurad die-cast construction. The forged type is considered superior in strength. Either a threaded end or a threaded hole receives a high-tensile bolt which securely pulls the crank onto the axle square taper. This

Fig. 7.8   Shimano Dura-Ace cotterless three-piece crank-set with single Allen wrench mount and dismount and no-tool take-apart chain (bottom).

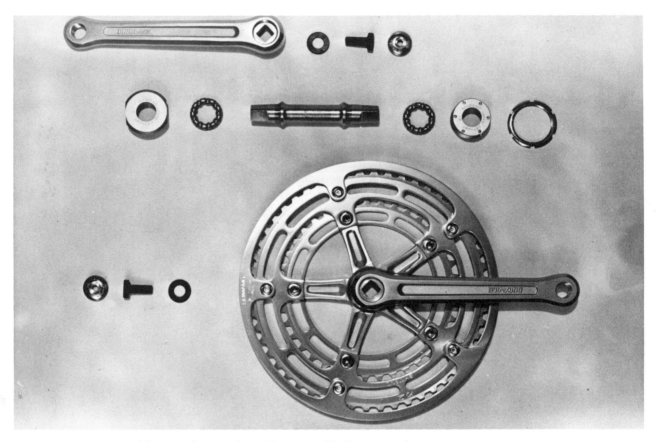

Fig. 7.9   Components of the cotterless crankset. *(Courtesy of R. Timmerman)*

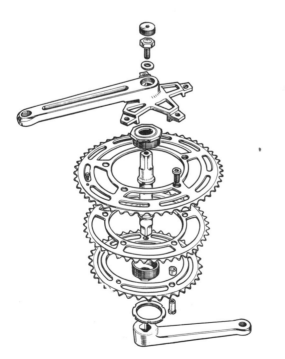

Fig. 7.10   Stronglight 93 triple sprocket cotterless racing
set (inside sprocket has 40 teeth).

type of construction is made by T.A., Nervar, Campagnolo, Zeus, Stronglight, and Williams in Europe; Shimano, Sugino, and Sakae Ringyo, in Japan. Campagnolo, Shimano, and Sugino are interchangeable. The other makes have limited interchangeability, but the fit may not be proper, and the chainline produced by interchanging cranks may vary considerably.

Stronglight originally made (and Campagnolo has reintroduced) a steel cotterless crank which, while a bit heavier, does not suffer from the initial loosening that occurs with aluminum-alloy cranks. It is important to tightly seat aluminum cranks before riding and to then carry an axle bolt wrench for the first several rides. Retighten the bolts after 10 or 20 miles. The bolts may require retightening four or five times, after which the cranks will stay tight for a long period. If not tightened in time, the crank will loosen completely and can eventually fall off. A special bolt socket wrench for tightening and an extracting tool for removing the cranks are provided with the crank and axle set.

Different makes of sprocket mountings are often noninterchangeable. Campagnolo, Sugino, and Shimano Dura-Ace are exceptions. For moderate ranges of chainwheel size, T.A. provides several series, with minimum sizes of 44, 36, and 26 teeth. The T.A. Cyclo-touriste set for double or triple chainwheels (see Fig. 7.11) provides large chainwheels of up to 70 teeth on special order. Stronglight and Zeus likewise produce sets that permit the use of these small sprockets for cycle touring use. The Campagnolo dual sprocket set provides a minimum chainwheel size of 42 teeth; the triple sprocket model has a minimum size of 36 (many other sets provide a 36-tooth minimum). Determine the range you desire, then select a set that will provide it.

Phil Wood in California, makes sealed precision ball bearing sets of axle, bearings, and threadings (Fig. 7.14), while Lambert in England, makes complete insert, bearings, and cranks. Insert assemblies are provided complete and ready to install by several makers. The Sakae Ringyo set is shown in Figure 7.15.

The threading of the cups must be selected to suit the frame. The axle length will vary to provide a proper chainline for use with single, double, or triple front sprockets. Typical dimensions are shown in Figures 7.12 (cotterless type) and 7.13 (cottered type). These dimensions are for the Stronglight model; other makes will differ. Note the differences among the thread diameter, thread pitch, and fixed cup thread direction, in the English and Japanese, French, and Italian series, and proposed international standards.

Steel sprockets provide a longer wearing life, with greater weight, than the light alloy types. With a high-strength light alloy, wearing life is reasonably good, and most high-grade bicycles now use the strong and rigid forms. However, there is a marked difference in the strength and rigidity of cranks and axles.

Fig. 7.11   T. A. Cyclo-touriste triple wide range, five-bolt standard crank mounting. Putting mounting holes closer to center permits smaller (26-tooth) inside sprocket.

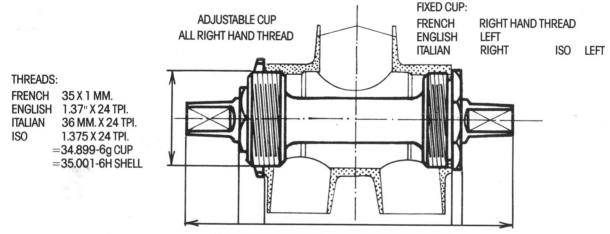

Fig. 7.12   Cotterless crank hanger set showing variations of thread direction and dimension and proposed international standards.

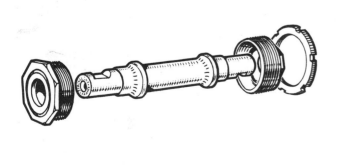

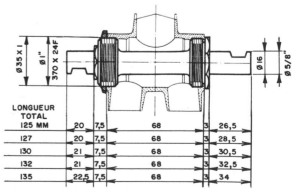

Fig. 7.13   In cottered or cotterless cranksets, cup thread, thread hand, axle length, and diameter must match and suit the crank and sprocket set. A 70-mm shell width (left) is used in some makes.

Shimano Dura-Ace in Figure 7.17, shown complete with "quick release." Campagnolo also makes a superior model that is widely acclaimed for its easy running qualities.

The internal construction of a typical front hub with a solid axle and hexagonal wrench nuts is shown in Figure 7.18. The locknut (item 7) is tightened after the cones are adjusted to prevent the cones from tightening or loosening while riding. Excel Mfg. Co. makes a hub with knurled axle threads that hold their adjustment without this extra operation.

It is important when replacing cones to be sure that the inner bearing diameter, slope, and concavity

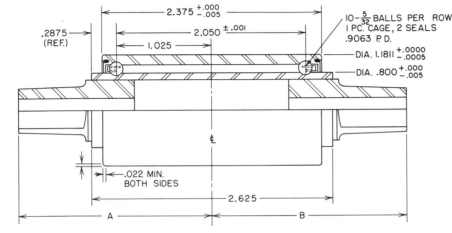

SHAFT LENGTH	DIM. A	SHAFT LENGTH	DIM. B
1	2.125	1	2.125
2	2.156	2	2.281
3	2.250	3	2.437
4	2.344	4	2.593

ALL DIMENSIONS ARE IN INCHES.

Fig. 7.14 Phil Wood sealed-bearing crank hanger with precision, sealed ball bearings.

HUBS

Phil Wood, Hi-E, Viscount, and Maxicar (in France) make the highest-grade hubs, using precision ball bearings. Other American firms, ACS and EBM have also introduced this type. The Phil Wood type uses a large diameter tubular axle strong enough to resist deflection by imperfectly aligned frames (see Fig. 6.30 and Fig. 7.16). This has been a cause of difficulty. The Phil Wood and Hi-E hubs use sealed bearings, which keep out road grit and water and require neither lubrication nor adjustment for extended periods.

A commoner construction universally used in bicycle hubs is the cup-and-cone bearing. This construction accommodates some deflection and misalignment. The finest quality hubs use chrome-molybdenum steel axles for greatest strength and resistance to permanent bending under impact or heavy chain pull. The cones and axles are precisely threaded, the cones carefully hardened and ground, and seals are fitted to exclude grit and water. Flanges are pierced to reduce weight to a minimum, and the entire hub shell is made of a light alloy. Hub flanges are placed at an angle toward the rim and are thick enough to give good spoke support without excessive bending. A fine example is the

Fig. 7.15 Sakae Ringyo replacement three-piece, preassembled crank hanger assembly. Slip-in type replaces one-piece crank assembly.

(Courtesy of R. Timmerman)

match the part replaced. If not, the bearing may lose its adjustment quickly and will have a very short life.

Figure 7.19 shows the construction of a "quick-release" rear hub. Note the hollow axle of larger diameter (10 mm versus ⅜ inch or 9.5 mm) for the solid axle of the rear hub, or the 5/16-inch or 8-mm axle of the solid axle front hub. The spindle of the quick release is eccentric, and when turned it will create a very strong clamping pressure. If made too tight, it can provide enough force to actually bow the axle and cause rapid bearing wear.

The hubs illustrated are termed "large flange." A large flanged hub weighs a bit more, provides a laterally stiffer wheel due to greater angularity of the spokes, and creates somewhat less driving tension when accelerating or climbing. The small flange hub is lighter and less expensive, and it provides a softer ride. It is often used by experienced racers, particularly on rough roads.

Makers of lower quality hubs pay less attention to accuracy and choice of material and to sealing dirt and grit out. The axles may bend under severe loading; the finish on the cones may be rough and not ground after hardening. A considerable reduction in bearing friction is obtained with higher quality hubs, worth the manyfold increase in cost to the enthusiast.

Size of hub flange fitted has a bearing on the length of spoke that is needed when building wheels. For guidance, tabulated below are actual measured flange diameters of representative hubs, selected at random.

Table 7.1
FLANGE DIAMETERS

Japanese small flange front	35 mm
Atom and BH, small flange front	42 mm
Campagnolo front, Japanese low flange rear	45–46 mm
Coaster brake, rear	50.8 mm (2 inches)
Campagnolo, small flange rear	52 mm
Tandem front, and small flange rear	54 mm
Phil Wood Standard Flange front and rear	57 mm
Atom, large flange front and rear	72 mm
Sturmey Archer, Campagnolo, & Phil Wood, large flange rear	76 mm
BH, large flange rear	90 mm
Prior, large flange front and rear	93 mm
Hub brakes, various	102, 110, 112, 116 mm
Tandem hub brake, rear	140 mm

Flange widths measured, which affect the spoke fit, varied from 0.062 inch to 0.147 inch.

STEERING HEAD SETS

Steering head sets are made of turned cones and stamped steel cups in the less expensive, less precise bicycles, and of smoothly and accurately turned types with accurate bearing surfaces, alloy steel material,

Fig. 7.16   Phil Wood sealed, precision bearing rear hub and hollow large-diameter axle.

Fig. 7.17   Shimano free hub with outer hub bearing located at right end of freewheel member, compared with standard rear Dura-Ace hub. Cogs slide onto body. Six speeds in space for five.

and small increment locking adjustment (as shown in the Stronglight set at the left, Fig. 7.20).

The most precise types with better steel, sufficient depth of case hardening, controlled atmosphere heat treating, accurately ground ball rolling tracks, mounted with greater accuracy will give longer life, more precise steering, and greater resistance to indenting under impact load. Dented races can cause unsteady and unsafe steering.

Sealed precision bearing head sets have been introduced by Phil Wood and H. Jasik.

An even lower cost construction, the three-plate type, with the fork stem tube brazed into the crown, is shown in Figure 7.21. The open top of the tubing of the fork blade is covered with a pressed steel cap. The fork crown bearing race is a pressed steel washer

1   Complete front hub (36H)
2   Complete axle unit
3   Axle (⁵⁄₁₆ × 5¼ ")
4   Steel balls (³⁄₁₆ ")
5   Dust cap
6   Cone
7   Locknut
8   Lock washer
9   Axle nut

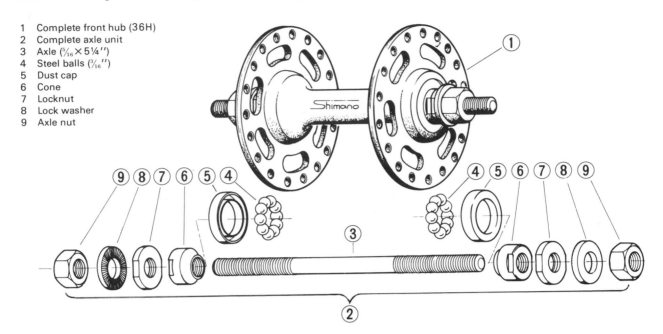

Fig. 7.18   Front hub—solid axle. *(Courtesy of Shimano American Corporation)*

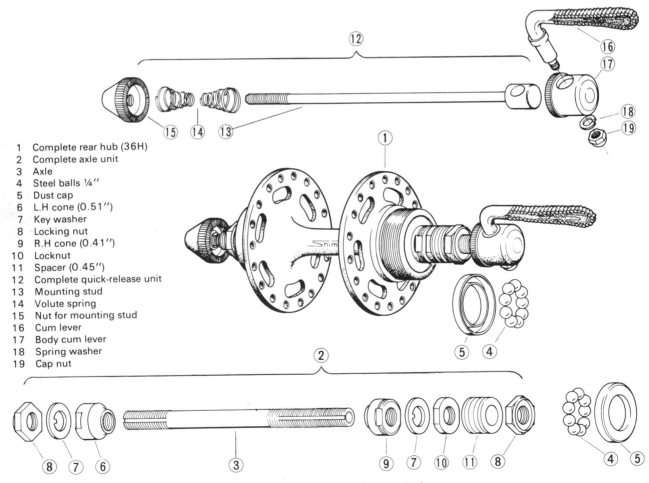

1   Complete rear hub (36H)
2   Complete axle unit
3   Axle
4   Steel balls ¼ "
5   Dust cap
6   L.H cone (0.51 ")
7   Key washer
8   Locking nut
9   R.H cone (0.41 ")
10 Locknut
11 Spacer (0.45 ")
12 Complete quick-release unit
13 Mounting stud
14 Volute spring
15 Nut for mounting stud
16 Cum lever
17 Body cum lever
18 Spring washer
19 Cap nut

Fig. 7.19   Rear, quick-release hub. *(Courtesy of Shimano American Corporation)*

Fig. 7.20 Extrahigh quality steering head bearings. Stronglight, Campagnolo, and Shimano have accurately hardened and ground ball tracks for maximum durability and minimum friction.

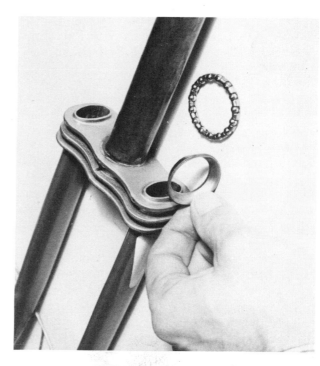

Fig. 7.21 Headsets. A, Lower head bearing with pressed steel cone—bearing balls held in retainer; B, Jasik self-aligning sealed bearings.

(Courtesy of H. Jasik)

formed to a conical shape. The space from the crown top plate to the fork stem tube spans a 45° angle. Since none of the three pieces are machined after assembly, accuracy of alignment of cone and head bearing cups depends on the quality of workmanship.

This head bearing uses balls in a steel ball retainer which, since there are no loose balls to be lost or miscounted during assembly and servicing, permits rapid assembly and easier servicing. A full set of balls without a retainer makes servicing more difficult, but it does increase bearing capacity.

Bearing capacity is proportional to the number of balls fitted and to the square of the ball diameter. Some head races are fitted with ⅛-inch balls, others with 3/16-inch or with 5/32-inch balls. Ball cups and races in which the surfaces are contoured to more closely conform to the shape of the ball provide greater capacity and resistance to brinelling or denting of the races under load. Stronglight's Competition uses a four-point contact race which also provides additional load bearing capacity. A major advantage over the two-point type is its ability to better retain grease and resist water washout, since the direct force of driven water when riding in the rain without fenders is deflected from the bottom bearing. However, it requires the frame seating surfaces to be extremely accurate.

Instead of cups pressed into the head tube, a long-used English construction uses a machined lower and upper head race with spherical turned surfaces where fitted into the frame. The top and bottom frame lugs are similarly shaped, and ⅛-inch balls are used. This spherical shape, however, allows the frame races to align themselves perfectly with the top and bottom fork races. Thus all balls share the load equally. This construction has been proven very effective despite the theoretically lesser capacity.

A fork stem damaged by impact (see Fig. 7.22) can be bent so that bearing alignment is severely jeopardized. Ball loading will be uneven, and binding results.

BICYCLE BRAKES

Modern bicycle brakes can be generally placed in two categories: the foot-operated type on the rear wheel which is powered by reversing the direction of the pedals, and the hand-operated types which either apply pressure to rubber blocks against the sides of the rim or pull up against the rim's inner face. Other hand-operated types include the internal-expanding automotive-type shoe brake, and the caliper disc brake, a recent innovation.

Hub Brakes

The foot-operated coaster brake uses an internal screw-actuated clutch in the rear hub. When the chain is turned forward, the clutch tightens against a tapered face in the hub shell and grips it tightly. When turned in the opposite direction, the clutch reverses, disengaging from the shell and pressing against a set of interleaved discs, of which half are keyed to the hub shell and half to an exterior torque arm attached to the bicycle frame. Friction between the discs slows the bicycle.

On reversal in another design, the clutch presses against two cammed surfaces which spread a set of friction shoes against the hub shell. This creates friction, which again slows the rear wheel speed (see Fig. 7.24).

These brakes are relatively weatherproof, but they demand the proper lubricants for good functioning under severe braking. In Figure 7.24 the driving screw (item 8) actuates the clutch (item 11) and the expanding shoes (item 13) which ride on the cammed surfaces of parts 11 and 15. The braking torque is transferred to the frame from part 15 through the torque arm (17). Wear in the friction parts causes excess play and pedal motion, requiring parts replacement. This type of brake is combined with gear shifting mechanisms in some Torpedo, Bendix, Shimano and Sturmey Archer two and three-speed hub gears.

Caliper Rim Brakes

Caliper rim brakes are supplied in pull-up types and side-of-the-rim types. Strictly, the pull-up type might be made a separate class. It is generally used on the cheaper types of utility bicycles in some European countries and is little seen in the United States where a wider rim with the spokes placed close to its center is used. Stirrups guide the brake shoes, which are pulled up onto the interior rim surface by means of rods and pivoted levers mounted under the handlebar grips. The action is fairly direct. There are no cables to stretch, little can go wrong, and the brakes are fairly effective, but the heavier wide rim and the difficulty of wheel removal have caused them to lose favor.

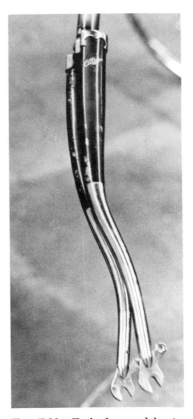

Fig. 7.22   Fork damaged by impact. Note that stem is bowed; this will result in bearing misalignment.

Fig. 7.23   Coaster brake.
(Courtesy of Shimano American Corporation)

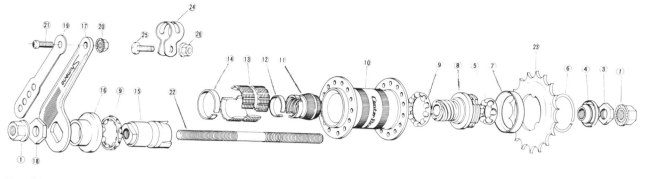

Fig. 7.24   Coaster brake (exploded view).
(Courtesy of Shimano American Corporation)

1	Hub nut	15	Brake cone
3	Locknut	16	Dust cap
4	Hub cone	17	Brake arm
5	Ball retainer and balls	18	Arm nut
6	Snap ring	19	Brake arm clip
7	Dust cap	20	Clip nut
8	Driver	21	Clip nut
9	Ball retainer and balls	22	Hub axle
10	Hub shell	23	Sprocket
11	Clutch cone	24	Brake arm clip
12	Clutch spring	25	Clip bolt
13	Brake shoe	26	Clip nut
14	Shoe spring		

There are four classifications of caliper brakes. The side-pull brake operates by a casing-enclosed cable connected from brake lever to brake. The brake lever pulls against one brake arm, bringing it around a pivot bolt to the rim. The reaction of the cable tension in the casing compresses the casing, which pushes against the opposite arm of the brake and forces it against the rim. The combined pressure against the rim sides causes friction which slows the moving rim and thus the bicycle.

A modification in the design of the side-pull is used in the Altenburger, Excel, GB Synchron brakes, in the Beborex (Italian), and in Magic Compe 812 (Japanese) and Weinmann Symetric brakes. These also pull from one side, but a lever or projection attached to the primary arm transfers force to the opposing arm, helping to drive it toward the rim.

The third type is the center-pull. The brake cable casing terminates at a fitting mounted from either the seat bolt in the rear or a bracket mounted on the top of the front steering head. The cable extends to a cable carrier, which is connected to the ends of the two brake arms by a cross cable or linkage. The brake cable transfers the force applied at the brake lever to the brake. The casing compression exerts force on the head bracket, which under severe braking deflects considerably.

Whereas on side-pull brakes the pivot point is also the point of attachment to the frame, on the center-pull type, two pivot bolts are mounted on a U-shaped bracket which is attached to the frame at its center. The pivot bolts are carried lower and closer to the brake shoes on the U bracket, thus providing the additional mechanical advantage of applying greater force to the brake shoes (see Fig. 7.28). By evenly applying the action of the center-pull to both brake arms directly, a one-sided pull that sometimes causes the side-actuated types to shift is avoided. However, the more secure mounting provided in Campagnolo and Shimano side-pull types have negated this disadvantage.

The fourth type is actually a center-pull. However, the brakeshoes are attached to a bell-crank, at the center of which is a pivot bolt attached to a boss that is brazed or clamped directly onto the fork blade or rear seat stay. This type is very simple and very effective, but brazing the attaching bracket adds to the cost. Since there is no cross bridge on the frame at this point, if the seat stays are feeble, they can deflect under brake pressure. The photos show four types, the original Resilion "Cantilever" with the double length brake blocks so effective in wet weather, the Shimano, and the Mafac types K and H. The latter, with 25% longer brake blocks and 25% more leverage, is excellent for heavy demands, such as those placed on tandems and touring bikes, as well as in the rain. On a single bicycle, brake block wear is reduced. Due to its minimum interference and complexity, the cantilever Mafac is widely used on cyclo-cross bicycles which operate in mud (see Figs. 7.30–7.33).

The side-pull was the brake most used until the 1950s, when the very popular Mafac Racer brake was introduced. Mafac set a new trend with its centered action, adaptability to wavy wheels, and good mechanical advantage. Italian frames, however, were traditionally built with a close clearance between the wheel and fork crown or rear-brake bridge, so short-reach side-pull brakes could be used to gain mechanical advantage. The "reach" of the brake is shown on the exploded view of the Dia-Compe and Weinmann brake in Figure 7.30. As can be recognized, the mechanical advantage of the brake system is equal to the mechanical advantage at the brake lever, times the brake-pivot-to-line-of-action distance B, divided by the reach A. As the reach required for the brake block to meet the rim location increases, as shown—from 43 mm to 108 mm, the mechanical advantage decreases

54   Acorn nut for pivot bolt, brake
        shoe
62   Locknut (outer) for pivot bolt
8–18 Outer brake arm
9–19 Inner brake arm
48   Spacer washer for pivot bolt
52   Locknut for pivot bolt
46   Spring only
58   Radius bushing for rear—bridge
56   Pivot bolt washer
42.1 Rear pivot bolt only
40.1 Front pivot bolt only
60   Serrated washer for pivot bolt
50.1 Name plate washer for pivot bolt
76.1 Brake shoe

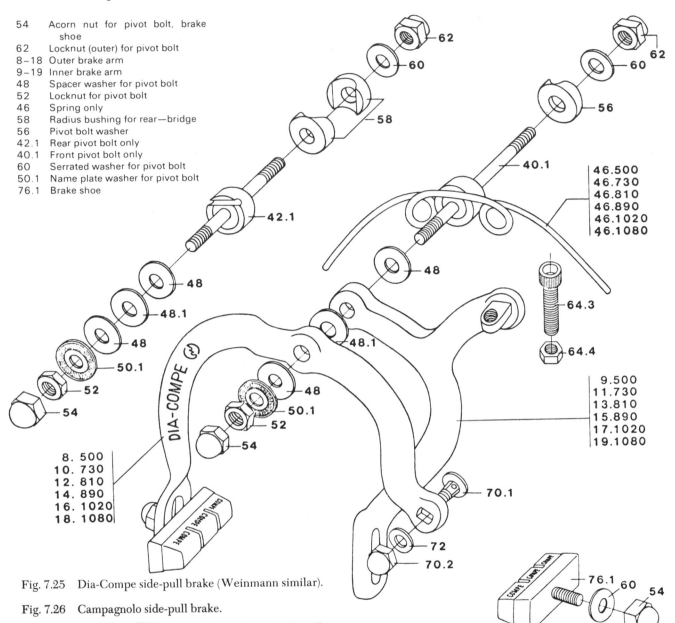

Fig. 7.25   Dia-Compe side-pull brake (Weinmann similar).

Fig. 7.26   Campagnolo side-pull brake.

to 40% of the maximum value at 43 mm reach! (Actually, a slight increase in B may be provided but this is minor).

The lowered pivot points in the exploded views of the Tourney Center-pull brakes in Figure 7.28 are typical of the construction of Mafac, Universal, Weinmann, and other center-pull types. The introduction in 1968 of the accurately made and finely finished Campagnolo side-pull brake (see Fig. 7.26) started a return to the less expensive to manufacture side-pull brake. The side-pull, having fewer parts, is simpler to make as well as to install. Campagnolo built its brake for very close clearance frames in order to obtain the maximum mechanical advantage and provided an offset mounting bolt for frames with a bit larger clearance. However, the short reach makes it unadaptable

Fig. 7.27   Magic Compe 812 double-action side-pull brake.

1   Nut for center bolt
2   Toothed lock washer
3   Washer
4   Radius bushing (front)
5   Square seating pad (front)
6   Lock nut for pivot bolt
7   Arm bridge
8   L.H. arm return spring
9   R.H. arm return spring
10   Flanged thrust washer
11   Inner brake arm "M" type
       Inner brake arm "S" type
12   Outer brake arm "M" type
       Outer brake arm "S" type
13   Bushing
14   Pivot bolt
15   Center cable 90mm (3½")
16   Cap nut for brake shoe
17   Brake shoe (left)
18   Brake shoe (right)
19   Cap
20   Sleeve

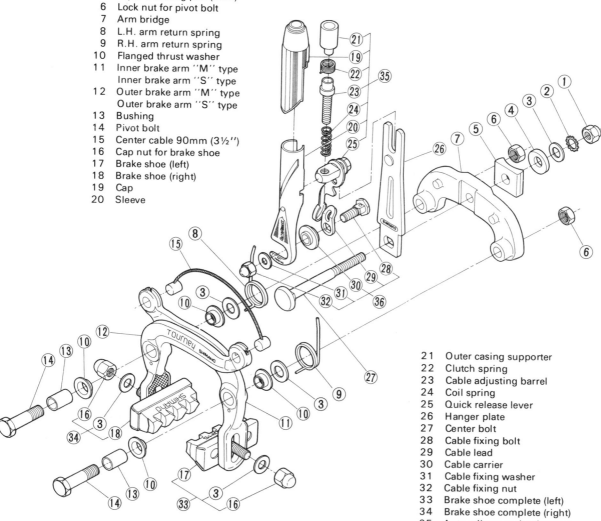

21   Outer casing supporter
22   Clutch spring
23   Cable adjusting barrel
24   Coil spring
25   Quick release lever
26   Hanger plate
27   Center bolt
28   Cable fixing bolt
29   Cable lead
30   Cable carrier
31   Cable fixing washer
32   Cable fixing nut
33   Brake shoe complete (left)
34   Brake shoe complete (right)
35   Auto adjust mechanism set
36   Cable fixing bolt set
37   Radius bushing (rear)
38   Square seating pad (rear)
39   Spacer

Fig. 7.28   Center-pull brake with auto-adjust mechanism.
A, Front brake; B, Rear brake.
(Courtesy of Shimano American Corporation)

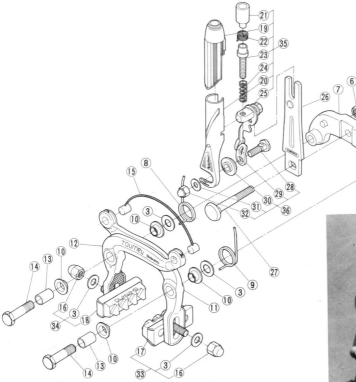

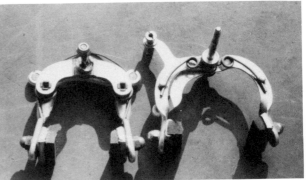

Fig. 7.29 Center-pull and side-pull brakes of same make and reach. Notice lowered pivot points and greater mechanical advantage of the center-pull.

to frames requiring mudguard clearance or clearance for larger section tires. With the Cantilever brake, mounted where the rim requires, neither frame clearance nor tire size matters.

In order to determine the facts on braking efficiency, the research laboratory of a leading American bicycle and racing bicycle manufacturer conducted a series of experiments under controlled conditions, both wet and dry. These experiments showed, not surprisingly, that brake effectiveness depends not on center-pull or side-pull action, but on the mechanical action provided by brake design and frame clearance. The typical center-pull brings the pivot point of brake arm 20 mm closer to the brakeshoe.

Other factors affect the braking performance of caliper brakes. We must consider the brake as a "system." Grease, oil, or mud on the roads, water on the rims and blocks may reduce braking effectiveness as much as 80%. The excessive deflection of a weak head-mounted brake cable casing support under hard brake application under wet conditions may permit the brake lever to bottom out against the handlebar. Brake cables and casings vary considerably in diameter and casing flexibility. Stretch of cable and casing compression can limit the braking force applied. Improved casing, and full-sized 1.8-mm diameter brake cables are a "must" for safety. The cost to obtain these is negligible.

Fig. 7.30 Resilion Cantilever of the 1930s. Compare double-length brake block to the normal brake block in the background.

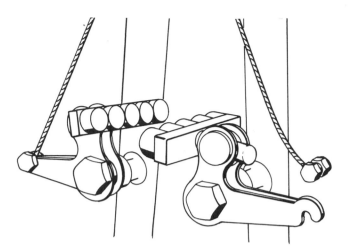

Fig. 7.31   Mafac Ref H cantilever with 25% longer block.

Fig. 7.31a   Mathauser extra-length bonded blocks curve to fit the rim. Heat-transfer fins on the shoe reduce rim temperature and brake fade.

Fig. 7.32   Mafac Ref K.

Fig. 7.33   Shimano cantilever brake.

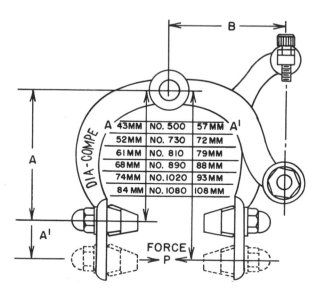

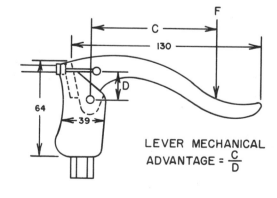

Fig. 7.34   Mechanical advantage of lever equals C/D. Force at the pad, P, equals $F \times C/D \times B/A$ — (the return spring force plus cable friction).

When hand caliper brakes are applied, the blocks grip the rim. Friction pulls the block, shoe, and brake arm forward. This is resisted by the stiffness of the arm in twisting. The arm also tends to bend as a beam from the applied pressure. Quite naturally, the flimsier the brake construction and the longer the reach, the more motion is lost in the brake system; security and controllability will also be diminished. Loose adjustment and play in the parts increase this effect. Chatter and noisy braking can also result.

The frame members, particularly the seat stays, must resist the twist of the brake through the mounting bolt and the pressure applied to the blocks. If the frame members are small in section, or if the brake bridge is not fashioned for resisting twist, the brake will again be less secure.

The reach of the brake must provide clearance between mudguard and tire, the thickness of the mudguard, and the diameter of the tire. These must be spanned before the rim is reached. The racing bicycle is designed for use on mud free roads. Lacking mudguards and having small-diameter tires, it uses brakes with a small "reach." As a result, greater mechanical advantages can be obtained. Campagnolo, Shimano, Dura-Ace, Weinmann 500, Universal 68, and equivalent side-pull designs are made with an extra short reach for maximum rigidity and effectiveness. But for touring use, their application is limited by their limited clearance.

For panic stops, the rigid, close-reach brake has the advantage. Its action is firm and hard. If the rim is perfectly true, without wobble or dents, it gives the strongest action. However, the self-centering action and the additional flexibility of the center-pull result in a somewhat softer action. In well-designed and accurately built brakes this provides sufficient brake force for pitch-over or wheel skid, and no more is needed, except with wet rims. With the softer action, however, the wheels need not be perfect. It provides a greater range of force application and more precise control under difficult conditions. The discerning rider can try both and select the action he prefers.

For weather protection and the prevention of tire trouble from overheated rims, the hub brake can be used. Figure 7.35 shows an automotive-type internal-expanding hub brake disassembled. These are effective, but they respond differently to brake lever action than does the harder acting caliper brake. Therefore, direct coupling with a rear caliper brake using a double-cable brake lever is not advised. On a tandem, the caliper brakes can be coupled together on one lever and the hub brake operated separately.

Disc Brakes

The disc brake is a recent development. The Phil Wood brake proved very effective when test-mounted on a Paramount tandem (see Fig. 7.36). Its single sintered disc is more effective for braking and more warp resistant. The Shimano disc brake (Fig. 7.37) is available in both cable and hydraulic operation. It requires a more rugged seat stay but has the advantage of easy wheel removal for tire repair.

Disc brakes have excellent heat dissipation and are less affected by wet weather. Tests have shown a reduction in braking power when wet of from 20% to 50%, compared to reductions as high as 80% for caliper brakes. However, recovery is several times as rapid as with caliper brakes, and they are therefore safer in the rain. Their one disadvantage is that a special narrow-flanged hub must be used to accommodate the disc. On small-diameter wheels this is a minor problem. On 27-inch wheels, the shallow flange width creates a narrow wheel with reduced side load resistance. Spoke breakage creates an unsteady condition. Extraheavy spokes should be used to correct for the extra braking load and for wheel strength.

Figure 7.38 shows a variety of brake levers that are available. The levers located on the hand grip of flat or raised pattern handlebars have an outward slope to increase the clearance when squeezed. A reversed pattern which fits on the bar end interior is available. For dropped pattern bars, the Guidonnet can be supplied. This can be operated from the bars tops, or by pivoting the hand, when on the "drops." More usually preferred is the Hooded lever (Fig. 7.39) which is attached just slightly above the center of the forward bend. The bend gives ample clearance for lever action, and the hood provides an extra hand position for climbing hills. The shape of the hood should provide a comfortable grip. An adjusting screw for brake block wear adjustment may be included in the lever or in the cable stop. In any event, this feature should be demanded.

Increasing in popularity is the "safety lever," an additional lever that can be attached to the hooded lever to permit braking from the top of the handlebar riding position. There are several constructions; one is shown, another is a separate attachment that attaches with one external screw. It is imperative that attention be exercised to keep this screw tightened or it may come loose in service. The lever can be lost when needed.

Safety levers are generally made to a common pattern and used with handlebars of varied throw and pattern. In some patterns, the lever pulls straight against the underside of the bar. With greater or lesser bar throws, the lever may pull up to an awkward position. The Altenburger lever has an angle of attachment adjustable to the most comfortable and effective position.

Brake Misfitting

Figures 7.40–7.42 show brake defects photographed on brand-new bicycles. In Figure 7.40, the brake reach fitted is insufficient. Even at their maximum extension

Fig. 7.35   Automotive-type internal expanding hub brake.

Fig. 7.36   Phil Wood disc brake, front or rear use.
(*Courtesy of Phil Wood*)

Fig. 7.39   Finely finished and shaped Campagnolo brake
lever.

Fig. 7.37   Shimano G self-energizing disc brake with automatic cable adjuster.
(*Courtesy of Shimano American Corporation*)

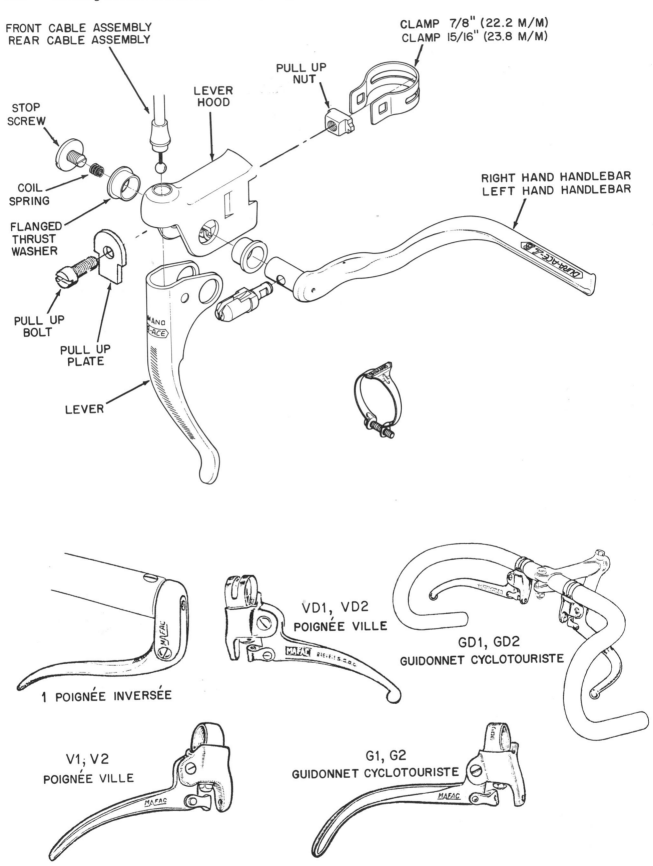

FRONT CABLE ASSEMBLY
REAR CABLE ASSEMBLY

CLAMP 7/8" (22.2 M/M)
CLAMP 15/16" (23.8 M/M)

PULL UP
NUT

STOP
SCREW

LEVER
HOOD

COIL
SPRING

RIGHT HAND HANDLEBAR
LEFT HAND HANDLEBAR

FLANGED
THRUST
WASHER

PULL UP
BOLT

PULL UP
PLATE

LEVER

1 POIGNÉE INVERSÉE

VD1, VD2
POIGNÉE VILLE

GD1, GD2
GUIDONNET CYCLOTOURISTE

V1, V2
POIGNÉE VILLE

G1, G2
GUIDONNET CYCLOTOURISTE

Fig. 7.38   Brake levers.

the brake blocks hit the tires. One common error is the use of a side-pull brake in which the cable attachment arm strikes the frame when the handlebar is turned (see Fig. 7.41). This arm can be easily bent, interfering with the brake action. In Figure 7.42 the cable attachment is misplaced, abrading the cable.

The brake levers fitted must suit the finger reach of the user. Ladies with short fingers should check this carefully. If the lever fitted is not within reach, a spacer may be made to hold your lever within your grasp.

Government standards require effective braking using a maximum lever force of 40 pounds (possible for a 10-year-old boy or an 11-year-old girl). The selection of a brake with a sufficient mechanical advantage is important for the rider of ample weight who has a below average finger grip.

Braking Effectiveness

Wet and dry braking effectiveness varies considerably for equal braking lever force applied. Brake block material, mechanical advantage, and rim material have an effect. Wet and dry weather performance can vary considerably. Brian Hanson at MIT found that the brake block giving the best dry friction dropped to only 5% effectiveness when wet. Another with 1/3 the dry friction of the first, dropped 50% when wet (to 17% the effectiveness of the first when dry). Oscar Abell at MIT found that the available brake friction at 30 mph was only from 70% to 80% of that available at 9 mph. Used rims give a poorer initial braking force, but less is lost when wet. Slots and grooves in the brake blocks gave poorer, not better wet performance. Dimpled rims which provide water traps wear brake blocks more and give a less predictable wet performance.

Tests in other laboratories have shown that when

dry, aluminum rims provide about 2/3 the braking effectiveness of chromed steel rims. About 50% more lever force is needed for equal stopping ability.

For equal performance in wet weather, though, the chrome steel rim requires about 60% more force at the

Fig. 7.41 This side-pull brake arm strikes frame when handlebar is turned. Bending can render brake inoperative.

Fig. 7.42 This factory-misassembled brake has a misaligned cable and will wear rapidly.

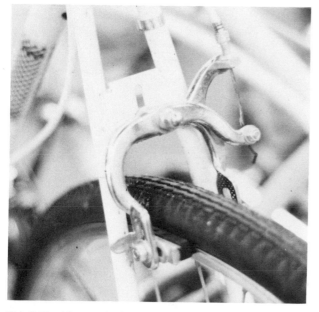

Fig. 7.40 Mismatched brake does not meet rim.

Fig. 7.43   The Harris Hill Test Site, a mile-long, 15% grade, used to torture test brakes to failure by the Bendix Company.
(Courtesy of Bendix Div.)

Fig. 7.44   A power-driven brake fade tester used at U.S. Testing Laboratory.
(Courtesy of Bicycle Institute of America)

Fig. 7.45   Measured forces can be applied to hand brake levers or to hub brake actuators repeatedly, and the time to stop under various loads measured. Brake fade under repeated loads, or under driven load to simulate down-hill braking is measured and continuously recorded. Water spray can be applied to measure wet-weather braking efficiency.
(Courtesy of Schwinn Bicycle Company)

brake lever than aluminum rims. The wet-weather fall-off in performance is less severe with aluminum rims. Even though the dry performance is inferior, the improved wet weather performance gives less chance of loss of control when the rain starts.

Internal friction, deflection of loaded parts, and block composition influence brake efficiency. Under equal conditions, however, one make of brake provided 1/3 greater stopping ability than a second make. Each was equipped with the factory-fitted blocks.

The block compressibility, especially when pads are severely slotted, can be so great that the lever may bottom when the extra force needed for wet stops is used. For block wear and effectiveness, Mafac gives excellent overall performance. The Campagnolo block is less effective at low loads but slightly better under the extreme loads used in wet conditions.

In 1973 Angenieux-CLB of France developed a self-energizing brake block and shoe, both having ramped surfaces. Under braking action as the wheel rotates, the block slides forward slightly and is forced more tightly against the rim. Less brake lever movement and force are required for equal stopping ability. In addition to their greater compressibility, slotted brake blocks with an interrupted braking surface wear and require readjustment more rapidly. While widely used, the slotted and nibbed block should be replaced with a more solid pattern for best overall performance.

A comparison has been made measuring the reach and mechanical advantage of a number of brakes now supplied. Used with close clearance frames, the racing brakes of side-pull design, such as Campagnolo and Weinmann 500, had a mechanical advantage of about 1.1. The Campagnolo had an available "reach" of from 42 to 54 mm and the Weinmann of from 43 to 57 mm. The CLB Hilife and Universal 68 were only slightly less.

Weinmann and Dia-Compe and Ballila side-pull brakes have reaches more usable on frames with mudguard clearance. Their mechanical advantages varied from 0.75 to 0.80. The position of the brake block in the adjustable slot changes the mechanical advantage.

Center-pull brakes with a reach sufficient for use with mudguards (the reach in the center of the adjusting slot of 68 to 70 mm) had a mechanical advantage of about 1.0 due to their lower pivot points. Weinmann 610, Mafac Racer, and Universal 61 brakes were measured.

Brake lever ratios (see Fig. 7.34) ranged from 3.9 for the Universal to 4.4 for Mafac and Weinmann and 4.5 for Campagnolo. The higher the ratio, the greater the force applied to the brake block will be for a given finger pressure. But the greater the ratio, the more lever motion is needed. Extra care must be taken to keep the brake blocks closely adjusted to prevent the lever from bottoming on the handlebar.

You can engineer the brake performance you desire for your weight, the wear characteristics, hand strength, brake sensitivity you desire, by combining different types of brake and lever. Don't expect any one combination to be the best under every condition.

SADDLES

The saddle has been called "the rider's most intimate point of contact with his bicycle." You can lose a handlebar and ride no-handed or damage a pedal or crank and still provide power with one foot, but riding for any appreciable distance without a saddle is murderous. When walking, the feet are lifted from 3 to 4 inches, and all the weight is on the foot on the ground. In cycling, the legs move in a 13 to 14-inch circle, and except when hill climbing, only a portion of one's weight is needed on the pedal. Without a saddle the balance of your weight must be on the rising pedal to balance the effort needed. This almost doubles the work output. Try riding a short distance with your saddle off, and you will gain additional love and respect for it.

Saddle problems are common with both neophyte cyclists and experienced racing professionals. Dr. Gaston discusses saddle soreness in Chapter X. Let's look at the mechanical aspects more closely.

Riding Position

The riding position affects the distribution of body weight between saddle and handlebars. An upright position with raised bars places almost 100% of the body weight on the saddle. Impact on the delicate and moving body parts in contact with the saddle is at its greatest. For the large person with upright bars, a saddle width at the rear of as much as 7½ or 8 inches is used with the saddle's top tilted toward the back. Additional springs will cushion the road shock.

As the handlebars are lowered to the position that permits the body to lean about 30° from the vertical,

Fig. 7.46   Mattress saddle with extra coil springs to reduce road shock, and bar frame. No longitudinal adjustment.

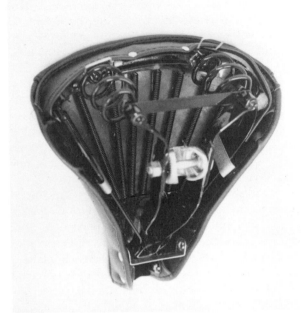

Fig. 7.47   Underside of mattress saddle. Single-sided clamping bolt. *(Courtesy of R. Timmerman)*

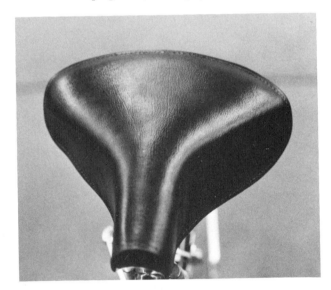

Fig. 7.48   The broad mattress saddle used on bicycles for an upright riding position.

load balance begins to be a bit improved and a saddle of from 6¾ to 7¼ inches is fitted. When the classic touring position is used—the body leaning forward at 45°—a saddle width of from 6¼ to 6¾ inches is most prevalent. Weight on the saddle is reduced, the nose of the saddle can be narrower, and friction between the saddle sides and the legs is lessened. Leaning the body farther forward reduces air resistance and higher riding speeds with faster leg movement are attained. Saddle friction, developing heat and chafing, combined with the potential for longer trips makes these factors important.

The portion of the pelvic bones (ischial tuberosities) supported on the saddle is spaced in men about 4¼ inches apart. For women, this distance is a little larger, say about 4⅞ inches. The saddle must provide flexible, yielding support surrounding these areas.

As the riding pace increases to the speeds attained in fast touring or racing, the body is leaned even farther forward and pedal pressure is increased. Both of these factors reduce the weight carried on the saddle, and a saddle width of from 6 to 6¼ inches is used. With the narrower width, friction is further reduced. And for highest speeds on the track, where friction must be at a minimum and road impact is less a factor, a saddle width as little as 4 inches may be used.

As the body is leaned farther forward, the angle of the saddle top tilts forward to compensate. While the upright rider may use a 2° or 3° backward tilt, the tourist may prefer his saddle top dead level, and the racer will have the nose of his saddle tilted down a bit at the front. The exact angle is of paramount importance. A degree or so can make a lot of difference in riding comfort. The exact pitch depends upon the riding position and the intensity at which you ride—this can vary from day to day, or even within the day.

With the narrower saddle, your bicycle will appear to be propelled more easily. Reduction of chafing reduces soreness and lessens heat and friction. Too narrow a saddle will provide insufficient support for the buttocks when riding in the upright position and will promote saddle soreness. Yet some import bicycles come equipped—even in the ladies' models—with saddles of track bike width!

Care of the saddle is essential. A leather saddle, if ridden while wet will deform badly and sag. As saddle top material stretches in use, the nose bolt must be extended to maintain tension. Otherwise it will sag, pinching the rider in the valley that is created.

Saddle Types

There are many types of saddle material available. Developments in plastics have resulted in all-plastic tops, in plastic-covered padded tops over a yielding plastic base, and in plastic-padded tops over an unyielding plastic or steel base. These are relatively weather-resistant, and some are made narrow for freedom. I have found the padded saddles with unyielding steel or nylon bases entirely too uncomfortable for all but short-distance rides on good roads. Troxel has, however, recently introduced a double-padded steel-framed saddle in which the steel frame has depressions accurately placed to cradle the ischial bones. Mesinger provides a spring-supported yielding base covered with a pad and a plastic cover (see Fig. 7.49).

Many experienced riders prefer the leather top saddle. With proper care it eventually breaks in to the exact shape of the rider's undercarriage. If well taken care of and kept dry, and if made of high-grade

Fig. 7.49   Mesinger saddle with yielding spring-supported nylon base. Longitudinal adjustment provided.

Fig. 7.50   Unicanitor saddle with extra holes for flexibility.

Fig. 7.52   Ideale TB-14 (top) and Avocet (bottom).

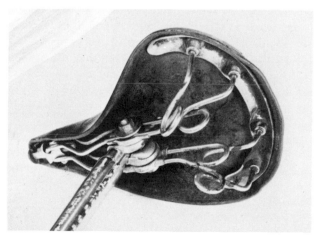

Fig. 7.51   Brooks four-wire, 6¾-inch saddle.

Fig. 7.53   Track saddle with plastic top.

Fig. 7.54   Novel furniture-webbing sling saddle proven in tens of thousands of miles of mountain touring since 1966. *(Courtesy of Dan Henry)*

leather, it will last for years. It breathes and so reduces saddle soreness due to perspiration. A leather saddle when new, however, is extremely hard, and its cost is high. It must be treated with neat's-foot oil from the underside, carefully kneaded and rolled before use. This takes time and effort, and many new cyclists will not endure the pain of breaking it and themselves in to each other. Nor do they appreciate the stained clothing resulting from riding a treated leather saddle.

The self-supporting plastic saddle made by Unica, Ideale, and others has gained in favor. It may be obtained with a thin leather covering over the plastic. Light in weight and weather-resistant, it gives minimum friction. I have found that drilling additional holes in its top enhances its flexibility and breathing and makes it satisfactory for touring use (see Fig. 7.50).

Figure 7.51 is a 6¾-inch width leather saddle on a four-wire underframe. The four-wire frame is more resilient and shock absorbing, yet it provides a firmer support than the coil spring types. Excessive springing reduces road shock but results in changing the distance from pedal to saddle top. This reduces pedaling efficiency.

Figure 7.52 shows the Ideale TB-14 and Avocet ladies' saddles with divided top and narrow nose. They are very popular with their feminine users.

Seat Posts and Seat Clamps

The seat post and seat clamp are very important components. They permit the adjustment of the height of the saddle to the exact position desired by the rider. The seat clamp permits adjustment of the saddle position forward or rear for best functioning and adjustment of the saddle top angle for greatest comfort. The clamp adapts from the seat post upper diameter to the saddle frame used.

The saddle frame may be of flat steel stock, of four-wire construction, or of two-wire construction. In the two-wire construction, there are two spacings of the wires; 36 mm is standard, but a narrower spacing available on some saddles permits a greater range of back and forth position adjustments. This requires a special narrow clamp, as made by Campagnolo, on their combination post and clamp (see Fig. 7.55).

Seat post length and diameter must fit. With the post raised to the proper saddle height, at least 2½ inches should remain in the frame tube. Any less is unsafe. For secure clamping and to avoid rocking, the seat post should closely fit the inside diameter of the seat tube. The gauge of the seat tube determines its inside diameter. Most tubing used in other countries is 28 mm (Continental Europe) or 28.6 mm (1⅛ inches—American, English, and Japanese). Many regular production American bicycles use 1-inch OD tubes with 1/16-inch wall thickness. These use ⅞-inch diameter posts or 13/16-inch diameter posts with either a bushing or heavier gauge.

For the 28 and 28.6-mm diameter tubing, seat posts are provided in every diameter from 25.8 to 27.4 mm in graduated steps of 0.2 mm. Thus tubes whose gauge varies from 0.3 to 1.4 mm in thickness (from 0.012 to 0.056 inch) can be fitted. An expander bolt post is available for American bicycles with 1-inch OD tubing. This has a wedge bolt similar to that used on handlebar stems at its base and eliminates the need for a seat tube clamp on the frame.

Seat posts with horizontal top extensions that gave additional back and forth adjustments were formerly available. To accommodate the need for greater ranges of saddle location, the clamp, which is normally placed behind the seat post, can be reversed to a forward position. This can be used if the seat tube is very inclined, or if a short rider wishes to adapt a frame or a handlebar extension that is too long. The rider's ideal position in relation to the crank hanger will of course be compromised.

The seat post should be closed on top. An open top forms a conduit for water and grit to the bearings. Even with a well-fitted closed top post, I apply a silicone sealant around the joint between the post and top seat lug to prevent the entry of moisture. The slotted opening at the seat post clamp in the frame must also be sealed. Riding without fenders in the rain allows much moisture to enter at this point.

Seat post lengths are usually provided from 13 to 25 cm in length, although lengths of up to 19 inches can be found on high-riser bikes. If over 3 inches remains in the tube, the surplus can be sawed off to save weight.

Mount the seat at the top of the seat post. If the reduced section is too long, the saddle may bottom on the extended post, and this is uncomfortable.

Seat post tops are usually ⅞ or ⅝-inch diameter.

The ⅞ inch is preferable by far. The smaller diameter gives insufficient resistance to prevent the saddle from turning. As a result, the clamping bolt is often tightened too much, and this results in bending or stripping the bolt or stretching the clamp (see Fig. 7.57). Seat clamp bolts may be either single or double ended. The double-ended type projects a lesser distance, and both nuts should be tightened equally. The single-threaded type may extend so far that the side of the saddle or the rider's leg may be scraped.

The saddle clamp has matching serrations to adjust for tilt. These vary in number from 24 to 54, and the number of serrations on each part must match. The clamp must be sufficiently loosened when adjusting, or the serrations will be rounded off. They will not then hold the saddle, and it may shift when the rider hits a bump and destroy his equilibrium. Figure 7.58 center shows a worn-off clamp. At the right are three clamps, each with a different number of serrations.

With 24 serrations, the minimum change of adjustment is 15°, while with a 54-serration clamp, the tilt will vary by only 7°. The larger the number of serrations, however, the more easily these may be stripped. I find that a 7° variation is still far too great for optimum comfort, and the highest quality bicycles use either a micro-adjusting seat clamp, such as the Ideale

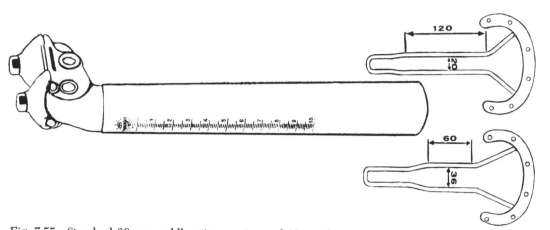

Fig. 7.55   Standard 36-mm saddle wire spacing and 60-mm longitudinal adjustment and narrow (20-mm) spacing with 120-mm adjustment.

Fig. 7.56   Five-eighth-inch diameter, four-wire seat clamp and frame seat post clamp.

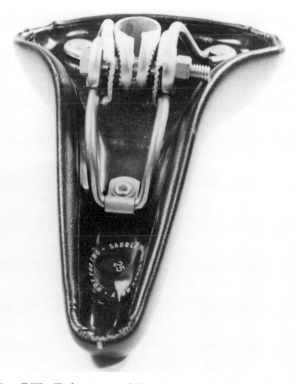

Fig. 7.57   Tightening saddle clamp too tightly will collapse the clamp, diminishing support.

SC, or a combination seat post and clamp—these are highly recommended.

Several types of micro-adjusting clamps are available. There is the Nitor cam-adjusting type. Very light in weight are the Nitor and the Japanese Compe and Zeus with plastic inserts which can be set to the exact position desired. These deform under clamping pressure to make a tight fit (see Fig. 7.60).

The Campagnolo seat post (see Fig. 7.55), and its competitors, Zeus and SR (Japanese), are widely used in competition. Clamping bolts also adjust the slope of the saddle top. Milremo grooves the post exterior and uses titanium bolts to reduce weight.

The Simplex seat post (see Fig. 7.62) is now also available with an aluminum-alloy top for lightness and is widely used in competition. It has a unique advantage (as does the Ideale clip mentioned above) in that the nuts can be snugged down just sufficiently tight to be secure, yet loose enough to permit adjustment while riding. In this manner, the saddle top angle can be changed to suit and its effect on comfort noted without dismounting. It can be moved back and forth until the best position is found and then tightened fully. On long trips with varied wind and terrain, I have found that this feature helps considerably to reduce saddle soreness. The pitch can be changed to suit the conditions of riding or to alleviate developing soreness. Of course it must not be left so loose that a bump will cause it to shift to a dangerous degree.

PEDALS

Pedal Types and Quality

The selection of pedals for your bicycle requires some forethought on your part. Price, of course, is a factor. A wide range exists: permanently assembled rubber pedals are available at $2.75 and the highest grade racing pedals may cost $40.00 or more. Luckily, the entry of the Spanish and the Japanese into the high-grade field has made some excellent pedals available at more moderate costs.

Consider the size and width of the shoes in which you plan to ride. Will you want to ride in street shoes that you can wear directly to the office or shop? Will you be doing considerable walking, and do you wish to dispense with carrying a spare set of shoes into which to change after riding? Do you wish to use toe clips and straps, which have a tendency to mark or wear the shoe at the point of contact? Do you feel ill at ease in heavy traffic, when you may want to put your foot down in an instant? Have you learned the knack of getting into and out of toe clips? These factors may lead you to select a rubber block pedal. A plastic-faced pedal, if the plastic provides sufficient friction when wet, may also be used.

The metal pedal without toe clips is widely used. It is lighter, but it doesn't give as much friction between shoe and pedal, so your foot is liable to slip in some circumstances. The pressure on your foot may be painful when wearing thin-soled shoes, particularly on a hard pull without toe clips. The width of the pedal should suit the size of your feet. Don't make the mistake of getting one too narrow.

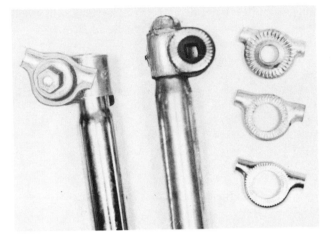

Fig. 7.58   Assembled and disassembled seat clamp. Clamp on right has worn serrations. (Some clamps with varied number of serrations.)

Fig. 7.59   Ideale Super Competition—micro-adjusting seat clamp.

Fig. 7.60   Nitor or Compe seat pillar with polypropylene inserts.

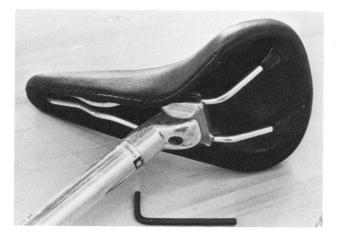

Fig. 7.61   Laprade micro bottom adjusting seat post.

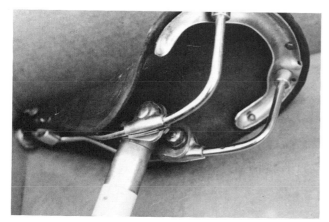

Fig. 7.62   Simplex micro-adjusting seat pillar.

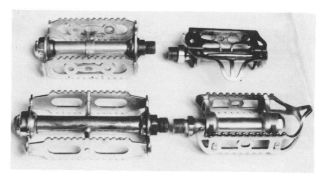

Fig. 7.63   Pedals. Lyotard light-alloy rattrap (left top); Marcel Berthet platform (right top); Lyotard wide rattrap (left bottom); Atom 700 quill (right bottom).

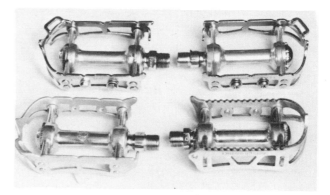

Fig. 7.64   Top quality racing pedals. Campagnolo road (left top); Kyukoto Pro Ace (right top); Zeus light alloy (left bottom); Lyotard 65 (right bottom).

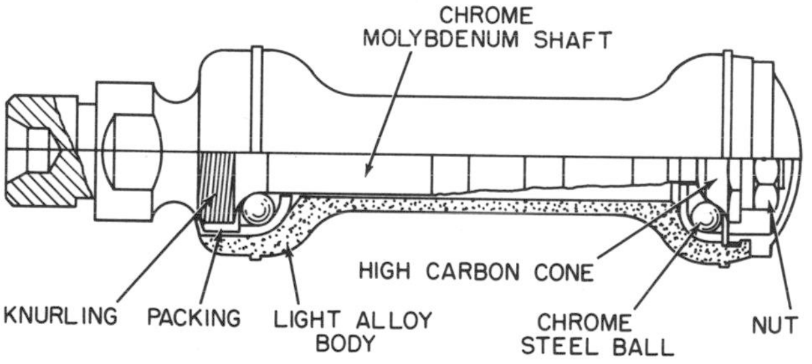

CHROME MOLYBDENUM SHAFT

KNURLING   PACKING   LIGHT ALLOY BODY   HIGH CARBON CONE   CHROME STEEL BALL   NUT

BODY : DROP FORGED LIGHT ALLOY
SHAFT : CHROME MOLYBDENUM STEEL
BEARING : CHROME STEEL
CONE : HIGH CARBON STEEL
CUP : HIGH CARBON STEEL
SCREWS : STAINLESS STEEL
WASHERS : STAINLESS STEEL

A

669 Left hand pedal axle
670 Right hand pedal axle
672 Inserted race
673 Pedal axle washer
674 Pedal axle cone
675 Pedal axle lock nut
676 Toe clip bolt
677 Toe clip washer
678 Inner dust cap
679 Pedal dust cap
2103 Pedal special ball races

669   670   B

672   673   674   675   676   677   678   679   2103

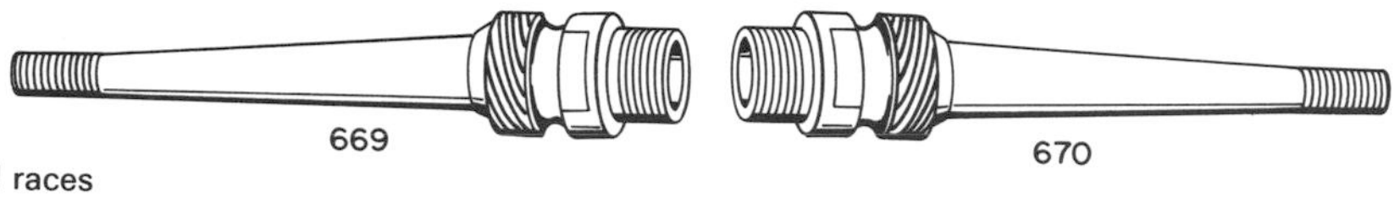

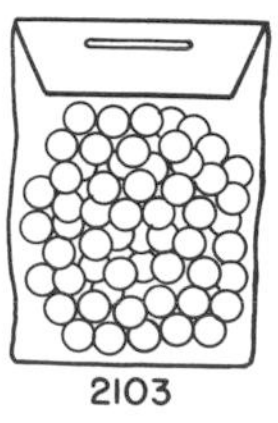

Fig. 7.65   The pedal. Top, Cross section of high-quality racing pedal; bottom, Parts of a pedal (Campagnolo).

If you plan to use toe clips, select the proper size. These come in three sizes: short, or Ladies'; medium or standard; and extra long. If none of these fit the shoes which you plan to use, extra length can be obtained by using longer bolts and inserting washers between the front of the pedal and the clip. Be certain that with the longer pedal-clip combination, you have sufficient clearance between your clip and the mudguard or front wheel. If there is interference at this spot, it can spill you unceremoniously when maneuvering in traffic or when turning the bars as you slowly climb a hill. Otherwise, you must learn the technique of pointing your toe down at this point of interference. In racing at high speeds, this interference is of less concern, since the amount of handlebar turn is small and the point of interference not usually reached.

What pedal pressures do you expect to apply? Will you be climbing hills or sprinting with high-power outputs? Will you be using your toe clips to enable you to pull up with the opposite foot—thus pushing with additional force on the downside pedal? Since your foot is about two inches outboard of the point of pedal attachment, tremendous bending moments must be resisted by the pedal spindle. If this spindle is made of mild steel, stresses can readily exceed the 40,000 psi yield strength of the spindle, and you can actually bend it. A stronger, alloy steel may be needed.

Do you want to be able to rest your foot on either side of the pedal? A symmetrically shaped pedal is needed. On the other hand, a racing pedal (always used with toe clips) needs only one surface for the foot. The other side can be cut away, particularly at the ends, to give increased ground clearance. This is important when turns are made at high speeds. If a pedal end hits the ground as it is being pressed down on the forward stroke, it can lift your front wheel off the ground for an instant and cause you to lose control.

Racing pedals are made narrow with the outer bearing set farther in to provide additional ground clearance on turns. This design may cause the outside tab which limits foot side movement to interfere with the shoe you use for touring and walking. Be certain to check this point.

How about bearing quality? Pedals work at poor conditions for lubrication. Their speeds are low—from 40 to 140 rpm, compared to the 250 rpm that wheels turn at 20 mph. Lubrication is of extra importance for reasonable bearing life. Due to the small bearing size, the cup and cone must be made of clean, hardened, high-quality alloy steel to accurate tolerances for minimum friction. Even at best, unless the bearing is kept free of water and grit, the friction and wear are greatly increased. Pedals must be designed to seal out dirt and moisture. Bearing surfaces must be accurately centered and their contours ground precisely.

Frank Whitt of London has measured the friction of various pedals under load. One high-grade racing pedal had a coefficient of rolling resistance of only 0.007, while a cheaper ball bearing pedal had a friction of three times this amount. Even worse, a sintered plain-bearing pedal (that had at that time been placed in service by Raleigh Industries) had a friction resistance twenty times that of the high-grade pedal.

Are you looking for weight reduction? This means less rotating weight and a snappier handling bicycle that is easier to accelerate in sprints. A great difference exists in this department. Here are some examples:

Table 7.2

WEIGHTS OF VARIOUS PEDALS

	Grams Per Pair
East Rochester Super, Al-Ti	235
Lyotard 460 or 45 CA	340
Campagnolo #1037 and Zeus Alloy racing pedals (extra-strong)	350
Lyotard 65 Road, or Zeus track pedals	400
Marcel Bethet	400
Campagnolo and Kyukoto KAW-1400 steel road pedals (extra-strong)	about 456
Atom 700	380
Lyotard steel, double sided	470 to 515
Schwinn rubber bow pedals	585
Union rubber pedals	620
Raleigh solid rubber, plain bearing	700
Torrington rubber pedal	840

The Zeus, Campagnolo, and Kyukoto pedals are made of chrome-molybdenum steel. The Lyotard 65 uses chrome-molybdenum steel for their pedal axle and bearing. The outer end of the Lyotard pedal has an accurately screwed-on cover which seals out dirt and water and permits quick access for bearing adjustment, cleaning, and lubrication. The crank end, being long and grooved for grease retention, bars the entry of dirt and moisture. Thus, the finest pedals are stronger, have less friction, are more resistant to weather, will last longer, are more sturdy against impact, and can be repaired and lubricated.

Cheaper pedals often are nondismantleable. They are not readily cleanable. Thy can be lubricated at the inner end, so grit will flow into the outer bearing if oiled. There is no attempt to seal the bearings—indeed, the inner set of balls can often be seen openly. However, they are inexpensive, and a new pair costs little more than the labor cost to dismantle and clean other pedals.

Fig. 7.66   Reflectorized rubber tread bow pedal.

Fig. 7.68   Cinelli pedal and special shoe plate reduces weight and eliminates toe clip and strap. Shoe plate attached is shown at bottom.

Fig. 7.67   Reflectorized rattrap pedal.

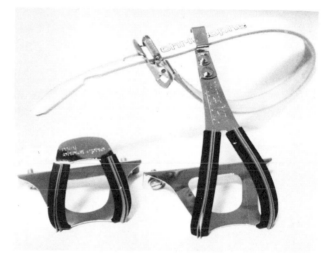

Fig. 7.69   Mini toe clip used without strap for city riding (left) and standard toe clip with strap—both equipped with plastic shoe protectors.

The sintered, non–ball bearing types have high coefficients of friction and are not recommended.

Federal and many state regulations now require that pedals be equipped with reflectors on front and rear. In California, these must be built into the pedal.

Toe Clips and Straps

Should I use toe clips and straps? At slow speeds on balloon tire bikes, the toe clip can be eliminated when stops and starts are frequent, when dressy street shoes are used, and when the terrain is level. A shoe larger than the close-fitting cycling shoe can be too large to fit comfortably into the clip and may not permit the ball of the foot to center on the pedal. Extralong clips can be used, but these do not give enough support with proper cycling shoes. Grooved sole shoes may lock into the pedal plates, preventing easy removal in a hurry.

Tightly strapped clips are needed only for very high-speed, forceful pedaling. Aluminum shoe plates whose slots fit into the pedal side plates are helpful in allowing the foot to be pushed forward and pulled back on hills or in sprints, but they make walking difficult. Unless smooth, hard-soled shoes are used, it is unnecessary to tighten the straps. Adequate ankle action will provide most of the advantages of clips and straps, yet feet can be withdrawn in an instant.

The sense of security provided by knowing that with toe clips and straps the foot will not slide off the pedal if a bump is hit and that one can press, pull, and lift with the feet makes riding both easier and safer. I would strongly recommend their use except for the special conditions listed. Take the time and effort to learn the knack of getting your feet in and out at once and you can reap the dividends.

GEARS AND GEARING

Gear shifting devices enable you to match your pedal speed and pedal pressure to suit the steepness of the hill you encounter, the load you are carrying, the direction and the speed of the wind that aids or opposes your efforts, and your own desires or capability at the moment.

Hub Gears

There are numerous methods used. The automatic two-speed gear made by Bendix and Fichtel and Sachs provides a lower gear for startup, and a higher gear for speed and easy running. These rear hub gears are combined with a coaster brake. Gear shifting is accomplished by momentarily back pedaling. The Shimano Automatic 5 is either combined with a five-speed derailleur or with a single rear sprocket. It automatically goes into low range as the pedal speed decreases and up-shifts as the wheel speed increases. The speed at which the drop into the 25% lower gear takes place can

be adjusted to suit the rider's ability and the terrain encountered by an external spring tension adjustment.

The Bendix Yellow Band drops to a 32% speed reduction upon back-pedaling, while the Bendix Blue Band engages into "overdrive" on back-pedaling, which gives a 47% increase in speed. All these types use planetary gearing to obtain the difference in output speed. Bendix also makes a back-pedaling coaster brake.

3, 4, and 5-speed planetary gearing systems are available in rear-wheel hub units, and some are combined with a coaster brake in the same unit.

Front crank hanger mounted transmissions have been made by Dana Corporation in the United States and Tritenne in France. The Dana has 3 speeds (normal, 33% increase, and 25% decrease from normal), similar to most 3-speed hub gears. The overall range of 1.78:1 compares to 1.47 of the 2-speed. This unit (see Fig. 7.73) can be combined with 3, 4, or 5-speed rear hubs, or with coaster brake units, or with 5-speed derailleur units to provide a range of 9, 12, or 15 speeds.

Combined with a 3-speed rear hub, the front transmission will provide a total gearing range of 3.2:1 with nine steps. Used with a 5-speed rear hub of 2.25:1, it

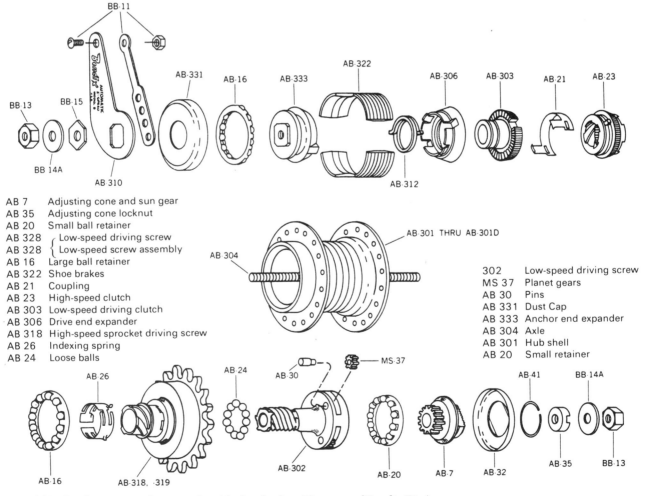

AB 7	Adjusting cone and sun gear
AB 35	Adjusting cone locknut
AB 20	Small ball retainer
AB 328	Low-speed driving screw
AB 328	Low-speed screw assembly
AB 16	Large ball retainer
AB 322	Shoe brakes
AB 21	Coupling
AB 23	High-speed clutch
AB 303	Low-speed driving clutch
AB 306	Drive end expander
AB 318	High-speed sprocket driving screw
AB 26	Indexing spring
AB 24	Loose balls

302	Low-speed driving screw
MS 37	Planet gears
AB 30	Pins
AB 331	Dust Cap
AB 333	Anchor end expander
AB 304	Axle
AB 301	Hub shell
AB 20	Small retainer

Fig. 7.70   Bendix two-speed automatic with shoe brakes. *(Courtesy of Bendix Div.)*

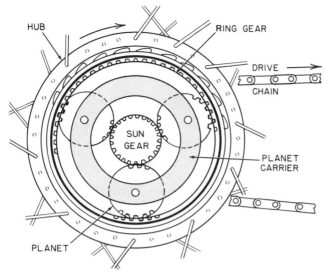

Fig. 7.71   Planetary gearing system.

1   Bell Crank Complete
2   Axle Nut (⅜")
3   Lock Washer
4   L.H. Lock Nut
5   Brake Arm
6   Arm Clip (⅝")
    Arm Clip (¹¹⁄₁₆")
    Arm Clip (¾")
7   Arm Bolt (M6×15)
8   Arm Nut
9   Arm Clip Bolt (ISO thread)
10 Arm Clip Nut (ISO thread)

11 Dust Cap L
12 Brake Cone
*13 Ball Retainer B
14 Brake Shoe
15 Brake Shoe Spring
16 Return Spring
17 Spring Guide
18 Slide Spring
19 Carrier
20 Pawl Pin D
21 Pawl Spring D
22 Pawl D

23 Pinion Pin
*24 Planet Pinion
25 Thrust Washer
26 Stop Nut
27 Non-turn Washer
28 Lock Nut B
29 Clutch Spring B
*30 Push Rod (4⁹⁄₃₂")
31 Axle (6⅝")
32 Axle Key
33 Sliding Clutch
34 Clutch Washer
35 Clutch Spring A
36 Hub Shell 28H
    Hub Shell 36H
37 Ring Gear
38 Pawl Spring E
39 Pawl E
*40 Pawl Pin C
41 Cam
42 Stop Ring
43 R.H. Ball Cup
44 Driver
*45 Ball Retainer A
*46 Dust Cap A
*47 Dust Cap
*48 Sprocket Wheel 16T
*48 Sprocket Wheel 18T
    Sprocket Wheel 19T
    Sprocket Wheel 20T
*49 Snap Ring C
*50 R.H. Cone
*51 R.H. Lock Nut
52 Guide Roller Assem. 1"
    Guide Roller Assem. 1⅛"
53 Stopper Band Assem. 1"
    Stopper Band Assem. 1⅛"
    Stopper Band Assem. ⅝"
    Stopper Band Assem. ½"
54 Trigger Lever Assembly
55 Grip Control Assembly
*56 Bell Crank Locknut

* All parts asterisked are interchangeable in Shimano 3-speed hub.

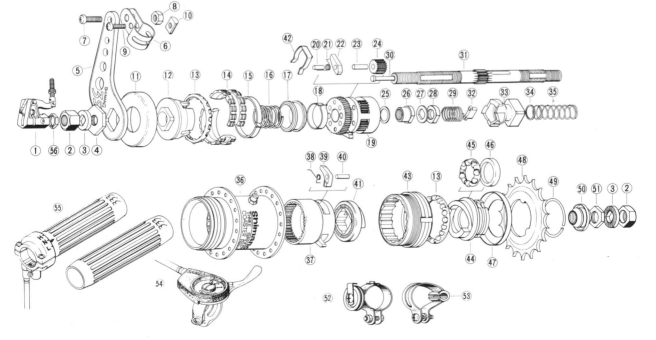

Fig. 7.72   Shimano three-speed hub and coaster brake combination. (*Courtesy of Shimano American Corporation*)

gives a total range of 3.96:1. Used with a 5-speed rear derailleur with 14 to 34 sprockets, the gearing range will be an impressive 4.35:1. The Dana unit is rather bulky and heavy; the Tritenne has been used in racing.

An interesting drive has been developed by IPD Corporation, Carson City, Nevada (see Fig. 7.74). Cranks drive rotating cams. These in turn engage cam followers attached to two center-pivoted bell cranks. The opposite arm is notched along its length. A follower can be positioned by a hand control where desired along this rack, reducing or amplifying the cam motion over a range of 5 to 1. Chains attached to these followers drive

a rear hub mounted freewheel. The width, weight, and cost are moderate. The driving-cam shape can be designed and selected to make maximum effectiveness of muscular ability at various points in the crank rotation. Higher effective gearing is thus possible.

3, 4, and 5-speed hub gears are made by Sturmey-Archer of England, while only the three-speed is made also by Shimano of Japan, and Fichtel and Sachs of Germany. The internal-geared hub is well protected from rain and road grit. They are operated either by frame or handlebar-mounted controls or by a handlebar twist grip control. If kept well oiled, they will

Fig. 7.73   Dana three-speed front planetary transmission.

Fig. 7.74   IPD infinitely variable cam-actuated bellcrank drive. *(Courtesy of IPD Corporation)*

Fig. 7.75   Internal construction of Shimano 333 three-speed hub. *(Courtesy of Shimano American Corporation)*

1	Left hand axle nut	27	Driver
2	Axle lock washer	28	Sprocket dust cap
3	Locknut	29	Sprocket 13T ½ × ⅛'' for RSW
4	Axle washer, ⅛'' thick	29	Sprocket 14T ½ × ⅛''
5	Cone with dust cap	29	Sprocket 15T ½ × ⅛''
6	Outer dust cap combined	29	Sprocket 16T ½ × ⅛''
7	Ball cage with 8 ball bearings	29	Sprocket 17T ½ × ⅛''
8	Shell—40 hole—and ball cup combined	29	Sprocket 18T ½ × ⅛''
		29	Sprocket 19T ½ × ⅛''
9	Shell—36 hole—and ball cup combined	29	Sprocket 20T ½ × ⅛''
		29	Sprocket 22T ½ × ⅛''
10	Lubricator, plastic	30	Sprocket spacing washer
11	Axle—5¾''	31	Sprocket circlip
12	Axle—6¼''	32	Cone lockwasher
13	Dowel	33	Right hand axle nut
14	Sun pinion	34	Axle key
15	Low gear pawl	35	Indicator coupling 5¾'' axle
16	Pawl pin	36	Indicator coupling 6¼'' axle
17	Planet cage	37	Thrust ring
18	Planet pinion	38	Clutch washer
19	Pinion pin		*Special Parts*
20	Clutch sleeve	39	Clutch spring
21	Clutch	40	Clutch spring cap
22	Gear ring	41	Indicator coupling locknut
23	Gear ring pawl	42	Plastic protector cap
24	Pawl spring	43	Indicator coupling, short
25	Right hand ball ring	43	Indicator coupling, long
26	Inner dust cap		

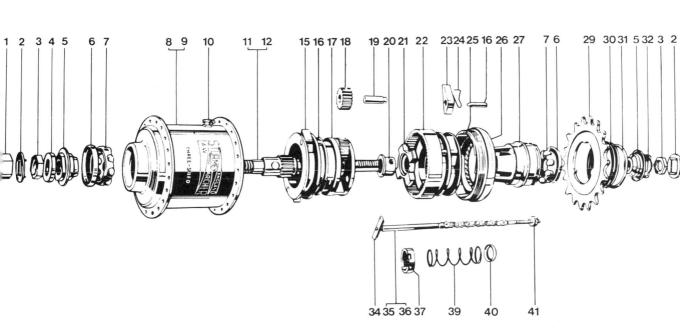

Fig. 7.76   Internal construction of Sturmey-Archer AW three-speed hub. A, Driving pawl and spring; B, Driver and assembly; C, Driving pawl and spring; D, Correct midposition adjustment of the indicator spindle.

work under all weather conditions for long periods without complaint. The fact that they can be shifted while at a standstill is an advantage if the downshift was not made prior to a stop. However, their range and speed-change steps are a fixed function of their design. By changing rear sprockets, the entire range can be shifted higher or lower, but the step ratio is fixed. Efficiency through the gear range is lower than for a clean derailleur. This reduction is amplified for a dual internal-geared system.

How the Hub Gear Works

While the internal parts are many and complicated, the planetary gearing system used in a hub gear need not be mysterious. Gear teeth on the axle of the hub do not rotate. The axle is prevented from rotating by flats on its ends which fit into the rear fork end slots. (see Figs. 7.71 and 7.75). The axle carries both the wheel bearing cones which permit wheel rotation and the weight applied to the wheel (the same as in an ordinary hub). Three small gears, called "planet gears," each on its own small axle, are mounted into a planet carrier housing which surrounds the axle or "sun" gear.

The ring gear encloses the planet gears—which mesh with the sun gear and roll around it. The ring gear is a ring with internal gear teeth which also mesh with the planet gears. Spring-loaded pushers, called "pawls," are mounted on the outside of both the ring gear and the planet carrier. The chain-driven drive sprocket, which accepts the rider's power output from the pedals, is mounted on a ball-bearing-mounted "driver."

A clutch which can be moved to the left or the right by the gear selector transfers the rider's power to the proper parts. Notches in parts attached to the hub shell receive power through the proper "pushers," or pawls.

Referring again to Figure 7.71, if the clutch connects power directly to the ring gear member, its pawls will drive the hub shell at the same speed as the chain-driven rear sprocket. This is called direct, or "normal," gear.

Power applied to the planet carrier forces the planet gears—through their stub axles—to roll around the central sun gear. Their teeth also mesh with the ring gear teeth, which is at a greater diameter than the planet gear axles. You can see that the ring gear is pushed with what might be termed a "whiplash" effect at a speed faster than that of the sprocket-driven planet carrier. Thus the pawls on the ring gear increase the speed of the hub shell.

If we now change our clutch position to connect the driving input power to the ring gear and disengage its pawls, the ring gear will drive the planet gears. As the planets roll around the "sun" gear through their stub axles, they drive the planet carrier. The planet carrier then runs at a slower rpm than that of the ring gear. If we connect the pawls on the exterior of the planet car-

rier to the hub shell, the hub shell rotates at this lower rpm. This is what happens in low gear.

Friction between the heavily loaded gears and the stub axles causes some power loss, but this is minimized by a good, clean lubricant. Since dirt and lack of lubrication can measurably reduce hub gear efficiency, extra care must be taken in the design to maintain cleanliness and prevent oil leaks.

The five-speed SC hub possesses a second set of planetary gears. The sun and planet gears are made in different proportions than those in the primary set. Thus, the whiplash effect differs in magnitude when these gears are selected through the gear selector control. A "super-high" and a "super-low" gear selection is thus available in the place of the original high and low gears.

DERAILLEUR OR CHAIN GEARS

"Gear," the speed of rotation of the rear wheel compared to that of the pedals, can also be varied by changing the relative sizes of the sprockets on the rear hub and on the pedal cranks.

If the front sprocket is enlarged, its toothed surface runs faster at a given pedal rpm than it did when smaller. If you turn a roller skate wheel at the same rpm as a bicycle wheel, it would travel much less distance on the ground. Since the chain rides on the toothed, outer circumference of the sprockets without slipping, making the front sprocket larger, or the rear sprocket smaller, increases rear wheel rpm. To decrease rear wheel speed in relation to pedal speed, we may increase the rear sprocket diameter (or the number of teeth), decrease the front sprocket diameter, or fit one with fewer teeth, or both.

A series of sprockets mounted side by side on the rear wheel (as many as six in number) provides the desired changes in derailleur gearing. Another set of sprockets is mounted on the pedal cranks. There may be one, two, or three of these, although more have been tried experimentally. By suitable mechanisms, the chain can be shifted—or derailed—to any desired combination of sprocket sizes. If there are two in the front and five in the rear, we can have two times five, or 10 speeds. If we have three front sprockets, we can have three times five, or 15 possible combinations.

A spring tensioning device provides a means to "use up" the extra chain length required if the largest front and rear sprockets are engaged when smaller-sized sprockets are in use. These chain-shifting and tensioning devices are called "derailleurs."

Instead of using multiple side by side sprockets, the same effect could be obtained if the front and rear sprocket sizes were varied. This would permit the chain to run in a straight line from front to rear, instead of at the odd angles that occur in some combinations of derailleur gears. The Tokheim transmission

Fig. 7.77   In the Huret derailleur, cage pivots at a distinct angle to the horizontal moving downward as it moves inward toward the larger sprockets. Positions of actuating roller and guide cage remain relatively constant in relation to the freewheel cogs, even with wide-range change in size of the front chainwheels. Suntour GT has a similar action.

Fig. 7.78   In the Campagnolo Nuovo Record derailleur, cage travel in and out parallel to hub axle, and jockey rollers axis offset; up and forward on outer, small rear cogs; and down and back on large rear cogs, giving additional clearance for the larger cogs. This is excellent when used with front chainwheels of limited size range, however, when used with wide-range front chainwheels, shifts to a small front chainwheel cause cage to move forward and up, independently of rear cog size, resulting in improper jockey pulley-rear cog spacing under some conditions.

Fig. 7.79   Shimano Eagle derailleur has heavy protecting shroud and "cable saver" spring to minimize accidental damage.
(Courtesy of Shimano American Corporation)

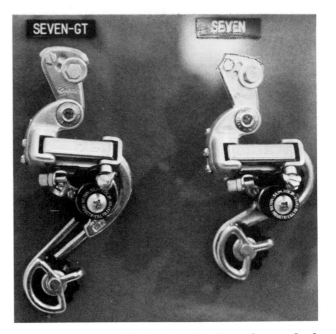

Fig. 7.80   Suntour GT Touring derailleurs feature fixed cage location and slanted cage travel, easy chain removal, and chain wrap adjustment.

(Fig. 7.88) permits five rear segmented-tooth sprocket sizes to be selected by moving the sprocket segments into or out of engagement with the chain.

The expandable chainwheel, or front sprocket, has been used to a limited degree for many years. In 1936, the Nealeson expandable chainwheel was introduced in England. Chainwheel sections could be moved while riding into five separate diameters, with a range of action of two to one, say 26 to 52 teeth. In 1973, the Hagen Infinitely variable drive was introduced by Don Hagen, of the TCM New Products Division of Minneapolis, Minnesota. It was designed for replacement on standard three-piece cottered cranksets. A series of small one-direction cogs forms a sprocket. Their action radius is controlled at will by the rotation of a disc with a scroll-shaped groove. This is done by rotating the pedals forward to raise, or backward to lower, the gear ratio. Two-and-one-half pedal turns accomplish the full range change of 2.85:1, which is equivalent to an effective front sprocket size of from 19.5 to 56 teeth. Used with a three-speed rear hub or a rear derailleur, even higher gear ranges are obtained, with the exact ratios desired a possibility. Gear shifting can be done while riding or at a standstill (see Fig. 7.142).

Gear Size

The term "gear" is generally expressed in two manners, and in racing circles sometimes by a third—the actual sprocket sizes used, such as 52 × 14.

In America and England, the ratio of the number of actual revolutions that the rear wheel turns for each crank revolution is multiplied by the diameter of the rear wheel in inches. This gives a number, called "gear," which represents the size of a driving wheel that would travel the same distance if turned one revolution by the pedals. In metric countries, the term "development" is used. This is the actual distance in meters that the driving wheel moves along the ground in one revolution of the pedals. Thus, sprocket size ratio is multiplied by π (3.1416) and by the wheel diameter in meters.

Gear or development may be calculated by dividing the number of teeth on the front sprocket in use, by the number of teeth in the rear sprocket. If a hub or crank-hanger gear train is used, the sprocket ratio is multiplied by the internal gearing increase or decrease. Then multiply by the wheel diameter, or wheel

Fig. 7.81 Shimano 600 derailleur uses inside-the-chain guiding on upper pulley, permitting closer spacing to wheel and reduced wheel dish.

Fig. 7.82 The wide-range Crane GS has a much lower cage. The upper jockey pulley moves out and down for greater clearance and capacity to handle wider ranges of gearing.
(Courtesy of Shimano American Corporation)

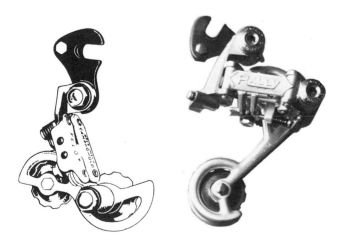

Fig. 7.84 Campagnolo Velox (on left) and its companion, the extra-wide-range (42-teeth capacity) Rally touring derailleur.

Fig. 7.85 Simplex SX 400 GT touring derailleur (left) with 36 tooth cog, 40 teeth difference. AR 637P (right) with 30 tooth cog, 30 teeth difference capacity.

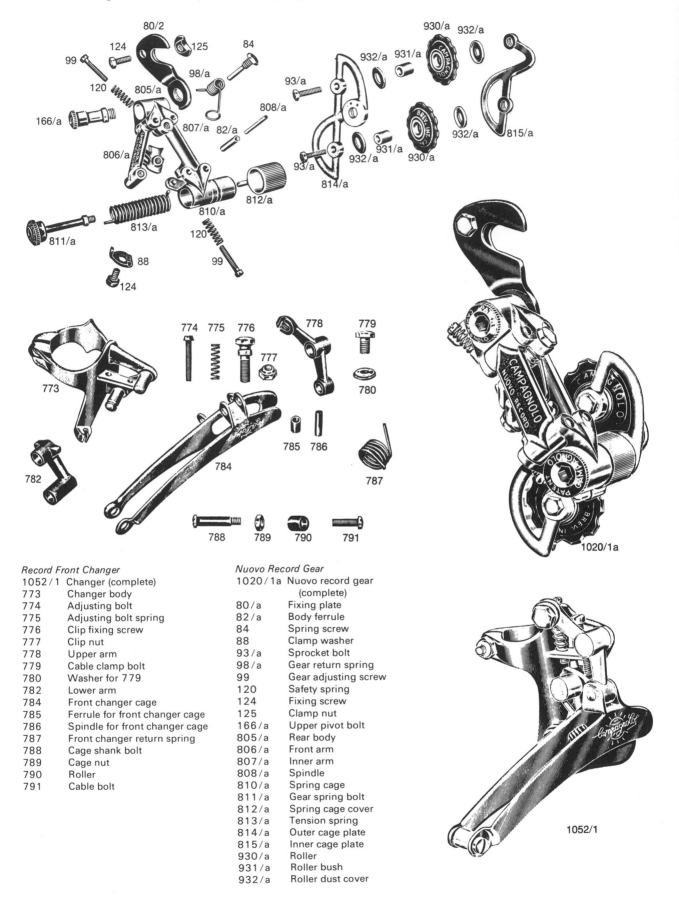

Record Front Changer

1052/1	Changer (complete)
773	Changer body
774	Adjusting bolt
775	Adjusting bolt spring
776	Clip fixing screw
777	Clip nut
778	Upper arm
779	Cable clamp bolt
780	Washer for 779
782	Lower arm
784	Front changer cage
785	Ferrule for front changer cage
786	Spindle for front changer cage
787	Front changer return spring
788	Cage shank bolt
789	Cage nut
790	Roller
791	Cable bolt

Nuovo Record Gear

1020/1a	Nuovo record gear (complete)
80/a	Fixing plate
82/a	Body ferrule
84	Spring screw
88	Clamp washer
93/a	Sprocket bolt
98/a	Gear return spring
99	Gear adjusting screw
120	Safety spring
124	Fixing screw
125	Clamp nut
166/a	Upper pivot bolt
805/a	Rear body
806/a	Front arm
807/a	Inner arm
808/a	Spindle
810/a	Spring cage
811/a	Gear spring bolt
812/a	Spring cage cover
813/a	Tension spring
814/a	Outer cage plate
815/a	Inner cage plate
930/a	Roller
931/a	Roller bush
932/a	Roller dust cover

Fig. 7.83   The superbly made Campagnolo Record set is shown assembled on right and its parts detailed.

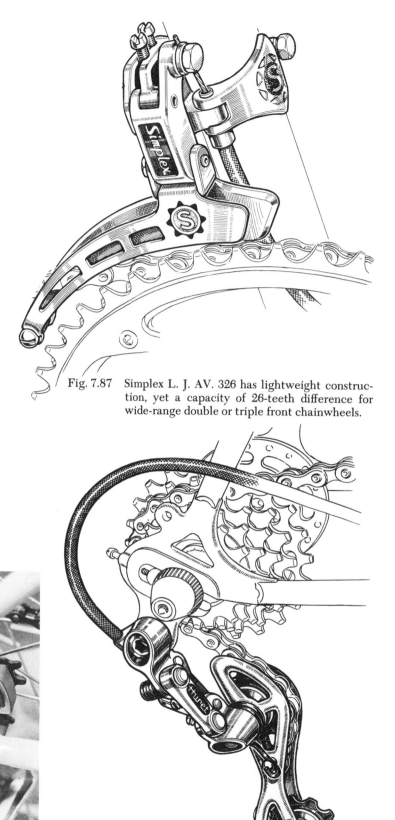

Fig. 7.86 Simplex Super Prestige AR 615 racing rear derailleur.

Fig. 7.87 Simplex L. J. AV. 326 has lightweight construction, yet a capacity of 26-teeth difference for wide-range double or triple front chainwheels.

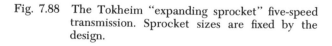

Fig. 7.88 The Tokheim "expanding sprocket" five-speed transmission. Sprocket sizes are fixed by the design.

Fig. 7.90 Huret Jubilee Touring derailleur is ultralight in weight. The short cage racing model is even lighter. *(Courtesy of Ets Huret et ses Fils)*

Fig. 7.89   Shimano Positive Preselect system uses a rigid transmission cable through the full length casing, which places the 5-position indexing member into the desired gear position. Spring tension on the cage moves it into alignment with the freewheel sprocket when the drive chain is in motion.   *(Courtesy of Shimano American Corp.)*

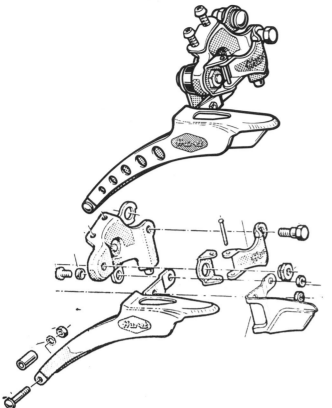

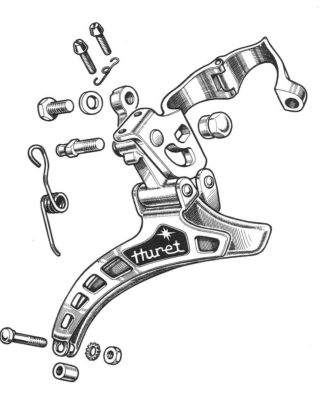

Fig. 7.92 Lightest weight front derailleur—Huret Jubilee. Carefully shaped body eliminates one parallelogram arm. *(Courtesy of Ets Huret et ses Fils)*

Fig. 7.91 Huret CPSC front derailleur has closed top with rounded edges. Separate inner chain deflecting piece "gives" as chain is contacted for smooth shift. *(Courtesy of Ets Huret et ses Fils)*

circumference to obtain development. This is a lot of work, so to make it easy, gear tables are provided at the end of this chapter. With these, you need only decide on the sprocket sizes. For the wheel size selected, gear can be looked up in the tables.

Tables of sprocket sizes, gear calculated for 27-inch wheels follow at the end of this section. Correction factors are indicated for figuring development, or calculating gear for other wheel sizes. Gear tables for three-speed and five-speed hub gears are separately listed.

There is an art to shifting gears properly. It involves both technique and timing. Prior to using your gears for the first time, the bicycle should be hung up from hooks so that the pedals can be turned to drive the rear wheel. Turning the pedals easily, shift both front and rear changers in sequence, a step at a time. Check for adjustment at the extremes, for overshifting or sluggish shifting. On three-speed hubs, an indicator usually indicates proper alignment in the center position. See that this is properly adjusted. Check derailleurs for loose or broken parts and for misalignment or for sloppy fit of the parts, which indicates wear. With both derailleurs on their largest sprockets, shift off and again onto the large front sprocket while turning the pedals. The derailleur should not bind due to too short a chain when climbing

Fig. 7.93 Suntour Ratchet Down Tube Shifter. Down tube operation permits minimum complexity, cable length, weight, and friction.

(Courtesy of Maeda Industrial Corporation)

onto the front sprocket teeth. Likewise, put the chain on the smallest front sprocket, and shift onto and off the largest rear sprocket. There must be no binding or interference of the cage with the sprockets under these conditions. Some types of derailleur will give interference under this condition.

Closely observe the derailleur action both front and rear, as described in the series of photographs which follow. This will help you to understand the action, and the precautions in use will become obvious.

Generally, as the chain is shifted closer to the center line of the bicycle, the gear is reduced. In most derailleurs, but not all, moving the left shifting lever—for the front derailleur—forward moves the chain toward the low-gear position. Moving the right lever—for the rear unit—forward places the chain in the high-gear position.

Refer to your owner's manual or count the number of teeth on both front and rear sprocket sets. Then make a table of actual gear values in the various combinations and cement or attach it to the frame top tube with clear tape. Until you memorize the values, it

Fig. 7.94   Suntour Stem Shifters permit shifter to be operated from top of handlebars.
(Courtesy of Maeda Industrial Corporation)

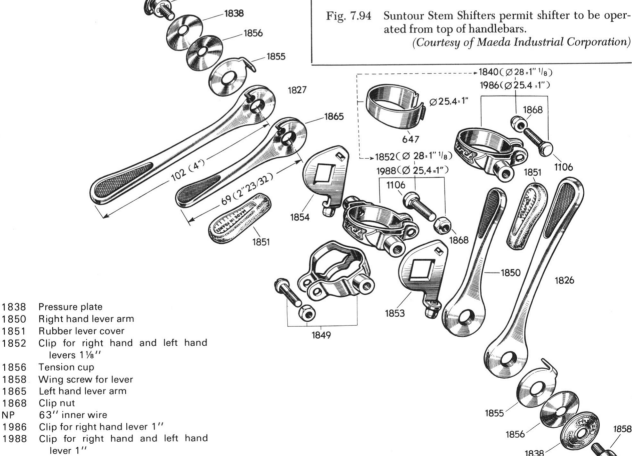

1838	Pressure plate
1850	Right hand lever arm
1851	Rubber lever cover
1852	Clip for right hand and left hand levers 1⅛''
1856	Tension cup
1858	Wing screw for lever
1865	Left hand lever arm
1868	Clip nut
NP	63'' inner wire
1986	Clip for right hand lever 1''
1988	Clip for right hand and left hand lever 1''

Fig. 7.96   Standard down tube derailleur shifting mechanism (Huret). Screw (1858) is tightened to compress Belleville spring (1856) and create sufficient friction to withstand the derailleur movement shifting spring tension. Two choices of lever length are provided. *(Courtesy of Ets Huret et ses Fils)*

Fig. 7.94a Six and seven speed freewheels in aluminum and titanium with minimum cog size of 12 teeth.

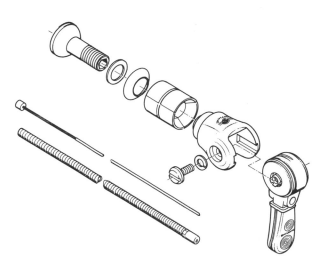

Fig. 7.95 Handlebar-end derailleur controls that are very handy when the hands are on the "drops" are preferred by some riders. An extra loop of operating cable and casing, under the handlebar tape, is needed.

(Courtesy of Ets Huret et ses Fils)

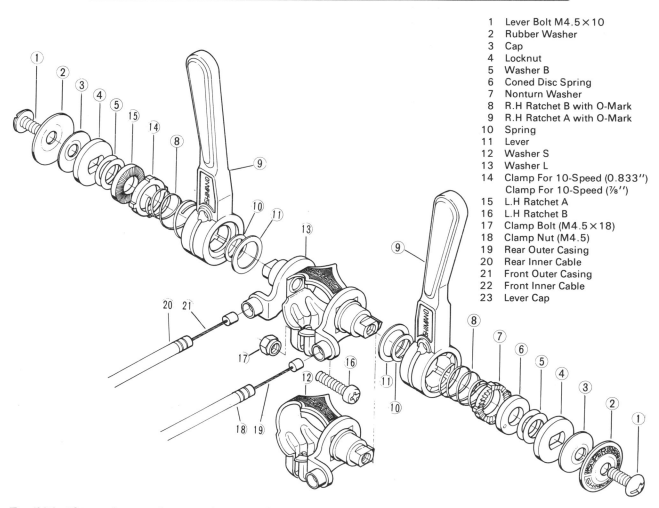

1	Lever Bolt M4.5×10
2	Rubber Washer
3	Cap
4	Locknut
5	Washer B
6	Coned Disc Spring
7	Nonturn Washer
8	R.H Ratchet B with O-Mark
9	R.H Ratchet A with O-Mark
10	Spring
11	Lever
12	Washer S
13	Washer L
14	Clamp For 10-Speed (0.833")
	Clamp For 10-Speed (⅞")
15	L.H Ratchet A
16	L.H Ratchet B
17	Clamp Bolt (M4.5×18)
18	Clamp Nut (M4.5)
19	Rear Outer Casing
20	Rear Inner Cable
21	Front Outer Casing
22	Front Inner Cable
23	Lever Cap

Fig. 7.97 This ratchet-type lever mechanism reduces shift lever effort by holding the lever in position against derailleur shifting spring tension. *(Courtesy of Shimano American Corporation)*

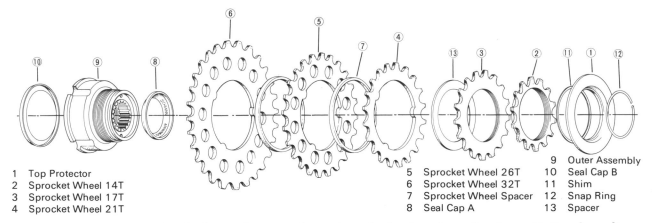

1	Top Protector	9	Outer Assembly
2	Sprocket Wheel 14T	10	Seal Cap B
3	Sprocket Wheel 17T	11	Shim
4	Sprocket Wheel 21T	12	Snap Ring
5	Sprocket Wheel 26T	13	Spacer
6	Sprocket Wheel 32T		
7	Sprocket Wheel Spacer		
8	Seal Cap A		

Fig. 7.98   While most multi-freewheels must be removed to replace wheel spokes, the modern type with three large slip-on sprockets requires unscrewing only the outer two cogs. Sealing discs (8 and 10) keep grit and water out of bearings and pawls. *(Courtesy of Shimano American Corporation)*

Fig. 7.99   Derailleur cage presses chain against outer chainwheel. At this point, the area contacted is moving upward at an angle, and the chain is actually lifted upward.

will guide you to the value of gear for each step, and will tell you which lever position to use. If your gearing range does not meet your needs, you will be able to determine what modifications can be made to reduce or widen the gear range or to change the size of intermediate steps. Note that if you do increase or decrease the sizes of either the largest or smallest sprockets, you must determine (1) whether the derailleur mechanism can clear the larger sprocket, (2) whether the tension adjuster can handle the increased difference in number of teeth accommodated (too slack a chain may result), (3) whether additional chain may be required if the sprocket sizes are made larger.

Principles of Derailleur Operation

The chain must move to effect a shift, but it must not be transmitting power. When shifting, relax pedal pressure at the instant of shifting. The faster it moves, the quicker it shifts. Shifting under power, the chain tries to remain seated in its former position, and extra strain and wear on the derailleur results.

Never shift derailleur position if the feet are being turned backward. The derailleur cages can be distorted or broken.

The shift lever should be moved firmly but without forcing; shift in succession one step at a time. This governs the speed of the shift lever. Moving the lever too fast may jam or derail the chain (as shown in Figs. 7.131–133).

When pedal pressure is relaxed, going uphill or against the wind, your bicycle speed will reduce quickly. If a shift is attempted on a hill or when going very slowly, the bicycle speed may drop to the point that balance is affected or that the shift cannot be completed. Notice the terrain ahead, and plan to shift while you have sufficient speed to complete it. Shift rapidly but without excess force. If you slow up too much, either stand on the pedals to gain speed and then reshift, or get off and walk.

Practice your gear shifting on a level street with little traffic. Get the feel of the levers. Listen for rubbing sounds either front or rear that indicate that your chain is rubbing on the derailleur cage. Try all possible gear combinations to learn the proper lever positions for each. Shift the full range in both directions to get the feel.

You will soon learn to time your shifting to the exact moment needed. Survey the terrain ahead and feel the force of the wind. The shift should be made before pedal effort has appreciably changed. When you shift at the proper point, there is no noise or clatter, nor any noticeable change in foot speed. If you wait too long to shift down, or you shift too large a range, your rhythm will be destroyed. Overspeeding the feet from too large a gear change will cause fatigue; maintain your pedal speed and let the bike slow down to your foot speed. *Don't* shift your gears to the bottom on every little change of slope! Climbing in higher gears will develop muscular strength and im-

Fig. 7.100 Chain lifts up near top of its travel. Rivet heads start to catch in tooth spaces, helping to drive chain forward and up.

Fig. 7.101 Tooth tips propel chain forward. Lifted chain disengages from inner chainwheel and is carried up and around outer wheel as rotation continues.

Fig. 7.102 Rear view of chain engaged on both sprockets. Driving power is still supplied by smaller chainwheel.

Fig. 7.103 Chain may start to settle into matching tooth spaces.

Fig. 7.104 Chain may also carry around due to mismatch in chain and tooth pitch.

Fig. 7.105 As the bottom is approached, the chain is lifted clear of engagement. Naturally these disengagements are resisted by rear derailleur chain tension adjustment.

Fig. 7.106 When chain is completely clear of inner chainwheel, power can be applied in the higher gears.

Fig. 7.107 Engagement completed.

Fig. 7.108 Chain is displaced at rear to a point on the inside of the chainwheel teeth.

Fig. 7.109 Unsupported, but under some tension, chain settles lower until it touches tooth of the inner chainwheel.

prove your ability. At a hilltop, if the going has been hard, let your feet speed up and relax the pressure for several dozen revolutions before speeding up. It limbers up the muscles and will allow you to rev up for a faster downhill dash.

With experience and improved technique, the value you get from your gears will increase. You will find that you can acquire the technique of shifting the rear derailleur without relaxing much power and the front with only an instant of relaxation. Your timing will improve. Practice makes perfect.

Hub gears are shifted with pressure relaxed, but they have the additional advantage of downshifting when stopped. At a traffic light, your derailleur must

Fig. 7.110 As chain settles into inner tooth spaces, its new position is stabilized. Slower speed of top position tends to pull front loop towards inner chainwheel at lower front.

Fig. 7.111 Tension from rear changer pulls lower chain into engagement. Shift is completed.

Fig. 7.112 Derailleur testing machine at Schwinn Laboratory. Derailleur is continually shifted under power to determine points of weakness.
(Courtesy of Schwinn Bicycle Company)

be downshifted before you come to a stop if you want a lower gear to start up.

Using and Understanding Your Derailleur Gears

The rear derailleur shifts from the under, or unloaded side, and with care can be shifted by an expert rider even under considerable power.

The front derailleur on the other hand, also shifts as the chain approaches the sprocket, but in its case, the chain approaches on the upper or tension side. Thus as it attempts to lift onto the larger size sprocket, its weight and the chain tension produced by the rider forces it to remain in its lower position. It is necessary to maintain motion of the chain to effect a shift, but pedal pressure must be relaxed. Otherwise the derailleur cage may be badly damaged. Chain rivets and plates will catch on the shifting fork edges resulting in forces greater than the derailleur can withstand.

Coordination in maintaining pedal speed and pressure while manipulating the derailleur lever is an art that can be obtained with practice. When properly done, noise and strain are at a minimum. The chain travels quietly and precisely to the desired cog and settles silently or with a pleasant "plunk."

A quick, firm (but not forcing) motion of the gearshift lever is required. The rider's forward speed must be maintained during the shift, and a sluggish shift may allow the rider's speed to fall to the point where power is needed to maintain balance with the result that the shift cannot be completed. Resumption of power can tear off the derailleur mechanism in this case.

Figures 7.113–7.121 will help you to visualize what is happening as you shift gears, and the proper methods will be quickly learned.

Upshifting Your Rear Derailleur

In easy movement of the rear derailleur from low gear (large cog) to high gear (small cog), the chain is led off the bottom of the larger cog by the derailleur jockey cage and pulley. As it travels to the successively smaller sprockets, the jockey cage rotates backward by means of its spring, to maintain an even chain tension. The chain travels smoothly from low to high without disturbance (see Figs. 7.113–7.116).

If, however, the derailleur shift lever is thrust suddenly from low to high position, the chain will feed rapidly on the underside onto the small rear cog, while still remaining on the larger cogs on top (see Figs. 7.117–7.119).

As the chain disengages from the top of the large cog, it can snap outward and downward onto the small cog. This, being of smaller diameter, is traveling at a lower tooth speed (see Fig. 7.120). Figure 7.121 shows the tremendous whip which develops on the chain as viewed from the rear.

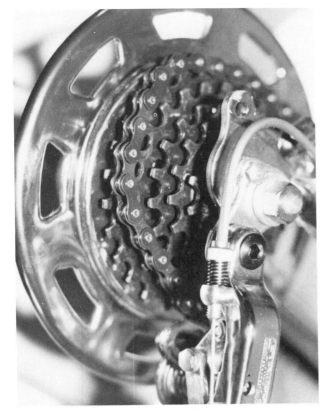

Fig. 7.113   Normal rear upshift—1.

Fig. 7.115   Normal rear upshift—3.

Fig. 7.114   Normal rear upshift—2.

Fig. 7.116   Normal rear upshift—4.

Fig. 7.117   Fast rear derailleur upshift—1.

Fig. 7.120   Action of chain in rapid upshift.

Fig. 7.118   Fast rear upshift—2.

Fig. 7.119   Fast rear upshift—3.

Fig. 7.121   High-speed photo of chain when upshifting rapidly.

Figures 7.122–7.125 are high-speed photos showing the action, viewed from the side, as the chain is completely derailed from the front chainwheel.

Other Chain Derailment Problems

A chainwheel bent or mismounted sharply out of true laterally can lead to chain derailment, but the chain can remain seated even with a considerable even wobble. If the wobble is sharp at any spot, if one or several sprocket teeth are bent out of line even a small amount, the chain may ride over the tooth tips. If a bump is struck, or if the chain is on the outside or inside rear cogs, it may feed off the front sprocket quite readily (see Fig. 7.126).

Downshifting Your Rear Derailleur to Low

The pressure of the jockey cage and roller on the side of the chain, as the gearshift lever is pulled back toward the low position, forces the chain against the next larger size cog face. Jockey pulley tension opposes friction, which lifts the chain. As the chain is led farther to the inside, a tooth space meshes with a chain roller and carries the chain along on the desired cog. The action continues until the chain is fully seated in the new position.

This action can be continued rapidly, step by step, until the full span of the rear cluster has been shifted.

Lever pressure must be firm but moderate, and power should be relaxed for best results (see Figures 7.127–7.130).

Fig. 7.124 The wave travels with the chain and may lift it clear from the front chainwheel. Due to angularity, chain can drop beside front chainwheel.

Fig. 7.125 Chain thus becomes completely disengaged.

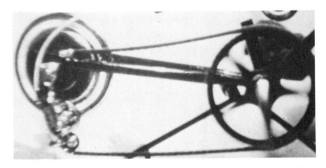

Fig. 7.122 As chain drops down from large cog to small, it attains a downward momentum at the rear as well as an outward momentum.

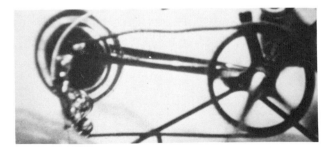

Fig. 7.123 Until rear-wheel speed increases, chain on small cog travels slower; a wave develops.

Fig. 7.127 Rear derailleur normal downshift to low gear—1.

Fig. 7.126   Sprocket teeth out of line or bent can cause   chain hop and derailment.

Fig. 7.128   Normal rear downshift—2.

Fig. 7.129   Normal rear downshift—3.

Shifting toward low gear on the rear cluster at too rapid a rate causes the chain to travel at an angle to the vertical, riding off the outside rear cog, and wedging itself between the small outside cog and the seat stay. Further pulling will not disengage the chain. Power is completely lost, and you may have to disengage the wheel nuts to free the chain. Figure 7.132 clearly shows the effect (see Figs. 7.131–7.133). Some freewheels have an outer ring which prevents this override.

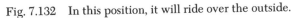

Fig. 7.132   In this position, it will ride over the outside.

Fig. 7.130   Normal rear downshift—4.

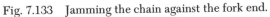

Fig. 7.133   Jamming the chain against the fork end.

Selection of Gearing Range

The range and spacing of the gears you select is based on the terrain you travel, the strength of wind you expect, your physical condition, and your age. If you are very strong and like to pull with all your strength, if your cadence is nimble and you can pedal fast, a relatively narrow range will suffice even in hilly country—say from 50 to 100 gear. If you are less athletic, or simply getting older, your strength and agility may be less, but with wider range gears, you can continue to climb and descend mountains.

Some riders recommend a geometric progression of gears of constant difference in ratio. For example, with succeeding gears 10% lower, a 10-speed would

Fig. 7.131   Downshifting rapidly bends the chain.

provide a 100–90–81–73–66–59–53–42–38–34 progression. Using the gear tables, at the end of this chapter, front and rear sprocket combinations can be selected to approach these values. I prefer the closely spaced midrange shown with larger changes at each end of the range. The constant ratio provides almost equal change of "feel" with each successive shift.

When 15 gears are fitted—a triple front sprocket and a 5-speed rear—or a 12-speed—double times a 6-speed rear—the chain angle comes into play. With short rear chain stays, the chain may rub on inner front/outer rear combinations or give excess friction on the outer front/inner rear combination. It may be more practicable when making your selection to avoid these extremes of angularity, or the top two front sprockets will have a small gap—5 or 6 teeth—with a much larger jump to the small inner front sprocket. This is then used with only the three large rear cogs to give a 10-speed of quite good selection plus three "granny gears" for the long, steep climbs. The extra weight of the small, third chainwheel is little.

The six-speed rear freewheel requires more distance between the fork ends—125 instead of 120 mm—and gives greater chain angle, a more "dished" wheel of less rigidity laterally. However, some riders prefer the ease of a front changer with only two positions, which is less troublesome for the racer or the newcomer to gearing.

When making your sprocket selection, front and rear, the "capacity" of each derailleur must be considered. This is termed the difference in number of sprocket teeth that the front derailleur can handle. A 22-tooth capacity will permit a 52–30-tooth, or a 48–26-tooth, chainwheel. The rear derailleur with its chain-tensioning mechanism must be able to "soak up" the sum of the difference in sprocket sizes both front *and* rear. For example, with a 14–30-tooth rear cog and a 52–30-front, the derailleur must handle 16 plus 22 or 38 teeth total difference. It must also be able to clear all rear cogs with the front chainwheel in either high or low range (see Figs. 7.77, 7.78 and 7.82).

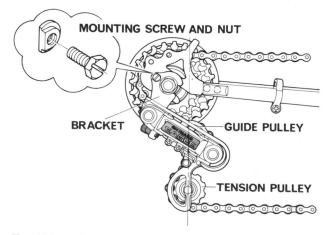

Fig. 7.134   Proper mounting and chain tension are required.

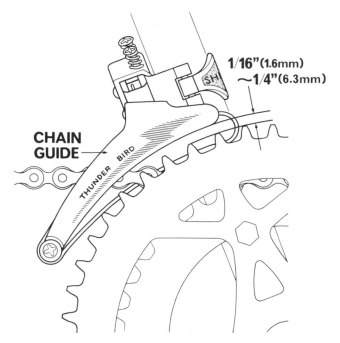

Fig. 7.135   Proper location of front derailleur cage.

To get the total range desired, you may choose between a wide-range front chainwheel set plus a small-range rear cog or a wide-range rear set plus a small-range front. The second method requires less rear derailleur "soak-up" capacity for the same total gear range. The wide-range front sprocket shifts less precisely when used with the offset pivoted cage rear derailleur, but it is quite satisfactory with the Huret and Suntour GT types. These use a slanted motion of the cage parallel to the sprockets. The shifting guide pulley remains in a constant position when front chainwheels of differing size are engaged.

If the chain rubs the front outer sprocket when the outer rear cogs are engaged, moving the front sprockets out a bit farther can reduce the difficulty. This may be prevalent with the six-speed rear. Remove the right-hand crank hanger cup and insert a 1⅜ inch inside diameter, ⅛ inch thick Sturmey-Archer cog spacer between it and the bracket shell.

Front changers vary in capacity. The Simplex 326 has a cage long enough to change a set of sprockets differing in range by 26 teeth. Huret 700 and Campagnolo are limited to 22 and 23. However, with a little ingenuity and some silver solder you can modify a front derailleur cage to increase its length. I use a modified Huret which smoothly handles a 55–49–26-tooth range (29 teeth). The Huret Jubilee 500 will handle a 26-tooth or greater difference with ease on a triple, but less on a double, due to its lifting movement as moved to the outside.

A wide inner shifting fork, as used on Campagnolo, some Simplex models, also some Shimano, Suntour and

Fig. 7.136   An improperly tightened or adjusted gear shift lever will wear out the front derailleur cage by allowing the chain to continuously rub.

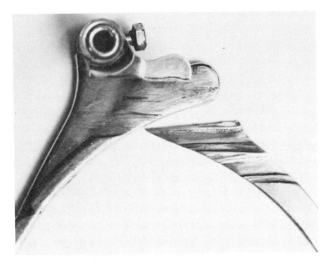

Fig. 7.137   Effect of chain rubbing derailleur cage.

Fig. 7.138   Forcing the shift or back pedaling with rear derailleur misaligned can cause extensive damage.

Triplex model front derailleurs, provides a more reliable shift from low to high than do narrower types.

Rear changers also vary considerably in the size of the maximum sprocket that can be handled and in the capacity in number of teeth difference accommodated. Racing gears feature close spacing to the freewheel for a crisper shift and reduced take-up capacity to eliminate bounce at speed on rough roads. However, there is a growing tendency for wider range capability on current models.

The Suntour GT, Shimano Crane GS, Campagnolo Gran Turismo accept a 36-tooth rear cog, Huret Super Allvit 34, and Campagnolo Nuovo Record 30, while Huret's lightweight Jubilee models 2254 and 2258 are designed for a 24-tooth cog.

Take-up capacities range from the Campagnolo Gran Turismo at 48 teeth, Simplex Maxi Prestige at 42, Super-Allvit at 40, and the Shimano GS and Suntour GT models at 38. Huret Allvit and Campagnolo

Nuovo Record stretch their ability at 29, while Huret's Jubilee models will handle 32 and 28. The Simplex Prestige will accept 37.

Weights vary considerably. The Campagnolo Gran Turismo weighs 440 grams, Shimano Eagle 400 grams, Suntour GT 400 grams, and the Simplex Maxi Prestige 300. The Shimano Crane GS is lighter at 280 and the Simplex Prestige lighter still at 230, while the Huret Racing Jubilee is 170 grams.

The use of dirt seals to reduce service difficulties and the use of slip-on inner cogs, so that all sprockets can be removed without the need to remove the freewheel body, are improving freewheel construction. Maillard in France, Zeus in Spain, and Maeda in Japan, are pioneers in the use of light-alloy freewheel bodies and cogs. Parts for the Maillard freewheel are forged and then machined for strength and accuracy. The aluminum alloy is then electrolytically treated to give it a hard surface.

The weight comparisons of six-speed, 13–18-tooth freewheels are: steel, 370 grams; titanium, 220 grams; and light alloy, 135 grams. Larger cogs would give a greater weight saving.

There are differences in freewheel threading. The French hub thread standard is 34.7 × 1-mm pitch (1.366 inches × 25.4 threads per inch). The English and Japanese standard (also used in the United States,

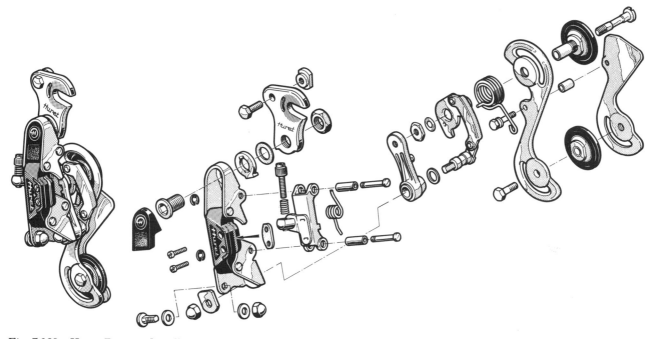

Fig. 7.139   Huret Duopar derailleur uses both lateral and longitudinal parallelograms to obtain extremely precise shifting even at low speeds under load. Capacity 36 tooth rear cog, 44 teeth difference. *(Courtesy of Ets Huret et ses Fils)*

Fig. 7.140   Shimano Uniglide chain (left) uses offset outer link plates to reduce sprocket and shifter pulley wear and facilitate shifting. Uniglide angled tooth freewheel reduces chain jamming and facilitates shifting into larger freewheel cogs. Conventional freewheel is shown on the right.   *(Courtesy of Shimano American Corporation)*

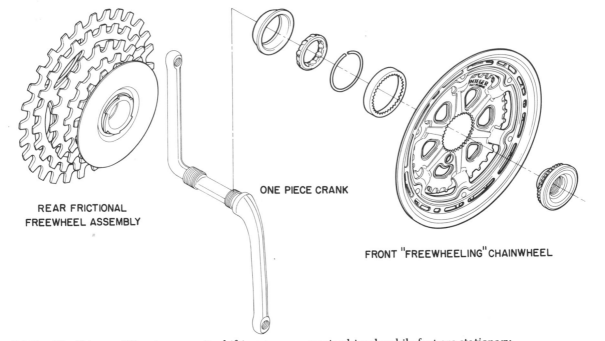

REAR FRICTIONAL FREEWHEEL ASSEMBLY

ONE PIECE CRANK

FRONT "FREEWHEELING" CHAINWHEEL

Fig. 7.141   The Shimano FF system permits shifting gears on moving bicycle while feet are stationary.

(Courtesy of Shimano American Corporation)

Fig. 7.142   Hagen expandable chainwheel drive. Left, Maximum ratio; right, Minimum ratio.

is 1.370 × 24 threads per inch. Do not attempt to interchange these, or you will ruin your hub threads. If you have an imported bicycle, make certain which threading is used before buying a new freewheel.

You will become accustomed to your derailleur if you make a table of gears and gear positions and cement it to your top tube in easy view. For example: with 52–46 front and a 13–16–20–25–31-tooth rear (see gear tables), you have:

108		88		70		56		45	
	96		78		62		50		40

GEAR TABLES

These tables are based on 27-inch diameter wheels of the "high-pressure road racing" type.

For tubulars and 700C tires, multiply by 0.99.

For full section 27 × 1¼ multiply by 1.01.

For 26-inch wheels, multiply by 0.94. For 24-inch wheels, 0.89; for 20-inch wheels, 0.74. To approximate "development" (meters per pedal revolution) multiply by 0.08. This is the actual number of meters traveled with one revolution of the pedals, and is the measure most common in continental Europe.

Table 7.3

GEAR TABLE FOR 27-INCH WHEELS (STANDARD)

Rear Sprocket Size	Chainwheel Size												
	26	28	30	32	34	36	38	39	40	42	43	44	45
12	58.5	63.0	67.5	72.0	76.5	81.0	85.5	87.2	90.0	94.5	96.7	99.0	101.2
13	54.0	58.1	62.3	66.5	70.6	74.8	78.9	81.1	83.1	87.2	89.3	91.4	93.4
14	50.1	54.0	57.8	61.7	65.6	69.4	73.3	75.2	77.1	81.0	82.9	84.9	86.8
15	46.8	50.4	54.0	57.6	61.2	64.8	68.4	70.2	72.0	75.6	77.4	79.2	81.0
16	43.9	47.2	50.6	54.0	57.4	60.7	64.1	65.2	67.5	70.9	72.5	74.3	75.9
17	41.3	44.4	47.6	50.8	54.0	57.1	60.3	61.9	63.5	66.7	68.3	69.9	71.5
18	39.0	42.0	45.0	48.0	51.0	54.0	57.0	58.5	60.0	63.0	64.5	66.0	67.5
19	36.9	39.7	42.6	45.5	48.3	51.1	54.0	55.4	56.8	59.7	61.0	62.5	64.0
20	35.1	37.8	40.5	43.2	45.9	48.6	51.3	53.0	54.0	56.7	58.1	59.4	60.7
21	33.4	36.0	38.5	41.1	43.7	46.2	48.9	50.3	51.4	54.0	55.2	56.6	57.8
22	31.9	34.3	36.8	39.3	41.7	44.2	46.6	47.0	49.1	51.5	52.7	54.0	55.2
23	30.5	32.8	35.2	37.6	39.9	42.2	44.6	45.8	47.0	49.3	50.4	51.6	52.8
24	29.2	31.5	33.7	36.0	38.2	40.5	41.8	43.4	45.0	47.3	48.3	49.5	50.6
25	28.1	30.2	32.4	34.6	36.7	38.8	41.0	42.1	43.2	45.4	46.4	47.5	48.6
26	27.0	29.0	31.2	33.2	35.3	37.4	39.5	40.5	41.5	43.6	44.6	45.7	46.7
27	26.0	28.0	30.0	32.0	34.0	36.0	38.0	39.0	40.0	42.0	43.0	44.0	45.0
28	25.0	27.0	28.9	30.8	32.8	34.7	36.6	37.6	38.6	40.5	41.4	42.4	43.4
29	24.2	26.0	27.9	29.8	31.6	33.5	35.4	36.3	37.2	39.1	40.0	41.0	41.9
30	23.4	25.2	27.0	28.8	30.6	32.4	34.2	35.1	36.0	37.8	38.7	39.6	40.5
31	22.6	24.3	26.1	27.8	29.6	31.3	33.0	33.9	34.8	36.5	37.4	38.3	39.1
32	22.0	23.6	25.3	27.0	28.7	30.3	32.1	32.9	33.8	35.5	36.3	37.1	37.9
34	20.7	22.2	23.8	25.4	27.0	28.6	30.1	31.0	31.8	33.3	34.1	34.9	35.7
36	19.5	21.0	22.5	24.0	25.5	27.0	28.5	29.2	30.0	31.5	32.2	33.0	33.8

Rear Sprocket Size	Chainwheel Size												
	46	47	48	49	50	51	52	53	54	55	56	57	58
12	103.5	105.7	108.0	110.2	112.5	114.7	117.0	119.3	121.5	123.7	126.0	128.2	130.5
13	95.5	97.6	99.7	101.8	103.9	105.9	108.0	110.0	112.1	114.2	116.3	118.3	120.4
14	87.7	90.6	92.6	94.5	96.4	98.3	100.3	102.2	104.1	106.0	108.0	109.9	111.9
15	82.8	84.6	86.4	88.2	90.0	91.8	93.6	95.4	97.2	99.0	100.8	102.6	104.4
16	77.6	79.3	81.0	82.7	84.4	86.0	87.8	89.4	91.1	92.8	94.5	96.1	97.9
17	73.1	74.6	76.2	77.8	79.4	81.0	82.6	84.1	85.7	87.3	88.9	90.5	92.1
18	69.0	70.5	72.0	73.5	75.0	76.5	78.0	79.5	81.0	82.5	84.0	85.5	87.0
19	65.4	66.8	68.2	69.6	71.1	72.4	73.9	75.3	76.7	78.1	79.5	81.0	82.4
20	62.1	63.4	64.8	66.2	67.5	68.5	70.2	71.5	72.9	74.5	75.6	76.9	78.3
21	59.1	60.4	61.7	63.0	64.3	65.5	66.9	68.1	69.4	70.7	72.0	73.3	74.6
22	56.5	57.6	58.9	60.1	61.4	62.5	63.8	65.0	66.2	67.5	68.7	69.9	71.2
23	54.0	55.2	56.3	57.5	58.7	59.8	61.0	62.2	63.4	64.5	65.7	66.9	68.0
24	51.8	52.9	54.0	55.1	56.3	57.3	58.5	59.6	60.7	61.8	63.0	64.1	65.3
25	49.7	50.8	51.8	52.9	54.0	55.1	56.2	57.2	58.3	59.4	60.4	61.6	62.7
26	47.8	48.8	49.9	50.9	51.9	53.0	54.0	55.0	56.1	57.1	58.1	59.2	60.2
27	46.0	47.0	48.0	49.0	50.0	51.0	52.0	53.0	54.0	55.0	56.0	57.0	58.0
28	44.4	45.3	46.3	47.2	48.2	49.1	50.1	51.1	52.0	53.0	54.0	54.9	55.9
29	42.8	43.7	44.7	45.6	46.5	47.5	48.4	49.4	50.3	51.2	52.1	53.1	54.0
30	41.4	42.3	43.2	44.1	45.0	45.9	46.8	47.7	48.6	49.5	50.4	51.3	52.2
31	40.0	40.8	41.8	42.6	43.5	44.4	45.3	46.2	47.0	47.9	48.7	49.6	50.5
32	38.8	39.7	40.5	41.3	42.2	43.0	43.9	44.7	45.6	46.4	47.2	48.0	49.0
34	36.6	37.3	38.1	38.9	39.7	40.5	41.3	42.0	42.8	43.7	44.5	45.2	46.0
36	34.5	35.2	36.0	36.7	37.5	38.8	39.0	39.7	40.5	41.3	42.0	42.7	43.5

Table 7.4

DEVELOPMENT, METERS PER PEDAL REVOLUTION, 27-INCH WHEELS

No. of Teeth in Front Sprocket	*Number of Teeth in Rear Sprocket* 12	13	14	15	16	17	18	19	20	21	22	23	24	25	26	27	28	29	30
28	4.98	4.59	4.27	3.98	3.75	3.51	3.32	3.14	2.99	2.84	2.71	2.60	2.48	2.39	2.30	2.21	2.13	2.06	1.99
29	5.14	4.76	4.42	4.12	3.88	3.64	3.44	3.25	3.09	2.94	2.81	2.68	2.57	2.47	2.38	2.29	2.21	2.13	2.06
30	5.34	4.92	4.58	4.27	4.01	3.77	3.56	3.36	3.20	3.05	2.91	2.76	2.68	2.55	2.46	2.36	2.29	2.20	2.13
31	5.51	5.08	4.73	4.41	4.14	3.89	3.68	3.48	3.31	3.15	3.01	2.84	2.75	2.64	2.54	2.44	2.36	2.28	2.21
32	5.69	5.24	4.89	4.55	4.27	4.02	3.80	3.59	3.41	3.25	3.10	2.92	2.84	2.72	2.62	2.52	2.44	2.35	2.28
33	5.87	5.41	5.04	4.69	4.40	4.14	3.92	3.71	3.52	3.35	3.20	3.00	2.93	2.81	2.71	2.60	2.52	2.42	2.35
34	6.04	5.57	5.19	4.84	4.53	4.27	4.04	3.83	3.63	3.45	3.29	3.09	3.02	2.90	2.79	2.69	2.60	2.49	2.42
35	6.22	5.74	5.34	4.98	4.67	4.40	4.16	3.94	3.75	3.56	3.39	3.17	3.11	2.99	2.87	2.76	2.68	2.57	2.48
36	6.40	5.90	5.49	5.12	4.80	4.53	4.27	4.05	3.85	3.66	3.49	3.25	3.20	3.08	2.95	2.84	2.75	2.64	2.56
37	6.58	6.07	5.75	5.27	4.93	4.65	4.38	4.16	3.95	3.76	3.59	3.34	3.29	3.17	3.03	2.92	2.83	2.72	2.63
38	6.77	6.23	5.80	5.41	5.07	4.78	4.50	4.27	4.06	3.86	3.70	3.42	3.38	3.25	3.11	3.00	2.90	2.79	2.70
39	6.94	6.40	5.94	5.55	5.21	4.90	4.62	4.38	4.16	3.96	3.79	3.62	3.47	3.33	3.20	3.08	2.97	2.86	2.77
40	7.12	6.57	6.10	5.69	5.34	5.02	4.74	4.50	4.27	4.07	3.88	3.71	3.56	3.42	3.28	3.16	3.05	2.94	2.84
41	7.30	6.73	6.25	5.84	5.47	5.15	4.86	4.61	4.37	4.17	3.98	3.80	3.64	3.50	3.36	3.24	3.13	3.01	2.92
42	7.47	6.90	6.40	5.98	5.60	5.27	4.98	4.72	4.48	4.27	4.07	3.90	3.75	3.58	3.45	3.32	3.20	3.08	2.99
43	7.65	7.06	6.56	6.12	5.74	5.40	5.10	4.83	4.59	4.37	4.17	3.98	3.82	3.67	3.53	3.40	3.28	3.16	3.06
44	7.83	7.23	6.71	6.26	5.87	5.52	5.22	4.94	4.70	4.47	4.27	4.08	3.91	3.76	3.61	3.48	3.36	3.24	3.13
45	8.01	7.39	6.86	6.40	6.00	5.65	5.34	5.05	4.80	4.57	4.37	4.18	4.00	3.84	3.69	3.56	3.43	3.31	3.20
46	8.18	7.55	7.01	6.55	6.14	5.78	5.45	5.17	4.91	4.67	4.46	4.27	4.09	3.93	3.78	3.64	3.51	3.39	3.28
47	8.36	7.72	7.17	6.69	6.27	5.90	5.57	5.28	5.02	4.78	4.56	4.36	4.18	4.01	3.86	3.72	3.59	3.46	3.35
48	8.54	7.88	7.32	6.83	6.40	6.03	5.69	5.39	5.12	4.88	4.66	4.45	4.27	4.10	3.94	3.80	3.66	3.53	3.42
49	8.72	8.05	7.47	6.97	6.54	6.15	5.81	5.50	5.23	4.98	4.75	4.55	4.36	4.18	4.02	3.87	3.75	3.60	3.49
50	8.90	8.21	7.63	7.12	6.67	6.28	5.93	5.62	5.34	5.08	4.85	4.64	4.45	4.27	4.10	3.95	3.82	3.68	3.56
51	9.07	8.38	7.78	7.26	6.81	6.40	6.05	5.73	5.44	5.18	4.95	4.73	4.54	4.35	4.19	4.03	3.89	3.75	3.63
52	9.25	8.54	7.93	7.40	6.94	6.53	6.17	5.84	5.55	5.29	5.04	4.83	4.62	4.44	4.27	4.11	3.97	3.82	3.70
53	9.43	8.70	8.08	7.54	7.07	6.66	6.29	5.95	5.66	5.39	5.14	4.92	4.71	4.52	4.35	4.19	4.04	3.90	3.77
54	9.61	8.87	8.23	7.69	7.20	6.78	6.40	6.07	5.76	5.49	5.24	5.01	4.80	4.61	4.43	4.27	4.12	3.97	3.85
55	9.78	9.03	8.39	7.83	7.33	6.90	6.52	6.16	5.87	5.59	5.34	5.10	4.89	4.70	4.51	4.34	4.19	4.04	3.92
56	9.97	9.20	8.54	7.97	7.47	7.03	6.64	6.29	5.98	5.69	5.43	5.20	4.98	4.78	4.59	4.42	4.27	4.12	3.98

Table 7.5

FICHTEL & SACHS MODEL H-3111 THREE-SPEED HUB BRAKE

26-Inch Wheels *Number of Teeth* *Chainwheel*	*Sprocket*	*Low*	*Normal*	*High*	**27-Inch Wheels** *Number of Teeth* *Chainwheel*	*Sprocket*	*Low*	*Normal*	*High*
44	16	52.2	71.5	97.2	44	16	54.2	74.3	101.0
	17	49.1	67.3	91.5		17	51.0	69.9	95.1
	18	46.4	63.6	86.5		18	48.2	66.0	89.8
	19	43.9	60.2	81.9		19	45.6	62.5	85.0
	20	41.8	57.2	77.8		20	43.4	59.4	80.8
46	16	54.4	74.7	101.6	46	16	56.6	77.6	105.5
	17	51.3	70.3	95.6		17	53.4	73.1	99.4
	18	48.5	66.4	90.3		18	50.4	69.0	93.8
	19	45.9	62.9	85.5		19	47.7	65.4	88.9
	20	43.7	59.8	81.3		20	45.3	62.1	84.5
48	16	56.9	78.0	106.0	48	16	59.1	81.0	110.2
	17	53.7	73.5	100.0		17	55.6	76.2	103.6
	18	50.6	69.3	94.2		18	52.5	72.0	97.9
	19	48.0	65.7	89.4		19	49.8	68.2	92.8
	20	45.6	62.4	84.9		20	47.3	64.8	88.1
50	16	59.3	81.2	110.4	50	16	61.5	84.2	114.5
	17	56.1	76.8	104.4		17	57.9	79.3	107.8
	18	52.4	71.8	97.6		18	55.0	75.4	102.5
	19	49.6	68.0	92.5		19	52.2	71.5	97.2
	20	47.5	65.0	88.4		20	49.3	67.5	91.8

Table 7.6

BICYCLE GEARING NOMOGRAPH

(Courtesy of F. H. Matteson)

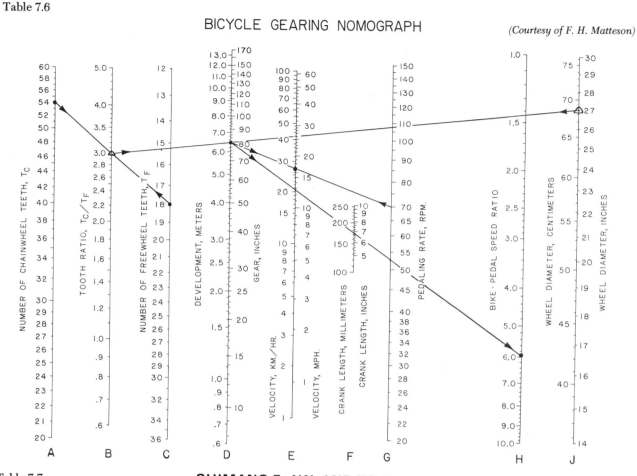

Table 7.7

SHIMANO F, AW, AND TCW AND
STURMEY-ARCHER
THREE-SPEED HUBS
33% Increase, 25% Decrease from Normal

26-INCH WHEELS

Number of Teeth				
Chainwheel	Sprocket	Low	Normal	High
44	16	53.6	71.5	95.3
	17	50.5	67.3	89.8
	18	47.7	63.6	84.8
	19	45.2	60.2	80.3
	20	42.9	57.2	76.3
46	16	56.0	74.7	99.6
	17	52.7	70.3	93.7
	18	49.8	66.4	88.5
	19	47.2	62.9	83.9
	20	44.9	59.8	79.7
48	16	58.5	78.0	104.0
	17	55.1	73.5	98.0
	18	52.0	69.3	92.4
	19	49.3	65.7	87.6
	20	46.8	62.4	83.2
50	16	61.0	81.2	108.2
	17	57.2	76.8	102.1
	18	53.9	71.8	96.3
	19	51.0	68.0	91.2
	20	48.6	65.0	86.8

27-INCH WHEELS

Number of Teeth				
Chainwheel	Sprocket	Low	Normal	High
44	16	55.7	74.3	99.0
	17	52.4	69.9	93.1
	18	49.5	66.0	87.9
	19	46.8	62.5	83.3
	20	44.5	59.4	79.1
46	16	58.2	77.6	103.4
	17	54.8	73.1	97.4
	18	51.7	69.0	91.9
	19	49.0	65.4	87.1
	20	46.5	62.1	82.7
48	16	60.7	81.0	107.9
	17	57.1	76.2	101.5
	18	54.0	72.0	95.9
	19	51.1	68.2	90.9
	20	48.6	64.8	86.3
50	16	63.2	84.2	112.0
	17	59.7	79.3	106.0
	18	56.2	75.4	100.0
	19	52.2	71.5	94.8
	20	50.6	67.5	89.9

Table 7.8

S5 STURMEY-ARCHER FIVE-SPEED HUB GEAR

26-INCH WHEEL   27-INCH WHEEL

| Number of Teeth | | 26-Inch Wheel | | | | | 27-Inch Wheel | | | | |
Chainwheel	Sprocket	Super Low	Low	Normal	High	Super High	Super Low	Low	Normal	High	Super High
40	14	49.5	58.7	74.3	94.1	111.5	51.4	61.0	77.1	97.7	115.7
	15	46.2	54.7	69.3	87.7	104.0	48.0	56.9	72.0	91.2	108.0
	16	43.3	51.3	65.0	82.3	97.5	45.0	53.3	67.5	85.4	101.3
	17	40.8	48.3	61.2	77.5	91.8	42.3	50.2	63.5	80.4	95.3
	18	38.5	45.7	57.8	73.2	86.7	40.0	47.4	60.0	76.0	90.0
	19	36.5	43.2	54.7	69.2	82.1	37.9	44.9	56.8	71.9	85.2
	20	34.7	41.1	52.0	65.8	78.0	36.0	42.7	54.0	68.4	81.0
	22	31.5	37.4	47.3	59.9	71.0	32.7	38.8	49.1	62.2	73.7
44	14	54.4	64.5	81.7	103.5	122.6	56.5	66.1	84.9	107.5	127.4
	15	50.8	60.3	76.3	96.6	114.5	52.7	62.6	79.2	100.2	118.8
	16	47.7	56.5	71.5	90.5	107.3	49.5	58.6	74.2	93.9	111.3
	17	44.9	53.2	67.3	85.2	100.6	46.6	55.2	69.9	88.4	104.9
	18	42.4	50.2	63.6	80.5	95.4	44.0	52.1	66.0	83.5	99.0
	19	40.1	47.6	60.2	76.2	90.3	41.7	49.4	62.5	79.1	93.8
	20	38.1	45.2	57.2	72.4	85.8	39.6	46.9	59.4	75.2	89.1
	22	34.7	41.1	52.0	65.8	78.0	36.0	42.7	54.0	68.4	81.0
46	14	56.9	67.5	85.4	108.1	128.1	59.1	70.1	88.7	112.3	133.1
	15	53.1	63.0	79.7	100.9	119.6	55.1	65.4	82.8	104.8	124.2
	16	49.8	59.0	74.4	94.5	112.1	51.7	61.3	77.6	98.2	116.4
	17	46.9	55.5	70.3	89.0	105.5	48.7	57.7	73.0	92.4	109.5
	18	44.3	52.5	66.4	84.0	99.6	46.0	54.5	69.0	87.3	103.5
	19	41.9	49.7	62.9	79.6	94.4	43.6	51.7	65.4	82.8	98.1
	20	39.9	47.2	59.8	75.7	89.7	41.4	49.1	62.1	78.6	93.2
	22	36.3	43.1	54.5	69.0	81.8	37.7	44.6	56.5	71.5	84.6
48	14	59.3	70.4	89.1	112.8	133.7	61.7	73.1	92.6	117.2	139.0
	15	55.4	65.7	83.2	105.3	124.8	57.5	68.3	86.4	109.4	129.6
	16	52.0	61.6	78.0	98.7	117.0	54.0	64.0	81.0	102.5	121.5
	17	49.0	58.0	73.5	93.0	110.3	50.8	60.2	76.2	96.4	114.3
	18	46.2	54.7	69.3	87.7	104.0	48.0	56.9	72.0	91.1	108.0
	19	43.8	51.9	65.7	83.2	98.6	45.5	53.9	68.2	86.3	102.5
	20	41.6	49.3	62.4	79.0	93.6	43.2	51.2	64.8	82.0	97.2
	22	37.8	44.8	56.7	71.8	85.1	39.3	46.6	58.9	74.5	88.4

Fig. 7.143   Karasawa Seisakusho externally contracting band brake.

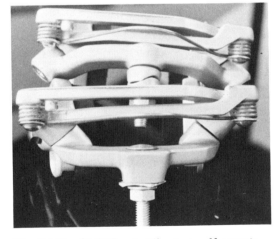

Fig. 7.144   CLB-Huret 45° pivot self-energizing caliper centerpull brake.

CHAPTER VIII

Rims and Tires

THE rim and tire act together as a flywheel. Their weight is not only carried along—as is the cyclist's body, the bicycle frame handlebars, and luggage—but it also has a rotational momentum.

Try an experiment. Turn your bicycle upside down. Give the front wheel a spin and then try to stop it with your gloved hand. You will find it takes a considerable effort. Now turn the pedals fast with the bicycle in high gear. Note the effort required to accelerate the wheels. Apply the brake and note the effort needed to stop the rapidly rotating wheel.

Because of this double effect a lightweight wheel contributes greatly to bicycle performance; it is easier to accelerate, maneuver, and stop. A little effort produces distinctly greater results with lightweight wheels, and a lightweight wheel rim combined with a lightweight tire provides the ultimate in handling.

Again we have a compromise: lightweight rims and tires are more easily damaged. When loaded, impact from hitting a bump, the edge of a pothole, or from inadvertently bumping into an object can cause too light a rim to bend or collapse. In effect it is an arch bridge upside down, which transfers the road load to the supporting spokes.

If you bump sideward against a curb or against the side of a pothole, the rim must also resist this sideward bending. It is braced to some extent by the spokes; these also pull sideward, but in opposite directions.

Try another experiment. With your bicycle stationary, press your fingers from the side at the point where the wheel goes between the front or rear forks. Notice how much deflection you obtain. While this is affected considerably by spoke tension, the rigidity of the rim has a definite effect. A wider rim, one of heavier gauge material, or one with a tubular cross section can better resist bending and final collapse. Steel is heavier, but more durable.

RIMS

Figures 8.1 and 8.2 show several constructions of lightweight rims. Note the differences in section that contribute to rigidity both vertically and sidewards. A laboratory test comparing two of the wired-on aluminum rims shown in the picture, but not the most rigid section, showed the medium-rigid tubular construction had a 17% greater vertical load capacity and over 85% greater resistance to side impact than the least-rigid wheel of substantially equal weight.

Two tubular steel rims tested in comparison provided respectively 100% and 200% more vertical load rigidity than the weaker aluminum rim and 35% and 90% more resistance to side blows. The 27 × 1¼″ rims vary in weight from about 16 to 24 ounces each.

The moral is: Select your rims for the performance you want. Heavy loads, or a heavy rider, on rough roads need stronger rims. A nimble rider who lifts his weight over bumps, avoids running into potholes, and stays on smooth roads can use the lightest rims to obtain maximum performance. The club rider can use the in-between construction.

Not having to withstand tire sidewall forces, the rims for sew-up tires can be lighter. For racing and touring purposes, these vary from 7 to 14 ounces each.

Using the factor for a rotating weight effect of 2:1, a 2-pound weight saving per pair (using 9-ounce sew-ups on 10-ounce rims) has the same effect on bicycle

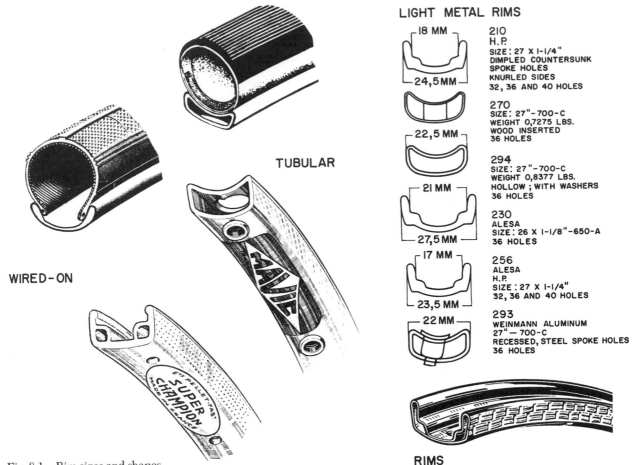

LIGHT METAL RIMS

18 MM / 24,5 MM	**210** H.P. SIZE: 27 X 1-1/4" DIMPLED COUNTERSUNK SPOKE HOLES KNURLED SIDES 32, 36 AND 40 HOLES
22,5 MM	**270** SIZE: 27"–700-C WEIGHT 0,7275 LBS. WOOD INSERTED 36 HOLES
21 MM	**294** SIZE: 27"–700-C WEIGHT 0,8377 LBS. HOLLOW ; WITH WASHERS 36 HOLES
27,5 MM	**230** ALESA SIZE: 26 X 1-1/8"–650-A 36 HOLES
17 MM / 23,5 MM	**256** ALESA H.P. SIZE : 27 X 1-1/4" 32, 36 AND 40 HOLES
22 MM	**293** WEINMANN ALUMINUM 27" — 700-C RECESSED, STEEL SPOKE HOLES 36 HOLES

TUBULAR

WIRED-ON

SUPER CHAMPION

RIMS

Fig. 8.1   Rim sizes and shapes.

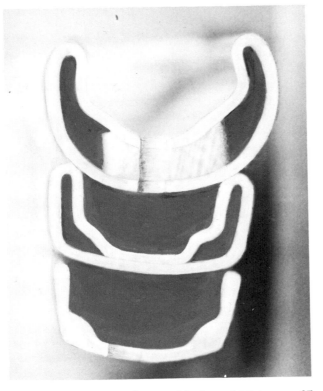

Fig. 8.2   Mephisto wood insert, Mavic, and Weinmann 27 × 1¼″ rims.

performance as a 4-pound reduction in bicycle weight. It is up to you to weigh performance against durability and freedom from trouble.

Wired-on or "clincher" tires are used on two general types of rim: the straight-sided rim, on which the bead wire rests on the bead seat of the rim, or the "hook bead" rim, which is made of a rolled section (see Fig. 8.1). Air pressure forces a projection on the exterior of the tire under the inwardly rolled hooked edge. These use tires whose dimensions are expressed in decimal inches and are not interchangeable with straight-sided rims and tires. A plastic filler strip which has now been introduced permits the use of certain straight-sided tires on hook bead rims.

SELECTING YOUR BICYCLE TIRES

At any gathering of cyclists, the subject of tire and rim selection waxes warm and heavy. The tubular tire, whose rolling resistance has generally been considered the least, has its strong adherents because it can be used with a rim of minimum weight. Tubes and tires of minimum weight and small in cross section are not restricted by the rim sides, and flexibility is at a maximum. When punctured, the tubular tire can be stripped off and a new one—easily carried as a spare—installed in short order. Repairs, though tedious, can be made at a later time. In a "tubular," or "sew-up" tire, the thin inner tube is contained in a cotton or silk casing. The casing is actually sewn together with a fine linen thread at the center of the rim. A fabric strip separates the tube from the stitching, and another strip on the rim surface protects the stitching and acts as a base on which to cement the tire.

Tubular tire weights range from 120 grams (about 4½ ounces) for the complete tire and tube, to 450 grams for training tubulars, to 24 ounces for a completely vulcanized all-weather side wall unit. The extralight tires have silk casings and are used for cement race tracks. Five-ounce tires may be used on wood tracks and tires weighing from 7 to 9 ounces for road racing work. Twelve-ounce tires are best for training or cyclo-cross, where durability and weather resistance are more important factors.

However, silk tires similar to Clement's Campionato del Mondo in the 10-ounce range are excellent for light touring use. The silk tire can use a heavier tread due to the light weight of the casing, and numerous riders have expressed satisfaction with their long life and reasonable wear.

Tubular tires are expensive. They are handmade, and worldwide demand exceeds the capacity of the builders. Repetitive monetary crises, European inflation, and heavy demand have strained prices and availability. Except for racing use, or where cost is no object, tubulars are a luxury. For detailed descriptions and the prices of available tires, see your local high-grade bicycle dealer. The catalogs and price lists of Cyclopedia, Wheel Goods, Big Wheel, or Kitching, referred to in the section on "Sources of Information" at the end of this book contain descriptions and prices as well as detailed information on methods of attaching, care, and repair of sew-up tires.

Attaching sew-ups requires careful attention. Track tires are attached with several layers of shellac and allowed to harden thoroughly before use. Unlike the wire-on, or "clincher," here it is the cemented bond that prevents the tire from rolling off on turns or from slipping around the rim and tearing out the valve under accelerating and braking forces.

A sticky cement (Mastice Gutta), which will permit removal and replacement of a punctured tire, is used for road work. Replacement without recementing and allowing the cement to dry is at best a touch-and-go procedure when demands on adhesion are heavy. By rolling off the rim a tubular can cause a serious crash. Heating of the rims due to the continued use of the brakes on a downhill course can soften the cement and cause a well-cemented tire to roll or slip. Wet weather replacement of a cemented-on tubular can be unsatisfactory.

The members of the New York Cycle Club often attach sew-ups with the double-sided ¾ inch wide plas-tic-backed adhesive tape used in hospital X-ray rooms. This can be carried in a small roll cut to the proper length for a tire change. It takes little space and is quite handy to use.

Let's look at the pros and cons of wired-on versus tubular tires.

Advantages of the tubular tire:
1. Minimum wheel and tire weight increase responsiveness when accelerating and make hill climbing a bit easier. Rolling resistance can be minimized, although the advantage for ordinary riding is small when compared to the best of wired-ons.
2. A punctured tire can be replaced with a spare most rapidly. "No puncture" liquid can be used.
3. If traveling in areas where racing predominates, spare tires can be obtained in America, Europe, and parts of Asia (this may only be true in major towns.)

Advantages of the wired-on:
1. They are less vulnerable to punctures, less affected by weather, and easier to maintain.
2. Their initial cost is considerably less.
3. A spare tube and a patch kit weigh less and take up less space than a spare tubular. It can be used again and again in case of multiple punctures.
4. Punctured tires are more easily repaired. Tubes can be patched with a minimum of shelter.
5. The slightly heavier rims and tires are less liable to cause pinch punctures, fabric breaks, and collapse under impact loads.
6. Extra lightweight casings whose rolling resistance is as good as some road weight tubulars are being made available in several popular sizes (see Fig. 8.3). The Milremo 27 × 1⅛ weighs 10½ oz., the Michelin 12½ oz., and the Schwinn 14 oz.   21, 25, and 28 mm sections can be used.
7. Spare tires and tubes are more generally available.
8. Wired-ons are safer. The are less liable to roll off or to slip under braking and cornering loads, particularly in hot areas or under long braking. Adhesion and braking are generally better; skid resistance is usually better.
9. An interrupted trip can often be completed successfully by repairing casing damage on the spot with canvas, Band-Aids®, tire tape, or rubberized repair fabric.
10. Costs are reduced.

If your cycling will take you far afield across wet or rough road surfaces, paving breaks, pebbles, or road debris, use wired-on tires. If your own weight or the load you carry is heavy, use wired-ons. If responsiveness and acceleration, and maximum ease of riding are

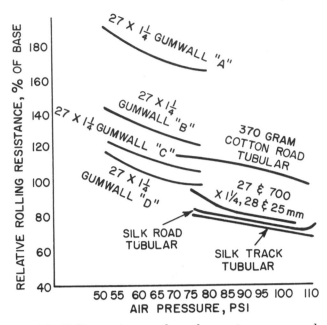

Fig. 8.3   Rolling resistance depends on air pressure and tire used.

Fig. 8.4   Automated brake and tire testing machine at Schwinn Bicycle Company Research Laboratory. Tire rolling resistance can be measured under varying loads and inflation pressures.
(Courtesy of Schwinn Bicycle Company)

worth more to you than the additional cost and vulnerability, use tubulars and enjoy them.

WHEEL AND TIRE SIZE

It is possible to obtain wheels from 12 to 28 inches in diameter, with tire cross sections from 1 to 2 inches in width. Of course the frame arrangement and dimensions must accommodate the difference in size. However, the most common wheels are 20, 24, 26, and 27 inches (or their metric equivalents). The most common tire widths run from 1 to 1¾ inches and 2⅛ inches in ⅛-inch graduations. Metric sizes are in many cases not interchangeable, so if you plan to travel abroad, it is wise to obtain a set of wheels which will be available in the country you plan to visit.

Tubes are less of a problem. Metric sizes are generally interchangeable with English and American sizes in the same general range, but valves may differ. The standard Schrader valve is widely used, and the smaller diameter Presta valve is common in parts of Europe. The valve hole in the rim can be reamed out if necessary. Conversely, the Presta valve can be used with an extra tire patch at the valve hole in place of a Schrader valve tube. Be sure to carry valve adapters that will convert your tube to the opposite type. An adapter weighs little and can be worth its weight in gold.

Tires fit rather precisely according to rim bead seat diameter. Tires that are a bit too large will blow off or have their tube pinched under the bead. Mounting tires a bit too small will break the bead wire.

The table of rim sizes and tire markings at the end of this chapter (see Table 8.2) will enable you to select a corresponding, usable size if you are stuck in a foreign land.

If you plan to visit metric countries, the investment in metric wheel sizes is not a waste. The extra wheels can be used as spares upon your return and will extend the life of your present equipment.

EFFECT OF WHEEL SIZE ON ROLLING RESISTANCE

The small-wheeled bicycle has returned to favor for portability. Sixteen, 20, and 24-inch sizes are marketed. They take less room, and for equivalent sections, wear is greater. The rolling resistance of the smaller wheels, however, increases proportionally with size decrease; a 20-inch tire at equal pressure may have 30% more road friction than a 27-inch tire.

To a lesser degree, wider tires also increase rolling friction. Tests indicate that the wider contact area increases friction by about ⅓ of the percentage increase in size. Using a 1-inch tubular as a base, the resistance of 1¼-inch tires would be 8% greater, that of 2¼-inch tires, 40% higher. Under actual road conditions, the effect may be less. For instance, if the roadway is soft or graveled, the wider tire will float over the surface with greater ease.

The larger section tire will "swallow" larger bumps and stones, thereby increasing comfort and greatly decreasing tire problems. At moderate speeds, the slightly larger resistance on hard-surfaced roads can be a minor factor.

VALVES

The Schrader valve cores supplied with most valves make it extremely hard to pump up a tire with a hand pump when on the road. The usual pump connection allows a great deal of the air to escape while it is being unscrewed. However, valve cores can be had that make pumping Schrader valves as easy as pumping a Presta. Zefal (French) makes a rapid connection of the type used on racing Presta valve pumps that fits a Schrader valve and does a satisfactory job.

Valve cores come in two lengths—¾ and 1¼ inches. A #9480 Schrader core improves pumping with the shorter length. If you can fit a longer core, the #6000, #6100, and #7250 cores are progressively easier to use. You may have to remove and clean the lighter cores once or twice until the talc in the tubes dissipates. (If you can't find these cores in shops, write to Schrader at Dickson, Tennessee 37055.)

SERVICEABILITY AND ROLLING RESISTANCE

The tire quality and rolling resistance are hard to determine exactly without scientific equipment, but differences can easily be felt on the road. Figure 8.3 gives the results of tests made in an American laboratory on 27 × 1¼-inch tires and tubulars. Tires similar in appearance at the same pressure of inflation exhibited differences in rolling resistances of 2½ to 1. The highest quality wired-ons with thin nylon cord were actually lower in road friction than some of the tubulars. The strong nylon fabric, moreover, has proven quite durable. Some indication of the relative ease of riding can be obtained by depressing the uninflated tires with the fingers. The difference in flexibility can be felt.

The 26 × 1⅜-inch blackwall tire can be expected to have a rolling resistance 40% greater than that of a good 27 × 1¼-inch tire. Eight percent of this is due to size difference, but the balance is due to the heavier walls and treads used to give more service. A balloon tire with a lower inflation pressure may require that the cyclist expend from 2½ to 3 times more energy. The estimated resistance to rolling on smooth, hard road surfaces on this chart is about 0.005 the load on the tire. Softer road surfaces, such as asphalt in the sun, and rougher-textured surfaces increase power demands.

The tire design varies with the intended service. A tire designed for speed will have fine cords angled close to the direction of motion; a tire built for flexibility and comfort will have threads more perpendicular to the motion. Improperly proportioned wall thickness can lead to cracks due to localized bending as the wheel revolves. Cord size and quantity will determine the strength and rolling resistance. I have counted tire cord from 22 to 56 threads per inch. The finer thread will be fast, but may break under impact loads.

A flatter tread which places more rubber on the road is used for durability and long life. Continuous ribs provide safety in cornering. A thin, smooth pattern will be used for speed. A safety tread with a studded design improves braking and cornering. A flat cord angle may give more comfort, but it gives a less-sure steering re-

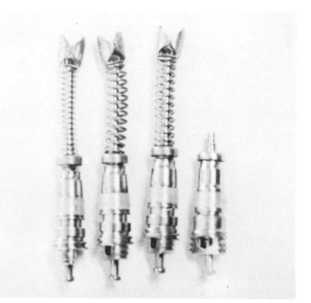

Fig. 8.5   Comparison of Schrader valve cores (easiest one to pump is on left).

sponse due to its extra flexibility. Nylon cords provide extra strength and durability and will not rot if cut. While about 5% less efficient for easy rolling, their extra strength makes up for this by allowing the use of lighter sections. Using light nylon tires, I have hit potholes that dented both rims till the tubes protruded without tire damage.

Rubber compounding and quality are important. Tires built for speed may have decreased adhesion—important when cornering or braking. The use of reclaimed rubber or fillers in the rubber compound can decrease the tire cost, but it decreases speed, life, and wearing quality as well. Insist on the highest quality, and examine the tires offered before you buy. You may decide on two different tires, one for commuting and one for club-riding.

INFLATION PRESSURE

Table 8.1 indicates the recommended inflation pressures for tires of various cross sections. The actual pressure used will depend on the load. Note that rolling friction decreases as pressure is raised, but shock and vibration also increase. Too high a pressure may overstress the bead wire and blow the tire off the rim. The extra stress can lead to more punctures and to fabric breaks when riding over small stones.

Underinflation not only makes the bicycle harder to push, but it allows the tire to "bottom" against the rim when a bump or stone is hit. This can not only pinch and rupture the tube, it can even dent the rim beyond repair. A rim dented inward or out on each side so that the brakes grab as they pass the bulge is a good indication of underinflation. The extrasevere flexing with underinflation can also crack sidewalls.

STAR BREAKS FROM HITTING STONES AND CURBS

RIMS CUTS FROM UNDERINFLATION OR BUMPS

BROKEN BEADS FROM IMPROPER TOOLS
IN MOUNTING

BLOWOUT FROM OVERINFLATION,
BREAKS, OR MOUNTING

RUPTURES AND CUTS FROM GLASS, METAL,
AND STONES

UNEVEN WEAR FROM MISALIGNMENT,
SKIDS, BRAKE GRAB

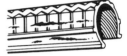

MISALIGNED VALVE FROM UNDERINFLATION

LEAKS AND CRACKS FROM OLD AGE,
OXIDATION RIDING UNDERINFLATED

Fig. 8.6   Tire problems.

Table 8.1

RECOMMENDED INFLATION PRESSURE FOR TIRES (AVERAGE)

Tire	Pressure	Tire	Pressure
2.125″	40 psi (2.7 ATU)	1.75 (1¾)″ 42 & 45 mm }	50 psi (3.4 ATU)
1.375 (1⅜)″ 35 & 38 mm } Tubulars	65 psi (4.4 ATU) 90–115psi (6.1–7.8 ATU)	1¼″ 30 mm & 32 mm } Schwinn Letour 27″ & 700 mm—20, 25, 28	70 psi (4.8 ATU) 85 psi (5.8 ATU) 85–95 psi (6.5 ATU)

NOTES: Actual tire pressure used will vary with load on tires. Rear tire can use 10% to 15% greater than front tire. For heavy riders or heavy loads increase pressure 5 to 10%. When in doubt, the pressure used should not permit over 30% section deflection under full load.

ATU = 1 atmosphere = 14.7 psi.

WIDTH OF RIM AT BEAD

Rigidalu	13/15mm(0.51″/0.59″)	Rigida 13 × 19	23mm exterior width
Pellet	16.5/18mm(0.65″/0.71″)	Superchampion 480-13	23mm exterior width
Mavic	12.5/15.5mm(0.49″/0.61″)	Module E	20mm exterior width
Weinmann	14/15mm(0.55″/0.59″)	A-124	20mm exterior width
French Etroit	16mm (0.65″)		
British K section	17mm (0.68″)		
French Mi-large	20mm (0.80″)		
British Endrick E-1 to E-6 EA-1 to EA-4 }	20mm (0.80″)		
Schwinn S-6			
French "large" 28	24.5mm (0.96″)		
British F-3, F-4, F-10, F-12 }	25mm (0.970″)		
Schwinn S-7			
American Middle- weight (1.75)			
American Balloon Tires (2.125″)	27mm (1.062″)		

If you are in a situation where tires of your size marking are not available, this guide will help you to decide alternate choices. With care tires of similar bead circumference can be employed on rims of differing width.

NOTES: Hookbead rims are used with decimal size tires, straight-sided rims with fractional inch sizes.

While similar in marking, e.g. 26 × 1.375 and 26 × 1⅜, these are not interchangeable.

To get outer circumference of straight side rims, and 22mm for 1¼ and 1⅜ sections, 43mm for 1¾ sections. Circumference under bead of hookbead rim, subtract 25.5mm from the outer circumference.

The above listings are for bead seat circumference of straight side rim (B) and hook rim circumference (OD).

In addition to the above, a 27 × 1¼″ tire is made in Argentina.

Table 8.2

GUIDE TO TIRE AND RIM INTERCHANGEABILITY

Rim Circumference (mm)	Proposed Uniform Marking°	British	American	French	Italian	German	Swedish	British Rim Size
986 OD	47-305		16×1.75 16×2.125 16×1¾					
996 B								
1068 B	37-340			400 A				
1097 B	32-449	16×1⅜			16×1¼ 16×1⅜			E3J
1125 B							17×1¼	
1225 B	37-390			450 A				
1257 B	32-400	18×1⅜ 18×1½ 18×1¾ 20×2			450×32A 18×1¼			E4J F4J
1315 B			20×1¾					
1327 OD	47-406		20×1.75					
1345 B							20×2	
1382 B	37-440			500 A				
1416 B	32-451	20×1⅜	20×1⅜ 20×1½ 20×1.25 20×1.375		500×32A 20×1¼	20×1½ beaded		E5J
1441 OD								
1539 B	37-490			550 A				
1563 B							22×1⅜ 22×1¼	
1575 B	32-501	22×1⅜			550×32A 22×1¼			F2 F6
1646 OD			24×1.75 24×2.125					
1695 B	37-540	24×1⅜			600×35A 24×1⅜			F8 F3, E5
1700 B	37-541			600 A				
1715 B			24×1¼			24×1½ beaded		
1717 B			24×1⅜					
1755 B	47-559					26×1.75 26×2.00	26×2 Transport 26×2.25	
1764 B								
1794 B	47-571	26×1¾			650×45 C 26×1¾			F12
1805 OD			26×1.75 26×2.125					
1835 B	40-584	26×1½		650B STD 650B-38 650B-42 650B-50	650-38B 26×1½ 650-42B 650-45B	26×1⅜ 26×1½		
1837 B							26×1¾ Transit 26×1½	
1854 B						26×1½ beaded		
1855 B	37-590	26×1⅜		650 A				E3, EA-3 F-4
1876 B	-597	26×1¼	26×1¼ 26×1⅜					K-1 E-1, EA-1
1906 B			27×1½					
1920 OD			26×1.375 26×1.25					
1955 B	32-622			700-30C 700-35C		700-30C° 700-32C 700-35C 28×1¼ 28×1⅜ 28×1⅝		
1956 B		28×1⅝ 28×1¾			700-32C 700-35C 700-38C 700-42C	28×1.75		F13
1958 B							28×1⅝	
1978 B	30-630	27×1¼	27×1¼	27×1¼	27×1¼	27×1¼		K2
1982 B							27×1¼	
1992 B				700-28B 700-35B				
1994 B	40-635			700B STD	700-38B	28×1½	28×1⅝ 28×1½	
1995 B							28×1½	F-10
2015C B	37-642	28×1⅜	27×1⅜	700 A	28×1¾ 700-35A			F5 E4-EA4
2016 B							28×1½ 28×1⅜	

°Nominal size

Fig. 8.7   Tire impact tester at Schwinn Laboratory. A power-driven wheel subjects the tire to severe impact under heavy load to determine the effects on tire, rim, and spokes.
(Courtesy of Schwinn Bicycle Company)

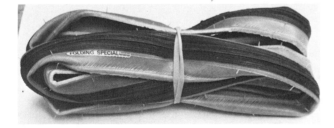

Fig. 8.8   Foldable tires makes carrying a spare casing on tour easy.

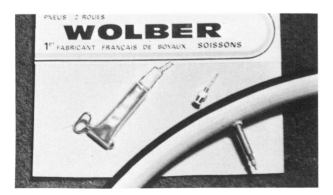

Fig. 8.9   New tubeless tire and simple kit for repairing punctures without dismantling the tire.

Inflating the tire too rapidly can cause mysterious tube failures. You fill a new tire and tube at the filling station, and the tire blows before it is ridden. Air rushing into an uninflated tube stretches it excessively at one point before filling the entire tube. When inflating a tire, add air slowly. Examine the tire all around the bead. There is usually a ridge of rubber on the tire sidewall near the rim. If this is not evenly spaced from the rim, deflate the tire a bit and press it down into the rim all around on both sides. Then inflate slowly to the desired pressure.

Glass and sharp metal can cut the tread, and the exposed fabric will rot. Fill any cuts, after you have cleaned them and dug out any imbedded glass, with tread filling compound.

Misalignment, grabby brakes or bent rims, and careless brake application—skidding the tire—will all cause uneven tire wear.

Hitting stones can cause X-shaped fabric breaks which may not be visible on the outside except for a suspicious bulge or a worn spot on the tread. This is a sign of abuse. A repair can be made using rubber solution and rubberized fabric.

Nails and sharp wire will penetrate both sides of the tire and tube if ridden flat. Thoroughly check the entire tire before removing a flat to find the nail or glass that may have been the cause.

A small bike tire repair kit is a wise accessory that may save a long walk!

Table 8.3

ALLOY RIMS FOR 27″ AND 700MM × 20, 25, AND 28MM HIGH PRESSURE TIRES

Tire	Rim Tape
Rigidalu	10mm × 1.2 rubber
Rigida 13 × 19	12mm cloth adhesive + 10mm rubber
Superchampion°	10mm × 1.2 rubber
Mavic Module E°	17mm cloth adhesive
Weinmann A-124	10mm × 1.2 rubber

°Suitable for use with foldable bead tires.

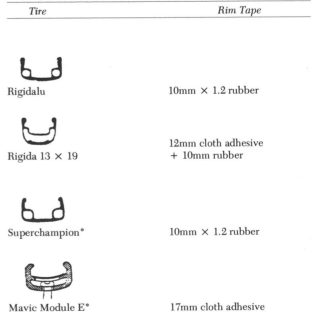

CHAPTER IX

Wheel Building

SELECTION OF SPOKE PATTERN

Spoke breakage and dented or wavy wheels are two of the cyclist's most common problems. The bicycle wheel is a marvel of engineering; a two-pound wheel may be loaded steadily to a hundred times its weight; but road impact can create local stresses of several times these values! Though it is rugged, severe damage can easily occur through lack of care.

At the road surface, the rim is an arch—like that of a bridge—which must transfer the load to the top, from which the weight on the hub is suspended by the spokes. It has a great vertical strength, but much less strength from the side. Sharp and heavy impacts, such as those from the edge of a pothole or curb, can bend in the arch—even though the rest of the wheel structure carries the shock.

Take a rim without spokes, lay it over the edge of a table, hold down one side on the table, and put your weight with the other hand on the unsupported portion. You will be amazed at the side deflection a little pressure will give. Consider the effect when you skid sideways against a curb, or when you bank sharply on a high-speed turn and hit a bump at the same time. Take your complete wheel, place its axle on the floor, and press downward simultaneously on opposite sides. Note the flexing of the rim. Remember this when you ride!

Impact from a stone, a railroad track, or a pothole, may flatten the rim. Some spokes will loosen, others become over-stressed. The sides of the rim may spread outward at the point of impact so that you get not only a bump-bump-bump as your wheel rolls over this flattened part each revolution, but also a snag-snag-snag of grabbing brakes when they are next applied. A side blow will create a wave in even a well-built wheel, and riding on wheels in this condition for a period of time can cause them to set. The uneven spoke tension that results causes some driving spokes to accept a greater share of the load—resulting in their rapid failure.

The rider who applies power unevenly—the "thruster," as compared to the "ankler"—alternately loads and unloads the driving spokes. By overloading the spokes at each thrust and underloading between pushes, the thruster greatly reduces spoke life.

Failing to lift your weight when you strike a bump and carrying heavy baggage loads—which certainly will not lift themselves at a bump—cause excessive spoke stress. Look first at your riding style to solve spoke breakage problems; it is the major cause. If your weight is heavy, give your spokes a break, and use a heavier gauge, but by all means "ride lightly."

Pick your rims and tires for the service you demand. Extralight rims and tires are lively, but they require greater care. If the roads you ride are rough and rutted, select rims and tires with larger section.

For hill climbing, use larger flange hubs; for resilience, use a small flange hub. European riders almost invariably use the lighter small flange hubs on rough road surfaces. Sprinters and hill climbers tie and solder their spokes at the crossings to distribute the load among all the spokes, but this makes a more rigid and unyielding wheel that rides harder on a rough surface. With their repeated sharp, high-speed turns, criterium courses demand the greater side and torsional—for the frequent accelerations—rigidity given by large flange hubs. Banked tracks require the extra rigidity of large flange hubs.

Pedal action and power flow are smooth in racing "against the clock," and therefore a lighter wheel can be used. Radial spoking and small flange hubs decrease both weight and wind resistance in the front wheel. The number of spokes can be decreased from 36 (the most common) to 32, 28, or even 24, if the spoke gauge is increased.

Wheel spoking is identified by the number of spokes crossed by a single spoke as it goes from hub to rim. In direct, or radial spoking, no spoke crosses another (see Fig. 9.1). This is the easiest to build and to true, but it is used only on nondriving wheels.

"Tangent spoking," in which the spokes leave the hub flange at almost 90°, gives most flexibility and pulling power. In this pattern, spokes are crossed four (X-4). We can also cross one, two, or three. Figure 9.2 shows cross-three spoking; the crossings can be counted in Figure 9.3 which shows the detail at the hub. In general, as the flange diameter grows larger compared to rim diameter, the number of crossings lessens. This reduces strain from the change of direction when the spoke runs along the flange and then angles toward the rim. With fewer crossings there are shorter spokes, a bit less weight, and less resilience. Cross-three is most common with high flange hubs.

Figure 9.3 shows spokes that pull "in pairs." The "pulling" spoke travels from the top of the flange to the left, or rearward, toward the rim. Most factory-built wheels have a pattern in which one spoke pulls from inside the flange, and the other pulls from the outside. This is fine for hub brakes, coaster brakes, or fixed wheels, in which power for both driving and braking is applied from the hub (see Fig. 9.4), but for freewheel hubs which pull only in one direction and apply no power in the other, expert wheel builders often build so that the spokes pull from the inside of the flange. Some builders prefer to pull from the outside of the flange. Either way will work, but in the event of unshipping the chain, the driving spokes are less liable to be damaged with the inside pull. This difference has gotten me home in a pinch. Also, filed head or Z-head spokes can be inserted on the inside of the freewheel side flange during emergencies (see Figs. 9.5 and 9.6).

Spokes must be properly inserted in the flange, and the flange thickness must match the length of bend of the spoke at the head. If the spoke holes are chamfered, the chamfer is placed at the bend of the spoke so that the spoke will not cut at the sharp corner (see Fig. 9.7). In the section on Hubs (Chapter 7), we discuss variations in hub flange thickness and diameter. Figure 9.8 shows the effects of mismatching spoke bend length and flange thickness and of mismatching flange hole size and spoke gauge. As can be seen, under load, the mismatched spoke will tend to straighten out at the bend, resulting in a loss of tension and wheel true. In this case, a washer can be placed between

Fig. 9.1   Large-flange radial-spoked wheel being trued in wheel truing stand.

Fig. 9.2   Small-flange hub with 36 tangent spokes.

Fig. 9.3   Close-up of hub of tangent spoked wheel. Spokes are "pulling in pair."

Fig. 9.6   Hub with keyhole slots on sprocket side flange permits spoke replacement without removing sprocket.

Fig. 9.4   Cross-three tangent spoking, one-side spoke placement. Spokes too small for hole diameter of flange.

Fig. 9.4a   Direct spoking reduces breakage. These streamlined Robergel spokes reduce air resistance. Pino Morroni spokes thread directly into hub flange.
(Courtesy of Stuart J. Meyers)

Fig. 9.5   Spoke emergency replacement. Left, Filed or shaped spokes for emergency use; right, Spokes inserted into flange of hub on freewheel side.

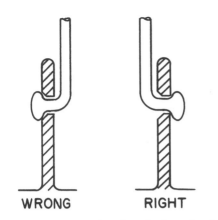

Fig. 9.7   Bend of spokes on chamferred edge of spoke hole.

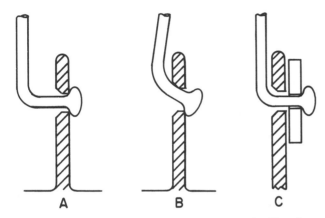

Fig. 9.8   Spokes must match hubs. A, Mismatched head length and flange;   B, Mismatched hole and spoke;   C, Use of washer corrects mismatch.

Fig. 9.9   Excessive spoke breakage may be caused by small differences in manufacture. Note the smooth radius full section bend (left) and the notched and stretched failure prone bend (right)—10× magnification.

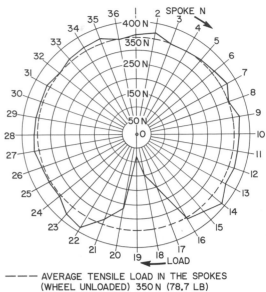

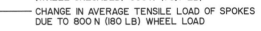

— — — AVERAGE TENSILE LOAD IN THE SPOKES (WHEEL UNLOADED) 350 N (78.7 LB)

———— CHANGE IN AVERAGE TENSILE LOAD OF SPOKES DUE TO 800 N (180 LB) WHEEL LOAD

Fig. 9.9a   Changes in spoke loading while riding causes spoke fatigue failure.(*Courtesy H.G. Bech*)

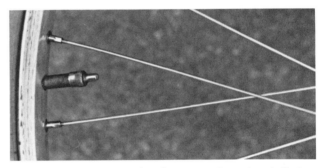

Fig. 9.10   Incorrect spoke lacing makes tire inflation difficult.

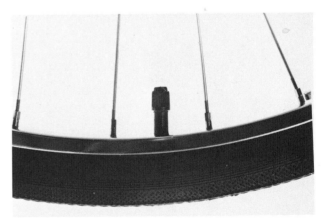

Fig. 9.11   Correct placement provides ample clearance for tire inflation.

spoke head and flange (see Fig. 9.9). Figure 9.4 clearly shows mismatched spoke thickness and bend length and spoke diameter and flange hole size.

Spokes must be placed so that they run parallel at the valve hole; otherwise it is difficult to inflate the tire. At the rim joint, the spokes should pull the joint together, not apart. The rim joint should be between the spokes where the valve is misplaced (Fig. 9.10). Fig. 9.11 shows too short a spoke. Threads extend away from the nipple; breakage at thread root is likely.

Many rims are not equipped with angled nipple seats that allow the spoke nipples to align themselves in the direction of pull. I usually set the nipples with a punch to align them in the proper direction during the initial construction of the wheel. This reduces the chance of spoke breakage at the point where the spoke leaves the nipple. Spence Wolfe uses a special tool to angle the nipple and tighten the rim ferrule staking prior to rim and spoke assembly.

Spoke and Nipple Length

The spoke length used depends on rim thickness, depressed nipple holes, rim diameter, the spoking pattern and hub flange diameter. Threads should be buried within the nipple and its threads. (Some come to the end of the nipple; some are recessed.) Under full tension (from about 80 to 100 pounds) and after straining and seating, the threads should be below the top of the nipple to allow for tightening after future use. Spokes on the freewheel side of the rear wheel are $\frac{1}{16}$ inch shorter.

On aluminum rims without an inside reinforcement between top and bottom surface, a washer is required to spread the nipple load, or else the nipple will eventually pull through the inner surface.

Nipple lengths vary depending on rim thickness. Wood and wood-filled rims take a longer length. Se-

lect the length that permits your spoke wrench to engage the flats when starting to tighten it.

The spoke length selected should provide at least 12 threads of engagement when the wheel is tightly trued. Normally, from 15 to 25 threads are engaged with the nipple screwed to its proper full depth. Softer nipple material requires greater engagement.

The following typical lengths are to be used only as a guide. The length can be calculated (see Robert Nelson's article in "Bicycling" magazine, August, 1972). Another method is to observe the spoke depth in the nipple in our existing wheel, to check the proper setting, remove and measure the spoke. If the pattern is to be different, use a tape measure to determine the change in length to the new location.

Spoke Gauge

It is obvious that the spoke gauge should suit the load applied. For persons over 150 lbs, 14 or 14/16 gauge is best (.080/.060-inch gauge). Lighter riders and cyclists with a smooth technique can use 15 or 15/17 gauge (0.072/0.056 inch). Remember that metric and American or English spoke threadings are different and don't try to mix spokes and nipples with unequal threading, even if the gauge is the same. Standard nipple sizes will fit 13, 14, or 15 SWG gauge spokes. For spokes 0.105 inch and larger, and for heavy duty or tandem use, use larger nipples. The hub and rim must accept these. If you drill a ferruled rim for larger nipples, you may destroy the ferrules that join the rim together.

Table 9.1 — TYPICAL SPOKE LENGTHS, IN MM

Rim type	Hub Flange: Spoke pattern:	LF 32 hole, X-3	SF	LF 36 hole, X-3	SF	LF 36 hole, X-4	SF	LF Radial	SF
26 × 1⅜		282	284	274	278	287	289	265	270
Tubular or 700 C wood filled		302	303	295	297	306	308	274	289
Tubular, 700 C ferruled or rolled		300	301	294	295	305	306	272	287
27 × 1¼ extruded or rolled		302	306	296	297	306	308	272	287

Table 9.2 — SPOKE GAUGES, NIPPLE SIZES, AND THREADING

Wire diam.: ISO, Jap. (mm)	(1.5)		1.8	2.0		2.3	2.6	2.9	3.2
Wire diam. (inches)	.060		.071	.079		.091	.100	.114	.126
TPI: ISO, English, Japanese			56	56		56	56	44	40
Nipple diam.: ISO (mm)			4.0	4.0		4.5	5.5	NA	NA
Nipple flats: ISO (mm)			3.3	3.3		3.8	4.5	NA	NA
SWG: English-American	17	16	15	14		13	12	11	10
Wire diam.: English (inches)	.056	.064	.072	.080		.092	.106	.116	.128
JP: French	10	11	12	13	14	15	16	17	18
Wire diam.: French (inches)	.059	.063	.071	.079	.087	.094	.106	.117	.134
Threads Per Inch: French			63.5	63.5	56.4	56.4	46.2	42.3	42.3
Nipple diam.: French (mm)			4.0	4.0	4.0	4.5	5.0	6.0	6.0
Nipple flats: French (mm)			3.2	3.2	3.2	3.7	4.0	4.6	5.0
Nipple diam.: Japanese (mm)			4.0	4.0		4.3	4.6	5.0	5.8
Nipple flats: Japanese (mm)			3.4	3.4		3.6	3.9	4.3	4.9
Wire diam.: USA (inches)			.072	.080		.092	.106	.120	.135
TPI: USA				56			56	40	
Spoke body: USA (mm)				3.7			4.57	5.71	
Nipple flats: USA (mm)				3.3			3.9	4.9	

NOTE: Butted spokes are thinner in the middle than at ends. A 15/17 gauge butted spoke is 0.72″ at the end and 0.56″ in mid-section. Streamlined spokes are broader but thinner in mid-section than at ends. ISO dimensions are proposed.

BUILDING THE WHEEL

First, check the hub axle (Fig. 9.12) for straightness and the bearings for proper fit.

There are numerous rules to follow when building a wheel. The easiest method for the newcomer is to obtain a similar wheel. Starting at the valve hole, but considering the factors above, follow the pattern of lacing.

If the original wheel is cross-three, but you wish cross-four, take your first spoke two holes farther than your pattern, or if cross-two—two holes less.

In a 36-hole hub, put nine spokes through every other hole in the upper flange using the holes with the chamfer properly located. Put one through the rim hole next to the valve hole (if the rim hole is on the flange side), then put on the nipple. Twist the hub in the driving direction to make sure it doesn't angle over the valve, as in Figure 9.10. If it does, place this first spoke two holes farther on the rim. The need will be obvious. The nondriving spokes come through the flange in the reverse direction, cross over, then under, the original set. Lace both sides loosely but evenly, turning all spokes to an even depth in the nipples. Continue around the wheel, tightening even amounts each time, until the wheel spokes are just snug. If properly done, the wheel will spin reasonably round and free of waviness.

Now your frame, fork, or a truing stand can be used to aid truing. Tap the spoke heads of all spokes with a hammer and soft punch to snugly seat the heads. Then stake or tap the nipples to align them. Retighten as before, adjusting so that "hop" or valleys as the wheel rotates are removed. Tighten or loosen on opposite sides as needed to take out waviness. Then with the axle supported at its end, take the wheel in both hands and press it gently but firmly sideways at the diameters, repeat this at several points, and on the opposite side. You will hear a cracking as the spokes bed in.

Retrue the wheel—it may have gotten out of true in the straining—then, being firmer this time, repeat the process. Use judgment, though. You can permanently bend the rim with too much side load. Retrue again.

Between each truing and during the initial building, use a rim-centering tool or a wheel-building stand to make certain that the rim is centered. On a derailleur rear wheel, the rim must be centered between the ends of the locknuts, not between the flanges. This is known as "dishing" (see Figs. 9.13 and 9.14). Figure 9.15 shows the procedure used to true up a wheel that has developed side wobble and is out of round.

Points to remember:

(a) Hold the spokes below the nipple when tightening them to avoid spoke twist which will cause loosening.

(b) For good life, tension must be even. After setting, straining, and truing, "pluck" the spokes like a violin string to check the tension. While

Fig. 9.12   Axle bending check. Rotate axle, check for radial movement in relation to pointer.

rechecking truth, readjust as close as possible to even their pitch.

(c) If the nipples aren't angled correctly, carefully reset them with a punch.

Maintaining your wheels round and true is worth the effort. The vertical and lateral oscillation caused by wheels out of true radially or side to side decreases control and stability, particularly at speed and on slippery roads. These vibrations result in wasted energy and make the bicycle less comfortable. Note the difference of riding ease on a rough and a smooth road surface.

BENT RIMS

If the rim is kinked in or sideways, it may not be possible to true using the spokes alone. Determine the location and the injury.

If the rim is dented in or out, loosen the spokes and tap the dents out with a block of shaped wood and a hammer. Be careful not to dent the rim surface itself. The wood should be shaped to the inside or outside shape of the rim. ANJ Enterprises, W. Carrolton, Ohio, makes a rim-bending tool to do this job easily.

Sidewise protrusions, such as those caused by hitting a pothole, can be straightened by very carefully using a vise grip pliers or a hammer.

A side bend or wavy twist takes more skill. In a pinch on the road, note where the bend is located and loosen the

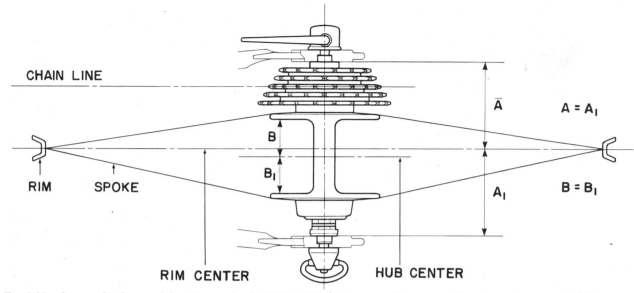

CHAIN LINE

RIM   SPOKE

B

$\overline{A}$

$A = A_1$

$B = B_1$

B₁

A₁

RIM CENTER   HUB CENTER

Fig. 9.13   On a multiple-speed derailleur, wheel is "dished." Rim is centered between fork ends, not between hub flanges.

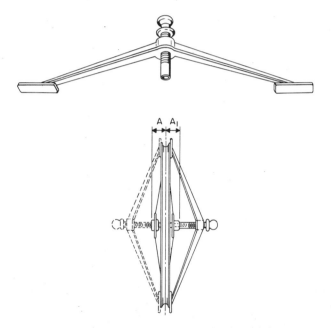

A A₁

Fig. 9.14   Rim centering tool aids in determining centering of rim.

RIM TRUEING

CORRECTING "SIDE WOBBLE"

(1) SPIN WHEEL SLOWLY AND LOCATE BUMPS WITH CRAYON ON EDGE OF RIM.

(2) LOOSEN SPOKES ON BUMP SIDE AND TIGHTEN ON OTHER SIDE OPPOSITE CRAYON MARK.

(3) NOTE: LOOSENING SPOKES ONE TURN ON ONE SIDE OF RIM AND TIGHTENING ONE TURN ON THE OTHER SIDE MOVES THE RIM ABOUT ⅛ INCH.

CORRECTING "OUT OF ROUND"

(1) LOCATE THE FLAT SPOT WITH CRAYON ON INSIDE OF RIM NEXT TO SPOKE NIPPLES.

(2) LOOSEN ALL SPOKES IN THE MARKED AREA, MIDDLE ONES MOST.

(3) LOCATE HUMP ON OUTSIDE OF RIM WITH CRAYON.

(4) TIGHTEN ALL SPOKES IN THE MARKED AREA, MIDDLE ONES MOST.

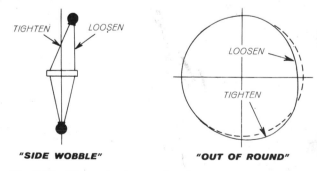

spokes in the affected area. Lay the wheel over a table-top, or even a log or fence rail, and firmly but gently try to push it into shape. Then retighten the spokes.

Straightening rims is an art that requires experience. Putting in a new rim may be easier, but new rims are not always available and these methods have gotten me home many times when damage occurred in a desolate area hundreds of miles from my destination. A serviceable, if not perfect, repair can be made using a fence rail or post.

Fig. 9.15   Rim truing instruction sheet.
(Courtesy of Columbia Manufacturing Company)

CHAPTER X

Health Aspects of Bicycling

By Eugene A. Gaston, M.D.

THE power that propels the bicycle and its rider comes from the human body, a truly remarkable machine that wears more slowly the more vigorously it is used. This chapter tells something of how that power is produced and expended. The various manifestations of heat disease are explained in relation to prevention and treatment. Diet, and the places of vitamins, minerals, drugs, and exercise in health and athletic efficiency are discussed. There is material on air pollution and the ways it affects the bicyclist. The section on Minor Health Problems of Bicycling includes discussions of saddle soreness, crotch and hand numbness, and problems with legs, knees, and feet.

MUSCLES

Bones and the joints that connect them form a system of levers that are, with a few notable exceptions, well designed for the uses to which they are put. These levers are activated by skeletal muscle, which makes up nearly half of the body's weight. The muscles apply force to the levers by contracting, or becoming shorter. The straightening of the knee, which produces part of the push on the bicycle pedal, results from the contraction of the quadriceps muscle on the front of the thigh. When the push is no longer needed, the quadriceps stops contracting and is passively elongated by the bending of the knee, which is produced by the contraction of the hamstring muscle on the back of the thigh.

A contracting muscle is able to exert a maximum force of about 42 pounds per square inch of cross-sectional area. The quadriceps muscle may have an area as large as 16 square inches and can apply a force of from 600 to 700 pounds to its tendon in front of the knee joint.

ENERGY

All bodily functions require energy, which is generated from the food we eat. During digestion, the carbohydrates, fats, and proteins contained in food are broken down into glucose, fatty acids, and amino acids. These nutrients are absorbed from the stomach and the intestines into the blood, which circulates them throughout the body.

The blood also absorbs oxygen from the lungs. In the muscle cells, oxygen combines with glucose to make adenosine triphosphate (ATP) and with fatty acids to make phosphocreatine (PC). These two remarkable compounds can instantly liberate energy as needed.

The reason moderate exercise can be performed over a long period of time is that ATP and CP are being produced as rapidly as they are consumed. In strenuous exercise, ATP and CP are used up at such a rate that not enough oxygen can be delivered to the cells to meet the demand. A response to the resulting oxygen deficit is the rapid, heavy breathing that continues for some minutes after the completion of exercise.

The chemical reactions that convert food to energy are not efficient. From 75% to 90% is lost as heat, and only from 10% to 25% is converted into usable energy for muscular work and other body functions. To maintain normal body temperature, the heat is dissipated in three ways. About 60% is lost by radiation, 18% by conduction, and 22% by evaporation. During vigorous exercise, heat production increases enormously, and heat and water losses through evaporation of sweat become increasingly important.

HEAT DISEASE

The bicyclist riding in hot weather may not appreciate the amount of water his body loses through sweating. The breeze keeps him cool by rapidly evaporating the sweat, and thirst is either not noticed or ignored. When exercising heavily in hot weather, ½ cup of water three or four times an hour may be needed to maintain the body's water balance. If too much water and minerals are lost through sweating, the onset of muscle cramps in the abdomen or legs may be the first indication that all is not well, but faintness and dizziness soon follow.

Heat cramps are the mildest form of heat disease. These painful contractions of muscles in the legs, arms, and trunk are caused by the loss of sodium and potassium in the sweat. Cramps can be prevented by increasing the amount of salt in meals before exercising or by the *judicious* use of salt tablets, which contain sodium and small but adequate amounts of potassium. Water loss must also be replaced, of course. And it is very important to take plenty of fluid, at least a quart of water with each salt tablet. To take salt tablets without adequate fluids makes matters worse by drawing water from the blood into the intestine, so less is available for sweating and cooling. Commercial preparations such as Gatorade, which combine minerals and sugar in a balanced solution, are a safe substitute for water and salt tablets.

Heat exhaustion is caused by a more severe degree of sodium depletion and by the loss of so much water that both the volume of interstitial fluid, which lubricates the cells in the body, and the volume of blood are significantly reduced. Symptoms include pallor, profuse sweating, muscle cramps, giddiness, difficulty with balance, and fainting, which is defined as the *momentary* loss of consciousness. Heat exhaustion responds rapidly to rest, which stops excessive heat production. In severe cases, water and salt may be given intravenously.

Heat stroke is the most dangerous form of heat disease, with a mortality rate that approaches 50%. It is most likely to occur when the weather is hot and humid, but is not limited to such days. Since only a small percentage of people exposed to the same conditions are affected, individual susceptibility is an important factor. Susceptibility may be due to lack of acclimatization, inadequate physical conditioning, obesity, fatigue, advanced age, or minor illnesses accompanied by fever and/or dehydration. Antihistamines, used in the treatment of allergies, and belladonna products, used for digestive disturbances, limit sweating and thereby increase susceptibility.

The first symptoms experienced by victims of heat stroke are severe thirst, profuse sweating, and dizziness. But the first sign that others note is loss of consciousness, sometimes preceded by confused, irrational behavior. Unconsciousness is soon followed by convulsions, vomiting, diarrhea, rapid pulse, and low blood pressure. In the early stages many victims sweat profusely, but others have dry skin. Body temperature increases rapidly, whereas it remains relatively stable with cramps and heat exhaustion. The victim's temperature can go as high as 108°F.

When unconsciousness and high fever are brief, recovery is usually rapid. When they persist four to ten hours, the patient generally will recover, but only after long illness due to severe, but repairable, damage to the liver and kidneys. Those who remain unconscious for longer periods usually die within three days. Death is caused by minute hemorrhages in blood vessels and defects in blood clotting, especially in the brain, liver, kidneys, and heart.

Heat stroke is an emergency which requires prompt treatment. This includes the immediate lowering of body temperature by the removal of clothing, and the use of shade, fans, and water or ice (or both) to cool the skin. However, dousing the victim with cold water may induce shock and greatly increase the possibility of death. If heat stroke is suspected, medical assistance must be obtained as soon as possible.

Common sense is a major preventive of heat stroke. To compete in a contest requiring exceptional endurance, one should be acclimated to the weather, in top physical condition, rested, and well hydrated. Avoid the use of all drugs, including antihistamines and belladonna products. Drink small amounts of water frequently during the contest and use salt tablets sparingly, not over one tablet with each quart of water consumed. If the flu or other minor illness comes on before the event, do not compete.

Proper training will reduce water loss. The cyclist should acclimate himself by riding increasingly longer distances prior to undertaking a long journey in hot weather. Excessive water intake should be avoided during this conditioning.

One popular misconception is that wearing heavy clothing during exercise to promote sweating eliminates "body poisons." Sweat contains no poisons, and the added difficulty of eliminating heat through heavy clothing adds to the burden of the heart.

DIET AND NUTRITION

An adequate diet includes water, minerals, and vitamins, plus sufficient Calories supplied as carbohydrate, fat, and protein. The average 150-pound man requires about 2000 Calories per day for the vital functions of the body, i.e., to maintain normal temperature and to supply energy for the muscles used in respiration, the beating of the heart, and the functioning of other organs. From 500 to 2500 additional Calories are needed each day to meet the energy demands of varying degrees of physical activity. When the Calories used by the body are exactly balanced by those supplied by food, weight remains constant.

Carbohydrates, chiefly starches and sugars, make up

the bulk of Caloric intake. They are absorbed from the intestines primarily as glucose, a simple sugar which is carried by the blood to all the tissues, where it is utilized by the cells. Excess glucose is converted to glycogen and stored by many tissues, but especially large amounts are stored in the liver and in muscles. When glycogen storage facilities are full, excess glucose is converted to fat.

When blood glucose falls below a critical level, liver glycogen is rapidly converted into glucose and poured into the blood to make up the deficit. The utilization of glucose is greatly increased during exercise, and when the exercise is prolonged and vigorous, the store of glycogen may be depleted. The blood glucose level can no longer be maintained, and under these circumstances, the brain is unable to function normally. This condition, known as hypoglycemia, is ushered in by the sudden onset of extreme fatigue and lassitude, followed by incoordination, difficulty with balance, and slurred speech. Eating candy or sugar is not advisable, however, because it draws water from the blood, where it is urgently needed, into the intestines. A sweetened, dilute salt solution, suitably flavored, is best, and such drinks are available commercially.

During moderate work, the energy for muscle contraction is chiefly supplied by the breakdown of fat. As the intensity of the work increases, fat is used less and carbohydrates more, until, with maximum exertion, all muscle energy is derived from the latter.

The daily requirement for protein is small because protein, when liberated from damaged body cells, is broken down into amino acids and resynthesized into new protein. There is always a net loss in this process, which is made up by eating about one gram of protein per day for each kilogram (2.2 pounds) of body weight. Some of this protein should be of animal origin (meat, fish, eggs) to supply the essential amino acids which are not all present in many plant proteins. When the diet contains an unnecessarily large amount of protein, the amino acids from the excess protein are broken down further, the nitrogenous part is excreted by the kidneys, and the remainder is converted to fat or carbohydrate. Exercise does not increase the need for protein, nor does consuming a lot of meat build strong muscles. Strong muscles are developed only by vigorous training and hard work.

VITAMINS AND MINERALS

Vitamins are necessary for life, health, and growth, but they do not supply energy. Diets that include meat, milk, and a variety of cooked and uncooked vegetables and fruits supply ample quantities of all vitamins for normal people. Outright deficiency of any of the vitamins is associated with fatigue and impaired physical performance, but the opposite is not true: excessive consumption of vitamins does not improve physical performance, and some vitamins taken in large doses can be dangerously toxic.

Vitamins are of two kinds, the fat soluble (A, D, K, and E) and the water soluble (B and C). Hypervitaminosis A (the illness caused by excessive intake of vitamin A) is characterized by nausea, vomiting, and diarrhea, a scaly skin rash, patchy loss of hair, and bone pain. Hypervitaminosis D is associated with weight loss, calcification of many soft tissues, and eventually, kidney failure. Hypervitaminosis K causes gastrointestinal disturbances and anemia. The toxic effects of excessive intakes of vitamins A, D, and K are so well known that they are seldom abused.

Much less is known about vitamin E. Because it is available in so many foods, a deficiency of vitamin E has never been identified, and research to determine whether increased dosages will improve athletic performance has been inconclusive.

Vitamins B and C are water soluble, and any excess of intake over body requirements is excreted by the kidneys. Vitamin B is a complex of several chemicals, each having a different function. One of these, thiamine, is utilized by daily body metabolism. Because physical activity increases the metabolic rate, it also increases the daily requirement for thiamine. Physical activity demands an increase of Calories and a balanced diet automatically provides additional B complex vitamins. Supplementation is unnecessary, though probably harmless.

Vitamin C occurs in nearly all fruits and in many vegetables. Many recent studies suggest, but do not prove, that vitamin C supplementation may help improve fitness. The final answer is not known and more extensive and better-controlled studies are needed. Until the issue is settled, if one wishes to try it, double or triple the daily requirement of 70 mg should not be harmful.

Huge doses of vitamin C, 1000 mg one to several times daily, have been advocated for the prevention and treatment of the common cold. There is no approved medical evidence that such massive doses are effective for this purpose, and recent studies have shown them to be positively harmful. Biochemical reactions are increased, causing the destruction of vitamin B_{12}, which is necessary for the formation of blood cells. Anemia results.

A number of minerals must be ingested daily to maintain health. These include iron, copper, iodine, and calcium, all of which are supplied by a diet that includes milk, meat, and iodized salt. Trace amounts of magnesium, manganese, cobalt, bromine, and zinc are also required but are easily supplied by a diet that is adequate in other respects.

DRUGS

Amphetamines and anabolic steroids (male hormones) are the drugs most commonly used in attempts to improve athletic performance.

The amphetamines are sold, illegally for competitive athletics, as Benzedrine or Dexedrine or combined with barbiturates. They have powerful effects on the central nervous system; fatigue and depression disappear and are replaced by euphoria and self-confidence, but athletic performance is worsened. As tolerance to amphetamines develops, ever-larger doses are required to obtain the psychic lift of the drug. The dangers of addiction and permanent damage to the nervous system are very real.

The anabolic steroids present another type of danger. At least 18 different steroid hormones are secreted by various glands for the control of specific body functions, some of which are essential to life. These normal hormones are integrated and balanced with each other in a complicated way that maintains the internal milieu necessary for normal health, growth, and development. Anabolic steroids are synthetic hormones that work on the utilization of protein, and the rationale for their use is that stronger muscles might thereby be developed. No evidence exists that this is true in normal people, although it may be partially true in those wasted by disease or starvation.

Anabolic steroids are dangerous because they upset the delicate balance between the normal steroid hormones and have various and unpredictable effects on future health. In addition they are androgenic (or masculinizing) and when taken by boys or young men, they can stop growth by causing the premature closing of the epiphyseal growth plates in bones. Atrophy of the testicles, loss of libido, and hypertrophy of the prostate may occur when they are taken by mature men.

Dr. Donald L. Cooper's condemnation of drug use to improve athletic performance (*Journal of the American Medical Association*, August 28, 1972, v. 221, pp. 1007–1011) is an excellent summary of medical opinion:

> "Normal" is the best there is. Drugs of any type should only be used in disease, deficiency states, or injury. Any other use is only a form of internal pollution, and there is no valid evidence that any drug ever improved any athlete's performance. The real difficulty is that many drugs make people feel they are better, but it is an illusion. This myth is perpetuated by the limited testing occasionally done on only the winners. When all the contestants have been tested, it has been found that more of the losers dabble in the drug area.

EXERCISE AND THE HEART

We live in a dangerous age. The mortality rate from coronary heart disease has increased steadily since the turn of the century until one out of every five men in the United States now has a heart attack before the age of

60, and two-thirds of these die before effective treatment can be started. Several factors have contributed to this increase. The most important among them are obesity, cigarette smoking, and lack of exercise.

Perhaps the most important cause of coronary heart disease is the sedentary life style to which 85% of the adult population is committed. The automobile, the elevator, the electric golf cart, the snowmobile, and the motorcycle have almost completely removed physical activity from daily living and even from some sports.

Studies of occupational groups have demonstrated the importance of exercise for the prevention of heart attacks. Conductors on two-story buses that ply the streets of London are physically active during the working day, moving on and off the buses, up and down the steps. They have about one-third less coronary heart disease than the drivers of the same buses who are seated and physically inactive during the working day. Similarly, North Dakota farmers have less than half as many heart attacks as their neighbors who are not farmers; farm laborers, those who do really heavy physical work, have only 18% as many.

The most convincing evidence, if more is needed, comes from a recently completed 20-year study by the United States Public Health Service of a cross section of the population of Framingham, Massachusetts. Over 5000 adults were examined for heart disease every two years and its incidence compared to degrees of physical activity. The incidence of coronary disease in men who were classed as sedentary was twice that of the moderately active, and these in turn had a higher incidence than the very active.

The basic defect in coronary heart disease is atherosclerosis of the coronary arteries which supply blood to the heart. High blood cholesterol levels are associated with a high incidence of atherosclerosis, or hardening of the arteries, and this disease, by narrowing the vessels, causes coronary heart attacks, cerebral strokes, and other serious circulatory problems. The implication for the diet is clear: insofar as is practical, dietary fat should be limited to the polyunsaturated variety. Fortunately for the bicyclist, regular vigorous exercise also tends to lower the blood cholesterol, helps diminish the incidence of coronary disease, and helps to ward off obesity.

Exercise helps prevent heart disease, including angina pectoris and heart attacks, not by preventing atherosclerosis (although its progress may be slowed) but by building up collateral circulation—new blood vessels—in the heart muscle. These take over the circulation of blood as the older vessels become obstructed. Even when a major coronary artery is suddenly obstructed and a heart attack occurs, the presence of collateral circulation improves the chances of survival and rehabilitation.

The middle-aged, obese, cigarette-smoking, sedentary man can do a great deal to minimize his chances of having coronary heart disease. He can stop smoking, he can reduce his weight, and he can initiate a gradually progressive exercise program that will eventually make him physically fit. To do all of this is not easy. But regular exercise will build morale that helps with the smoking and diet problems. Many individuals find group psychology helpful; groups are often sponsored by the Y.M.C.A. and similar organizations.

The type of exercise is less important than its regularity. People continue activities they find pleasant, and the fun and convenience of bicycling are among its important advantages. It can be done alone or in a group; the intensity and duration are easily varied. It gets one out of doors in good weather but can be done indoors, on rollers, when the weather is bad. From the health standpoint, it is equal to jogging or swimming.

Before any exercise program is started, one's physical condition should be evaluated by a physician and the intensity and duration of the beginning exercise established. Thereafter it should be gradually increased in duration or intensity or both, as physical fitness improves. The program should be continued past the period of aches and pains and in spite of frustrations and inconveniences because, in a few months, the quality of life will be improved by better sleep, tranquillity, renewed energy, and a feeling of being on top.

Once physical fitness has been achieved, it can and should be maintained indefinitely. Healthy people can continue vigorous physical activity well into old age, but to do so they should become physically fit early in life and stay that way.

AIR POLLUTION

Pollutants in the air irritate the respiratory tract and change its structure and function. Changes include slowing down or even stopping the action of the cilia, the hair-like projections that line the bronchial tubes. Their sweeping movement propels mucus, and the dirt and bacteria caught in it, to the outside. As the cilia function less efficiently, the quantity of mucus increases, becoming thicker and more difficult to expel. Foreign matter, including bacteria, is not effectively removed, and respiratory infections result. Obstruction of the flow of air into and out of the lungs increases because of a progressive constriction of the bronchial tubes. Emphysema, a common and very disabling condition, is caused by obstruction of the outflow of air, with resulting breakdown of the tiny air sacs of the lungs. Finally, the cells lining the bronchial tubes may be destroyed, and the continued destruction and regrowth of these cells leads to lung cancer in susceptible individuals.

Among the major air pollutants are sulfur, present in fuel oil and coal, and the oxidants, or photochemical smog, which are produced by radiant energy from the sun acting on hydrocarbons and oxides of nitrogen. The most important ingredient of smog is ozone, a highly toxic gas that can cause acute changes in lung function. Fortunately, hazardous levels of ozone occur only at midday and are of short duration.

Particulates are solid or liquid particles floating in the atmosphere. Those larger than two or three microns (a micron is about 1/25,000 of an inch) are trapped in the air passages, but smaller particulates penetrate deeply into the lungs, carrying bacteria and toxic chemicals which adhere to their surfaces.

Carbon contributes soot, which is particulate matter resulting from incomplete combustion, and two gases, carbon dioxide (CO_2) and carbon monoxide (CO), to the atmosphere. Carbon dioxide is used by plants for photosynthesis, and the rising amounts produced by human activities are not dangerous.

Carbon monoxide, a colorless and odorless gas, is, however, very toxic. It is present in high concentrations in cigarette smoke, but the chief source is exhaust from motor vehicles and heating fuel. Its toxicity results from the ease with which it combines with hemoglobin, the red matter of the blood which carries oxygen to the tissues. The affinity of hemoglobin for carbon monoxide is over 200 times greater than its affinity for oxygen; and to the extent that the former combine to form carboxyhemoglobin (COHb), oxygen cannot be transported. Once COHb is formed, several hours are required for its removal from the blood. Nonsmoking city dwellers have from 0.62% to 1.24% COHb in their blood, moderate smokers from 4.0% to 6.0%, and heavy smokers up to 12%. Alertness is reduced in healthy persons at COHb levels of 6.6% and progressively worsens up to concentrations of 20%, when exercise performance is greatly reduced.

Weather and geography are important factors in air pollution. Wind rapidly disperses and dilutes air pollutants so that, under typical conditions, they are not health hazards. When a layer of warm air overlies cooler surface air so the latter cannot rise and mix, a temperature inversion results. There are several causes of inversions, which are more common in valleys and during the colder months. In industrial areas the stagnant surface air, trapped by an inversion, accumulates increasing amounts of pollutants. When the temperature then falls, water vapor condenses into fog, oxides of sulfur and nitrogen are converted into acids, and the stage is set for respiratory disasters, which chiefly strike the elderly and chronically ill. In 1952 the noxious air of such an inversion caused the deaths of 4,000 people in London.

The health effects of air pollution depend on the concentration of pollutants, the duration and frequency of exposures, and the rate and depth of respirations. The exercising bicyclist inhales more air in a given time than the physically inactive automobile driver. Commuting by bicycle in moving traffic when there is some wind to dilute and disperse pollutants is not dangerous. However, on foggy, windless days when temperature inversions increase the concentrations of pollutants, especially in dense, stop-and-go traffic and in industrial areas, it is wise to use other means of transportation. Bicycle commuting at off hours, or using less congested routes even though longer, are alternatives to consider.

Pollution of ambient air by automobile and industrial exhaust presents a negligible risk to health when compared to inhaling cigarette smoke. Smoking a pack a day more than doubles the risk of developing coronary heart disease, increases the chance of emphysema about 300 times, and 95% of lung cancers occur in cigarette smokers. Cigarette smoke is the most concentrated and dangerous of all common pollutants.

The Minor Health Problems of Bicycling

Like all sports, bicycling is associated with minor physical disabilities which if untreated or mistreated can progress to discouraging proportions. The following are those problems most commonly encountered.

Saddle Soreness

Saddle soreness is a miserable condition that has two basic causes, pressure and friction. Pressure causes two types of injury, *ischial compression* and *numb crotch syndrome*. The injury caused by friction is called *saddle burn.*

Ischial compression is caused by pressure on the soft tissues which are squeezed between the saddle and the ischial tuberosities, the portion of the pelvis on which you sit. The compression is aggravated by the inability or failure of the bicyclist to change positions frequently, as is done in normal chair sitting. Softening the saddle with padding, springs, or both, delays the onset of pain and possibly reduces its severity, but causes other problems, including increased friction and wasted energy. Many bicyclists agree that the best saddle is one covered with leather which has been treated by prolonged soaking in neat's-foot oil or other leather softener. The tension bolt of the saddle should be tightened enough to prevent sagging, while allowing the areas of support to be resilient without being soft.

On long rides, however, some ischial pain is almost inevitable. It can be relieved by a slight change in the tilt of the saddle—one or two degrees or perhaps even less. When the pain returns, as it eventually does, another shift of angle will again give relief. Changing the tilt duplicates the natural shifts of position which are part of normal sitting.

A quick-release tilt control can be easily made by substituting a shortened, quick-release hub spindle for the bolts that normally secure the tilt adjustment on an Ideale Super Competition, micro-adjusting seat clamp.

A detailed description was published in the March 1976 issue of *BICYCLING!* magazine. This device makes frequent changes of angle possible without the use of tools and, with a little practice, even without dismounting.

Another problem, known as the numb crotch syndrome, involves numbness of the penis, scrotum, and nearby areas after long rides. The numbness usually lasts only a few hours, but it may persist for a month or more. It can be prevented by not allowing the narrow part of the saddle to slide up. Tilting the saddle forward, raising the handlebars, and shortening the distance between handlebars and saddle all help in shifting body weight to the wide part of the saddle. If this is not satisfactory, a platform-type saddle such as the Lemet Rok, made in Holland and available in this country, may solve the problem. Another possibility is a Dan Henry sling-type saddle.

Saddle burn is caused by the friction of underwear rubbing against the skin of the crotch. Saddle burn usually involves only the outer layer of skin, the epidermis, which is in turn made up of multiple layers of cells. The initial injury in saddle burn is mechanical destruction of cells which lie immediately above the deepest layer of the epidermis. Fluid collects in the areas occupied by the destroyed cells, forming tiny blisters which coalesce into larger blisters. An inflammatory reaction is started, with dilation of local blood vessels and escape of fluid from the blood into the surrounding tissues. This results in swelling, pain, and tenderness. The next step is infection. Overcoming the infection, and draining the pus from abscesses when they are present, makes possible the repair of damaged tissue during which scar tissue replaces the destroyed dermis.

The treatment of saddle burn consists almost entirely of prevention. But once the injury has taken place, the most effective treatment is to stop riding until the inflammation has subsided and healing is complete. When there is no infection bland ointments, such as Vaseline, give some relief. When infection is present antibiotics may be helpful, but they should be prescribed by a physician.

Saddle burn can be prevented by eliminating as much as possible the friction between the underwear and skin. In mild cases only a lubricant may be needed, such as talcum powder or cornstarch. Carry some on the bike and use it as frequently as needed. Vaseline is also good, but it is messy and may stain your clothing.

Ideal undershorts for the bicycle rider are made of soft, absorbent material which is knitted to fit snugly and with as few seams as possible. It should cling to the skin so friction occurs only between underwear and outer clothing. The parts covering the thighs should be snug, tapered, and sufficiently elastic to stay down where they belong. Unfortunately such garments are not easy to find. Of those that are available, the ones made of synthetic fibers seem to retain their elasticity, have less tendency to crawl up, and have seams that are softer and less abrasive than garments made of cotton.

Outerwear pants should fit snugly and be sufficiently elastic to allow freedom of movement without wrinkles or folds. They should glide freely over the surface of the saddle, seams should not be bulky enough to become abrasive, and they should be easy to clean. Garments made of doubleknit, wash-and-wear material probably come closest to meeting these specifications.

Even with minimal friction between saddle and pants, there is always some motion between pants and underwear when pedaling a bicycle. The resulting friction will do no harm as long as underwear clings to the skin. But if sweat makes underwear and pants stick together, the friction is transferred to the skin. Inserting a lining of acrylic pile, the artificial fur used to line winter coats, into your outerwear pants is remarkably satisfactory in keeping underwear and pants from adhering to each other.

Backache and Neck Strain

Many beginning cyclists note discomfort in the lower back because their muscles and ligaments have not yet become conditioned to the riding position. The discomfort usually disappears with continued riding, but it can often be prevented with simple stretching exercises. Touch the fingers to the floor with the knees straight (or try to) 20 or 30 times before rides. During rides, change the position of the hands on the handlebars frequently, from the down to the up, to the middle, and back again. The spinal curve is thereby changed and discomfort relieved. This feature makes drop handlebars popular. Professional advice should be obtained if back pain is severe and persistent, especially if it radiates down one or both legs.

The down position of the handlebars does, however, make it necessary to hyperextend the neck to see the road ahead. The muscles and ligaments on the back of the neck may become sore and extremes of flexion and rotation painful. This discomfort is also prevented by frequently changing position on the handlebars. Chronic stiffness usually disappears spontaneously, and the local application of heat and limbering-up exercises of the neck before rides speed recovery.

Leg Cramps

Leg cramps which come on during a ride may indicate potentially serious depletion of water and salt. If this is not the case, the cramps are probably due to pushing too hard on the pedals. Try using a lower gear.

Leg cramps which persistently come on with mild exertion, such as walking, and disappear promptly when the activity ceases, usually indicate a blockage of one of the main arteries to the leg. See your doctor.

The cause of leg cramps that come during sleep is not known. Some people are much more susceptible than others, and no treatment is universally successful. Some are helped by quinine, which should be prescribed by a physician. Tonic water contains quinine and a glass of this is worth trying.

Knee Strain

As already noted, the quadriceps muscle on the front of the thigh can exert a tremendous force. As a result, a few fibers of the quadriceps tendon, which inserts into the leg just below the knee, are occasionally torn. If this happens, there is pain and tenderness just above or below the knee cap. The lateral ligaments, on the inside and outside of the knee, may receive similar tears from hard pushing when the foot is improperly positioned on the pedal. These injuries may be quite disabling and are slow to heal.

Ease off at the first symptom. Do not push hard enough to cause pain—pain may indicate more injury being done to the tendon or ligament. If the pain is on the inside or outside of the knee, change the position of the foot on the pedal; for most people the foot should point straight ahead or be very slightly pigeon-toed. Over the long haul, aspirin by mouth and heat locally will help, but the basic treatment is rest until the healing is complete. It is probably safe to bicycle for moderate distances, without hard pushing, if there is no pain during or after the ride. The penalty for overexertion is prolonged disability, often lasting six months or more.

Chondromalacia of the knee cap (softening and degeneration of the cartilage) has only been recently recognized as a common source of knee pain. Its cause is not known, but it often begins abruptly with a dull pain in the front of the knee, and swelling is common. Usually there is no obvious injury or change of activity. Young adults are the most vulnerable, but it can occur at any age. The pain is aggravated by prolonged sitting with the knee flexed, and especially by increased pressure of the knee cap against the end of the thigh bone, as when descending steps or pushing a bicycle pedal. Chondromalacia may spread and permanently cripple the knee, but early treatment usually assures complete recovery. Treatment consists chiefly of avoiding pressure under the knee cap until pain and tenderness are completely gone, which may take weeks or months. Supervision by an experienced and interested physician is of first importance. He may prescribe treatments such as exercises, anti-inflammatory medication, or surgery in extreme cases.

Numbness of the Hands

Almost every bicyclist notices that his hands occasionally "go to sleep." Usually of short duration, this becomes quite annoying when it persists, and it can lead to inadequate control. The cause is pressure on the ulnar or median nerves that carry sensation from the hands.

The ulnar nerve extends along the side of the wrist and hand to supply sensation to the little finger and the adjacent half of the ring finger. These areas become numb when this nerve is subjected to pressure. Pressure on it can also temporarily paralyze small muscles of the hand with resulting awkwardness in the fingers. Pressure on the ulnar nerve results when the fingers grip the vertical part of the handlebar and weight is borne on the little finger side of the wrist and hand. Symptoms are relieved by avoiding pressure on this area.

The median nerve supplies sensation to the thumb, index, and middle fingers, and the adjacent half of the ring finger. It lies in the middle of the wrist and palm. Pressure may be applied either directly or by riding with the wrists bent forcibly back. The latter can be avoided only by self-discipline.

Direct pressure can be relieved by padding, but the pads on commercial bicycling gloves are too thin. Preferring well-padded gloves, I sew shaped pads, made of foam rubber one inch thick, into pockets on the palms of cotton gardening gloves. Some riders pad the handlebar. Foamed tubing, used for insulating refrigeration pipes and available at plumbing supply stores, is convenient for this purpose. The best size, ⅞-inch OD or ½-inch IPS, is slightly too large and tends to slip unless the bar is first covered with adhesive tape. The surface of the installed tubing can be protected with twill handlebar tape or adhesive tape. Bailey III handlebar tape, with thick soft center and tapered edges, is effective and easily applied.

The Randonneur handlebar helps to eliminate hand numbness by giving better weight distribution. This bar has a slight upward bend from the center to each side, and the top and bottom grip positions are nearly parallel. The angle of the bar can be critical, and a very slight adjustment, made by rotating the bar in the stem, will often help.

Painful Feet

A normal foot has three weight-bearing points: the heel and the heads of the first and fifth metatarsal bones (near the bases of the great and little toes). The transverse arch prevents weight from bearing on the heads of the second, third, and fourth metatarsal bones, but when the arch is flattened by hard pushing on the pedal, these may become painful. The discomfort disappears when a suitably shaped pad is properly placed in the riding shoe to support the arch. Adhesive metatarsal pads, for sticking in shoes, are available at many drug and shoe stores.

Pain on top of the foot usually is caused by a bent toe clip or by a strap or shoe that is too tight.

The soles of riding shoes should be sufficiently stiff not to buckle under pressure. Bicycle racers use specially made metal sole plates to prevent this, but the tourist will find them uncomfortable for walking, and they mar the finish of wooden floors.

Riders sometimes have a problem with the sole of the foot falling asleep on a long journey. Many riders keep constant foot pressure on the pedals, letting the pedal push the idle foot up on its upstroke. Quite naturally, this requires increased pressure from the working foot. Lifting the leg consciously on the upstroke momentarily restores circulation to the sole of the foot. This load-unload technique may result in complete freedom from this complaint.

FINALLY

Physical fitness comes only at a price. Deconditioned muscles are stiff and sore for several days following exercise, but this nuisance is progressively eliminated by the conditioning process. All muscles, conditioned or not, hurt when the work load exceeds certain limits, but this disappears almost immediately when the load is eased. The bicyclist learns to tolerate this discomfort until even long, steep hills are climbed with feelings of accomplishment and satisfaction. Perseverance is the key to enjoyment.

CHAPTER XI

Spacecraft with a Human Engine

OUR CYCLING "SPACECRAFT"

Skillful cyclists vary their choice of equipment and method of riding to obtain the best performance with a minimum of energy. As in spacecraft, we have only a limited amount of fuel, and this can be used up quickly with high demands. The graphs in Figures 11.1 and 11.2 give some idea of the power we need at different speeds. Figure 11.3 shows the power our "Human Engine" can provide.

Rolling resistance from bearings, tires, and chain can vary greatly. An extralight sew-up tire will have the least resistance, although some new wired-on types are almost as good. Inflation pressure has a considerable effect (see Chapter VIII, the section on tires and tubes). Derailleur gearing can be quite efficient, if the chain tension is kept to the minimum, say from 92% to 96%. Experiments made by Frank Whitt show that three-speed hub gears in low gear range from 85% to 90% efficient, depending on the load applied.

Of the controllable factors, air resistance has the greatest effect on cycling effort. Experiments performed by T. Nonweiler in the wind tunnel at Cranford University in England have shown that the deeply crouched racing position greatly reduces the effort required. The cyclist riding in an erect posture, which was once most common, will use twice the power used by a crouched rider for overcoming air resistance. Clothing can have a big effect. The racer wears tight-fitting, smooth-surfaced togs, cuts his hair short, and carries a minimum of air-catching impedimenta. His tires and rims are small in section. He may even reduce the number of spokes.

Tests on skiers have shown that a low, crouched position with arms held in close and extended reduces air resistance to a value only 27% of that encountered when skiing in the erect posture. Holding the arms away from the body doubled the air drag! Nonweiler's tests showed that some positions of the arms increased drag of bicycle and rider by 30% and that loose and flapping clothing caused another 30% increase.

The bicycle itself causes from ⅓ to ¼ of the total drag. The addition of bags and brake and derailleur cables, bottles, fenders, and carriers all exact their toll.

William Curtis, Director of Research and Development for Fairchild-Hiller Aircraft and an avid cyclist, has shown the air resistance of a recumbent posture bicycle to be as much as 1/3 less than that of a normal racing bicycle (when riders are included). Figure 11.8 shows Dan Henry on a recumbent riding with companions. The difference in frontal area is evident. Mr. Curtis estimates that a streamlined enclosure could cut the air resistance of a normal bike in half, while a recumbent cycle in an especially designed streamlined enclosure could eliminate ⅞ of the total drag encountered by a cyclist riding in an upright position.

At about 10 mph on level road, 50% of the power output is used overcoming air resistance, but above 25 mph, more than 90% of the effort you apply goes to overcome wind drag (see Figs. 11.1 and 11.2). Headwinds increase losses to air resistance in proportion. The erect posture riding position, baggy clothing, outspread elbows, and bushy hair or beards all add to the requirements shown.

The weight of the bicycle is not nearly as large a factor as is commonly conceived. An increase of 10 pounds to a total weight for bike and rider of 170 pounds on a 5% grade increases effort by only 4% or 5%. On the level this 10-pound difference increases

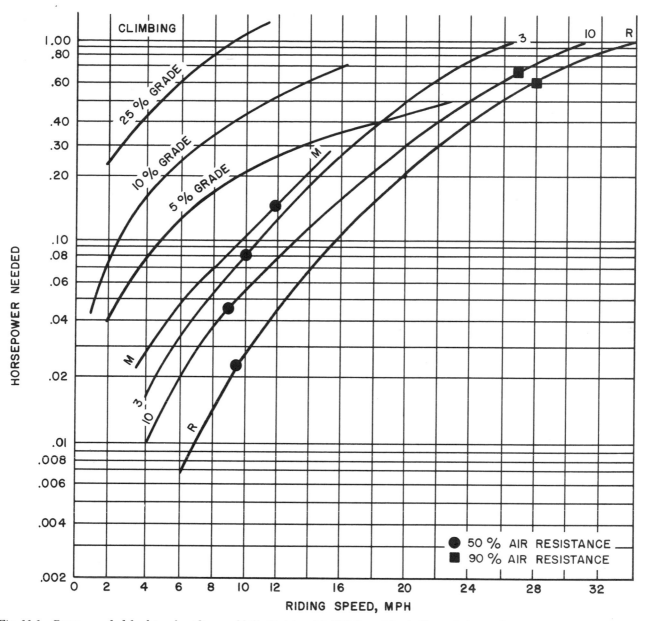

Fig. 11.1   Power needed for bicycle riding and hill climbing. M, Middleweight, balloon; 3, 3-speed tourer, 26 × 1⅜; 10, 10-speed tourer, 27 × 1¼; R, Road racer, crouched.

the load less than 3% at 10 mph, while at 25 mph the effect is well under 1%—far too little to detect. If part of the weight gained provides a more rigid frame, an actual gain in efficiency may result.

The speed maintained on hills and the amount of the slope encountered can be a "killer" to the cyclist not in excellent condition. Figure 11.1 also shows the additional power needed to climb grades of 5%, 10%, and 25%. It is small wonder that as grades increase, your "granny gears" help so greatly to maintain an efficient pedaling speed, even though your forward travel may slow to walking speed.

Even if partially from behind, a quartering wind can greatly increase your load. Riding in formation, echeloned if the wind is from the side, will greatly re-duce air drag. Search for proximity to road banks, tree shelter, or any other means of even slight shelter when you fight against the wind. Keep your position low, your outer clothing buttoned or removed, and your arms in close.

THE HUMAN ENGINE

As we ride, we can study ourselves and determine tactics and methods to get the best performance, the most speed, to climb hills the easiest, or to ride with minimum effort. A coach is helpful, but the more we learn about ourselves, the more rewarding riding be-comes. An automobile engine can be tuned and tested with a dynamometer to predict the best performance; we are not as easily defined.

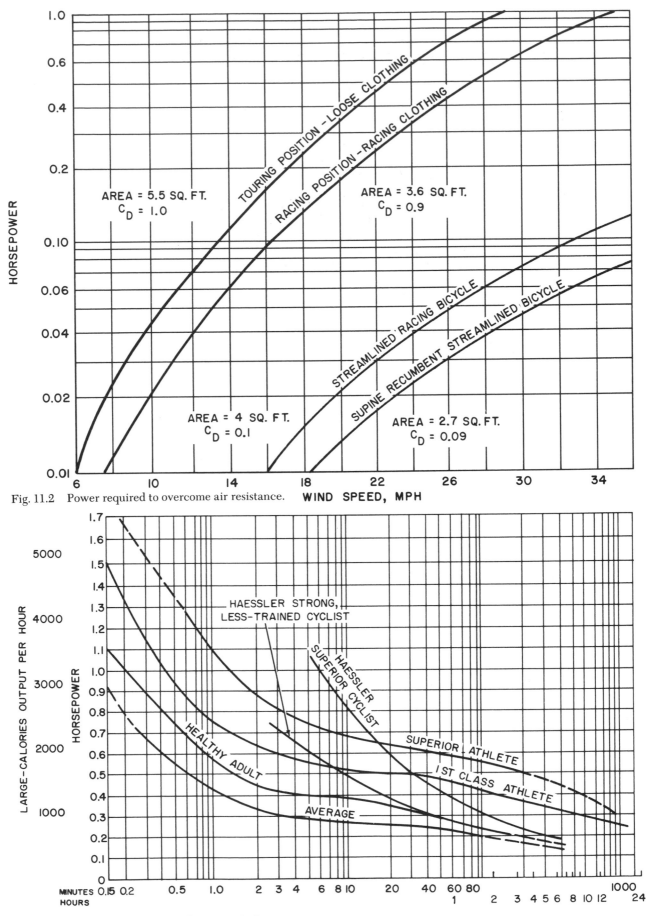

Fig. 11.2   Power required to overcome air resistance.   **WIND SPEED, MPH**

Fig. 11.3   Human power output: duration of effort.

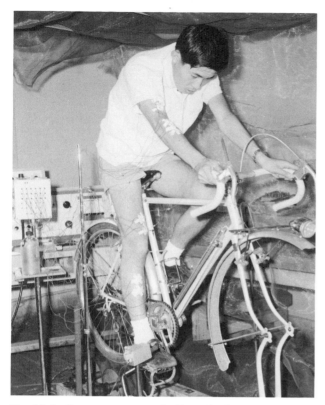

Fig. 11.4 Instruments record effect of riding load of rider on ergometer. *(Courtesy of Shinichi Toriyama)*

Fig. 11.7 Oxygen consumption and muscular efficiency being measured with variations in riding position, gearing, and crank length.

(Courtesy of Shinichi Toriyama)

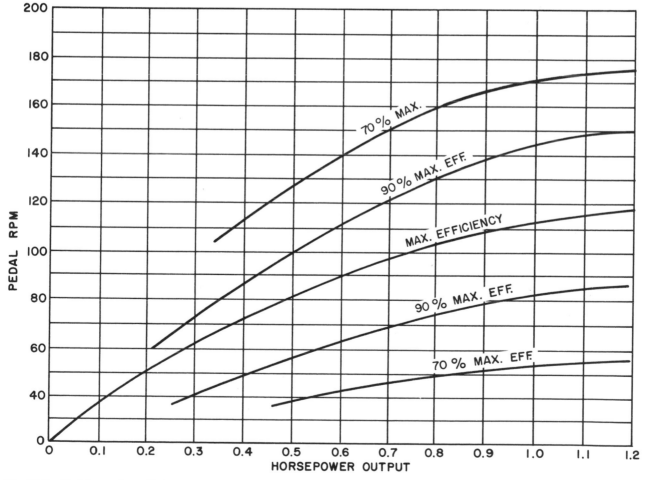

Fig. 11.5 Pedal speed vs. efficiency.

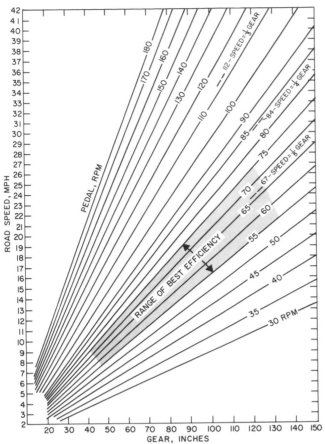

Fig. 11.6   Road speed, mph, vs. gear and pedal rpm.

The auto engine "breathes" in air and then adds gasoline in proportion to the air supplied. "Stepping on the gas" is actually opening the throttle so that more air can enter.

To accelerate from a standing start, we use a lower gear and run the engine fast to suck in more air and give more power. But a limit is soon reached. If we stay in low gear, the power needed just to run the engine increases until no more is left to accelerate the car. Then a higher gear is used, and the engine runs slower until a new peak is reached, at which point a third gear is used. But if the higher gear were used at the outset or on a hill, the engine would not provide sufficient torque, "twisting power," to get up speed or climb the hill. Horsepower output is the product of torque *and* speed; it is what is left over after the power to run the engine has been developed.

In our "engine," it takes power to turn our legs even if no output power is being given. If we race down a hill, or on the rollers, we can get tired and overheated even though there is no output. Even with no load, each of us has a maximum pedal revolution speed we cannot exceed. Likewise, there is a maximum force our legs can produce. If the hill is too steep, we may use both legs with our toe clips, but eventually we may have to get off and walk.

Increasing the length of our cranks increases our pedal torque; we can then climb steeper hills. But back on the level, the extra leg movement may tire us or limit

Fig. 11.8   The decrease in air resistance afforded by Dan Henry's recumbent bicycle is obvious. *(Courtesy of V. Hershfield)*

Fig. 11.9   Bicycle with long cranks. Note extended wheels and high crank hanger.

Fig. 11.10   Long cranks.

the rate at which our legs can spin. In a lower gear, we use less force more often, but on the level, leg spin will limit speed. Selection of the combination of crank length, gearing, pedal force, and speed of pedaling best for you is a part of "learning to know yourself."

Let's not assume that both legs work equally well. The Japanese Research Institute tested cyclists at various speeds and loads. The pedal pressure, pedaling speed, torque produced, and bicycle speed were measured. Crank lengths varied from 145 to 190 mm, both with equal lengths on each side and with left and right side lengths differing over this range. The riders' opinion of "how it feels" was recorded. It was discovered that one leg might produce as much as 10% difference in output compared to the other. Large differences in crank length were not favored, but a difference of as much as 10 mm reportedly "feels good." For the same

bicycle speed, pedal force should decrease as crank length increases. This force varied unequally for left and right legs. In some subjects pedal force even increased at greater crank lengths, indicating less efficient pedaling.

Our "Human Engine" uses some oxygen and food just to keep us alive and warm. Above this minimum, one liter of oxygen absorbed per minute should be able to produce 4/10 horsepower, but at best our engine is only about 25% efficient. Three-quarters of the oxygen and food absorbed is burnt heating us up and producing perspiration to keep us cool. Each liter of oxygen, obtained from five liters of air, produces only 1/10 hp.

An average man's lungs can absorb three liters per minute; he can work for long periods at half this rate. Physical training and hard exercise can increase this capacity, and seasoned athletes can work at 80% to 90% of their maximum capacity for long periods. You too have this potential.

Our "Human Engine" has another remarkable characteristic (see Fig. 11.3). Several researchers on human power output have found that by burning oxygen reserves in the tissues, power can be generated at amounts well above the maximum capacity for up to about 5 minutes. For periods of from 10 to 60 seconds, almost twice the continuous capability can be generated. We can use this reserve in a sprint, to climb a short, steep hill, or to escape from danger, but if the effort is too prolonged, collapse and loss of control result.

The capacity to absorb oxygen decreases with age. At age 80, it is only half what it was at age 20. The rate at which blood and oxygen are carried to the tissues depends on the size of the heart and heartbeats per minute. Training at sufficiently high outputs increases heart capacity and size and improves breathing capacity. The average person's heart beats 72 times per minute. At exhaustive output this may increase to 175. But training increases the heart's capacity so that at rest, lower heart rates will supply the body's needs. Many racing cyclists have resting heart rates in the mid 40s. Some long-distance runners have resting heart rates in the 30s and a high degree of training can increase the maximum tolerable heartbeat rate to well over 200.

The maximum pulse rate that is safe also decreases with age. If you plan any intensive effort, it is prudent to have a doctor determine your limit. The maximum heart rate decreases from 220 to 200 between ages 10 to 15, and to 165 at age 65. Dr. Herman K. Hellerstein, well-known cardiologist of Cleveland, writing in the "Schwinn Reporter," recommends that you exercise three to four times per week for 30 to 45 minutes (continuous) at a heart rate of at least 70%, with peaks of 85%, of your maximum heartbeat rate. Your maximum heart rate up to age 45 is about (230 — your age), 170 at 55, and 165 at 65. For a 60-year-old cyclist, this would be 118 average and 142 peak beats per minute, for 20-year-olds, 140 average and 170 peak beats per minute.

With the proper gearing to reduce the effort required, cyclists in good condition can enjoy the sport well into their 70s and high 80s. They can climb mountains steadily at a reasonable speed. They may arrive at their destination a bit behind their younger companions, and they may avoid sprints for the top, but they will see more on the way. The joy and challenge of cycling remain; the knowledge of nature and the countryside increases.

Women are men's equals. William Adams, at the Human Performance Laboratory, University of California at Davis, showed in 1966 that sex had no effect on energy expenditure in cycling. The subjects studied ranged in age from 20 to 53.

Other research may guide you in your study of yourself, whether you race, or in your private competition against wind, hills, or riding companions. Benedict and Cathcart in 1913; Campbell, Davis, and Hobson in 1920; Garry and Wishart in 1931; researchers at the Kaiser Wilhelm Institute of Germany, and at the Japanese Bicycle Research Institute in recent times, to name a few, have all studied cycling performance in depth.

Their experiments have shown that to obtain the maximum performance with greatest efficiency the pedal speed must increase as the power output rises. Due to size and build differences, an individual's most efficient speed range may vary. A composite of test results is indicated in Figure 11.5. The pedal speeds for maximum efficiency at various outputs are shown, as is the pedal speed range for 90% and 70% of maximum efficiency. As pedal speeds are raised, more power is needed just to turn the legs; but as pedal speeds are reduced, more muscular force is required to give equal power.

Garry and Wishart found that untrained cyclists reached a point of no external power output at 120 rpm. At this rate all their energy was needed just to turn their legs, but some nimble cyclists have been able to reach speeds of almost 200 rpm.

A study of record holders' pedaling speeds for the hour record, for time trialing in the Tour de France, for time trialing in England, and for other road racing events has shown a remarkable consistency, with speeds ranging from 88 to 109 rpm, with the majority being around the midpoint of this range. Maximum short-term power output occurred at about 115 rpm. Anquetil's hour record was set at 92 rpm. Merckx set his hour record of 49.41 km in 1972 at 105 pedal rpm and his fastest 10 km at 106 rpm using 175-mm cranks and a 98 gear.

Researchers agree that the highest (almost 25%) efficiency of muscle use at moderate outputs, the best "output power per pound of oatmeal consumed," is obtained at pedal speeds in the range of from 42 to 55 rpm. In a recent Japanese study, four cyclists were tested at various speeds using a wide range of gearing. Comparisons of oxygen consumption at each speed with different gears showed consistent results. Most efficient outputs were obtained as follows:

12 mph	42 rpm (pedal speed)
15 mph	49 rpm
18 mph	61–66 rpm
21 mph	65–70 rpm

Figure 11.6 will enable you to find the right gear to use for the pedal rpm you select at various road speeds.

CRANK LENGTH

Since the 1880s there have been many debates on the subject of proper crank length. In 1897, Monsieur Perrache wrote about experiments he had made on a fixed course in France using 160, 190, and 220-mm cranks. He found that he could develop maximum power with all the cranks at from 110 to 115 rpm. Exceeding this rate with the longer cranks caused power to fall off more quickly, and the maximum power developed decreased with increased length. However, he concluded that the heavy cyclist in mountainous country could profit by using longer cranks with equal gearing.

Carlo Bourlet, famed cycle engineer in France at the same period, calculated that the maximum length that a rider can effectively use is one-half the thigh length from hip socket to knee joint. James Farnsworth of New Hampshire states that this length has been found excellent for himself; F. C. Frazine of Florida reports similar findings; and Milton Morse of New Jersey has increased his average speed on tour with longer cranks. Eddy Merckx—who is tall—has used 180-mm cranks on time trials and mountain ascents in the Tour de France and 175-mm cranks for his world's hour record. The "normal" crank length is 170 mm (6.7 inches).

In tests conducted at the University of New South Wales, Australia, in 1970, J. Y. Harrison found that though his subjects, who were not skilled cyclists, preferred a longer crank, there was no significant performance variation with crank lengths up to eight inches (about 203 mm).

Tests at the Japanese Bicycle Research Institute in which times were compared for a 1,000-meter course with cranks of from 165 to 178 mm showed that a novice did best with 170-mm cranks. A time trialist did equally well on all sizes, and a professional road racer had best performance with both the shortest and the longest cranks. With lower gears, he did best with shorter cranks; with higher gears, longer cranks gave best times.

Mr. Farnsworth has introduced the concept of "effort ratio" to replace the usual method of expressing "gear." Effort ratio is a calculation of road speed compared to foot speed expressed in percentages. (Table 7.6 permits calculation of effort ratio, gear development, and road speed.

The use of longer cranks requires modifying the bicycle design (see Figs. 11.6 and 11.7). The crank hanger must be raised to provide ample ground clearance, or else the pedal will hit the ground on sharp turns. The front wheel must be extended, or its diameter reduced, to provide clearance between toe clip and front wheel when turning. The rear must be likewise extended so that the pedal and the rear of the feet do not strike the chainstays and luggage.

My own experience is inconclusive. Having used standard lengths for many years, I did not find longer cranks satisfying even after four or five hundred miles. I would strongly suggest that you make your own trial to determine what is best for you.

DUAL POWER

For those readers seriously interested in competition and record breaking, the results of Dr. Harrison's experiments at the University of New South Wales in 1970 will be of interest. He found that the legs alone can use more oxygen than the blood can supply them with. Of course, the use of other muscles simultaneously, such as those of the hands, arms, and body, diverts available blood flow from the heart to several members.

The use of a modified rowing motion with fixed seat position and linkages obtained remarkably high power outputs. The linkages fed energy back into the system at the ends of the stroke, from changes in the speed and direction of movement of body parts. Two horsepower was obtained for six seconds, one horsepower for one minute, and ¾ horsepower for two minutes. This is far more than can be obtained using the legs alone. Using as large a mass of muscle as possible helped. Using force to slow down and change the direction of body parts at the end of the stroke actually wastes useful energy.

Dr. Harrison tested oval chainwheels, and these gave somewhat better performance. The chainwheels tested were of great ovalness.

For years, I have used the Thetic oval chainwheel developed in Belgium in the 1930s. After a mile or two, it feels smoother in motion than a round sprocket. Its smaller diameter is at the bottom of the pedal stroke, giving a lower gear at this point. At the center of the stroke, its diameter is about 8% larger than the mean. Thus a higher gear is available when the leg is in a position to give maximum power thrust. The Thetic oval was used both in competitive racing and for long-distance touring. It improved acceleration and made hill climbing definitely easier. Its proportions are more practical than the chainwheels used in the Harrison tests.

Fig. 11.11   Durham elliptical sprocket. Eccentricity ± 25%.

Fig. 11.12   Rocket oval front sprocket. Angle between the largest diameter of sprocket and the crank can be altered.

Fig. 11.13   Thetic oval front sprocket with a hollow, steel lightweight oval-section crank. Sprocket made in Belgium. Ovality ± 8%.

Bridgestone Cycle Co. in Japan has recently reintroduced a double oval sprocket which may be used with a front derailleur. The position of the crank with respect to the large diameter differs from the Thetic, and tests will determine the results of this. Durham Bicycles, Los Angeles, makes one designed to give almost constant foot speed away from the rider's center of gravity for 82° of crank rotation. It has ± 25% ovality.

Dr. Harrison concluded that a constant speed of

Fig. 11.14   Bridgestone (Japanese) double oval front sprocket set.

foot travel over an elliptical path with the major axis vertical would give even better performance. Some years ago, a very favorable test of this type motion was carried out in Russia, and results were reported as being excellent.

Dr. David Wilson at the Massachusetts Institute of Technology describes a pivoted lever motion with a variable attachment point for the driving chain which would provide an infinitely variable gear range.

Pivoted lever drives have been tried in the past, but they have always been supplanted by rotary pedals. In 1973 Harris Dynamics developed a greatly improved design which corrects previous deterrents to even motion and allows the most effective use of the leg muscles at each instant without the dead centers that characterize the usual rotary drive (see Fig. 11.15). Tests to date have been encouraging.

By use of a rocker arm which connects the levers, pressing one pedal lifts the opposing pedal—as in rotary cranks. The lever motion can be preset anywhere up to a 15-inch (380-mm) stroke to meet individual needs. This is equivalent to a maximum rotary crank length of 190 mm. Toe clips allow the pedals to be pushed and lifted to provide power with both feet. On turns one pedal can be powered while high and the other low.

The design includes a speed-change mechanism. The rear-wheel driving cable's point of attachment to the

Fig. 11.15   Pivoted lever drive. *(Courtesy of Harris Dynamics)*

lever can be varied while in motion or at rest to 20 different locations, in effect giving 20 different "gear" combinations.

A cam-shaped pulley driven by the pedal is connected to the rear-wheel drive pulley on each side. The shape of this cam pulley can be varied to produce the most effective relationship between the pedal pressure at each foot position and the torque transmitted to the rear wheel.

The circular chainwheel to which we have become accustomed has proven its worth and efficiency for a century, but future advances in design will further enhance cycling pleasure.

HEIGHT AND POSITION OF SADDLE

There has been considerable difference of opinion among skilled cyclists concerning the saddle position which allows maximum performance. Differences in pedaling action among champions habituated by long use to their own particular saddle resulted in stoutly defended opposing ideas. In 1966, Vaughan Thomas, at the Department of Ergonomics, Loughborough University, England, determined to make a scientific investigation. One hundred cyclists took part. Among these were 3 novices, 3 women, 2 national champions, 21 juniors, 20 each in the first and third category of racing proficiency, and 30 in the second category—a large range in ability. Thomas himself was the hundredth rider. The tests were made for short durations at maximum possible power output. After analyzing the tests, Thomas compared them to road performance. Since the results of these tests have been widely quoted without explanation, the facts should be reviewed.

The tests were made on a Mueller ergometer; the seat tube angle was about 68°; the seat used was a Unicanitor plastic saddle.

Saddle height was measured from the pedal spindle to the top of the unloaded saddle along the line of the seat tube. The saddle clip was set behind the post, about in the center of its front-to-rear adjustment. Cranks used were 6¾ inches long. The length of the rider's leg was measured while standing erect in stocking feet. It is the distance from the floor to the lowest bony part of the pelvis, the pubic symphysis palpation. Saddle heights were set at four heights ranging from 105% to 117% of this leg length. Riders rode in cycling shoes and used long toe clips. Their work load was 500 kg-meters.

The overall power output averaged highest at the 109%-of-leg-length saddle setting. There was a 5% improvement in power at this setting over positions either 4% lower or higher. Foot length, which also combines with the amount of ankling to determine leg motion, was not considered, and this explained individual variations from the average.

This height generally produced the minimum angle of thigh motion in pedaling. Since comfort is to a great extent what you are accustomed to, Thomas suggests that new riders set their saddle at this point initially. Long-term riders should approach this value, if it differs from their present position, by changing their saddle height ¼ inch at a time, at monthly intervals.

In using this guide, remember that an extraflexible saddle or a longer foot both require a bit greater height. A different saddle angle or longitudinal position adjustment likewise requires some compensation, but we have a base from which to start.

SOUPLESSE

The term "souplesse" describes the silky or supple action of the skilled rider. Power appears to flow without effort; his action is smooth. Note the action of an experienced racer. No motions are wasted. He doesn't rock from side to side or bounce. A lesser rider may shake his head and shoulders as he labors. An unskilled rider rides an erratic course, leaning from side to side as he progresses. He makes climbing even a moderate hill look like hard and tiring work, while the experienced rider breezes past effortlessly. Conditioning plays a part, but smooth and effective coordination of muscle movement is the real secret.

Use low gear training to develop a wider range of leg speed. You should be able to ride down hills in a lower gear without bouncing and discomfort. High-gear training up the hills develops strength and the ability to push around the circle using your ankles effectively. You can even use your arms and body, pulling your body back and forth to follow your feet around the power stroke on slow, hard climbs.

Coordination can be achieved in combination with low and high-gear training by training at the pedal speed you find best and at the gear you find most effective, particularly for racing.

ANKLING

The cyclist applies power by placing the ball of his foot on the pedal. Inexperienced riders are often seen with their instep on the pedal, but this allows only direct leg push to be applied. Since pressure on the pedals is most effective in propulsive effort when applied at right angles to the crank, a straight push is only about 60% effective. The balance goes into extra bending stress in the bicycle frame and causes the bicycle to accelerate and decelerate a bit between each leg push. This wastes energy.

It has long been recommended that the ankles be used to permit the foot to press more nearly at right angles on the crank and to permit the crank to be pressed forward at the top and clawed backward at the bottom of the stroke. In this manner, both feet apply power at the bottom and the top of the pedaling circle, where direct leg thrust gives no motion. The flow of power is thus more uniform and smoother, energy losses from frame deflections are reduced, and the whole bicycle is more efficient.

Short bursts of pressure tend to lift the body weight from the saddle and let it settle again between thrusts. Indeed, when riding on a tandem with a partner who has a poor pedal action, the entire bicycle rear seems to be bouncing up and down. The other rider can oscillate back and forth on his saddle due to the accelerations and decelerations in the pedaling circle to the point that he can get saddle irritation, while the bouncing makes it more difficult to control the tandem.

Frank Whitt of London, England, has measured pedal forces when ankling is well done. He found that he could increase effectiveness to about 75% (100% would be even power flow around the entire circle). However, this high percentage was possible only at low power outputs and at the most efficient pedaling speeds of from 50 to 60 rpm. As power demands and speed increased, the effect was less. The average pressure divided by the peak pressure decreased to 40%. However, it was found to be possible to press forward and pull backward with the feet at the top and bottom of the stroke. Thus it appears that, for moderate speeds and power, the tourist and casual cyclist should practice effective ankling. For higher speeds and outputs, pictures of racers at speed show a more forward saddle position and greater digging into the toe clips.

Continental racers on rough road surfaces tend to push forward at the top of the stroke, keep the heel down at the bottom, and claw up from this position.

Effective ankling reduces the length and speed of the leg stroke. The heavy parts do not accelerate as fast and do not have to be "braked" as hard as without ankling, and a higher saddle position can be used. Hill climbing is easier due to the elimination of "dead-power" areas at the top and bottom.

Figures 11.16-11.21 show the action of both feet when ankling. Figures 11.16-11.18 record measured pedal forces at various pedal speeds.

Fig. 11.17   Pedal can be pressed far past center.

Fig. 11.18   Ready to reverse position.

Fig. 11.16   Near bottom, ankle tilts foot down.

Fig. 11.19   Foot tilted up near top of stroke.

Fig. 11.20   With foot raised, pedal can be pressed forward.

Fig. 11.21   Foot follows pedal, pressing 90° to crank.

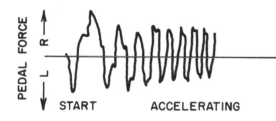

Fig. 11.22   Pedal forces accelerating from a standing start.

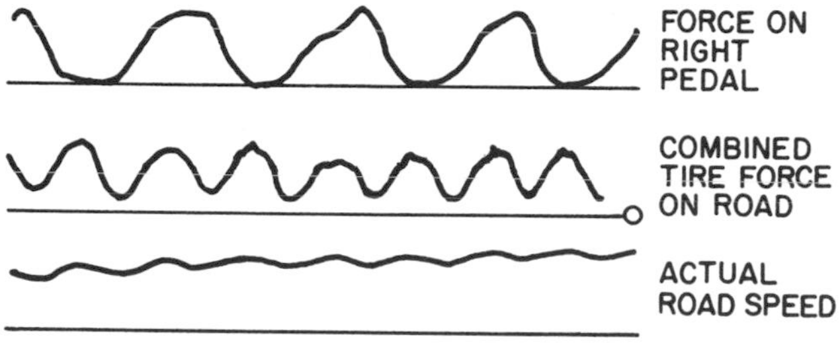

FORCE ON
RIGHT
PEDAL

COMBINED
TIRE FORCE
ON ROAD

ACTUAL
ROAD SPEED

Fig. 11.23   Force magnitude (one pedal only). Force applied
to road by rear tire. Actual bicycle road speed
variation. *(Test data from Lawrence G. Brown)*

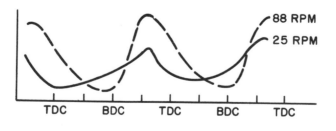

Fig. 11.24   Pedal forces over two revolutions.

Hill Climbing

"Honking" is the technique used in hill climbing of getting out of the saddle, putting the body directly over the crank hanger, pulling with the arms, and pulling up on the toe clip with the rising foot to get maximum output power. It provides a change of position, gives good circulation in the sitting region, and allows the latter to cool at times of high stress. Honking is an occasional practice and is not done all the way up a hill. It is a technique that takes practice; some riders ineffectively throw their bikes from side to side and waste energy by placing their bike and body in a new position with each stroke so they can press directly on the pedals. When climbing hills, the experienced rider selects a gear which he can pedal smoothly sitting down. It is the inexpert rider who gets out of the saddle on the slightest grade.

When he is properly prepared, the cyclist welcomes hills. A hill is a challenge to be met and bested. A feeling of accomplishment awaits you at the summit, perhaps mixed with a sense of relief. Hills add variety to a ride and reward you with a thrilling effortless descent upon completion.

Climbing techniques vary with the wind, your speed, your purpose, and length and steepness. Your strength and fitness and your gearing are also factors. Races are often won or lost on hills, where an "attack" separates the strong from the weak. Near the top, a gap can be opened, and when the summit is reached, the lead riders can widen their advantage greatly. Pursuers must regain the distance lost at high speeds when air resistance is a major disadvantage.

When touring, gradients may mean merely a lower speed using a lower gear. Size up the hill at the start and plan your approach. Never fight a hill; never contemplate its height as if it were an adversary.

If the grade is short, as in rolling country, approach the hill in a higher gear at speed. Your momentum and a little hard work for a few moments may carry you over the top with ease. If the wind is against you, however, this may be a lost cause. You can tire, and you will have to shift gears once your rhythm has been lost.

Don't drop gears too quickly, or your feet will speed up to a point where you can't follow through. You will lose momentum and rhythm this way. Downshift in successive steps that keep your pedal speed constant. Stress ankle action; keep your power flow smooth.

If the hill is long, or if head winds are a factor, change down to a gear that requires a moderate pedal pressure which you can maintain, if not for the entire length at least throughout local variations in steepness. Pace yourself to avoid stopping. It's twice as hard to get going again. If there are no obstacles, cross-streets or traffic, it helps at times to watch your feet turning. It is easier to check your ankling when you see them turning steadily.

The top is your goal, but it may seem far away. It is far easier to pick interim goals at moderate intervals. As you successfully pass each one, set your next attainable objective—this tree, that pole, the next rock outcrop—and the summit arrives unexpectedly soon.

Remain seated and pedal smoothly. Leaning forward transfers your body weight to your pedals through the back muscles and allows your arms to assist. On a long hill, prolonged pulling in one position may produce back pain. Shift to a higher gear, get out of the saddle, stretch forward, and walk (honk) on the pedals. Select a gear that has ample resistance without forcing. After a bit, return to your sitting gear and continue. Change your hand position at changes in slope to utilize other muscles. On a long, hot grade, however, a stop for a sip of water or to take in a view may pay dividends.

Finding Your Normal Riding Pace

There is a speed at which you ride where things feel just right. You must learn this by experience. Riding too slowly can be tiring. Your pedal speed will vary, and without a rhythmic motion, cycling is just not as satisfying. This is why cyclists like to ride with others of equal pace. Too slow a pace feels sluggish and detracts from any feeling of accomplishment. Too fast a pace may wear you out and make the ride a drudge. The actual pace varies with wind and grade and with your condition and training, and it will increase as your condition and ability grow.

Wind is a constant adversary if it is against you on a long trip. If you have a choice, plan your trips so that the wind is at your back on the return leg. When it comes from the direction in which you are going, reduce your pace and gear to maintain a steady rhythm; then plug steadily ahead. Lower your body to lower air resistance. Pushing too high a gear may drain your energy reserves so that your muscles no longer respond. A stop for refreshment is then required. Riding too slowly, however, can be self-defeating. The ride becomes monotonous and never-ending. If when pressing against the wind, or cold, or hills pain in legs or knees announces itself and makes every stroke a burden, further travel is inadvisable. "Running out of gas" from insufficient food is a real and terrifying experience, affectionately termed by cyclists who have experienced it as "the Bonk."

Conditioning

A lack of willingness to exert yourself a bit greatly limits the joys that cycling can bring you. Stretching your limit may make you tired, but it brings its rewards. Learning to accept some pain will increase your strength and endurance and make your next ride easier. It will also enhance your capability for fun and exploration. Riding at over 80% of your capacity increases the abilities of your muscles, heart, and lungs. Exercising ever more strenuously expands your ability.

There are many training techniques which advance your ability. You can progressively ride farther, faster, and climb more grades. Start with from two to five miles a day, but get it regularly and increase the distance weekly. Get used to sitting on the saddle—for long trips this conditioning is necessary. The hills will become easier, the miles shorter. When your pace speeds up, and you use higher gears, you know that you have arrived. The entire sphere of cycling enjoyment will grow beyond belief.

If you are in an active cycling club, Fartlek training (an American synonym for this Swedish export is "rat race") can be used. On a ride with your friends, maintain a comfortable pace which is punctuated frequently by sprints to a hill top, to the next telephone pole, attacks at unexpected times by any member of the group. This is fun for all but those whose ability hasn't developed and an incentive for them to develop it.

Interval training, in which bouts of all-out effort are interspersed with periods at a pace within your capacity, has proven very effective. This can be done alone or with a group.

Tempo training is a variation of interval training in which a set time for a given distance is interspersed with periods at reduced pace. Goals are gradually increased for speed, and the relaxation periods made shorter, until an entire distance is covered at top speed.

Time trialing is covering a given distance in a minimum amount of time. This is another competition in which you master a goal and then set a new goal. Time trialing improves your physical and aerobic fitness. It requires more will power to maintain the pace when tired than does interval training and thus takes intense will and concentration.

What can be accomplished on a bicycle may sound fantastic to the beginner. During 1972 in England, Ken Webb covered 80,647 miles in one year, while holding his regular job. He continued on in 448 days to 100,000 miles. The 24-hour time trial record is currently over 500 miles; the 25-mile unpaced road time trial has been done in about 53 minutes. In 1972 Eddy Merckx set a world's one-hour record of 49.408 km (over thirty miles). In Utah, Dr. Alan Abbott reached a speed of 143 mph paced by a racing car. You probably will not want to reach these heights, but then again maybe you will try to beat them. Set your own goals and when you reach them set new goals.

THE CYCLIST'S SEVEN COMMANDMENTS

Paul de Vivie was an outstanding cyclist, tourist, inventor, and leader in France at the turn of the century. He is credited with developing the derailleur gear and popularizing it against strong opposition. Many years ago, "Velocio" (his pen name) expounded in Le Cy-

cliste (a magazine he founded) Seven Commandments for the Cyclotourist which all should know. These are as follows:

1. Take short and infrequent rests so that you do not interrupt the rhythm.
2. Eat lightly but frequently. Eat before you become hungry, and drink before you become thirsty.
3. Never continue until abnormal fatigue manifests itself by lack of appetite and the inability to sleep.
4. Cover yourself before becoming cold. Uncover before becoming hot. Don't be afraid to expose your skin to sun, air, and water, within reason.
5. Eliminate, at least on the road, alcohol, meat, and tobacco.
6. Never force yourself. Ride within the body's reserves, especially during the first hours of the day, when your energy seems inexhaustible.
7. Do not force the pace—ride just to prove yourself.

These are based on the experiences of a master, the patron saint of cyclotouring, who knew mountains, weather, and long-distance "epreuves" till his 70s!

HOT WEATHER CYCLING

Reducing excess body heat is a requisite when the weather is hot and the effort intense. Dr. Gaston has explained that too warm or impermeable clothing burdens the heart by making it pump harder to increase the blood flow to the skin surfaces and dispel heat.

To obtain the most comfort, select a speed that generates a cooling breeze. A higher gear and lower pedal speed may help, if pedal effort is not too great; a lower gear and a normal pedal speed may cut speed, but it also cuts effort, reducing the heat you generate. The latter can prevent heat stroke on a steep grade with a hot, following wind.

Protect yourself from the sun, but leave as much of the "shaded you" exposed to the air as possible. Open your shirt front and roll up your sleeves and shorts to allow air access. Cycling clothes must breathe to hold down body temperature. But beware of open net clothing that admits and traps bees. Sunburn on your back can incapacitate you if you are exposed for a couple of hours.

A wet washcloth carried in a plastic bag in your handlebar sack is handy to freshen your face and wipe stinging sweat away from your eyes as you ride. Some riders find a sweatband helpful on hot humid days.

Avoid alcoholic beverages in hot weather. Alcohol gives a heating effect just the opposite of that desired from a cold drink.

Plastic capes and plastic rain suits increase the humidity around the body, even in mild weather, and result in a considerable loss of cooling ability. Open the front and roll up the sleeves to gain access to cooling air.

As you learn to use your human engine well, you become more aware of its fuel needs. Prunes, grapes, or raisins are used by some riders in periods of long and intensive effort. Others use honey, which contains needed minerals, vitamin B, and levulose sugars that are absorbed rapidly into the bloodstream.

ALTITUDE SICKNESS

Cyclists accustomed to lower altitudes sometimes extend their cycling range to regions of high altitude by means of air transportation. Racers who wish to set time or distance records travel to high altitudes because the thinner air provides less resistance to motion. Before the record attempt is made, however, they will spend almost a week getting their bodies acquainted with the effects of high altitudes.

At altitudes above 8,000 or 9,000 feet, some riders find themselves feeling lethargic and lack the energy to accomplish the challenging rides they came to enjoy. Headache, sleeplessness, loss of appetite, more rapid pulse rate, more rapid breathing under even relatively light effort may occur. Others may experience nausea, which can result in vomiting. You may feel chilled, even when dressed warmly. The unexpected effects may tempt you to abandon your high altitude vacation, never to go again.

Rolinda Baker suggests (in *Bicycling* magazine—July, 1973) that you ascend slowly, getting moderate, not overly strenuous, exercise. It takes three to five days to become accustomed to the higher altitude, but ascending gradually over a period of several days minimizes the effects. After a week or two at altitude, you are able to undertake heavier exercise. Mrs. Baker recommends taking aspirin prior to the ascent. Several other drugs are available to combat the symptoms; ask your doctor about these prior to your trip. If you must ascend to the higher altitude quickly, lie down and rest upon arrival and avoid strenuous exercise for a few days. Planning your itinerary and activities with this break in mind will make your anticipated pleasure a reality.

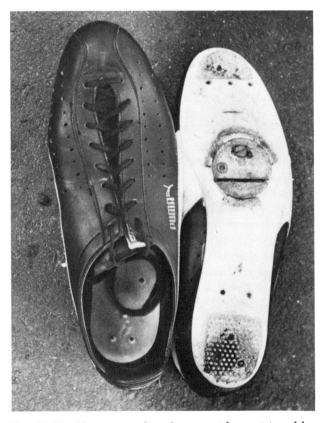

Fig. 11.25   Cleats on cycling shoes must be positioned by trial and error to place the foot at the proper location and angle for greatest power and least fatigue.

CHAPTER XII

The Art of Bicycling

BECOMING A MORE SKILLFUL CYCLIST

Billions of enjoyable cycling miles are ridden each year without incident, yet the National Safety Council tells us that as the number of bicyclists on the road is increasing, accidents are also increasing. However, at too many gatherings of cyclists throughout the country each year avoidable accidents will occur. Most have no connection with motor vehicle traffic. Falls, collisions between cyclists, and slipping on imperfect road surfaces are the more common causes.

Consider for a minute that cycling is a skill. As a mounted cyclist you do not have two feet on the firm ground, as you do when walking. Your body is at least four inches higher than when afoot. You normally travel three to six times faster, too. And if you fall, you possess from 9 to 36 times the kinetic energy, and you fall from a greater height. At these higher speeds, you only have between 1/3 and 1/6 the time to take action if an obstacle is in your path.

In addition, you share the roadway with other vehicles that may be traveling at speeds slower, equal, or up to six times faster than you. These vehicles are generally bigger, heavier, and better armored than your bike, and in the event of a collision, you will come out second best. The following program for enhancing bicycling skill was developed by the careful analysis of cyclists' needs by a group of riders with long experience. Many of these items were learned in the school of hard knocks—yet almost all can be learned in just a couple of days. Even experienced cyclists have found that this instruction sharpened their skills.

Those skills that had not been needed for a considerable period should be practiced during the course of regular riding. As an example, having witnessed several severe accidents involving gravel at road edges and on turns, I often practice riding and turns in gravel patches. Several years ago while touring in Germany, I was approaching a turn with graveled edges at the bottom of a steep hill, when an impatient motorist in the opposing lane pulled out of his line of traffic directly into my lane. Only the practiced experience of riding and maneuvering in gravel at speed kept an interesting experience from becoming a severe crash. The exact intermittent turning procedure used had been learned under controlled conditions, and when needed, it was automatic.

Note the figures showing potential causes of accidents. These photographs were not made with extreme contrast because potential hazards on the road are often not in distinct contrast—particularly when on a dark surface or back lighted. The inexperienced rider just doesn't see them. By learning to recognize them, we become more observant.

Practitioners of "preventive cycling," like those of "preventive driving," avoid accidents by looking more carefully at the road ahead, by watching what the other fellow is doing, and by anticipating what he is about to do. Watch for cross traffic, watch the speed and maneuvering of approaching drivers, be alert for sudden stops or turns, and, recognizing our own ability to start, accelerate, and stop, drive within these limits.

However, the cyclist has an additional responsibility. He must recognize that his speed and power are not equal to those of others on the public road and that automobile drivers are not attuned to maneuvering with vehicles at speeds greatly different from their own. All too often the motorist sees a cyclist as a stationary object and drives accordingly.

Riding considerately and carefully requires skill. The cyclist must thoroughly understand the handling characteristics of the two-wheeled vehicle. Some factors affect us more than they affect a heavier vehicle. A bump or pothole or foreign object in our path that has no effect on a car can upset us. Steering close to the edge of objects or road breaks requires precise handling. Poor handling can cause you to veer in an erratic riding path into the roadway, and if the motorist isn't expecting this, he may not pull aside in time.

The necessary handling skills become automatic through practice. You will acquire a sixth sense that enables you, without thinking, to ride smoothly, steadily, and confidently at all times, in all weathers, on quiet streets or on mountain roads, at leisurely speeds or in thrilling downhill dashes with the speed of the wind. You can practice these alone, but you can try them more effectively with a group of cycling companions.

Each of the tasks is performed first at low to moderate speeds. As one's confidence increases, it is tried again and again at increasing speeds.

It is important that your equipment be in tiptop shape so that it will not fail when stressed to the utmost (see Chapter VI). These equipment safety checks should become a habit. The skilled cyclist learns to detect while riding the little signs that indicate his equipment is not in tiptop condition: brake levers must be squeezed a little bit further than normal due to brake wear; a lack of absolute steadiness occurs when wheel bearings and steering head bearings are loose, overtight, or in need of lubrication; the bike bumps or wavers due to a loose or missing spoke, a rim dented or out of true, a tire malinflated or so worn that traction on sharp turns is less effective than may be necessary under emergency conditions. Loose bolts or saddle clamps, brake levers or handlebar fitment can also be felt.

Each of the proficiency tests provides you with a skill that you will almost certainly need at some time. Like the safety belt, it is wise to buckle up before you start, because there is no time to buckle up under emergency conditions.

In giving these tests to groups of cyclists, every effort is made to make the most effective use of every minute in the training time. The group is in constant motion and practice, except during periods of explanation or demonstration by the instructor. A previous skill is practiced while proceeding from one task to the next. The entire group takes part together, so there is no standing and waiting while others perform a task.

THE SKILL OF BALANCE

The primary skill in bicycle operation is the ability to ride straight and smoothly at both low and high speeds. Indeed, a cyclist who has learned to balance

well can remain motionless and upright for a considerable period of time without removing his feet from the pedals. Experienced cyclists often wait in this position for a traffic light to change. It enables him to apply full power and accelerate immediately when the light changes, or when the traffic flow permits. This way he is not a slow starter in a stream of traffic whose drivers have their eyes on the traffic light and the cars in front—*not* on the cyclist.

A great many of the tests, including the initial balancing test, are made on a straight-line course several hundred feet long and from four to six inches wide. This provides a gauge of the cyclist's skill which he himself can constantly measure and evaluate. The cyclist himself is the first to detect improvements. He himself can determine when further practice and correction are needed. A ready-painted straight line can often be found in a school or supermarket parking lot, or one can be laid out with a chalk line marker. In our initial test, the rider begins *off* the bicycle with the wheels on the straight-line course, his right foot on the right pedal. He propels himself with his left foot, attains a moderate speed, and then coasts while maintaining a course directly along and inside the guiding white line. This may sound easy, but even experienced cyclists have found it difficult. This develops the skill needed to maintain a straight and unwavering course, and with your body close to the ground, you will not fall if you lose your balance. This method will be used in many nontraffic situations to mount the bicycle (see Fig. 12.1).

Fig. 12.1   Balance test, dismounted. Maintain a straight-line course while scootering with one foot on the pedal.

NORMAL MOUNT AND DISMOUNT

Under normal conditions, and particularly when riding on traveled roads, for best control with least wavering upon start up, the cyclist starts with one foot resting solidly on the pavement, astride the bicycle and off the saddle, the opposite foot placed on the other pedal which has been rotated to a point 45° above the horizontal. His bicycle is solidly supported, and he can look over his shoulder for traffic approaching from the rear before he starts. He also looks to the front to make certain that there is no parked car or any other object which will turn him into the path of traffic approaching from the rear. When he sees that all is clear, he pushes off with the foot on the ground and simultaneously lifts his weight onto the 45° pedal. This gives him full starting power. As he pushes down the pedal, he lifts himself onto the saddle.

Fig. 12.2   Mounting and startup: with one foot on the ground and the other on the raised pedal, push forward, lift up and onto the saddle.

In this manner, you start in a perfectly straight line since a speed sufficient to maintain full control is developed at once.

Dismounting is done as above but in reverse. The cyclist applies his brakes, supports his weight on the downside pedal, pulls his body forward from the saddle, and lowers it with the opposing foot extended toward the front. As the bicycle is brought to a stop the extended foot is lowered to the ground to arrest his motion.

Both the start and the stop are made with full control and without swerving or wavering. The cyclist starts and stops along the straight-line course so that he can evaluate his ability to maintain the straight line (see Fig. 12.2).

This method is particularly helpful when starting on a bicycle loaded with luggage or when starting from the edge of a road in which the road shoulder is depressed or when the initial stretch of road is rough or bumpy.

This all seems simple, but if you watch cyclists, you will note a great difference in the ability to start smoothly without wavering.

STRAIGHT-LINE RIDING

A prime requisite for safe and efficient cycling is the ability to maintain perfect balance without a swerving path. When you gain this ability, you use your energy most effectively. Even more important, however, it gives you confidence in your ability to know that you can make the bicycle do what you wish. You can maintain a position close to the edge of the road out of the stream of traffic. When you approach a bicyclist in your car, aren't you often fearful that he may suddenly veer into your path—particularly if the road is narrow and traffic is coming from the other direction? The fear is mutual. The cyclist fears that the car will pass him at speed only a few inches away and throw him off balance. Yet the competent cyclist needs less than 24 inches of road space, particularly if there is no curb. Having learned to maintain a smooth and steady path for long distances, you can ride relaxed in this lane knowing you have maintained a true course. The motorist, noting your narrow straight course, drives more smoothly and is less likely to swing wide or to rush past you or to blast his horn.

The expert rider can be noted at a great distance. He doesn't bobble or wobble, swing or sway. He appears to be—and is—riding effortlessly. Surprisingly this skill can be learned in a matter of a few minutes. With a little practice you can smoothly and evenly place pressure on your pedals and avoid overcorrecting your steering or leaning when you deviate from a straight line. This is easiest learned if you ride along a straight line with space on either side—such as a line in a parking lot or on an unused street. Riding at the road edge is a bit more difficult. Upon completion of the initial ride down the line, return at the edge of the road, riding as closely as possible to the road edge or the curb. Of course, one trip will not do it. You must repeat this course again and again, noting your progress, until you are confident you can ride within the width of the painted line every time. Go slowly at first, and then increase your speed down the course and back along the curb. While you can do this by yourself and continue practicing during your normal periods of riding, you will find it a great deal more effective with a group.

With a group, maintaining a space of not more than two or three feet between your front wheel and the rear wheel of the rider in front of you will give you practice in controlling your speed and reacting

Fig. 12.3   Riders maintain straight-line course within the width of the line.

Fig. 12.4   Riders maintain alignment at the road edge and during a turn while in close formation.

quickly to changes in the speed of other traffic. Experienced cyclists ride at extremely close spacings in groups to take advantage of the reduced effort that results when the first rider breaks the force of the wind. The effect of this is quite considerable, and it enables a group of cyclists to travel much faster than they could individually with much less effort. However, one unskillful rider touching his front wheel against the rear wheel of the rider in front of him will trip up both riders and can send the whole group crashing to the ground. By practicing on the continuous return path course we have described and starting slowly, this skill can be learned. You will find it very useful throughout your cycling life.

Slight changes in grade over your course introduce a new dimension. On the upgrades you will have to increase power to maintain a formation, and on the downgrades you will have to use your brakes very lightly to avoid running over the cyclist in front of you. You will thus learn the precise amounts of braking and pedal pressure needed to maintain a steady pace, and you could not learn this nearly as well by riding alone.

Repeating this return path course again and again enables you to increase your speed until the entire group is riding pace at normal speeds. Even if you do not plan to take part in closely spaced group riding, group riding in this exercise will improve your reaction time to traffic speed fluctuation on the open road. You will learn to ride at a steady and uniform speed without energy-consuming accelerations and decelerations. This steady and smooth pace of riding will not only make your regular riding both easier and safer, but it will also enable you to take part in events with skilled cyclists.

REMOVING ONE HAND

When riding on the road it is often necessary to take one hand off the bars to signal a change in direction, to get a handkerchief to wipe a tearing eye, or to shift gears. This results in a sideward displacement from the straight line until you learn to move your hands without disturbing your equilibrium. As soon as you and your group are satisfied with your ability to handle the bicycle on a straight-line course, repeat the course removing and replacing both hands in turn. Repeat at ever-increasing speeds until you can ride the course at as high a speed as the group can maintain. You will find that at higher speeds keeping the spacing constant becomes more and more difficult. However, practice makes it easier.

BEING ALERT

Close-spaced riding practice reduces accidents on the road by teaching the riders to keep alert at all times and to react quickly to changes in spacing. When you are satisfied with your group's ability to ride at any speed in close spacings both with hands on the handlebars and with one hand off the bar, you can proceed to the alertness test.

Starting first at low speeds, a preselected rider makes an unannounced stop while in the line of traffic, and all the succeeding riders come to a halt behind him. If any one is not alert, a collision will occur. This

Fig. 12.5   Maintaining position on the line while giving hand signals. Removing a hand from the bars and still maintaining a straight course requires practice.

may sound like a drastic exercise—indeed it is—but remember: you are developing skills that may be needed in an emergency. Continue around the course again and again, and have different riders make the unannounced stop until everyone is satisfied with his reactions. Then you can further sharpen your reflexes by repeating this at increased speeds.

Ankling action should be introduced as a portion of straight-line training. Ankling allows the cyclist to apply power smoothly and enables him to more easily maintain a desirable arrow-straight course and is especially helpful at high speeds and in hill climbing. Ankling should be practiced first on the steady-state travel around the closed loop course. This and other methods of using the foot and body position to best adapt to varying levels of wind and grade will follow. Because of the concentration required for closely spaced riding, the study of foot action and pedaling techniques is more effective when full attention can be given to this alone.

While we still have the group together on our straight-line course one more skill should be introduced. Prior to making any turn into the stream of traffic or to the left across traffic, we must look over our shoulder and listen for the sound of approaching traffic. This maneuver should be practiced with the group at increased spacing—perhaps six to eight feet between bicycles. It is a natural tendency, when turning your head to look to the side or rear for traffic approaching, to travel in the direction you are looking. This can cause us to inadvertently swerve into the line of traffic. How-

ever, with a little practice you will find it easy to maintain your straight-line course while turning your head. Try this again and again along the straight-line course and at the very edge of the road, and you will very quickly master this technique.

AVOIDING OBSTACLES

To learn how to accurately control your path and pick your way through a series of obstacles and debris on the road, set up a series of closely spaced obstacles on either side of your straight-line course. Place these close enough so that the pedals can just clear them. Use small lightweight cans which will not damage your wheels if you hit them. When these have been set up, try riding along the line through the obstacles to see how you react. Most probably the first time you do this you will find that you hit one or two or more cans. Eventually you will be able to complete the course without striking a single obstacle. When you can, space the obstacles even closer to the line and increase your speed, until you are satisfied that on the road you will miss every obstacle every time. You will find much use for this skill in actual riding. When riding near the edge of the road where the pavement is broken, you will find it possible to ride to the very edges of cracks and bumps with great precision.

BRAKING

Having learned how to start, accelerate, and ride in a precise and controlled manner, it is now very important to learn how to stop properly and how to keep the bicycle from running away on steep hills. It will be

Fig. 12.6   The unannounced stop in close formation. A sudden stop tests the alertness of following riders.

Fig. 12.7   These two cyclists (count them) demonstrate the ability to ride consistently at the road edge out of the lane of traffic.

Fig. 12.8   When looking to the rear for oncoming traffic, the rider must not veer into the traffic lane.

Fig. 12.9   Following a straight-line course with obstacles or paving breaks to divert the rider's attention.

helpful to review some of the items that affect brake performance. Though many of these may be obvious they will help you to avoid many a fall or accident. As you practice precisely controlled stopping, you will learn to automatically take the right action in an emergency.

The distance and time it takes to stop depends on several things. Two of the most important of these are your speed and the steepness of the grade. Next in importance is the effectiveness of your brake system in stopping the wheels. Of course, the friction between the tires and the road is all important; stopping on glare ice is much more difficult than stopping on a good hard road surface. The bicyclist then encounters an additional factor: to maintain control of steering and equilibrium, he must keep his wheels from sliding. This is particularly true for the front wheel upon which steering control depends. Another factor which must be taken into consideration is pitchover. Before discussing road practice, let's consider the type and magnitude of the effect each factor causes.

The distance it takes to stop is the sum of the distances traveled before and after reacting.

First, the period of time that the rider travels while he recognizes the need to stop, and before he can apply pressure to the brake lever, is his reaction time. It varies with the individual and also with his attentiveness, but the average reaction time is about ¾ of a second. Now at 10 mph this means that he will travel, during his reaction period, a distance of about 11 feet before he starts stopping. At 20 mph this distance will increase to 22 feet, while in a steep downhill dash at speeds up to 50 mph, the rider will travel 55 feet before he is even able to apply pressure to the brakes.

Second, the distance required to stop after the brakes are applied varies with the cyclist's kinetic energy as the square of his speed. At 30 mph, for example, it takes nine times the distance to stop that it takes at 10 mph (see Fig. 12.10).

But now suppose that the road surface becomes wet, as after a rain. On a dry road not covered with sand or gravel, oil slicks or rain, an adhesion factor of about 0.8 can be obtained. If pitchover did not occur, this would permit a deceleration rate of about 0.8g, or a reduction in speed of about 18 mph each second.

While we may have a road friction available to our rolling tires of 0.8, if we apply our brakes so hard that the wheels skid, the available friction drops 25%.

The rider's braking effort, whether by finger pressure on the hand grips or foot pressure on the coaster brake, should depend on the condition of the road surface, the steepness of the grade, the type of tire used, and the total weight, including rider, cycle, and luggage.

Pitchover is a result of short wheelbase and a high center of gravity. The wheelbase of a bicycle is short—from about 39 to 42 inches (100 to 110 cm) compared to the 90 to 120-inch (230 to 300-cm) wheelbase of the automobile. The center of gravity of bicycle and rider is relatively high (from 36 to 42 inches) compared to that of the automobile, in which the heavy portions, engine, axles, and transmission are only one or two feet above the ground. Thus when the brakes are applied, the body and bicycle weight tends to keep going, to pivot about the front wheel contact point (see Fig. 12.12).

This transfer of weight reduces the weight on the rear wheel to the point that rear wheel skid can ensue. Once the tire begins to skid, it may skid in any direction, so that the rear end of the bicycle can swing uncontrollably toward the front unless the pressure on

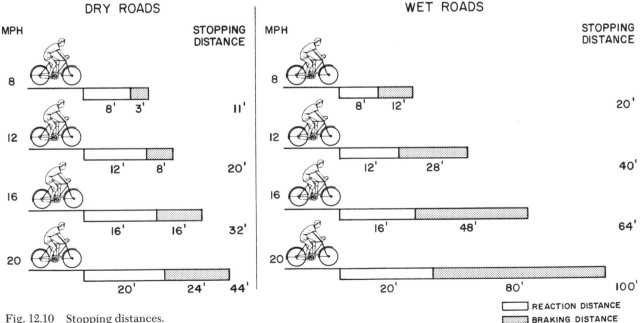

Fig. 12.10   Stopping distances.

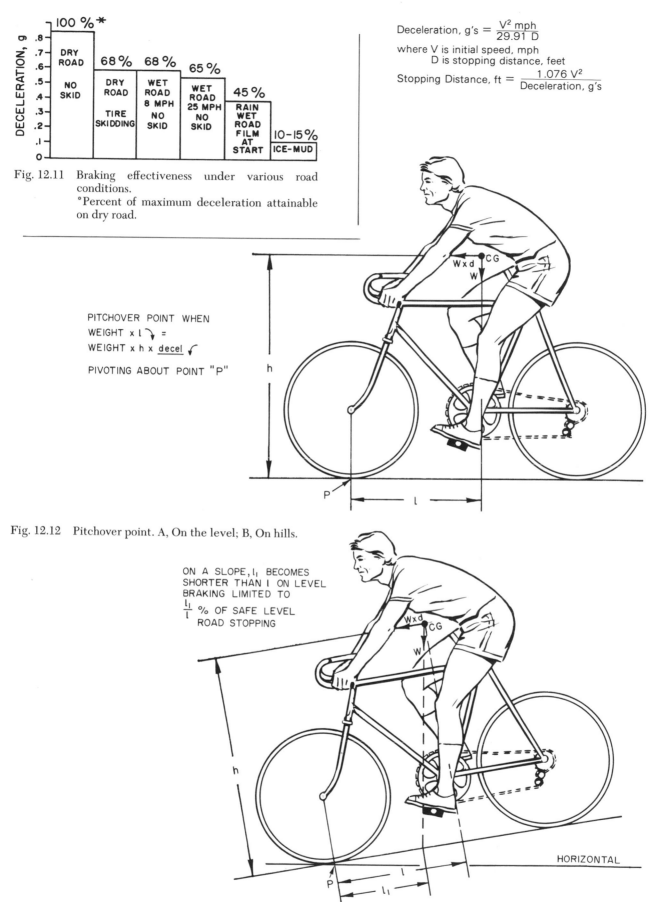

Deceleration, g's $= \dfrac{V^2 \text{ mph}}{29.91 \ D}$

where V is initial speed, mph
D is stopping distance, feet

Stopping Distance, ft $= \dfrac{1.076 \ V^2}{\text{Deceleration, g's}}$

Fig. 12.11 Braking effectiveness under various road conditions.
°Percent of maximum deceleration attainable on dry road.

PITCHOVER POINT WHEN
WEIGHT x l ↘ =
WEIGHT x h x decel ↙

PIVOTING ABOUT POINT "P"

Fig. 12.12 Pitchover point. A, On the level; B, On hills.

ON A SLOPE, l_1 BECOMES
SHORTER THAN l ON LEVEL
BRAKING LIMITED TO
$\dfrac{l_1}{l}$ % OF SAFE LEVEL
ROAD STOPPING

the brake is diminished. The weight transfer can be so intense that the whole rider and bicycle can pitch over about the front wheel, if the front brake is applied too harshly. On a downgrade, the effect is even greater.

The rider must develop a feel for all of these items through actual practice on the road. Due to weight transfer, if a rear brake alone is used, the maximum deceleration is only ⅓g—or even less if the tire skids.

These factors are particularly important on a turn. When turning, the available tire friction is used not only for stopping, but also for changing the direction of the bike. The rider must guard against loss of steering control when braking on a turn.

For a period of from 10 to 20 minutes after a rain starts, the oil and grime film on the road surface mixes with water to form a rather effective lubricant. This greatly reduces friction. As a matter of interest, this friction loss can be 50% or greater—cutting in half the friction available at the tires for both steering and stopping! Thus with equal force on the brakes, skidding and loss of control can occur without warning. The same can occur if one wheel rolls through a wet patch. The rider must anticipate these changes in handling.

At low speeds once the road surface has been thoroughly washed off, an adhesion of about 0.6g will be available for braking and steering control. But as speed increases—say from 8 to 25 mph—aquaplaning must be taken into account. As the water on a wet road surface is compressed underneath a rapidly advancing wheel, it tends to lift the wheel from the road surface. At high speeds this further decreases the wheel-to-surface friction available to the rider.

Ice or frozen moisture on the road surface also affects braking considerably. An extremely thin, invisible film of ice—called "black ice"—is one of the most insidious conditions that the rider will encounter.

Other factors that affect the ability of the wheels to hold on the road surface include wet leaves, a light sprinkling or film of mud, and slicks of oil spilled from auto crank cases—especially when slightly wet. Gravel, even in small and thin layers, sand, blowing straw, or other loose materials likewise reduce traction. If any of these are present on the road, their effect upon braking ability must be considered.

All of the items we have listed are considered part of the game, and the rider's eyes constantly search for them as he progresses on his trip. As his speed increases, the experienced cyclist searches the road at greater and greater distances ahead of him, so that he is not surprised by unusual conditions on the road surface. He anticipates things that will cause him to brake, things such as bumps, a car approaching his path, pedestrians, poor road surface, potholes, obstacles, or traffic lights.

BRAKE EFFECTIVENESS

As brake blocks wear, their clearance becomes greater, and the hand levers must be moved closer to the handlebars before they contact the rims. If this wear proceeds and the brakes are not readjusted properly, soon the brake handles will touch the handlebars before full braking pressure is applied. Thus, an otherwise adequate brake may not function adequately. Prior to the start of the next series of road tests, the brakes must be fully adjusted.

Brakes and brake cables improperly lubricated will also result in a reduction of the force applied to the brake blocks. It is not at all unusual to have a loss of as high as 50% or 60% of the effort applied at the brake lever by the time it reaches the brake pads themselves! Worn or loose pads, pads that have hardened from long storage or old age, pads not properly adjusted to meet the rims at the proper angle at the proper place all reduce brake effectiveness.

Internal hub brakes, such as a coaster brake, or internal expanding brakes are quite effective in both wet and dry conditions. Water affects a disk brake much less than a caliper brake, which is located near the road surface and is subject to splashes as well as to rain. Laboratory and road tests have shown that the effectiveness of caliper brakes under wet conditions may be as low as 5% of that when the brakes are dry! This effect is often not realized by the rider until he applies normal pressure to the brake and finds that his bicycle does not reduce speed. Then he must react further and apply greater pressure. In the meantime, however, he is proceeding toward the obstacle. Even with vastly increased pressure, until the rims have had a chance to dry, the brake may be only 60% efficient. In heavy weather or puddles this may not occur since the brake pads will be lubricated by the water film.

Understanding the effects of these items will help in anticipating the effort and the time required for braking under different road situations, but the magnitude of these effects cannot be understood and felt unless they are experienced.

TRAIN YOURSELF TO USE THE BRAKES

This next portion of our skill development program will enable you to learn the feel of your brakes under many different situations. We'll develop skill in stopping at a fixed point—this can be a painted line, or it can be a rope or a small stick placed across the path of the rider. Initially, traveling at low speeds along our curbside course and approaching the mark on the ground, we'll attempt to stop exactly with our front wheel on the marker. When your feel for the brakes is such that you can stop exactly at the marker each time, install a marker to one side of the rider to represent a stop sign or a street intersection. In this manner we have to stop at a guide to one side of us. These efforts give us practice stopping under conditions we would experience in normal traffic. Our aim is to develop accurate braking.

The next exercise involves a bit of "calculated risk." Before taking part, it is mandatory that the bicycle be equipped with a braking system in tiptop order with plenty of reserve lever motion available. Wheels and tires must be true and properly adjusted. It is strongly suggested that you equip yourself with heavy clothing and head protection so that if you do misjudge and have a fall, you will not be injured. However, remember that the entire purpose of this training is to learn to know your bicycle and its braking system. If properly done in steps of increasing severity, you will increase your handling skill along the way so that no accident should result.

You can do this alone or with a group. In a group, the riders are lined up side by side and spaced about five or six feet apart so that there is plenty of room to maneuver if a skid develops. A stopping line objective is drawn with rope or chalk or painted line at about 100 to 300 feet distance. Each rider is definitely on his own during this test since each rides as fast as he can, and speeds will differ among the riders of a group.

At the starting signal, each rider puts all his power into the pedals and rides toward the line. When he judges proper, the rider applies his brakes as hard as he feels safe in doing and attempts to stop exactly on the finish line. As soon as he stops, he starts up again and clears the line, so that the next person in the group can use the same course. At first this is done at moderate speed, but as the rider gets the feel of the bike and its braking system, he accelerates faster and tries to stop closer to the line. At these times the cyclist must be alert for the start of pitchover, that is, for excessive braking that could send him over the handlebars. As soon as this is noted, he must immediately release the brakes to prevent a fall.

In this exercise you will find how much pressure will cause a rear wheel to skid, and you will get the feel of relaxing the brake lever until this skidding is eliminated. Thus you will learn the maximum deceleration possible without losing control.

When satisfied with your progress, try wet weather braking. This is done most realistically on a rainy day, but you can simulate it on a dry day by wetting both the bicycle brakes and rim and the roadway on which the stop is to be made. You accelerate rapidly and stop as above. Note the difference between wet and dry braking action.

As Figure 12.14 shows, pitchover is more likely and will happen more severely on a downhill stretch. When the bicycle is inclined toward the front, the rider's center of gravity comes closer to the front

Fig. 12.13   To prevent pitchover when braking hard at speed, the cyclist thrusts his body back as far as possible while braking.

Fig. 12.14   Downhill braking in wet weather. There is a greater possibility of pitchover and skidding. Wet brakes may be only 20% effective.

Learning To Turn

When a cyclist sees an object in his path, his immediate reaction is to steer away from it. His bike, however, tends to move toward it. There is a good reason for this which is based on the way in which bicycle steering operates. When you turn your handlebars, the gyroscopic effect of the front wheel throws your machine in the opposite direction. To avoid losing your balance, you then instinctively reverse your steering, but this causes you to turn into the obstacle you were trying to avoid. Since this problem does not exist with the automobile, it surprises the newcomer to cycling.

Let's consider what happens when a bicycle turns. Say we turn right, from north to east. Try an experiment. Lift the front wheel of your bicycle an inch or two from the ground, supporting it by the handlebar stem near its steering pivot point. Give the front wheel a good spin forward. Now, with the wheel spinning, turn the handlebar sharply to the right. The bicycle banks automatically toward the left. Now, with the wheel still spinning, lean the bicycle toward the right. You will find a strong force turning the front wheel and handlebars toward the right—in the direction that the frame is banked. The gyroscopic action of the spinning wheel causes the bicycle to bank in the wrong direction when the handlebars are turned.

Now, let us think through turning a corner. At the start, you and your bicycle are heading north. When

wheel. Thus less weight is on the rear wheel, and this not only makes it easier to skid, but also causes pitchover at a much lower rate of deceleration than on the level. For safety's sake on a downhill run, allow yourself much more distance to stop than when going at the same speed on the level. To gauge, try the stopping test on hills of increasing steepness and at different speeds, until you learn just how hard you can apply the brake. On wet roads this limitation is even more severe, since losing control of front wheel steering can occur at the decreased friction levels available with wet roads.

One more caution should be expressed with wet weather braking. We saw earlier that due to the poor friction characteristics of the brake block on the rims, a much greater force is required to brake in wet weather. This results in increased cable stretch, increased casing deformation, and increased deflection of the brake bridges and brake arms. Unless the brakes are very closely adjusted, under panic or wet weather conditions, the brake levers may bottom against the handlebars even before the lesser available road friction limit is reached.

I would strongly suggest that you continue this training from time to time during your normal riding. This will enable you to keep your reflexes sharp, and in case of an emergency, you will know exactly what to do and how to get the maximum results.

Fig. 12.15   Gyroscopic effect on equilibrium. The spinning wheel maintains its direction.

your front wheel initiates a turn to the east, your weight and the weight of your bike begin rotating in a clockwise direction. When you have turned as far as you wish, this horizontal rotation must be neutralized.

If you were flying through the air, free of the ground, momentum would keep you traveling in your original direction. On a bike as you turn—with your tires gripping the ground and your weight many inches above ground—momentum throws you toward the outside of the curve. In our right turn example, centrifugal force tends to bank you toward the left.

By leaning your body toward the inside of the turn, you can counteract this force. When turning right, you bank to the right. The angle required depends on the sharpness of the turn and your speed. Figure 12.17 shows how this angle of bank can be determined. It also shows the outward forces which the tires must resist just to maintain the turn. For a 200-pound bicycle and rider (90 kg) turning at 20 mph (32 km/hr) on a 35-foot radius of turn (10.7 meters), side forces of almost 60 lb (27.3 kg) are needed to maintain the turn—even more to start it.

Too high a speed or too sharp a turn can force you to bank so steeply that—unless you raise it as you coast round the bend—your inside pedal can strike the ground.

Your tires must not only be able to withstand the side forces without sliding, they must also provide the front wheel steering force to make your turn. If you

are carrying a luggage load at the front and rear, or if you have a long bicycle, such as a tandem, with the weight distributed over a distance, this extra steering force is even more important.

When we discussed maintaining control while braking, we learned that the force of brake application has to be kept within available road friction. If not, we can skid and lose control. This is doubly true while turning. If your tires slip on a turn, they will continue

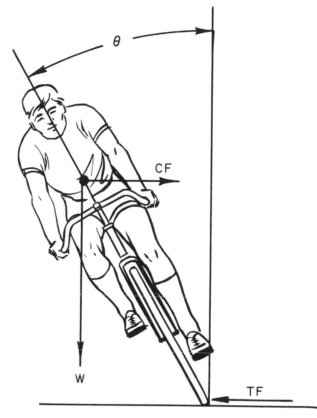

Fig. 12.17   Balance of forces in a turn. Tire friction must at least equal centrifugal force.

Fig. 12.18   Instrumented bicycle measures roll, yaw, and handlebar angle during test maneuvers in stability research at Calspan Laboratories, Buffalo, New York.

(Courtesy of Schwinn Bicycle Company)

Fig. 12.16   When the spinning wheel is turned to the right, gyroscopic force banks the fork to the left.

to slide outward, out of control. A rear wheel slide is somewhat self-correcting—it tends to sharpen the turn—but a front wheel side slip is self-defeating. Your momentum will tend to throw you to the ground, and the greater force needed for steering correction is not available from the slipping tire.

A bit of sand, a patch of gravel, an oil slick, or wet leaf, or wet tires or pavement will reduce adhesion. Thus, to keep control, either the radius of turn must be increased or the speed reduced before the slippery spot is reached. Using the brakes while turning can start the slide, and hitting a bump can bounce your wheel enough to do the same.

As the tire load is increased, the tires will provide proportionally less side and steering thrust. Thus, a lightweight rider may successfully make a sharp, high-speed turn, yet a heavier rider, riding the same course, may lose control at the same speed.

Table 12.1 shows the minimum permissible radius of turn with a 10% allowance to provide for starting forces and bumpy spots. Note the great increase in turning radius that is needed as the road surface changes. For heavier loads, the safe radius of turn will be even greater than those given.

Table 12.1

MINIMUM PERMISSIBLE RADIUS OF TURN, IN FEET

| Road Conditions | Turning Radius | | | | |
	@ 7 mph	@ 10 mph	@ 15 mph	@ 20 mph	@ 30 mph
Smooth, dry road (f=0.8)	4.5	9.1	20.2	38	90
Gravel, continuous rain (f=0.6)	6.0	12.2	27.5	51	118
Newly wet road (f=0.4)	8.8	18.2	42	76	175
Sand (f=0.3)	12.1	24.5	55	98	233
Ice (f=0.1)	34.6	73	168	Better To Walk	

As the skillful cyclist approaches a turn, he observes the road far ahead, noting obstacles that will cause him to increase the sharpness of turn at any point—stones, traffic, paving breaks. He looks for loose material and slippery spots that will reduce adhesion. He notes the camber, or slope toward the outside edge, which aids him on a right hand curve, but gives less friction on a left. Like the sports car driver, he selects the line of travel that allows the maximum turning radius. He watches particularly for treacherous turns that become sharper as they spiral inward. And if his judgment so indicates, he applies his brake *before* the turn is started.

If you encounter loose material or slippery spots on the curve, straighten your course for an instant as you pass over these spots.

The skillful rider develops a "feel" for the turn. He leans into the turn and lets his gyroscopic front wheel steer. To avoid tire bounce, he lifts his weight a bit from the saddle. He may move his body forward or back to obtain the most stable feel. He looks to the inside of the turn, never to the outside—looking to the outside will draw you in that direction.

Now that we've understood the mechanics, let's set up a practice course. The course should begin with a narrow line following wide-radius turns in alternating directions. This should lead into a 180° turn and then a turn whose radius decreases throughout the turn. The course should end near the starting point so that it can be repeated several times at increasing speeds. Keep exactly on course, using your brakes in advance if needed.

As your skill develops, increase your speed. Try lifting your body and shifting your weight to obtain the position that feels most secure on each turn. Then, at even higher speeds, select your own path through the turns at maximum speed.

TURNING TECHNIQUES

Turning the steering wheel twists the tire about the area of contact between the tire and the ground. Centrifugal force produces a sideload on the tire at its contact point. Since the steering axis, if extended to the ground through the steering head bearings, is normally to the front of the tire contact point, this side force tends to straighten the front wheel toward center.

The center of gravity of the handlebar, stem, front carrier load, and the wheel is usually located ahead of the steering axis center. Lift your front wheel off the ground with the bicycle stationary and lean it slightly to one side. Weight will turn the wheel in the direction of lean.

The combined effect of two forces provides the "cornering force" you need to make a turn. The angle between the actual wheel heading and the contact patch direction at the road is termed the "slip angle." Its friction provides the lion's share of the tire's turning force. If you leaned to the left when on a patch of ice, you would logically expect that your wheels would slip out from under you toward the right. On the road, this so-called "camber thrust" gives a side force reaction in the direction of lean. For our purpose, we can dispense with the mathematics, but there are three factors we should recognize:

(1) While the available steering force generally increases with the angle of bank, the available friction for the same applied weight can vary considerably for different tires on the same road surface (see Fig. 12.19A). Tire #1 gave very little increase as the angle of bank increased from 0° to 40°, while tire #6 gave a very marked increase. Tire #3 held the road much

more poorly than the others. All these tests were made at constant load.

(2) As actual tire load increases, the available turning force becomes a smaller proportion of the total weight (see Fig. 12.19B).

(3) Rolling resistance increases drastically as slip angle increases (see Fig. 12.19C).

Since the cornering force available increases with slip angle and bank to a certain maximum and then decreases again, turns must be made with "something to spare," otherwise at a point of no return, our wheels can slip out from under us.

Changing tires may enable you to make the same turn faster, depending on the tire. Since test data is not generally available, you will have to learn the capability of your tires for yourself.

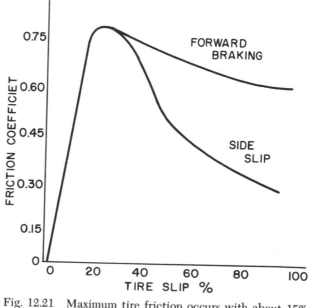

Fig. 12.20   Tire characteristics research at Calspan Laboratory. Reaction forces are measured for different types of tires under varying loads, camber angles, slip angles, and inflation pressures. *(Courtesy of Schwinn Bicycle Company)*

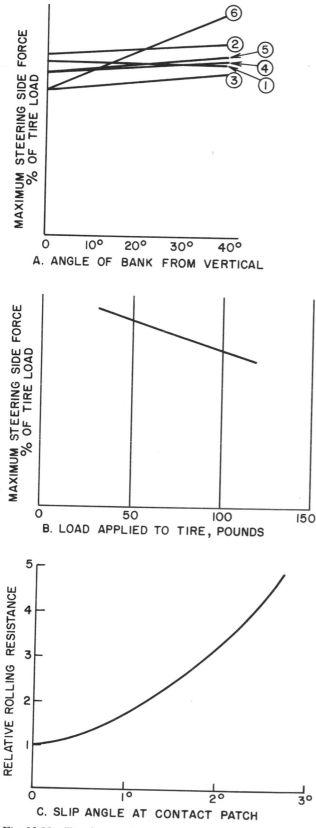

Fig. 12.19   Tire forces when turning.

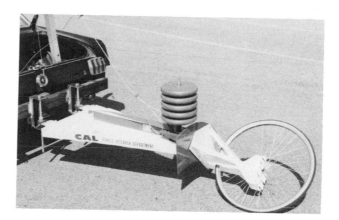

Fig. 12.21   Maximum tire friction occurs with about 15% slippage. Resistance to side slippage deteriorates much more rapidly as the skid increases.

If you are heavier or are carrying a heavier load than someone else on the same turn, you may not be able to negotiate the turn at the same speed and radius as he can.

Tire friction (and wear) increases with sharp turns and greater tire slip angles. This may explain in part why the steering tire of a tandem wears much more on either side of the tread center when riding on hilly, tortuous roads. (I have worn out a tire on tandem front on a week's trip, and yet the center of that tire's tread was good enough to permit exchanging front and rear!)

Lean In or Lean Out on Turns?

Pressing the handlebars down in the direction you want to turn starts the bank, and gyroscopic action then turns the wheel in the proper direction to give maximum turning capability. In case of back wheel slide, you will be able to correct the increase in bank by pulling the bicycle in line with your body. If, on the other hand, you want to maintain full power during a turn, leaning in will decrease the chance of your pedals striking the ground (see Fig. 12.22).

High-Speed Turns on Sound or Sight Signal

Because traffic has a way of suddenly and unpredictably shifting pace and direction, we can expect that sooner or later an automobile will turn directly into our path. Then too, eventually some pedestrian will step off the curb in front of us. Observe the front wheels of passing or approaching cars; a slight movement in your direction signals the need for instant action. Your ears are another major asset: changes in the sound of an automobile exhaust indicate a possible change in pace or speed, and vehicles approaching from a side street can be heard before they can be seen. But no matter how carefully you ride, you must still be able to automatically take evasive action, and you can only develop this knack by practicing rapid turns on signal.

We have learned that leaning into the turn or pressing down on the handlebar in the direction we want to turn, forces our bicycle to lean in the desired direction and allows us to turn sharply. Another turning technique relies on gyroscopic action. Momentarily steering in the opposite direction will throw us into a bank in the required direction. Reversing the steering then provides a rapid turn.

An instructor or a group of instructors is stationed along the straight-line course. The participants ride toward the instructor at speed. Suddenly, the instructor raises his arm in one direction. He has the option of calling "right" or "left." On hearing or seeing the signal, the rider turns as sharply as he possibly can in the

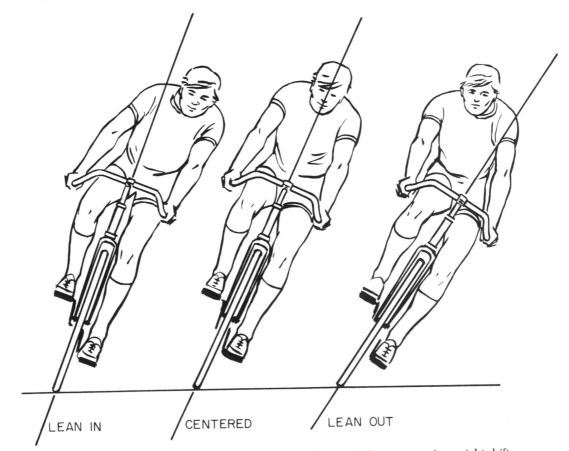

LEAN IN   CENTERED   LEAN OUT

Fig. 12.22   Techniques of cornering. Road camber or poor tire characteristics may require weight shift.

indicated direction. This is repeated many times over at increasing speeds until the rider gains confidence in his ability to master the emergency. The natural tendency to approach slowly and to turn lazily must be avoided.

In all the cycling proficiency tests we have undertaken, our objective has been to increase progressively our skills. Speed increases, but there must be no foolhardiness. Each person must be sure of himself, he shouldn't try to match the performance of another rider. The instructor should keep this thought uppermost and tailor the timing of his commands to suit each person.

PREPARING FOR TRAFFIC

In group riding on little traveled roads, companionship and conversation are made possible by riding two abreast at very close distances so that cars may pass. To do this at normal riding speeds without bumping handlebars and spilling, it is helpful to practice side by side riding.

A group of riders line up side by side with their handlebars only a foot apart and their front wheels in perfect alignment. Upon signal, all start together. Sighting constantly from side to side, the riders proceed to a predetermined point, while maintaining their wheel alignment. This repeats the straight-line start-up and stop we originally practiced.

At the start there will be considerable wavering until each rider learns close speed and distance control, but the speeds are moderate, and any slight bumping will prove harmless. In short order, all the participants will develop the ability to maintain excellent control. From 20 to 40 riders can practice this exercise at a time with good results.

RIDING IN THE BOX

We have previously learned to ride in close formation front to rear at different rates of speed and with changes in speed. Now we combine this skill with the side by side skill just learned. Again, for effectiveness, it is best to use a larger group: four or more rows, each of four or more riders. The riders maintain alignment from side to side as before, but now they also maintain close spacing between ranks. This duplicates conditions in traffic: vehicles are ahead and behind, and vehicles (or parked cars) are on either side. At first this double-attention task leads to ragged lines and ragged rows, but as the group proceeds, changes pace, stops, and starts, it will not take a great many tries before a considerable amount of skill develops. This exercise greatly increases your confidence when riding in actual city traffic. It will also make it easy for you to take part in group riding as practiced worldwide by cycling clubs in which two lines of riders riding closely spaced from front to rear maintain an orderly appearance on the road. The lead riders break the force of

Fig. 12.23   Automobile passes cyclist.

Fig. 12.24   Without warning, automobile turns right. The cyclist must make an emergency right turn to avoid collision.

Fig. 12.25   Automobile makes left turn without warning into cyclist's path.

Fig. 12.26   Maneuverability course.

Fig. 12.27   Rapid maneuver on signal.

Fig. 12.28   Sharp turn practice under wet conditions.

Fig. 12.29   Riding side by side in close-spaced alignment.

Fig. 12.30   Riding "in the box."

the wind for those behind and make higher speeds possible with less effort.

THE OPENED CAR DOOR

It is against the law in most states for a driver to open his door on the street side in the face of oncoming traffic. The opening of a curbside door several feet from the curb—far enough from the curb to permit a cyclist to pass on the right—is less illegal. Yet both these actions happen often. When passing cars which have an occupant on your side, anticipate that he might open a door in your path. Note any action—the motion of a shoulder or arm—that could signify he is about to open the door. The cyclist may be able to avoid a door if swung open without warning through his rapid maneuvering skill if no high-speed traffic is approaching from the rear. But all too often, the door is opened so quickly that a painful crash occurs. Thus the cyclist, being the one who can sustain more damage, must learn how to prevent this type of accident before riding on traveled streets.

In a series of parked cars, station several occupants who will open the door without warning in the path of riders taking the test. The riders should approach slowly at first and then at increased speeds. The little indications of an obstacle-to-be become apparent. The evasive maneuver, practiced shortly before in our rapid turn on sight signal, is here put to the test!

READY FOR THE ROAD

Having checked out bicycle handling on the level, we can learn more about the methods used to obtain the maximum motion for effort expended. Describing the effects of riding position, the use of the ankles to smooth the flow of power, hill climbing techniques, and the use of variable gears to minimize effort makes the return legs between successive exercises productive.

Fig. 12.31   Avoiding the opened car door.

Prior to riding in heavy traffic, review rules of the road. A cyclist is authorized to use the public roads, but as a legitimate vehicle, he must at all times obey traffic rules. He must:

1. Ride on the right side of the road. To ride opposing traffic is not only against the law, it is exceedingly dangerous. (We will discuss this later.)
2. Obey all traffic signs and signals. This includes stop signs, one-way streets, stoplights, and caution signs.
3. Ride in single file, except in low-traffic-level areas if the law permits. Always ride in single file at the far right of the road in faster traffic.
4. Ride in an arrow-straight line. Don't swerve from side to side or weave through traffic.
5. Be constantly on the alert and anticipate the movements of other traffic, particularly of cars which pull into your path, turn into or out of parking spots, driveways, or side streets. Be vigilant for the actions of pedestrians. Watch far ahead so that you will not be taken by surprise. Give pedestrians the right of way.
6. Listen constantly for traffic approaching from the front or rear or side out of your line of vision.
7. Slow down at street crossings. Look both ways to check approaching traffic before crossing.
8. Use hand signals to warn those behind of your intention to turn or stop. Use an audible signal to warn those in your path of your approach.
9. Maintain full control at all times. Don't carry items that interfere with your vision, or ride with your head down limiting your vision. Don't encumber steering by carrying objects in your hands.
10. Maintain your bicycle in mechanical perfection with brakes, wheels, tires, saddle, gears, nuts, and attachments securely tightened.
11. See and be seen. At night, have a light which will enable you to see and be seen. Use rear reflectors and preferably electric lighting. Use side reflectors on the bicycle, pedal reflectors front and rear if you will ride after dusk. Wear light clothing or reflective tape at night and bright colors or fluorescent tape by day.
12. Be courteous to other road users, but don't assume that all drivers you meet will be as well mannered and observant as you are. Remember always that you are the lighter vehicle. In case of error you may lose.

Which Side of the Road?

A little reflection will make clear the importance of riding in the same direction as traffic. Consider the mathematics. If you ride at 15 mph and the traffic speed is 40 mph, your rate of approach against traffic is 55 mph, while riding in the same direction, traffic approaches you at 25 mph. If a pothole, pedestrian, or stone causes you to swerve at this speed, a 10° turn of the handlebar will, allowing a ¾-second reaction time, take you three feet into the traffic lane. If a car is three car lengths in front of you, in his ¾-second reaction time he will reach you before he is able to apply his brakes. On the other hand, if you are riding with traffic, he will have 1 ⅔ seconds available, and this is ample time for him to slow his speed and to swerve away from you. If you are struck, the impact would be at most only 1/5 as great, and since he had already reduced speed, probably much less than this.

In Traffic

Despite the handling and observation training we have just outlined, once we actually take to the road and are subject to the "real thing"—traffic flowing and maneuvering close to us—there is a natural tendency to be overcome by the distractions and to make errors of judgment. Thus the first parts of the "on-the-road final exam" should be ridden on lightly traveled streets with a minimum of distractions, side streets, and heavily traveled intersections. Instructors must observe each rider carefully during the initial portion of this trip and particularly at intersections for good control, even riding pace, maintaining even spacing, and staying out of the line of traffic. If possible include sections where train or car tracks must be crossed. Include uphill and downhill sections—and if possible downhill turns—for practice in hill climbing and downhill braking. Call less-than-acceptable riding procedures to the attention of each rider at once. He probably will have not recognized his mistake and will be glad to have your help.

When the group has passed muster, head for more heavily traveled areas. At this point your training will be put to test. You can expect traffic to turn or stop in your path, or to pass you at close spacing. The group must master all that comes, but their skills should stand them in good stead. Their self-confidence will zoom as a result of the successful trial, and they will travel safely wherever they wish to go.

When overtaking and passing another vehicle, whether it is parked or operating at slower speed, determine if another vehicle is approaching from your rear, so that you will not pull into his path. If only an occasional car is parked at the curb, and you ride in the curb lane, approaching cars may not notice you. If cars are parked at frequent intervals, maintaining a straight path just to the left of the curb lane can actually be safer than weaving in and out between cars.

SLIPPERY ROAD SURFACES

Maintaining front-wheel steering control is especially important in two-wheeled vehicles. When the front tire contact point begins to slide, there is no longer any support under the weight of the rider.

Without support, the bicycle starts to fall on its side, and the rider's speed further accelerates the rate of fall so that the rider hits the street at almost his full riding speed. This can result in severe scrapes and possible head injury. The fall can be arrested only if the tire slides into an area of sufficiently increased friction before all control is lost.

There are a number of items that can initiate this loss of control. Some are obvious; others take skill and experience to recognize and counter.

Even riding straight without turning on a cambered road or with side wind requires extra care when surfaces are wet, muddy, icy, or oil slicked. Particularly insidious is "black ice"—water frozen on the surface of asphalt pavements in a film too thin to be seen. This is especially hazardous at dusk and at night when road visibility is lessened. When temperatures approach freezing and the streets are wet, a small low level cold air pocket can create a localized black ice spot that will spill the unwary rider.

WIND GUSTS

A sudden gust of wind from the side can produce severe results. Side wind pressure is exerted above the ground point of wheel contact, and it thus tends to roll the bicycle over on its side. Secondly, there is more area of the front wheel ahead of the steering axis than is behind it. Thus a wind gust tends to turn the front wheel in the direction it is blowing. Both effects combine to swerve the bicycle off the road, or into the traffic stream.

Large trucks or buses passing at high speeds close to the cyclist produce a similar effect. The magnitude of this effect varies directly with the speed of the vehicle and its frontal area and inversely with the distance between the vehicle and the cyclist. An instantaneous side thrust as high as from 10 to 30 pounds can be exerted on the cyclist. This may be even higher depending on wind speed and direction and truck speed.

The best defense short of dismounting is to anticipate these effects in windy weather. Listen for large vehicles approaching from the rear and brace yourself for the blast. Another effect to guard against is the suction that can pull you in under the rear wheels after the front wheels have passed. A trailing end wind also follows the moving vehicle.

Approaching trucks in the opposite lane of a two-lane road, with the wind coming from behind, is also a problem. Being braced for this effect once kept me and my partner from being forced off the road on a left hand curve as we descended a hill at high speed on a tandem.

In all these cases, knowing what will take place, the rider can prepare himself by studying this effect as vehicles pass him at reasonable speeds and distances during his regular riding.

THE STEEP, WINDING DESCENT

Rapid descents on winding roads are often required when touring in hilly country. Your bicycle rolls freely, turning and banking as it plummets.

But the sharp turns may decrease in radius as you round them. A car may be hidden around the bend. The road edge may be strewn with gravel. Only careful observation and the skill gained in training will then prevent accidents.

On hairpin bend roads, your weight is poised mostly on your legs, lessened on the saddle. Your body position is moved backward or forward on the saddle as you descend and turn. You sense the position which at each instant gives the maximum road-holding security. If the road surface is bumpy, the speed must be slowed, your arms flexed, and your body lifted to avoid wheel bounce.

A more forward position may "feel" better, but applying the brakes requires a quick backward weight shift. To maintain control, use the brakes selectively, more on the rear to prevent front wheel "wipeout," but with instant relaxation if wheel slippage occurs.

Watch and prepare constantly for turns that decrease in radius as you round them. Turn your head hard toward the inside of the curve. Looking at the outer road edge on a turn will lead you to the outside, and you may be unable to recover. Forcing yourself to look around the bend on the inside may permit you to recover. Looking inward is not automatic; you must force it.

Select your line of travel through the turn in advance to obtain maximum turn radius with due consideration for opposing traffic. Always assume that a car will appear around the blind corner. Prepare for this both in speed and your position on the road. A position farther to the left on a blind turn to the right gives more advance warning of slower moving traffic in your path. On blind curves to the left, stay to the outside of the turn, but observe carefully for gravel, stones, or loose road surface in your path. If road surfaces are damp, reduce your speed well in advance. A slight amount of water even hundreds of yards before the curve can wet your tires enough to cause a crash when you bank for turning.

OTHER ROAD HAZARDS

Gravel

Loose gravel gives a much less secure footing than hard-surface roadways. Unnoticed gravel at intersections where the rider's attention will be diverted by looking for cross traffic may cause a fall. If lighting is from the back, or if the roadway is shaded or in the dark, gravel is even less noticeable. Gravel at the edges of the road on curves can be hazardous if the rider is forced to turn on this material, but it may be possible to make the turn in steps, picking thin spots in the gravel. On fully graveled roads, a reduction in speeds is in order. Turns must be made gingerly (see Figs. 12.32–12.34).

Sunlight and Shadow

Alternate sunlight and shadow can affect the rider's judgment of road conditions and render gravel and potholes imperceptible (see Fig. 12.35). This is particularly true on high-speed downhill runs in partially shaded areas. Extra caution must be taken.

Fig. 12.32   Gravel on turns.

Fig. 12.33   Gravel and pebbles at intersection.

Fig. 12.34   Fully graveled road surfaces require picking a path through the thinner sections and keeping turns to a minimum.

Fig. 12.35   Alternate sunlight and shadow makes bumps and holes difficult to see.

Sewer Gratings and Expansion Joints

Sewer gratings with bars parallel to the direction of travel are criminally dangerous. In some areas these extend across a good portion of the road width and cannot be avoided. It may then be necessary to dismount.

Fig. 12.36   Parallel bar sewer grating can cause serious injury.

Fig. 12.37   Pennsylvania Highway Department's safety drainage grating is much less dangerous.

Full-width expansion joints are often fitted on long bridges. The unwary cyclist approaching these at high speed may not discern them in time to stop. The only solution is to expect these and look far enough ahead.

Tar Spots

Observe macadam roads carefully for areas or streaks where the tar has bled to the surface until it completely covers the stones. In wet weather, these small spots are more slippery than the adjacent surfaces. Use extra caution, especially at speed.

When the weather is hot and the sun strong, these tar spots though appearing quite normal may be soft and even fluid under the surface. When riding over them, rolling resistance perceptibly increases. The tire tread may pick up telltale tar and stones on its tread. When banking hard on a turn, the extra load on the tires may cause them to break through the surface skin to the more fluid area beneath, and this can result in the tire losing its grip on the road and an abrupt skid or fall (see Fig. 12.38).

Wet and Slippery Spots

Oil slicks, black ice, and wet leaves can act as lubricants on wet road surfaces, reducing braking ability and steering control.

Wet metal surfaces provide extremely low resistance to slipping. Wet manhole covers, sewer grates—even the relatively safe Pennsylvania 45° bar type (see Fig. 12.37)—and small-diameter, metal lane markers permit your wheel to slide sideward when you are turning ever so slightly. When the slide starts—even if only an inch—you may be unable to recover. Treat them as if they were spots of ice.

Railroad and Car Tracks

Normally, a cyclist crosses railroad or trolley car tracks at a right angle if this is possible. Wet trolley car and railroad tracks must be approached squarely. The uneven contour and extended length help to initiate and maintain uncontrolled side slippage; grooves beside them can trap the wheel. However, if the tracks are extra high or the paving broken away, there may be less chance of rim damage if the tracks are crossed at an angle. Grip the handlebars firmly when doing this.

In some instances, where the tracks do not cross the road perpendicularly, traffic may not permit veering across the road to steer across tracks at 90°. Figures 12.40–12.43 show a successful technique. Figure 12.40 shows angled tracks with rough road surface, a double hazard. In Figure 12.42, the front wheel has been rapidly turned so that it rolls over the track at a larger angle. As soon as the wheel has passed the track, it is again straightened. Once the front wheel is safely across, the rear will follow without incident.

Stones and Twigs

An unexpected small stone on the road can deflect the front wheel enough to cause a fall. Moderate-sized twigs parallel to your line of travel can roll your front or rear wheel sideward, particularly on a turn. Running over one end of a twig perpendicular to your path can flip it into the spokes, where it can be carried into the fork, effectively jamming the wheel and causing pitchover.

Breaks and Level Changes at the Road Edge

Figure 12.44 shows a paving break at the white line on the road edge. On this narrow road, with two-way traffic, the ability to skirt obstacles closely which we learned in the obstacle course test enables us to ride at the very edge of the break without veering out in front of traffic.

Fig. 12.38   Smooth tar spots on macadam pavement are more slippery when wet. If softened by the sun and hot weather, they will permit side slip on turns.

Fig. 12.39   Wet leaves on a wet road surface can considerably reduce braking and steering control.

Figure 12.45 shows a white line at the road edge painted over the actual paving edge. This line hides the change in the level of paving parallel to the line of travel. Such level changes can wrest the steering from your hands or prevent corrective steering back onto the higher level. Even though this difference in elevation is only about ½ inch, if you don't see it and brace for it, it can precipitate a fall.

Figure 12.46 shows pavement breaks parallel to the

Fig. 12.40   Diagonal railroad crossing.

Fig. 12.41   Front wheel approaches track.

Fig. 12.42   Front wheel turns sharply just before contact.

Fig. 12.43   Front wheel straightens immediately after crossing.

line of travel on the shoulder-pavement juncture along a normally heavily traveled, narrow two-lane road which can trap the front wheel and interfere with steering.

When in heavy traffic on narrow roads, the straight-line riding and obstacle course training provide a great measure of confidence and safety. Constant practice makes it easy.

Road repairs sometimes result in paving breaks across the entire usable pathway. These breaks must be seen far enough in advance for you to slow down to a safe crossing speed. In heavy traffic they may be hidden until the last minute. As the wheel enters the de-

pression, it is possible to break or dent a rim, pitch over the front, or lose control.

A skilled cyclist on a dropped-bar bike equipped with toe clips and straps may be able to "jump" his bicycle safely over the hole at speed without incurring damage, but his timing must be perfect. The arms pull up on the handlebars, the body is lifted, and then the feet are pulled up sharply. The entire bicycle is lifted into the air through the toe clips and straps enough to clear the obstacle. You may wish to practice this technique over lines in the paving from time to time in your regular riding.

Fig. 12.44   Paving break at the road's edge.

Fig. 12.46   Paving breaks on the shoulder parallel to the road can trap tire.

Fig. 12.45   Difference in level can trap tire.

Fig. 12.47   Rut running across road requires slowing down or "jumping" the bicycle.

Dogs

The unleashed dog is a common hazard for cyclists. Despite the fact that dog attacks are illegal, dog owners in many cases do not keep their dogs under control. A cyclist with his moving feet seems to be considered fair game and is more appealing to the dog than are the entreaties of his owner to halt. As a result the cyclist must resort to certain strategies for self-protection.

There are several categories of dogs, depending upon home training and temperament. We have the friendly type, who runs along parallel to you at a respectful distance and then returns to his property. We have the barker, who enjoys announcing his presence by barking lustily as he travels with you. Then we have the snapper, who enjoys using your moving feet as targets in which to sink teeth. Some larger breeds don't stoop to your foot level but snap at your upper legs instead. Then we have the doubly curious, who are inclined to see what you look like from the other side. Unfortunately, they do this by running at constant speed across your path; their mental computer doesn't warn them that this results in a diminishment of their original forward speed in your direction of travel. The result will be that either they run into your front wheel, or you run into their side. In either case, this is likely to bring you down. At high speeds, cyclists have been known to cut a dog in half and continue, speed undiminished, as projectiles free of their bikes. Finally, we have the jumper. This type jumps onto you from the side, knocking down your bicycle in the process.

There are as many protective strategies as there are cyclists. Some that I have found helpful are:

1. If no traffic is coming and you are ahead, move over to obtain maneuvering room, put on full power, and outdistance him—if this is within your capability. Then the problem is over and done with.
2. If he is alongside at your feet, grip the bars firmly, remove your foot, and aim a well-directed quick kick at his snout. This can be very effective if you are quick enough. If not, it gives him a larger target to latch onto.
3. Stop and place the bicycle between you and the dog to give him a chance to get acquainted. This method is generally the safest, but in the case of a vicious dog, it will only result in a more severe attack.
4. If the dog is ahead or to one side of you, slow down to his speed, turn toward him and ride at him, following him as he turns, and barking at him at the same time. This method is quite effective. Instead of being the aggressor, the dog now becomes the defender. His ego is deflated, and in most cases he will cease the attack. Of course, this requires an untraveled road upon which you can stop and maneuver.

5. Use Halt or some other brand of repellent spray. These sting the dog and temporarily incapacitate him from further attack, but the effect is not harmful and soon wears off. The one disadvantage is that you must remove a hand from the bars, and while you are doing this, you are more vulnerable to attack. If you do make a hit, it is unlikely that you or others in the group will be attacked again even on the return trip, but your aim must be good.
6. Another dog defense recommended by some cyclists is a squeeze bottle or water pistol filled with ammonia water. These discourage, without hurting, the dog. Al Spass of El Cajon, California, has written that a "gun" of this type made by Eldon contains enough fluid to protect a cyclist from more than 20 dogs.
7. Under no circumstances remove a hand from the bars and try to hit the dog with your pump or some other object. Swinging your arm can cause you to lose control and crash. Even if you hit him, you are likely to break your pump. At best you have little control if the dog should jump at you or run in your path.

Large Animals

At times on country roads, large farm animals can be found crossing or traveling along the road from field to field. If you pass a slow-moving horse and carriage, your silent approach can startle the animal. I find it best to speak softly as you come alongside so that you are noticed. Large field animals look like elephants to the cyclist when he gets close to them. Discretion usually causes me to halt, size up the situation, and then either proceed or let them proceed as judgment indicates.

WHEEL WOBBLE AT SPEED

When bicycles are operated at the high speeds attainable on the level and down hills by the modern ten-speed, an almost uncontrollable wheel wobble may develop. If not curbed, this oscillation of the front wheel from side to side can result in a high-speed crash. This phenomenon is not new in the two-wheeled field. It has existed for years with motorcycles and in the nose wheels of aircraft. A mathematical discussion of its causes are beyond the scope of this book, but the fact that this may occur should be recognized. Many factors are involved, which in combination may lead to this oscillation. Once started, the oscillation tends to increase in intensity. Some of the factors which influence the speed at which it starts include:

Wheel unbalance, out of round, out of true
Speed
Placement of loads on the bicycle

Pitch between road surface undulations and their height

Road camber (inclination toward the side)

Direction and intensity of side winds

Steering head steepness, fork offset, and the "trail" these factors provide

Stiffness or flexibility longitudinally of the frame

Relationship between the moment of inertia of the steering frame (wheel, fork, handlebars, handlebar extension, front luggage carrier weight and position ahead of the steering axis) and that of the rear frame (rear wheel, frame, rear luggage carrier and luggage, the rider's weight and position)

Size and type of tire used; inflation pressure.

On the same bicycle, different combinations of these many factors result in maximum wheel wobble intensity at different speeds. If the design and load distribution result in wobble peaking at a low speed, it may be possible to pass through this point and ride much faster with safety. Applying power may temporarily reduce wobble, but it will return when coasting is resumed. On the other hand, when the wobble starts, an increase in speed may bring the cycle closer to the critical speed for maximum wobble intensity. The following considerations will help in overcoming this problem.

Keep your knees close to the frame when coasting at speed. This makes you a part of the rear frame and allows you to control vibration.

If this vibration starts when you have removed one hand to reach for a handkerchief or wipe away a bug, immediately regrasp the bars near their outer extremities firmly with both hands.

Lower and extend your body by sliding back on the saddle to increase the rear-frame's moment of inertia.

Make certain that your wheels are well balanced.

Make certain that your luggage carriers are rigid, not flimsy, and that your front and rear luggage is firmly attached and supported so that it cannot sway. Keep your front handlebar luggage as close as possible to the steering axis—don't extend it far out in front of the handlebars.

Use the rear brake first to reduce speed to below the critical value, or apply power and increase speed. You will have to determine which is most effective.

Never descend hills at speed with one or both hands lifted from the bars. You may not have time to grasp both hand grips to regain control.

Fit a fork offset which brings your critical speed either below that at which you plan to ride or beyond your expected maximum speed. Generally at speed, smaller offsets appear to be beneficial.

HIGH-SPEED WEAVE

While rapid oscillation of the front wheel from side to side—wheel wobble—can occur at various speeds, "weave" of the bicycle increases in intensity with speed. "Weave" is an undulating path taken by the bicycle despite its rider's attempt to maintain a straight line. Its rate may be one or two cycles per second.

Research is being done on its causes and cure. Moving the center of gravity forward seems to help. Heavy luggage mounted far to the rear increases weave. A longer wheelbase—to keep the weight of front wheel, fork, and handlebar and front bag as close as possible to the steering axis—seems to help. Shallower head tube angles and moderate trail—ample fork offset—improve performance. Fitting tires with good cornering performance and keeping them well inflated also help. A frame of good lateral rigidity better resists weave (see Chapter V).

However, increased fork offset and low front-frame inertia amplify the wobble tendency. A balance must be struck for the best performance in your speed ranges. The trend to 27-inch wheels, narrow rims, and thin, smooth-tread tires may be a factor. Research in Germany has indicated that increased trail, the use of smaller diameter wheels, wider rims, thicker and flatter tire treads reduce shimmy.

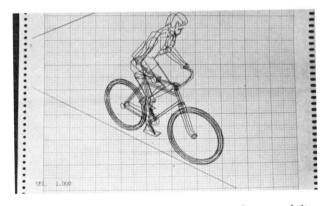

Fig. 12.48   Computer graphics output from stability computation
(Courtesy of Schwinn Bicycle Company)

Fig. 12.49   Rocket-powered stability disturbance test.
(Courtesy of Schwinn Bicycle Company)

GROUP RIDING TECHNIQUES

When riding closely spaced in a group, the lead and tail riders must act as eyes and ears for the entire bunch. If the lead rider sees any bumps or paving breaks or anticipates the need to slow or stop, he calls this out to the riders behind him. Likewise, the rider in the rear of the group signals approaching cars.

If you are following another cyclist closely to gain wind advantage, tell him so he will take extra care in maintaining an even pace. Do not overlap wheels. A very slight shift or deviation can bring down one, both, or an entire string of riders. Maintain an extremely even pace by smooth and even pedaling. Don't apply brakes without warning—you may cause the rider behind you to crash. Likewise, don't pull out of line without giving warning and don't reduce speed until you are certain that no one is following you. Don't try paced riding until you have trained yourself amply in smooth and efficient pedaling. When you do learn this, you will be rewarded by more effortless cycling.

Keep the rider in front of you in your eye pattern at all times. If you wish to look about, move back and allow more clearance.

When the group stops, clear the road completely. Keep off the pavement entirely. Don't obstruct driveways or sidewalks so that pedestrians must detour around you. Don't stop as an individual or as a group on blind turns. Keep beyond the outside edge.

Drafting

Drafting is an extension of paced riding that takes skilled handling, judgment, being attuned at all times to the bicyclist ahead of you, a deft touch on the brake when needed or an instant increase in pedal pressure to maintain a close and constant distance. The rider ahead may have a "crotch-ache" which may cause him to lift from his saddle for a moment. He may have to swerve a couple of inches to miss a stone. He may want to stand on the pedals and honk for a short pe-

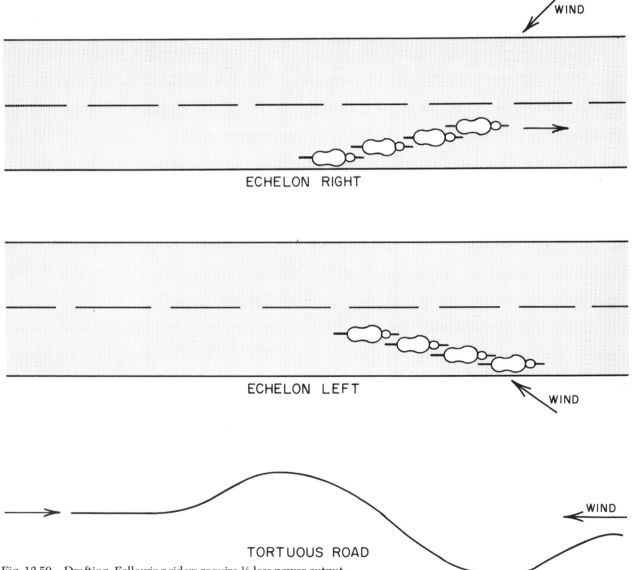

Fig. 12.50   Drafting. Following riders require ⅓ less power output.

riod to use other muscles. You must be tuned in for immediate action and response, yet the magnitude of your response must be slight. The rider to the rear of you may not be as alert or skillful.

The wind may be straight ahead, or it may be quartering from right or left. As the road winds, the actual direction of the wind against you will vary. In every case, there will be a pocket or position behind or to one side of the lead rider in which air resistance will be least. You can easily feel this point. If this point would cause you to lap his rear wheel with your front wheel, be sure of your ability and that of the rider in front.

If the wind is from the side, echeloning of the group of riders gives the best performance. But this takes extra space and should only be done if other road traffic permits. If the wind quarters from the left, the lead rider must ride farther out; if from the right, he will be close to the road edge.

The leader of a pace line must not hold his position too long or he may slow the group. When ready to change, he glances over his shoulder without swerve or pace change and checks on traffic and the position of the rider behind. If OK, he signals his intention, drifts off slightly to the left of the line (to the right in a left-echeloned line), and reduces his pedal pressure just enough to allow the rest of the group to pass. As he nears the end of the line, he increases pedal pressure enough to gain speed so that there will not be a gap to close after the last rider goes past.

The lead rider must anticipate the effect of changes in terrain on his followers. For example, if he comes to the base of a rise, he must apply additional pressure, otherwise the rear riders will bunch together as he slows. At the top of a hill, he must reduce pressure, or the group will open up gaps which the riders must then close. This forces them to accelerate and then brake. This "turbulence," as some riders term it, causes accidents.

Drafting has great advantages and great responsibilities. Under no circumstances when riding in large groups should you pull out of a line and then slow down. This tactic causes massive pile-ups such as those which recur regularly on the 2,000 plus riders TOSRV in Ohio, where untrained riders attempt the tactics used successfully by skilled members.

Crests and Rises

Keep to the right of the road at, and considerably before and after, the crests of hilltops, bridges, and rises on rolling terrain. Not only are you hidden from view at these points to oncoming traffic, but oncoming traffic may be hidden to you. If the cyclist in Figures 12.51–12.54 were riding out farther, he would have no protection from a car approaching from behind, and if another car were below the crest in the opposing lane, the following driver would be unable to swerve to avoid the hidden cyclist.

At crests, use your ears to listen for other traffic. They can warn you to pull off the road if necessary.

Figures 12.55–12.57 are unstaged photographs taken on group bicycle trips that show all too common unsafe practices. The first, taken on the same road upon which the truck surmounting the hill top was

Fig. 12.51   Cyclist approaching road crest.

Fig. 12.52   Cyclist at the crest.

Fig. 12.53   Truck suddenly appears.

Fig. 12.55   Cyclists riding across road near crest.

Fig. 12.54   Cyclist is invisible beyond the crest.

Fig. 12.56   Lone cyclist riding on the left and a group stopped on the roadway at a blind corner.

Fig. 12.57   Climbing a hill at slow speed while blocking traffic is inconsiderate.

photographed, shows cyclists approaching a crest riding across the entire road width! The second shows a group dismounted at the apex of a blind turn while a lone cyclist goes around the corner on the wrong side of the road! A car coming from either direction would have to strike either the lone cyclist or the group. The third shows a cycling club climbing a grade at low speed on a two-lane road. As can be seen, there is ample width in the lane for both cyclists to ride at the road edge and for automobiles to pass without going over the road center line. The inconsiderate practice of riding far out in the traffic lane and slowing traffic to a crawl is not only unsafe, but unnecessary. Sharing the road space so that both cyclist and motorist can travel unimpeded develops respect for the cyclist's legitimate right to use our road network, and the riding skills we have developed make this sharing possible.

COURTESY AND JUDGMENT

Under most circumstances on the open road, we ride as far to the right as is practicable, but sometimes the "facts of life" make it better or safer to break the normal rules. However, under no circumstances can we condone the "dog eat dog" philosophy that sometimes appears in the "letters to the editor" of cycling publications. (The "logic" of this philosophy is that since some automobile drivers are discourteous or downright aggressive, cyclists should retaliate in kind.) While aggressive actions and abusive language may momentarily soothe the reaction to driver discourtesy, in the long run it is self-defeating. Likewise, if we run red lights, stop signs, or impede traffic flow and speed, we hurt our own cause. This has already resulted in an ill-conceived regulation restricting cyclists to bike paths or the road shoulder—its condition not withstanding—and it further encourages steel-encased operators to "drive them off the road."

A saner course is to note the driver's license number and press charges. In the past, police response has all too often been in the motorist's favor—the cyclist's word being disregarded. This is one reason for participating in a recognized cycling "Proficiency Course." Having taken "driver training" can be used to combat the driver's most common defense: "He was wobbling all over the road." Police often construe this as fact, due to past experiences with irresponsible riding on the part of both children and adults.

Several intensive studies made throughout the country of bicycle and bicycle-motor vehicle accidents have shown that violation of basic traffic laws by bicyclists is the outstanding factor involved. In 70 to 90% of the cases, the cyclist was found to have clearly violated the rules of the road. Children under nine years old, it was found, are usually actually incapable of comprehending the implications of traffic laws and should not be permitted to ride on public roadways without supervision. Taking undue risks and riding at speeds in excess of the rider's emergency-handling capability were other major causes.

On short sections of narrow two-lane roads and bridges, where glass or debris at the edge of the road could result in falls or damage to our equipment, it may be necessary to ride out into the traffic lane. In slow or heavy traffic, especially on narrow two-lane sections, where the driver has a lot of distraction, this is especially true. When bicycling in heavy traffic, it is most important to be seen, and on a good ten-speed a cyclist can often keep up with traffic speed.

When the driver's view from intersecting streets and driveways is diminished by parked cars, posts, signs, and buildings, the cyclist must ride out a bit farther to be visible. When approaching corners, stay out farther so that drivers will know that you do not plan to turn right. Stay out of "right turn only" lanes.

When passing lines of parked cars, if the road lane width permits, stay out far enough to avoid opened car doors, or cars whose drivers pull out without looking.

When cars are parked spaced intermittently, maintain a straight and steady course. Don't dodge in and out—this makes you less visible.

When traffic is fast and the view from intersecting streets and drives is blocked, expect that drivers will nose out into your lane to better see the traffic.

When riding fast where the road lane is not too narrow, observe the normal path of traffic. Then take a position that does not impede the traffic, but which gives more room for maneuver.

Give pedestrians the right of way. Pedestrians may step off the curb, even against a red light, without noting your silent approach. At the speeds at which you travel you become a rather effective "guided missile." You and your bicycle weigh as much as two sacks of cement. Visualize the effect of being struck by two sacks of cement traveling between 15 and 25 miles per hour. If you strike a pedestrian squarely, you can hurl him completely across an intersection.

When passing slower traffic, unless your lane is open, pass on the left. If traffic is slowed or stopped, be especially aware of right side passengers who may open a car door into your path, even in midblock.

When moving into a traffic lane, however, whether to pass, or at a point where the road narrows, change your lane gradually and far in advance. Give the following driver plenty of warning so he has time to perceive your plan.

As you gain experience in bicycle handling, making left turns from the center lane the same as automobiles is much safer. The beginning cyclist, lacking confidence, may wish to proceed to the opposite curb of the intersection when in the right lane. At this point he can stop, turn his bicycle, then proceed when the road has cleared. While this method is often recommended by legislators and noncyclists, it is confusing to the motorist and the cyclist as well. Where poorly designed bikeways and bike lanes exist, this method is required.

In some areas and in some larger cities, driver discourtesy and impatience is a norm. In my daily rides to the office, experience has shown that in certain sections drivers will give no quarter. For example, to make a left turn onto some streets without traffic lights, it may be necessary to ride in the center lane for a city block or more. Otherwise, rush hour traffic will not permit you to turn. There are other points where traffic habitually crowds me to the curb unless I stay out far enough to prevent it. The experience gained in the Proficiency Training enables you to take these situations in stride and you soon adjust to riding in close quarters with vehicles. In many cities of Europe, where drivers have long been used to cyclists in the traffic mix, riding between lanes of slow traffic is an accepted commonplace that greatly speeds traffic flow.

On heavily traveled very narrow roads with a depressed or unrideable right shoulder, but a wide smooth shoulder on the left, the "never-ride-on-the-left" rule can be waived—particularly when visibility is poor or when wide and fast trucks or house trailers share your narrow lane.

Observe constantly the demands on the driver ahead of and behind you. Evaluate the distractions he faces and his probable line of travel through turns and corners. Then judge the action and course you must take for your safety. This "defensive driving" is a skill just as important as bike handling.

COURTESY

Reprinted from the
THREE RIVERS VELO-SPORT CLUB
Activity Log, 1972

Courtesy is essentially the Golden Rule in action. It makes cycling safer and more enjoyable for all concerned. It is also important if bicyclists are to retain the fine public image they now enjoy.

A. *Courtesy to other cyclists*
1. Don't ride too close.
2. Give hand signals.
3. Point out broken glass, grates and other road hazards.
4. Aid a cyclist having trouble.
5. Give warning of your approach. For example, say "Passing on your left."
6. Don't leave novice cyclists behind.

B. *Courtesy to motorists*
1. Don't hog the road.
2. Obey all stop signs and traffic lights.
3. Give hand signals.
4. Ride a straight line.
5. Give motor vehicles a wide berth.
6. Get all bikes off the roadway when you stop for a break.

C. *Courtesy to the public*
1. Give pedestrians a wide berth.
2. Don't block doorways or gas station entrances with your bicycle.
3. Don't park your bike against plate glass windows.
4. Don't take shortcuts across lawns or through private property.
5. For continued good public relations, why not greet the people you see along the way with a smile, a wave, and a cheerful "Good morning" or "Good afternoon."

CHAPTER XIII

See, Hear, and Be Seen

Be Alert

The average automobile driver is attuned to perceiving large moving objects, such as other automobiles, and smaller, very slow-moving objects, such as pedestrians, yet each year large numbers of accidents occur in which several cars or cars and pedestrians collide. Smaller, faster-moving vehicles such as motorcycles have an even greater accident-hazard experience, so that many states require motorcyclists to drive with their headlights on even in broad daylight to increase their visibility.

The bicycle is a small vehicle. When riding skillfully, the cyclist is a symphony of motion with no weave and wobble across the motorists' path. He thus attracts even less attention. The modern lightweight bicycle attains much higher speeds than those to which the driver's "bicyclist image" is attuned. He can approach a corner at a speed which places his original position out of the driver's conscious area of perception.

The driver who is not "in tune to cyclists" will make sharp right turns into a driveway, parking lot, or intersection immediately after passing the cyclist. He will also make left turns into the cyclist's path, and stop short or pull into parking spots in front of the cyclist. Until drivers recognize the great increase in bicycle riding and until the auto driver's responsibility for bicycle riders' safety is included in auto driving training and state driver codes, we must take responsibility for our own safety.

Ride as though the other drivers were unaware of you. Don't assume because you can see a car coming from the opposite direction from either side at an intersection, or because a vehicle has just passed you, that in either case your presence and speed have been recognized. Points of defensive riding include:

1. Watch the wheels of cars that approach or pass. Note the sound of the exhaust of the car in front. A change in exhaust tone or the slightest deviation of the front wheel indicates a change in speed or direction. The fraction of a second's extra warning can prevent an accident.

2. Recognize items that divert your attention from the road and consciously break away from them to glance ahead for an instant. This includes pretty girls, store displays, bright lights, or gorgeous views that merit lingering attention—but not when sprawled on the ground from hitting an obstacle.

3. Be extra careful when your visibility is decreased either by your clothing lacking contrast or by distracting foregrounds into which you blend.

4. Observe factors that will divert drivers' attention—narrow roads with opposing traffic, signs and displays, or scenic views.

5. Observe conditions that decrease drivers' ability to perceive you. These include approaching auto headlamps, particularly on narrow roads. Also particularly dangerous is the setting sun or the early morning sun. When low in the path of the motorist, the sun reduces greatly his ability to see. The cyclist is small, and in the field of reflected glare from the auto hood or the fireball of the sun, he may be practically imperceptible. When the sun is in the driver's eyes, the vehicle appears highly illuminated to you. This should alert you to the fact that you do not appear highly illumi-

nated to the driver, and he is therefore much more likely to turn into or to start up into your path than under higher angle illumination.

6. Look far ahead for intersections, driveways, and pedestrians who may step off the curb. Give yourself extra time to maneuver by constantly scanning the roadway from close in front to far ahead. It is particularly important to scan farther ahead the faster you ride. You can buy time with vision.

7. Watch for deviations and bumps in the road surface that will affect the handling of your bicycle. Remember that if the sun is directly above you or at your back, bumps, potholes, stones, and gravel are much less visible. When the sun is behind them, but not so low as to blind you, stones, holes, and gravel are silhouetted and become more perceptible.

8. As you approach a car coming toward you head on or from either side, try to catch the driver's eye to see that he perceives you. If he doesn't look at you for an instant, it's a safe bet that you haven't been noticed and extra caution is in order.

REAR VIEW MIRRORS

Rear view mirrors allow you to see traffic approaching from behind and to check on the positions of other cyclists in your group. Handlebar-mounted mirrors are partially effective, but handlebar motion and vibrations affect their field of view. A mirror mounted on your eyeglasses or cap visor is more effective. With this type, you can turn your head to see in any desired direction without taking your eyes from the road in front of you. Such a mirror can be fashioned from a dental mirror or purchased ready-made from Ultra-light Touring Shop (see Fig. 13.1).

THE CYCLIST'S EARS

On a road with limited traffic, the rider can use a bit more road space. However, he should regularly twist his head to place his ears fore and aft. This position intensifies the sounds of traffic approaching from both front and rear, and the rider should be able to hear even traffic approaching on intersecting streets (see Fig. 13.2)

Wind is a factor, however. With a following wind, traffic can be heard from the rear at a greater distance, but approaching or intersecting traffic will not be noted as soon. If the wind is from the front, the reverse is true. Winds from the front or rear mean you must listen more frequently and depend more on your eyes and your rear view mirror.

BE VISIBLE

Figure 13.5 shows an orderly group of touring cyclists riding in an orderly fashion well to the edge of the road in the early morning. The sun is ahead of them to the right. The riders' backs and left sides are shaded, and the sun is in the eyes of a driver about to take the road to the right. The cyclists can see well, and their lack of contrast to a driver approaching from the rear may not be apparent to them. The fluorescent safety flag carried by the rear rider is an attention getter.

With low sun and long shadows, glare and the limited lighting of the shaded objects may limit the approaching driver's vision. The shaded cyclists (see Fig. 13.6) are not very apparent, while the rider approach-

Fig. 13.1 Spectacles-mounted rear view mirror designed and built by Charles Harris. (Available from Ultra-light Touring Shop, Box 308, Brinkhaven, Ohio 43006—cost is $3.00.)

Fig. 13.2 The cyclist's ears are his best defense.

ing the sun direction is in a position where a driver would be blinded.

With the low sun at your back, an approaching driver may not see you even though you can see him clearly. Be prepared for him to turn in your path without warning.

If the sun is in your face, having no automobile hood in front of you, you can see the road readily, but a driver approaching from the rear is looking at an angle nearer to horizontal and is therefore more likely to be temporarily blinded. In addition, since the cyclist's back is in shadow, his visibility is lessened, and this compounds the danger.

Fig. 13.3   Fluorescent safety flags above riders' heads attract motorists' attention.

(Courtesy of D. Chaney)

Fig. 13.4   Orange fluorescent vest with reflecting-tape borders improves day and night visibility.

Fig. 13.5   Early morning shadows.

Figure 13.7 shows the actual conditions existing at a hilltop location in which one cyclist was struck by a sun-blinded driver. A car, approaching in the opposite lane in this picture, can be detected only by its shadow.

NIGHT VISIBILITY

Drs. Hazlett and Allen of Indiana University point out that vehicle-pedestrian (-cyclist) accidents result from a failure in the system composed of environment, vehicle and driver, and pedestrian. Even minor changes in the combination of these elements produce accidents. Nighttime, poor weather, or a drinking driver are three major contributors. However, these items have been further defined.

"Ample-visibility distance" must be greater than the distance traveled during the driver's reaction time plus the braking distance—both of which are factors of the speed of vehicle travel. With good brakes and pavement the minimum distance varies from 45 feet at 20 mph, to 350 feet at 70 mph.

In tests, highly reflectorized materials were found to be visible at the 70-mph distance, while gray clothing was fully visible at the a-v distance at only 30 mph. Black clothing was recognized in only 86% of the cases at even the 20-mph stopping distance.

Drinking drivers still recognized reflectorized subjects at 70 mph, but they saw the gray-clothed subjects at distances only safe under 20 mph. Drinking drivers need a stronger light to distinguish objects. Dimly lit objects may be discerned, but if dazzled by a light, they need a longer time to again see clearly. Their depth perception is reduced and their field of vision diminished. Thus, low-contrast objects at the edge of the road are detected much less easily.

Fig. 13.7   Sun blanks out car in left lane.

Fig. 13.6   Sun renders lead cyclist invisible.

A person on the road is visible as a silhouette or as an illuminated object against a dark background. Street lighting silhouettes figures, while auto headlights contrast them against a dark background. Snow or bright roads favor the silhouetted contrast, but well-lit areas combined with auto headlights produce opposing effects that may obliterate the rider or pedestrian!

The cyclist or pedestrian under low-light conditions adapts to the low level of illumination and can perceive an oncoming vehicle easily, even under difficult conditions. But since they can see the vehicle, many cyclists fail to appreciate the difficulty the driver has in detecting them.

With his low beams on, even an alert driver who is looking for a cyclist or pedestrian-sized object will not see it over 50% of the time if it is clothed in dark or gray fabric. White or reflective objects may be seen at 40 mph, but Drs. Hazlett and Allen report that if the driver has been drinking, only reflectorized objects are safely visible.

The doctors also quote Indiana accident records, which state that in 87% of the cases night drivers stated that they didn't see the person struck, while 50% of the drivers involved in accidents at twilight did not see the person in time. Only 12% of the daytime accidents resulted from the driver not seeing the person struck.

Reflective fabric, such as 3M Scotchlite tape is very effective at night, particularly if it outlines the form and shape of the rider. Establishing the shape of an object helps to distinguish it from a row of reflector buttons or lights or illumination in the background.

Figure 13.8 shows two cyclists whose presence is identified by reflective tire sidewalls. Figure 13.9 shows two cyclists with small patches of reflective tape on one rider, who is visible at 40 mph automobile stopping distance.

Silver or yellow tape in vertical and horizontal patterns, in one-inch or wider bands, gives excellent protection. The yellow tape improves contrast under dawn, daylight, and dusk conditions. Bands should be visible from the front, rear, and sides.

Front and rear reflectors on pedals have likewise proved to be of great value, and are now mandatory in many states. They are required throughout France.

Pedal reflectors create a moving beacon which flashes up and down on the two sides of the bicycle and attracts the driver's attention from a considerable distance. More important, they are always present, unlike protective apparel which may or may not be worn. However, the addition of reflector-banded clothing to increase the height and delineate the cyclist is highly recommended for maximum protection.

The strap-on French Matex leg lights are very effective. These shine in two directions, red to the rear and white to the front. Schwinn markets an improved model which is even more visible. These lamps have satisfactory life when fitted with alkaline D cell. The oscillating beam alerts motorists approaching from ahead and behind and, in the Schwinn model, from the side. They are made of lightweight plastic and are attached to the leg by straps. It is helpful, however, when pedaling fast, to add a safety pin to prevent them from moving. This lamp is not adequate for illuminating your path, but it will signal your presence.

HEADLIGHTS AND TAILLIGHTS

For adequate safety when riding at night, headlights

Fig. 13.8   Two brilliant hoops of light from reflective tires identify presence of cyclists.   *(Courtesy of MMM Company)*

Fig. 13.9   Cyclists with and without reflective tape at 120 foot distance from headlights. *(Courtesy of MMM Company)*

Fig. 13.10   3M reflective tape: visibility under dull conditions.

(Courtesy of MMM Company)

Fig. 13.11   Back-lighted jacket shines brilliantly, giving form to the rider.

(Courtesy of MMM Company)

and taillights are needed. With only reflectors and no lights, fatal accidents have occurred when cyclists collide at night. The headlight should be of ample size—it may still be light in weight—and you should be able to adjust the beam height while riding. When riding over potholes at moderate speeds with distracting illumination, the beam should be lowered closer to the front wheel. When riding at speed in pitch-black country on winding roads, the beam must be pointed farther ahead or you may overrun it and crash on a bend or into an object.

The combination generator-headlight does not give this flexibility, but it is extra light in weight. A headlight mounted on the fender ahead of the handlebar bag carrier is excellent. If your bike doesn't have a fender, you can attach a bracket to the handlebar bag carrier. This is far enough ahead that it is not hidden by your cape in the rain, and with a side illumination lens, the cyclist can be seen by drivers approaching both from ahead and from either side.

While a 50-mm headlight is good, a larger headlight gives much better visibility with the same generator power, and in lightweight materials, its weight is still minimal.

Generator sets are made in 3-watt, 3.6-watt, and 6-watt capacity. Naturally, both weight and effectiveness increase with capacity. Battery headlights and taillights produce no generator friction drag and are easily removed to save weight when riding in the daytime. They are effective for short trips, but their light level falls off with longer use. Newer alkaline batteries overcome this objection.

With no handlebar bag, the headlight can be located centrally in front of the handlebar extension. This gives best visibility for both cyclist and motorist.

British standards BS AU155, which increased the size, side visibility, and power of headlights and taillights, has resulted in much better side and front protection. Side reflectors, either reflective tires or wheel-mounted reflectors, are now mandated in most states. The bobbing motion of the wheel reflector when the bicycle moves attracts the driver's attention. Clear reflectors are the most night effective, yellow giving 20% less, and red 40% less luminence. However, the yellow wheel reflector also draws attention in daylight hours. Front, rear, and side wide-angle reflectors give protection if lights fail.

RAIN AND FOG VISIBILITY

The difficulties the motorist has on dimly lit, misty rain-soaked roadways are all too apparent. If you find it necessary to ride at night in the rain, remember that your "defensive cycling" band must extend far ahead and behind you. Be prepared to leave the roadway, don't rely on the motorist for your protection.

The motorist's headlights improve your own view of the road ahead, but they illuminate all the raindrops between you and him and decrease your contrast with the background. Raindrops which wet the windshield after the wiper blade passes form a diffused pattern softening the outlines of smaller objects. The headlights of approaching cars, streetlights in the foreground, traffic lights, and taillights of vehicles in front of the driver create long, lighted reflecting patterns on the wet road surface which are far larger than a cyclist and compete for the motorist's attention. On a wet night the prisms of raindrops on the windshield pick up these reflected lights and form another screen to obscure you. Let's face it—in the rain you should ride as if you were completely invisible to the driver ahead and behind. If you must ride, look for an alternate route with less traffic or wider roads.

The diffusion of images through the windshield contributes to the need for caution in the daytime as well. Lighting levels are lower in the rain, shadows are nonexistent, and the background contrast is reduced. The use of brightly colored rainwear of ample size is a must. On one of our summer trips, a group of cyclists dressed for protection in cycling rain capes was proceeding along a highway. Except for one, the capes were bright red or yellow. The exception was a conservative olive-drab army surplus garment. A car approached from the rear and successfully passed the brightly clad cyclists, then struck the one in the low-contrast cape. Upon questioning by police, the driver responded that he had seen the cyclists both behind and ahead of the unfortunate victim but had not noticed the rider he struck.

Fog and mist have quite similar effects. They shorten the visibility distance, diffuse the form of the cyclist, and lessen his contrast. It is possible to cycle with reasonable safety under the conditions mentioned, by considering the driver's visibility problem at each and every portion of our trip. Remember, accidents occur for three reasons:

(1) The cyclist isn't seen at all.
(2) "Something is seen," but it is not recognized.
(3) The cyclist is seen and recognized, but the driver is surprised and reacts less quickly than he would in the daytime.

Frank Warhurst of Annapolis, Maryland, suggests the use, in addition to leg-lights and reflective pedals, of strong lighting that shines on the bicycle and rider, who is outlined with reflective material, to provide extra care in a garish jumble of lights, such as those at a shopping center.

chapter XIV

Clothing, Rain Gear, and Head Protection

CLOTHING FOR BICYCLE RIDING

You can see bicyclists dressed in business suits, in attractive dresses, and in torn dungarees. Certainly a bicycle can be ridden in almost any garb to suit the occasion and the weather, but for cycling any distance, careful attention to togs pays dividends in easier and more pleasant travel.

Being completely exposed to the elements, the weather has a large effect on clothing selected. Temperature ranges to be encountered during the trip; the possibility of wind, rain, or snow; the places to be visited; and plans for other than pure cycling on the agenda must be taken into account. For example, racing gear is out of place when visiting in a city, viewing a cathedral in a foreign land, or stopping at a fashionable restaurant. For long, hard riding at top pace, use colorful racing attire. But if you expect to enter homes and buildings, cleated racing shoes are out, and a heelless shoe is downright uncomfortable.

Cycling clothing should be light in weight, should—except for cold weather use—permit cooling air to enter, should not bind or restrict motion, and should be close fitted. You ride with wind as an opponent. Loose, wind-catching clothing slows you down. Wind protection is needed in cold weather, but the other criteria still apply. Protection from the sun is vital in summer.

Select shorts, trousers, and underwear so that the seams do not come where the weight or motion is applied. Walking shorts are good for all-purpose summer use, but chamois-lined racing shorts give the utmost of freedom of movement and comfort. A Ban-lon jersey is neat, easily washed and drip-dried. A light pair of double-seated cycling knickers and knee-length stock-

ings is enough when the weather gets chilly; a track suit will do if only cycling is planned.

Shoes must be light in weight to minimize revolving weight and low to permit ankling. Both cycling shoes and lightweight firm-soled sneakers with thin soles are excellent. Unfortunately, you must look far and wide to find both. Either Pound-a-Pair or Hush Puppies afford a more dressy shoe with light weight and practical soles that are excellent for touring. To avoid foot and arch troubles, soles must be firm and must not slip on the pedals.

Customs are more restrained in Europe, and girls wearing shorts are likely to incite wolf whistles, especially in towns. Even in the United States, however, it is good to remember that all bicyclists may be judged by the appearance and actions of a few, just as motorcyclists suffer from the antics of a small minority of irresponsible and offensive riders. The cleated-shoe rider that clacks over finished floors and the noisy, perspired club group that disrupts other diners' mealtimes both harm the sport.

While actually riding, close-fitting wool cycling shorts with neat and colorful wool, cotton, or silk cycling jerseys are comfortable, give the least wind resistance, and make cycling most efficient.

On tour, a short-sleeved, drip-dry Dacron shirt and tie, weighs little and takes little space. A lightweight, dark-colored, Dacron-wool or other wrinkleproof cloth slacks and suitcoat should be carried for evening and in-town use. If carefully folded and packed in plastic bags, they take little space, and can be used for a month of dress occasions. A small tube of dry spot remover keeps it neat.

An extra set of drip-dry underwear, socks, and handkerchief permits a daily change. The day's drip-dry togs, washed on arrival, will be ready for morning. A pair of folding house slippers takes little space and can be worn at night if your day shoes are soaked by rain.

The bicycle boom has resulted in the marketing of neat and attractive cycling togs for the ladies. Select those that are practical, neat, and washable. On a sag-wagon tour, it may be possible to carry several changes of dress for all occasions. If, however, you are traveling all on your own and transporting all your gear on the bike, there is an unmentionable but practical point to consider. If you are on tour, you meet different outsiders each evening. Even though you have a minimum of changes, each evening you are "new" to your beholders. On tour with a bicycling group, everyone is in the same boat, and your friends are interested in you, not in your garb. Keep it neat; keep it light.

Under some conditions, rainwear can cause profuse sweating, so there is a choice between getting soaked from the outside or from the inside. When caped up, you need less clothing to remain comfortable, but being caped up on windy days can greatly increase wind drag and make the bicycle more difficult to handle.

If you expect chilly weather or large temperature changes during the day, a windbreaker or several lightweight garments that can be peeled off as needed must be carried. For example, when climbing high mountains—even only from three to four thousand feet—or when traveling in early morning and evening—and sometimes at noon—temperature changes can be wide. You may have to strip down when ascending a mountain, but on the high-speed descents from the top, a windbreaker, arm and leg warmers, and gloves will prevent chills and loss of control—especially in shaded and misty areas. Dr. Gaston has discussed cycling gloves—these are a "must" for the rider. Light, windproof mittens in winter or early morning are effective.

STRIPPED DOWN TOURING AS A GROUP

Some cycle tourists prefer the luxury of extreme lightness to the luxury of having all they might want. The final decisions of what to leave behind depend on the cyclist and his trip, but the following guidelines show how to get started.

Don't Duplicate

There is no need for everyone to have everything. One set of maps and guides, one compass, one dish towel, one supply of salt and matches do for all. Depending on the size of the group, you may want one or two sets of pumps, tools, patch kits, spare tires, cameras, and so forth. One shaving kit is enough for all the males.

Multipurpose Use

Many items can be used for more than one purpose. A T-shirt also serves as an undershirt or pajama top; swim trunks will double as underwear or pajama bottoms. A single jacket can be both a windbreaker and rain jacket. One kind of tape patches people and cycles. Scissors are more versatile than fingernail clippers; washing soap can be used for shaving.

Leave it at Home

Aim to find what you can leave at home by clever planning. Don't pack striped pajamas when other garments will do. Don't take a heavy towel—even if it starts light, it will soak up a lot of water. Wipe off with your washcloth; if you think this is tedious, you haven't lugged a wet towel over hills. Don't take a spare set of clothes. If your wash is not dry in the morning, don't stuff it in your bag; be a human clothes dryer. On weekend trips you can take only the shorts or trousers you wear. Realize that your bag mustn't be full at the start; leave room for food acquired on the road.

Check List

Personal: Shorts, trousers, underpants, swimsuit. Shoes, cotton socks, knee socks. T-shirt, Dacron shirt and tie, sweater, jacket. Cap, washcloth, toothbrush, razor. Passport and AYH pass—if hosteling or foreign touring. Bike, saddlebag, sheet sleeping sack. Plastic dish, cup, fork, spoon.

For the entire group: Dish towel, soap, salt, sugar, matches, knife, toothpaste, pump, patch kit, spare tire, guidebook, maps, camera, film, and watch. Sewing kit, first aid kit and light knapsack for food shopping.

HEAD PROTECTION

Head gear is advisable for protection from impact when cycling at speed. Yet speed alone is not a criterium. On one occasion, I rode over the end of a twig at night. It popped into the front wheel spokes and locked the front wheel as it went through the fork. Before I knew what had happened, I was thrown over the handlebars, landing full force on my head. On another occasion, a water-filled pothole at night gave a similar result at low speed.

This book should help develop your skill of observation and ability to maneuver, but an oil slick not perceived, or striking a pebble when your attention is diverted, can fracture the skull of the most experienced rider.

The United States Standards Institute specification Z-90 sets impact resistance standards, and the Snell Institute tests prototypes for approval in relation to these standards. Research on football helmets has shown that a hard shell with an inner liner of foamed, nonresilient plastic and a soft, slow-rebound plastic next to the head is most effective.

A stout chin strap is needed to hold it on in a crash, and a suspension harness for coolness is desirable. A cycling helmet, however, has other requirements. Since the cyclist's ears are his best protection from motor traffic, giving advance warning of the presence and of changes in speed and direction of cars close to him, a helmet must not create wind whistle or interfere with hearing—this is a defect in motorcycle helmets. Likewise, they must be extra light, or their overhung weight will be fatiguing. They must not cause your head to sweat—this is not only uncomfortable, it also results in a loss of vision. The standard lightweight racing helmet used by American racers gives some protection and is light—about 6¾ ounces. The Johnson's helmet, made by Jofa in Sweden, weighs about 12¾ ounces and costs about $22, but there is wind noise with it at high speeds. Some riders like the Kunoh Sports Cap, made in Japan, at 9¾ ounces. The CCM Hockey helmet and Sweden Cooper helmet have proven useful. The "Skid Lid" is lightweight, cool, and comfortable with a brim of tinted plastic, but is less resistant to shock and penetration. The Mountain Safety Research helmet and the Bell helmet (Fig. 14.3) both use a Lexan exterior shell to distribute shock loading and absorb impact force with crushable foam lining. I can testify to the effectiveness! Cooling air holes and suspension add comfort.

RIDING IN THE RAIN

A difference of opinion exists among avid cyclists on the subject of rain protection. We have the purist, who disdains mudguards for their weight and air resistance as well as for their effect on easy transport when wheels are removed. Come storm or slush, mud or grit, as head bearings, chain, and bottom bracket and pedals are bathed in grit-laden water, though grit and water stream up his back and soak his saddle, the purist slogs through smiling.

If the road is clean and the weather warm, the tires with a minimum of tread pattern, and the speed reduced, the ride will not be too distasteful. Indeed, once one becomes completely soaked in a summer shower, an interesting cycling experience results, which is not too unpleasant.

When it is possible, however, to stay relatively clean and dry, cycling in the rain becomes a really pleasant experience. Protected from splashes, you come alive to the patter on your cape; your face is gently caressed by the rain; your rainwear encloses you in a separate and sheltered, moving domain.

But when the weather turns colder, the wind sharper or the road surface dirty, a deluge of biting grit flung onto your body and into your eyes will be not only unsafe and unpleasant, it can be downright unhealthful. Mudguards are then a necessity.

Fig. 14.1   Cyclist's racing helmet.

Fig. 14.2   Kunoh sports cap.

Fig. 14.3   Bell helmet.

Mudguards come in varying widths, lengths, and designs. Widths vary from 43 to 60 mm, or even greater for balloon-tired bikes. Sections vary from flat to deeply channeled. Braces are either exterior or mounted on the interior. The length ahead of the fork may be a stub or may extend forward well beyond the wheel center. The distance from the ground to the fender bottom may vary from 5 to 15 inches in the front, from several inches below to several inches above the rear wheel center. Let's generalize on the differences.

A wider, closely fitted guard of deep channel shape with external braces will catch the water better and contain it for discharge to the ground. This, and increased length reduces fallout which is caught by the wind—particularly by wind from the side—and blown back on the cyclist. These guards are a bit more durable. A metal guard is more rigid and less likely to shake itself to pieces by oscillating from side to side. A metal guard permits front and rear lighting to be mounted neatly and provides a return current path and concealment in its rolled edge for the wiring.

Water spray from the front wheel will be directed back over the rider's feet unless a guard of sufficient length is fitted. A fender flap that extends almost to ground level is imperative, but this can get in the way and be torn off in normal handling. The Bluemels clip-on mudflap, which can be removed or slid up onto the fender when not in use, has proven itself quite practical.

Kleenfeet attachments, elastic-looped plastic segments that attach to the wheelnuts and extend over the fenders are very light in weight. They take very little room when folded and are quite effective in protecting the legs from windblown splash and fallout. Made in England, they are stocked in the United States by Shaker Velo-Sport of Cleveland.

An unrolled venetian blind slat carried on the rear carrier under the down tube will divert the stream from the tires, and when the rain stops, the slat can be rerolled and stowed out of sight.

Pointed tread tires and tires with a minimum of tread are less secure in wet conditions, but they throw much less water.

A plastic saddle is not affected by rain. A plastic saddle cover, however, takes little space, weighs little, and can be used to protect a leather saddle. Riding on a wet leather saddle can distort it and ruin it forever.

Wet weather clothing comes in several styles. A racing apron is the lightest, but it protects only the upper body. It consists of a front and rear flap that goes over the shoulders and ties about the waist. Racing capes have collars and sleeves; they fasten at the front, give little wind resistance, protect the upper body, and are warmer. The standard rain cape is made in varying lengths both with and without an attached hood. The longer the cape, the more it will droop down over the side. Longer capes having a greater bottom circumference provide freer handlebar movement as well as greater protection.

Capes come in 39, 42, 45, and 48-inch lengths. Shorter riders and riders with a short-length top tube and handlebar extension, or with raised handlebar machines, can use the smaller capes. Too short a cape used by a large rider is dangerous, as it can actually restrict motion.

A short cape also gives insufficient protection from the rain on the legs and no protection at all against splashes from passing cars and trucks, but this can be counteracted by the use of overtrousers or Spatees. The latter come with a string attachment to a belt loop to keep them from falling down. They cover the foot and the leg to above the knee. The open rear type is much cooler to wear; the foot protection keeps the feet from becoming soaked and muddy from automobile or front wheel spray. Overtrousers and sleeved jackets protect the rider, but they are hotter to ride in and give no protection to bicycle and saddle.

A sou'wester hat better protects the face, interferes less with side vision, and is cooler than the hood attached to a cape. The rear of a cape must be equipped with an inside string to hold down the rear, otherwise, the cape will fly out in the wind, creating air drag and giving little protection. Likewise, the sou'wester must be securely tied around the chin. If not, the rear end lifts up, and the front tilts over the eyes. At speed this is dangerous.

Remember the cautions given elsewhere about reduced braking capacity and tire road-holding ability in the rain. It is often helpful to ride out farther and to then pull in so that cars will splash you less. Always use a yellow or red cape for visibility.

CHAPTER XV

Packing for Touring

LUGGAGE CARRIERS

Front and rear luggage carriers vary considerably in weight, size, and rigidity. Most American manufacturers provide a pressed steel, platform-type carrier as an accessory on their middleweight lines. This carrier attaches to the seat-post-clamp bolt in the front and to the rear fork end or axle of the rear wheel. While heavy, it is quite sturdy and has sufficient space to support books. Another common type also bolts to the rear fork end, but a bolted clamp attaches this one across the rear seat stays. A third type, which uses a separate spring-loaded clip on the top, will secure material placed on it rather snugly, if the material is within its size range. Other carriers are attached by bolted clamps either to the bottom of the seat stays or to the rear fork ends.

Aluminum carriers, such as the Pletscher, are also supplied for fork-end and seat-stay clamping. Generally, all these types have two supporting struts. Their loads must be placed on top, since there is insufficient side protection to keep pannier bags from entering the spokes.

Rear carriers of these types generally supply sufficient support for a saddle-attached bag and for lightweight items supported on the carrier top while riding at moderate speeds on good roads. Unfortunately, the modern lightweight can travel at high speeds downhill on moderately rough roads, and the vibration in a load supported only on the carrier can loosen the bolts. On a tour, the carrier attachment on the stay-mounted types can slip down in front, so they must be frequently inspected. The lighter-weight types are often unduly flexible because their stays and attachments are not sufficiently rigid. At high speeds on a rough road

surface, sway in the unit can adversely affect bicycle stability and lead to loosening or breakage.

A twin-strut pannier bag carrier bolted rigidly to brazed-on attachments on the seat stays provides the most rigidity and security. Rigidity is reduced when this is made of thin steel rod. The Japanese carriers of this type are of heavy solid rod construction and extremely sturdy, but they are far heavier than they

Fig. 15.1   Wide platform, tubular rear Pannier carrier.

245

Fig. 15.2   René Herse Pannier carrier with brake-cable protection.

Fig. 15.3   Complete rear loading on Pletscher carrier.

more securely, without their rolling off the top and into the spokes on bumpy roads. The weight increase is minor for the short extra lengths of tubing.

PANNIERS AND SADDLEBAGS

The pannier bag carries the weight low and to the rear to increase stability and maneuverability. Some types even permit supporting the side bags at levels much closer to the road. The "long-range touring and camping bicycle" (see Fig. 2.12) has low-mounted panniers both front and rear, as well as a tubular front-mounted carrier for a handlebar bag.

Rear-mounted pannier bags should be carefully checked to make certain that there is sufficient heel clearance for the feet when pedaling. The front lower corners on some makes, such as Brooks, are cut at an angle to give the needed clearance.

Front-mounted panniers decrease maneuverability and handling ease, but they aid in balancing the load. With the rider's weight normally carried 60% on the rear wheel, the addition on the rear of all the baggage load results in undue tire wear and spoke breakage. Rim denting or breakage in rough terrain, or potholed roads can be reduced by more evenly distributing the weight. There is a trade-off here, maneuverability for less breakage, which each cyclist must decide for himself.

An amply sized rear saddlebag is another way to pack for touring. While the load is higher and further forward than with panniers, if solidly attached so that it does not sway, the saddlebag rides well—it also gets cape-protection in the rain. With a saddlebag, the bicycle is more difficult to wheel when dismounted. There is no protection to the rear derailleur such as that afforded, for instance, by panniers when the bike is air-shipped uncrated. There is a tendency to catch the leg when dismounting. If the frame is small, there is little room for a saddlebag of ample size, and panniers are in this case preferable. An "uplift" or hi-lift attachment supports the saddlebag from one to three

need be. Some English and many French constructors build tubular steel carriers that are firmly attached to brazed attachments and have welded-on tabs that attach to the rear fender. These are light in weight and terrifically rigid. The mutual support also stiffens the rear fender. With fully loaded panniers down rough, steep winding roads at high speeds, this type has perfect control and no sway.

The tubular carrier tops are generally made from three to four inches in platform width. A loop near the point of bolted attachment to the fork end allows the use of Sandows, elastic straps with hooked ends, or the holddown attachment on the pannier bags. My personal preference is for a wider top platform. When the bags are not in use, the carrier supports strapped loads

Fig. 15.4   In-the-frame tandem clothing carrier and spare tire roll.

inches higher than the saddle top on short frames. Of course, dismounting is affected.

A bag support which attaches to the seat-post bolt or rear stays will keep the saddlebag from hitting on the rear tire or the rear mudguard and dropping into the rear wheel. An excellent carrier of this type, which is marketed by Schwinn dealers, can be used as a spring top carrier for small loads or as a saddlebag support, and in addition, it protects the rear-brake cable from interference.

HANDLEBAR BAGS

The handlebar bag is a French cyclotouriste standby. If of ample size and used with the Randonneur handlebar which has adequate width, it is a most versatile accessory. The front pocket flap should be of ample size to keep out the weather. Rear pockets surround the handlebar extension, allowing space for tools and a spare tube and tire patch kit. Rainwear can be placed in front. The rearward opening main compartment is remarkably roomy. Since it opens to the rear, objects can be stowed and retrieved while riding, and they are less likely to fall out even if the top is not secured. We've carried liter sized bottles of milk, demi-loaves of French bread, and countless large articles in ours. Food can be munched from it while riding. The center panel top houses a plastic map pocket that can be viewed while riding.

This carrier requires a bottom support. Ets. TA, who markets the bag, also supplies a small front carrier which bolts onto Mafac, Weinmann, or Dia-Compe center-pull brake pivot bolts. A tubular-type carrier (see Fig. 15.7) is even better, being larger, yet as light, and more rigid.

This bag can be attached directly to the handlebar at the top. If you wish clearance between your fingers and the rear of the bag while your hands grip the center position on the bar tops, you need a stand-off device. There are several made. Schwinn markets one type, and Charles Mead in Marion, Massachusetts, markets an ingenious, but more expensive, type which is lighter in weight. Rene Herse and several other French custom builders provide proprietary models.

A smaller, lightweight but still ample bag made by Cannon has an ingenious strap attachment which suspends it and requires no carrier. It can be made rear opening by simply reversing it.

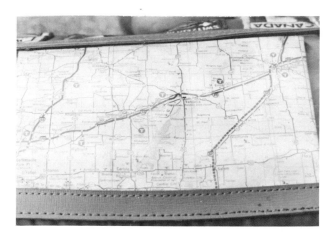

Fig. 15.6   Map pocket in handlebar bag visible when riding.

Fig. 15.5   Handlebar bag and panniers.

Fig. 15.7   Tubular front platform carrier for the handlebar bag.

Fig. 15.8   Tandem Touring—complete luggage for two with front and rear panniers, handlebar bag, and spare tire.

Fig. 15.9   Pannier carriers by Touring Cyclist Shop of Boulder, Colorado.

(Courtesy of Touring Cyclist Shop)

Some well-known names in America supplying front and rear touring bags are Cannondale; Touring Cyclists' Shop (Boulder, Colorado), and Hubbard, Stow-Away, and Frickman Mfg. Company. Carradice (English) bags are also well known. Most American bicycle manufacturers provide saddlebags of moderate size. The extraheavy canvas waterproofed bag is most durable, while nylon bags provide good service and protective coloring with the lightest weight.

Saddle and pannier bags come in a wide range of sizes and shapes. Consult your touring-oriented bicycle dealer or the sources of supply listed in the appendix for further information. Examples of available equipment are shown in Figures 15.9–15.11.

Cannondale has developed a novel method of transporting extra loads for bicycle touring and camping: a two-wheeled trailer attached to the bicycle at the seat post. Though it can carry up to 80 pounds, its center of gravity is low, and it therefore doesn't disturb the equilibrium or steering as does weight on the bicycle itself. In a trial, I was amazed at how easily it handled under all sorts of maneuvers (see Fig. 15.12).

Fig. 15.10   The Day Tripper—nylon, four-compartment bag.

(Courtesy of Touring Cyclist Shop)

Fig. 15.11   Cannondale touring bag set: handlebar bag, saddle bag, and two individual panniers.
(Courtesy of Cannondale Corporation)

Fig. 15.12   The Bugger bicycle trailer. *(Courtesy of Cannondale Corporation)*

CHAPTER XVI

Tandeming

THE TANDEM

For sheer fun, there is little that matches the joy of teamed effort directed toward a common goal on a tandem. The tandem combines the strength of two with the wind resistance of one. With a matched and spirited teammate, the tandem accelerates like a locomotive on the level and can hold speeds that make the tongues of exhausted companions on single hang out. And when the locomotive goes past, a string of single-bike "cars" will fall in line to be pulled along by the pounding pair in front.

On the downgrades, however, there is no contest. The longer wheelbase gives a smoother, steadier ride, and the lower resistance and greater weight let the tandem drop down hills like a stone, leaving the others far behind. (It's part of the tactics, though; on the upgrades, the double load on the longer frame invariably slows you down, so you run when you can, and crawl when you must.) Wider gear ranges, both up and down, are needed for the best performance.

Tandeming has many advantages. Being larger, the tandem is more visible to motorists and thus safer than a single. Likewise, it takes less space on the road than two bikes. Getting separated in traffic is no problem.

Also, sociability improves. Because there is no danger of crashing into each other due to inattention, a couple on tandem can converse with ease. An equally matched pair of riders is a rarity, but on a tandem each does his part to the best of his ability, and the differences average out. The stronger rider can take a larger share of the load; the rider who is less strong never gets left behind. The effect on morale is terrific. Usually the "crew" will provide utmost in performance, and if one does tire early, the partner is always there to carry as much of the load as possible.

Conversation isn't necessary; just the fun of working closely together, enjoying the view and the countryside, creates a feeling of harmony. No words may be spoken for miles, yet the feeling of togetherness is there. One amazing thing about tandeming is the degree to which the pedals telegraph feelings and moods without a word being spoken. Once a tandem couple has become used to riding together, the partner can detect mood changes and anxiety. He can feel the need for a bit of solace or the approach of tiredness which demands a refreshment stop. He can feel when to be silent and when to bubble with enthusiasm.

The tandem is an excellent way for a more-experienced rider to teach one who has had less experience because the teacher obtains instant feedback as to the effectiveness of the training. The techniques of ankling, of smooth application of pedal pressure, of climbing hills, and of timing gearshifts can be demonstrated, until the team learns to ride as one. One rider continuing to push while the gears are being shifted can result in gear damage or a difficult change. On the tandem, gearshifting is done just as if the bicycle were a single. Usually I don't give any warning, but my crew (and wife, Pauline) relaxes her pressure at the exact instant needed. Power needed for hills or acceleration comes automatically without urging.

Properly ridden, the tandem feels so much like a single, that I once went several miles before I realized, failing to get any response to a question, that Pauline must have stepped off at a curb.

TANDEMING TECHNIQUES

Tandeming techniques differ from those used handling a single, and both partners must learn them for safety's sake. Breaches of tandeming etiquette cause

Fig. 16.1   The author and his wife, practicing what they preach—and enjoying what they practice.

moments of strain. For instance, the crew must learn not to talk when climbing hills, as the captain then needs all the help available, and talking diminishes output. Likewise, the rule is "no talking in traffic." The captain uses his ears as well as his eyes to guide the craft and to sense impending danger, and speaking in traffic could disturb his judgment at a critical point.

The rear rider can noticeably steer a tandem. If a car comes close, a timid rear rider may shy toward the road edge. If the captain has just set course to skim the edge of a pothole, this movement can cause the bike to hit the pothole squarely and bend a rim. Any unannounced moving and turning around on the part of the rear rider is hard on the captain: I once twisted a handlebar stem out of shape trying to maintain control after a rear rider unexpectedly moved or leaned to one side.

When turning at low speed, the angle of bank may be such that the overhung weight of the rear rider will flip the tandem over. To prevent a fall, the captain should be prepared to rapidly pull his foot out of the pedal and extend it to one side. When first piloting a tandem, practice alone with a weight tied to the rear carrier or saddle. When the captain is holding the tandem upright at a halt with one foot on the ground, the rear rider must not shift his weight, particularly toward the unsupported side.

Nervousness at speed, especially on winding hilly descents, can cause the rear rider to start a very disturbing tremor which sets the whole machine to wobbling and interferes with control. A lack of faith in the captain's ability can cause an accident.

Pedaling styles must be similar. Nothing is as disheartening as the mating of a "plunger" and a "twiddler" as tandem partners. The pedal disappears at midstroke when the plunger applies his thrust. Then, as suddenly as before, at the top and bottom centers—when power is needed to keep the pedals turning—all help ceases. If the captain is a smooth pedaler, the difference in action throws him a bit off balance at every stroke. He must pull alternately with his arms to maintain balance, and of course after a short time, his arms and shoulders tire. Pedal action is impaired, and the ride cannot end too soon. Unbalanced pedal pressure also slides the other rider back and forth slightly. and continually on the saddle until he becomes saddle sore.

If one of the partners is a fast pedaler, the slower-moving plunger will find it impossible to cope with the pedal speed. His untrained legs will not bend quickly enough. At the top and bottom of the stroke, his body will move up and down, sometimes enough to make him lose the pedals. This bounce can also create so much vertical vibration that it feels to the front rider as if the whole rear of the tandem is jumping up and down.

Some riders with great variations in style are simply too individualistic and resistant to change to tandem together. Tandeming is also impossible with a less-energetic partner. Neither strength nor fitness matters. When riding with a partner who doesn't do his full part, the rear of the tandem feels like it is moving through treacle, and you cannot pull it loose. This differs so much from the feeling of a rear rider who is willing but tired that it must be experienced to be understood.

Riding together can improve technique and teamwork. In a great many cases, riders team admirably right from the start, and the fun starts at once. If it doesn't, both partners need kindness and understanding to learn the art of bicycling. Give it a chance. Encourage, don't criticize. It will pay dividends many times over.

It is sometimes helpful to stagger the cranks a few degrees to compensate for differences in pedal action. It has been suggested that placing the cranks out of phase makes hill climbing easier (see Fig. 16.2). I have found this helpful when starting or climbing grades at low speed, but when turning corners at speed, there is a chance of hitting the low pedal. The riding rhythm did not prove to be as smooth—even with a seasoned pair—as with the pedal strokes matched. However, you may wish to experiment on your own.

TANDEMING FOR THE BLIND

One particular joy of tandeming is being captain for a friend without sight. The blind can perform fully and admirably as a tandem crew. Unfettered by an insulating box of steel and glass, his keen senses hear all that is about.

The sightless partner can hear and smell his surroundings much more keenly than the sighted pilot. He can point out objects that the pilot has not noticed: the fragrance of the flowers, the rustle of the wind, the approach of another silent cyclist, the smell of cologne from the beauty shop you pass. The conversation of the others in the group makes him a full partner. A sprint to a finish line is understood, felt, and "seen" in full measure. Speak with your local Association for the Blind. You can bring sunshine into another's life.

SELECTION OF A TANDEM

A strong, sturdy, but light frame is even more important on a tandem than on a single bicycle. Because the extra length and double power impose greater strain and "whip" on the tandem frame, power needs increase when the going is tough. Likewise, the demand on the brakes is more than double, due to the lower air resistance. On level roads at moderate speeds, many of the low-cost tandems on the market will give a measure of fun, but for travel, a well-designed frame with large diameter tubing and an extra-wide gear range is needed. Higher gears—often over 100—can be used downhill. On the upgrades, however, lows in the 20s and 30s are frequently used.

Fig. 16.2   Cranks angled at 80° for continuous power flow.

Fig. 16.3   Riding with a blind partner.

This range requires 10 or 15 speeds. Derailleurs must have a tooth-difference capacity sufficient to handle the wider range. The chain drive interconnecting the two riders can be on either side of the machine. If on the left, it is called "crossover drive." Drive to the rear can be made from either front or rear crank hanger. Chain angularity is reduced from the front, and a triple front chainwheel for 15 speeds gives good results—particularly if you fit a close-coupled rear wheel. However, the extra chain length requires extrastrong spring tension of the rear derailleur, and chain whip is a problem. As shown in Figure 16.6, this arrangement puts less bearing load on the crank hanger bearing than the rear drive method.

One-side drive can be provided with proper modifications of chainwheel spacing, and a 10-speed drive with a reasonably wide range can be obtained with the 14 to 34-tooth freewheels now available. A 36–52 front combination gives a range of from 28.6 to 100. The Simplex touring derailleurs can manage this, or you can fit the Campagnolo Gran Turismo rear.

Figure 16.6 shows that maximum bottom bracket bearing forces for a load on each pedal of 150 pounds will be 610 pounds with the one-side drive, 940

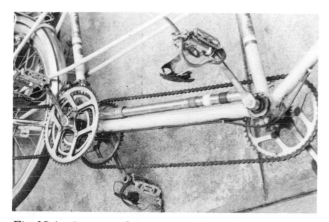

Fig. 16.4   Crossover drive permits 15-speed gearing.

Fig. 16.5   One-side drive train with 10-speed transmission.

pounds with the front crossover drive, and 1080 pounds with the rear crossover drive. The one-side drive gives considerably less maximum axle torque. Extrastrong tandem riders using a crossover drive may break the cotterless crank axle, or twist the heavily loaded axle so that the cranks move out of parallel, or shear the cotters on cottered crank assemblies. It used to be possible to purchase nickel-steel cotters, but these are no longer in production. One sheared cotter can immobilize your tandem, so if you plan to ride in hilly country on a cottered crank tandem, always carry spares and a means to change them. The only way to get around this is to invest in a set of specially treated custom-built and heat-treated cotters—any good machine shop can make them for you.

Short wheelbase tandems have a bit less whip and are better on hills, but they have their disadvantages. Due to the short centers, chain angularity is excessive, and with derailleur gearing, the front drive—with its extralong chain—must be used. Room for rear panniers is reduced; panniers may have to hang ungainly to the rear of the rear-wheel center. Tandems are particularly hard on the rear rider, who doesn't see the road bumps. Riding etiquette requires the captain to call "bump," when even a minor bump is negotiated, and a shortened rear tandem will break more spokes and bruise the rear rider more easily because of its higher road impact.

Tandem frame rigidity has already been discussed in Chapter V, but it might be helpful to add here that extralarge diameter or oval tubing between the crank hangers improves rigidity (see Figs. 16.7–16.9). A double gents' construction is, however, to be preferred.

WHEELS AND TIRES

With double the load, stress on tandem wheels is much greater. Spreading out the load creates far greater steering forces, so front-wheel spoke breakage is more common, and the front tire wears out rapidly on the sides—not the center. Rear tires also wear out quickly. For short distances, some riders prefer 27 × 1¼″ standard, single-bicycle wheels and tires, but these are not adequate for many uses. Rear tires of this size can wear clean through in only 750 miles. Due to the doubled weight and the fact that you can't jump a tandem over bumps, dented rims and broken tires occur much more readily. Rolling of tires due to rim heating is a hazard in hilly country with tubulars. I strongly recommend a larger section tire and a more robust rim. French tandemists consider the 650 B 42 (26 × 1⅝″) a must. A 1⅜-inch section should be considered the minimum, although the 1¼-inch section, used with extra care and good luck, can get you over smooth roads. Inflated hard, the larger tire gives a much greater feeling of control and security while detracting little from riding ease.

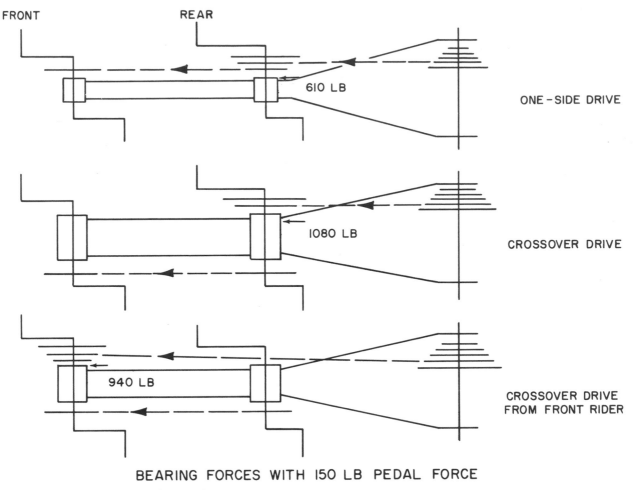

BEARING FORCES WITH 150 LB PEDAL FORCE

Fig. 16.6   Drive arrangement bearing force comparison.

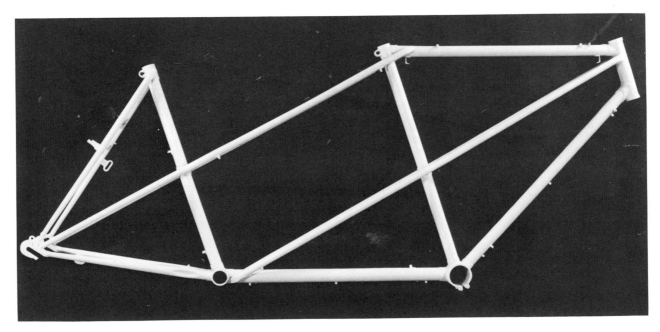

Fig. 16.7   Open rear frame.

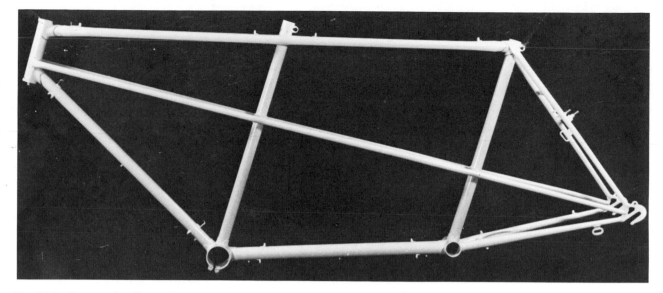

Fig. 16.8   Longitudinally reinforced frame.

Fig. 16.9   Twin-tube tandem frame construction provides lateral rigidity.

BRAKES

Excellent brakes are a must if hills or traffic will be encountered. With double the weight, rim brakes heat up very rapidly, and tire and tube failure at speed on long descents is far from uncommon. The Mafac extra-large Cantilever Reference H brake is considered the standard for caliper brakes—these brakes can be yoked together on a Mafac double-cable lever.

For safety, add a good hub brake. This can be operated by the other front lever, by a lever on the rear bar, or by a friction lever mounted to the frame. On grades the latter can be pulled into braking position—similar to the gear shift lever—and released at the bottom.

The tandem captain must learn to sense rim over-heating in hilly country by mentally taking note of the time and intensity of brake application. To avoid failure it may be necessary to stop and cool the rims or to walk down steep sections while the brakes cool. Extreme care must be taken in the rain when using only rim brakes.

CHAPTER XVII

Bicycling with Children

THE CHILD CARRIER

Bicycling is a family sport. Children over a year old are easily carried in a hiker's backpack or a "papoose pack" on trips of 20 or 30 miles (see Fig. 17.1), but when the child reaches three or four, it may be more comfortable to obtain a baby seat. Several types are available. Some fit on the handlebar; others mount on the frames between the handlebar and saddle. For safety, however, the seat that fits behind the cyclist has many advantages. It doesn't impede visibility, mounting, or dismounting. In it, the passenger's motion has less effect on the bicycle handling. Scientific tests have proven pliability and handling to be more favorable with the seat in this location (see Fig. 17.5). The child is also better protected from wind and chill. When tired he can lean forward, rest his head on the parent's back and nap.

THE PARENT'S EXAMPLE

Cycling is a fine way to teach children to enjoy and appreciate the world about them. At cycling speeds, the parent can point out the many things he passes, and the child can see the cows and horses in the fields, the flowers and the trees to either side, the stores, and the people. The scent of new-mown hay becomes an experience. A conversation can be had at cycling speeds without distraction. Unlike the motorist, whose higher speed and larger vehicle demand his concentration, the cyclist can see his surroundings to the fullest.

Frequent stops allow him to view the sights more closely. This gives the child a chance to stretch his legs every 5 or 10 miles and reduces fatigue. As the children grow older, their attention span naturally in-

Fig. 17.1   Back pack carrier for the younger child.

Fig. 17.2   Front carrier keeps the child in view and turns with the handlebars. Lack of spoke guards allows feet to enter spokes, which can cause a head-over-heels crash.

Fig. 17.3   Rain need not stop family touring.
(Courtesy of D. Knapshaefer)

creases, but experienced parents suggest that daily mileage not be over 30 or 40 miles. However, with routes planned for many points of interest, extended tours of a week or more are possible within this framework (see Fig. 17.3).

Prior to carrying a child in either a backpack or baby carrier, the parent should practice further on the "Proficient Bicycle Handling Course" (see Chapter XII). Before taking a child for the first time, mount the carrier or pack and place a dummy load in it equal in size and weight to the child you intend to carry. Then repeat the handling and braking tests. If you plan extended trips where rain is a prospect, complete the tests under wet weather conditions before you set out on the trip.

Make certain that your child carrier has some provision to prevent the child's feet being placed into the moving wheel spokes. Check to see that it has enough padding to absorb road shock and that it has safety harnesses to prevent the child from falling out or being thrown. Use either a safety flag or fluorescent

reflective material on the rear for additional security. While motorists are generally extra careful when passing a cyclist with a baby seat attached, it is always prudent to utilize every means of increasing visibility.

A child learns best through his parents' examples, and he should become accustomed to safe cycling procedures during his apprenticeship on the baby seat. Parents should point out as they ride the importance of maintaining a straight path on the road edge, of observing traffic, obeying traffic laws, and avoiding road hazards. Then by the time children are 6 or 7, they can accompany their parents on extended trips. A boy of 9 and a girl of 10 successfully completed the 210-mile Scioto River Valley weekend run in Ohio a few years ago, and others, even younger, completed substantial portions of the trip under their parents' guidance. I have observed several of these family tours on the road. Parents permitted no safe riding infractions; the children were proud of their ability to cycle well and outshone others less well instructed, though several times their age (see Fig. 17.4).

Fig. 17.4   Parents teach proficient cycling.

Fig. 17.5   This tandem with rear-mounted child carrier gives excellent riding stability, protection from wind, and doesn't affect steering if a body strap to the seat back prevents excessive motion. Note that parents and child wear head protection. The riders can carry additional children in back packs or in a "Bugger" trailer. Note foot guards which prevent feet getting into the spokes.

CHAPTER XVIII

Carrying and Protecting Your Bicycle

CARRYING YOUR BICYCLE

To get to quiet countryside, to go to rallies and bicycle club events, or on vacations, it is often more practical to drive to the starting point.

If your car has a large trunk, it is often possible to nestle two bicycles inside it by removing the front wheels. If the trunk is smaller, use a blanket to protect the bicycles and tie down the trunk lid so that it doesn't bounce. A couple of elastic-hooked straps, called "Sandows," will do the job, and you can use these later to hold items onto your rear carrier.

We have carried two tandems and two singles along with four of their riders in a standard station wagon. Locked inside, the equipment is protected not only from the weather, but also from rear-end collisions.

Many cyclists find it possible, by partially dismantling them, to fit two bicycles in the rear seat of a standard sedan. I've even seen two in a Volkswagen—although this required ingenuity.

To avoid the time and trouble of dismantling, many cyclists use top or rear-mounted carriers. Most good bicycle stores carry several different models. Some fit on top of the roof, others on the trunk or rear bumper.

You can easily build a sturdy car-top carrier equipped with bolted-on, weather-treated 2 × 4 inch timbers running across the width of the car. Drill ¼-inch or preferably larger holes (up to ½ inch) through the two timbers. Insert metal dowels which extend 2 inches in front and rear into these holes. Space the timbers to match the average handlebar-top to saddle-center position of the bicycles to be carried. Space one pair of dowels on either side of the saddle position and another pair on each side of the handlebar ends near the brake-lever position. By staggering the bicycles,

the outer ones facing the front and the center one facing the rear, three bicycles can be carried.

Cut a discarded truck inner tube into one-inch wide strips. Place the bicycles upside down on the carrier and loop the rubber bands around the dowels and over the saddle and handlebars. In this manner, a securely attached carrier will safely carry bicycles at speeds of 70 mph or more.

Fig. 18.1   Barre Crafters rear deck rack.
(Courtesy of Barre Crafters)

259

Fig. 18.2   JCI 2642-2 Rooftop carrier. *(Courtesy of JCI Industries)*

Fig. 18.3   JCI 2642-3 Cycle Caddy—Two-bike capacity.
(Courtesy of JCI Industries)

Fig. 18.4   R. D. Allen carrier on VW.
(Courtesy of R. D. Allen)

Fig. 18.5   R. D. Allen carrier on a station wagon.
(Courtesy of R. D. Allen)

A rooftop carrier has one or two disadvantages. Sometimes unthinking cyclists drive into a garage or under a low underpass with disastrous results. During rainstorms, forcefully driven rain may enter the bear-

ings or soak the saddle. Constant vibration on the timber top will break in the saddle to a form that doesn't fit the rounded bottom of its rider. Blowing sand or grit can remove the finest, even chrome-plated, finishes. The bicycles cannot be left unattended, unless they are locked to the carrier itself.

Rear-trunk carriers give a bit more protection, but they can limit rear visibility. In the trunk, bicycles are better protected from rear impact and when backing up.

Rear-fitted bumper-mounting carriers are very popular. There are many makes and models (see Figs. 18.8 and 18.9). The rear-mounted carrier is probably the easiest and quickest to load and unload since the bicycles are not dismantled. They are, however, most vulnerable to damage and to theft. They are better protected from driving grit and rain—a saddle cover can be fitted—but they get more grit splash from the road during rains. Often, the bicycles on rear carriers hang so low that they strike the ground when entering or leaving a steep driveway, and this can result in bent or broken wheels. You must be careful going over bumps and hollows. Hitting a bump hard enough can cause the rear of the car to dip and the bicycle wheels to hit. Be sure to allow for this and mount the bikes high.

Fig. 18.6   JCI bicycle and luggage carrier. *(Courtesy of JCI Industries)*

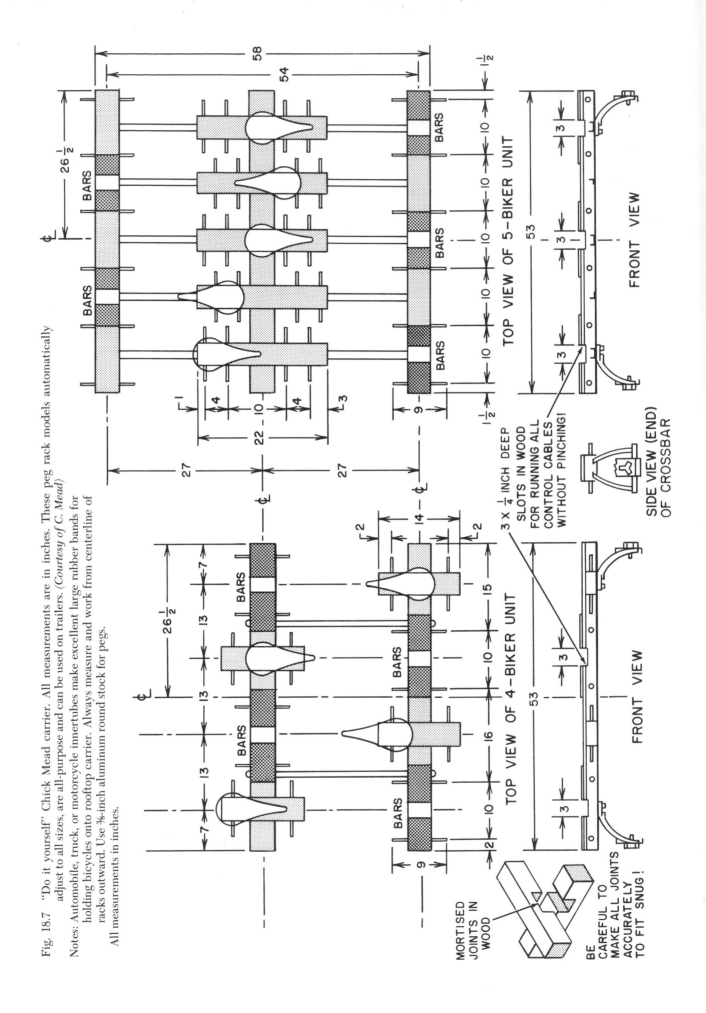

Fig. 18.7 "Do it yourself" Chick Mead carrier. All measurements are in inches. These peg rack models automatically adjust to all sizes, are all-purpose and can be used on trailers. (*Courtesy of C. Mead*)

Notes: Automobile, truck, or motorcycle innertubes make excellent large rubber bands for holding bicycles onto rooftop carrier. Always measure and work from centerline of racks outward. Use ⅜-inch aluminum round stock for pegs. All measurements in inches.

Materials needed for constructing a (4-bicycle) Peg Rack roof carrier

1 set (4 brackets) Sears' Best Catalog #28G-7216L rain-gutter type, "micro-adjustable."

2 pcs 2 × 4 wood for racks 96 inches long, preferably without knots and smooth (get 16 ft lumber).

1 qt of Penta-Treet wood preservative (soak wood by brush then let dry 3 to 4 times).

12 carriage bolts ¼ × 1⅝ inches long, countersink heads ³⁄₁₆ inch deep: 4 bolts for side-struts to keep measured distance and 8 bolts for attaching 4 roof brackets.

12 ft of ⅜ or ⁷⁄₁₆ inch aluminum roundstock for 16 pegs 9 inches long (Total 144 inches—2¼ lbs).

64 Large rubber bands for all pegs of whole carrier.

2 pcs, ⅛ inch thick and 1 × 32-inch long aluminum flat or ¾-inch angle stock (for adjustable struts). Get 64 inches.

4 tubes (or bulk) of weatherstrip adhesive to stick-on the "padding." (Mill ends of thick felt or carpeting for roof-rack protective padding for bicycles.)

1 pt Rustoleum paint (desired color).

1 qt liquid Neoprene for waterproofing top of padding (if desired).

Some Good Tips

For large rubber bands (also called, rubber-tension rings), get some old motorcycle, auto, or light truck inner tubes, or buy new inner tubes if you wish, and cut bands approximately 1 inch or more in width for stretching strength. Figure on 4 or 5 rings for each 9 inch peg, then multiply 4 or 5 times the number of pegs in your whole carrier! (Same for 5-bike unit.) Motorcycle inner tubes are excellent for the 5-bicycle carrier.

You may want to reflectorize; use 3M's Scotchlite white or yellow Codit aerosol spray cans or brush-on "reflective" liquid paint. You can use white or yellow Scotchlite tape on the metal parts to make your carrier "reflect" light in darkness! Get 1 pt or qt paint.

Mounting bicycles: Start with seat first; put one ring over seat to hold it in place. Next, put one ring over each side of handlebars, then add, as needed, more rings all around for greater holding tension and stability.

Caution: Do not drive into any garage or low-lying overhead roof with a bike or bicycles mounted upon roof carrier (for obvious reasons). Also, remember to secure "peg racks" very firmly to your vehicle! All control cables can be slipped through the 3-inch wide slots for handlebar stem (please note these on drawing).

Materials needed for constructing a (5-bicycle) Peg Rack roof carrier

1½ set (6 brackets) Sears' Best Catalog #28G-7216L rain-gutter type, "micro-adjustable."

3 pcs 2 × 4 wood 8 feet, 2 inches long for cutting 3 pcs 53 inches long for 3 racks and for 5 saddleboards, each 22 inches long (get smooth wood without knots at lumberyard).

1 qt of Penta-Treet wood preservative (keeps wood from warping & cracking out in the weather).

12 carriage bolts with nuts: 4 bolts ¼ × 2 inches long for rear-rack brackets mounted on the aluminum bar-stock track, and 8 bolts ¼ × 1¾ inches long for middle-rack (no bar-stock) and for the front-rack brackets (which are in line with the 3-inch wide grooves, especially on VW Squareback).

Note: Countersink all boltheads ³⁄₁₆ inch deep for smoothness.

28 wood screws (flathead) ³⁄₁₆ × 1¼ inches long for anchoring 5 nonadjustable aluminum struts.

32 wood screws (flathead) ³⁄₁₆ × 1½ inches long for bar-stock tracks on front and rear racks.

24 ft of ⅜ or ⁷⁄₁₆-inch aluminum roundstock for 32 pegs 9 inches long (Total 288 inches—4½ lbs).

128 Large rubber bands for all pegs of whole carrier.

16 ft of aluminum channelstock (1¾ × ¾ × ⅛ inch) for 3 struts 58 inches long, or 15 ft if you can get that length to cut up for less money.

10 ft of aluminum anglestock (¾ × ¾ × ⅛ inch) for 2 pcs 58 inches long each strut.

9 ft of aluminum flat-barstock (1¼ × ⁵⁄₁₆ inch thick) for 2 pcs 53 inches long each piece.

1 tube or 1 pt epoxy or wood glue for joining mortised saddleboard pcs to middle rack.

25 wood screws (flathead) ³⁄₁₆ × 1¼ inches long for joining mortised seatboards to middle rack.

8 tubes (or bulk) of weatherstrip adhesive to stick-on the "padding." (Mill ends of thick felt or carpeting for roof-rack protective padding for bicycles.)

1 qt of Rustoleum paint (desired color).

1 qt of liquid Neoprene for waterproofing top of padding (if desired).

Some Good Tips

Using large rubber bands, there are no knots to tie and untie, and they grasp and hold the bicycles better than anything else—there is always tension, never slack! Using 4 or 5 large rubber bands on each 9-inch peg is an insurance in case one should break (which is rare).

These carriers assist bicycling, and bicycling gives more dimension and perspective to the world around us by getting us outside for a closer look at the countryside. Everyone who owns a car or some motorized vehicle should have at least one good bicycle-carrying device to more fully enhance the pleasures of bicycling and for use at "big time" bicycle events.

Transporting by Bus

The Greyhound Bus Lines accepts bicycles at those stations where it operates a package express. (Inquire at your nearest Greyhound office.) The bicycle need not be accompanied, so you can travel in any manner you wish and send your bicycle on ahead. It must, however, be packed in a carton, and the maximum length permitted is 84 inches within a state, or 60 inches interstate—to meet the latter you must remove the front wheel. Your bicycle will be held at its destination for three days; for longer periods there is a fee.

Fig. 18.8   Schwinn 2-bicycle carrier.
(Courtesy of Schwinn Bicycle Company)

Fig. 18.9   Bike—ette carrier.

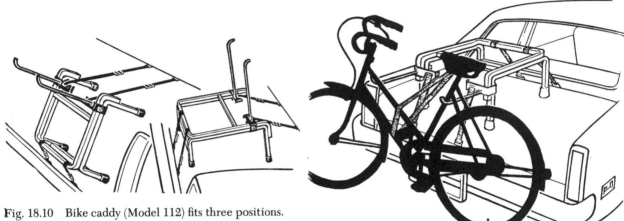

Fig. 18.10   Bike caddy (Model 112) fits three positions.

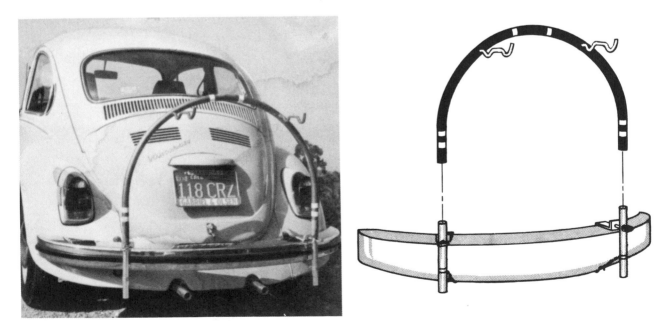

Fig. 18 11   Good Earth carrier is light and easily removed.

Rates are expensive—about $7 to $10 for 150 miles—and should be determined in advance.

TRANSPORTING BY RAIL

Amtrak permits bicycles as baggage for a $2 handling charge, but a bike can be substituted for one of the three pieces of baggage allowed. Preparation the same as that described for air travel is recommended. Avoid other luggage that makes the bicycle hard to handle.

It is sometimes possible to stow a collapsible bicycle in the overhead luggage rack if it makes a small-sized package.

Bike cartons are available in limited quantities in New York, Chicago, Minneapolis, Los Angeles and San Diego; these are recommended if the bicycle must be transferred from one train to another. Pedals must be removed and the handlebars turned. While only $25 liability insurance is accepted, additional insurance can be bought at a rate of $0.30 per $100 value.

Check schedules to see if your train has a baggage car. If your bike is to be placed on your train, check to see how long in advance it must be delivered; if it must go on another train, make sure it will arrive on time.

TRANSPORTING BY AIR

More and more airlines are presently accepting bicycles as personal baggage, though often at a not excessive, supplemental charge.

Special vinyl cloth bags in which bikes may be sent are available on the market. With its wheels removed and astride the frame the bicycle takes up less space, and its parts are protected from loss. However, in some instances, these "well-protected" packages, tossed or dumped by baggage handling personnel, incur more damage than an exposed bicycle.

Several airlines provide a bicycle carton free of charge. Pedals and handlebars must be removed and the seat lowered or removed to fit the bike in it. An excess baggage charge of $10 to $12 is often charged.

American and Delta provide a reusable poly-sack for about $3. The excess baggage charge applies, and the bike must be prepared to fit in it.

Eastern and some others have taken my bicycle, with pedals reversed and handlebars turned, with no sack. United may provide a carton or insist that the sharp parts be protected and cushion foam fitted to protect the bicycle and the luggage of others. Eastern also has cartons.

Cartons and sacks reduce theft and lost parts, protect the baggage of others, and facilitate handling.

Unless the frame size is small, an assembled bicycle with fenders will exceed the luggage size limits of the CAA. Properly prepared (with pedals removed, chain thoroughly cleaned, plastic brake lever sleeves, all projecting metal parts that may mar other luggage wrapped with rubber or foam, pannier bags in place, and the front wheel attached with a Sandow—an elas-

tic cord with a vinyl-covered hook at each end—to prevent swinging), the complete touring bicycle can be readily handled as a single package by baggage loaders and will not harm other luggage. Removing the pedals reduces width, conserves cargo compartment space, and prevents handlers from snagging their shins. It also prevents the pedals from digging into other luggage, and from snagging other travelers in a crowded terminal. With the front wheel swing restrained by a Sandow, the bicycle can be easily placed by baggage handlers wherever convenient. Figure 18.12 shows my bicycle thus prepared being put into the cargo hold. Fig. 18.13 shows a TWA bicycle carton and a bicycle prepared in the previous manner "at your risk" just as flown. Reversing one pedal and removing the other reduces chance of damage in uncrated handling.

1977 rules for overseas travel permit taking a bicycle prepared this way, with bars turned, plus one suitcase whose total dimension of height, length, and width do

Fig. 18.12 With pedals removed and front wheel secured with elastic cord, bicycle can be handled easily.

Fig. 18.13 Bicycle carton and bicycle ready for uncartoned, "at-your-risk" shipping.

not exceed 44″, and a handbag with total dimensions of 39″. Without the bicycle, you may carry two bags with total dimensions of the larger bag not over 66″ and total for both bags not over 106″. This might permit a take-apart bicycle in its sack if under 66″.

I usually leave the rear or front panniers in position, which protects the gears and also the luggage of others, and use the handlebar bag as my cabin luggage.

Compartmentalized luggage containers are generally too small for anything larger than a dismantled or a collapsible bicycle, but most planes reserve a section of their cargo space for bulky cargo. Small commuter planes, however, may not have enough baggage space for bicycles.

If the plane is large enough to hold it, but the airline has not filed for acceptance of bicycles, you can demand they accept it as air freight (at a higher cost). They may still request crating.

Tandems will fit in most planes of DC-9 size and larger, but not on commuter airlines and some smaller services within European countries. Check plane type when planning your trip.

Preventing the Theft of Your Bicycle

A bicycle is a lightweight, easily lifted and transported article with wide acceptance, a ready market, and appreciable value. As a result, bicycle theft in the United States has reached scandalous proportions. Since components can be switched and color easily changed, the recovery rate has been rather poor. Regular organized theft rings have been started. The New York Cycle Club warns against bicycling alone in many areas of New York City. Even in the parks, assailants will attack a rider, knock him from his bicycle, and take it away. Automobile and truck drivers have been known to do the same, putting the bicycle in the vehicle and driving away with it.

Leaving a bicycle unattended without a substantial lock and chain is an invitation to steal it. Bicycles are even being removed from garages in private homes. Never leave a bicycle unattended at night. If you must leave your bicycle, leave it in a busy, well-illuminated spot and, if possible, enlist the aid of a movie cashier or newsstand operator to keep an eye on it.

If you can, lock the frame and rear wheel and take the front wheel with you. Make arrangements at your place of business for a space for it. Lock it to heavy, immovable objects.

Your chain must be case-hardened. In New York and in some other cities, ⅜-inch section links are recommended. Maintain a rapid pace and try to ride where there is room for maneuvering. Keep a weather eye out for suspicious characters, and stay on well-lit and well-traveled streets at night.

Extra strong locks of special steels and a hoop length and width sufficient to surround frame tube and a post, such as "Citadel" or Kryptonite, are available. Schwinn has a frame lock of this type which combines with a recoil cable for added security.

Register your bicycle with your police department (if it provides this service). Arranging with the police department in your city or town to have your social security number engraved on the frame is a good deterrent that has improved recovery rates.

Record make, model, and a description of all accessories and components.

Record the serial number, color, and identifying marks and dents.

Pick a readily identifiable color, different from the run-of-the-mill, or add racing stripes or other nonstandard decorations.

Photograph your bicycle, in color if possible. Report any theft to your bicycle club as well as to the police. Unfortunately, bicycles are often transported to far-away areas, but state and nationwide registration schemes, plus your etched social security number, provide some security.

Never buy a used bicycle unless you obtain a signed bill of sale. Make sure the seller has a valid identification card that you can inspect and verify. If this is not given, report this and the bicycle description to the police. By helping to frustrate theft rings, you gain a measure of protection for yourself. Be involved! Buying a "hot" bike involves you in a crime, and you may be the next victim.

CHAPTER XIX

Bicycling Societies and Organizations

PERIODICALLY, bicycling clubs hold joint and regional events that attract enthusiasts from long distances. Joining one of these clubs enables you to meet with others and share experiences and riding skills while pleasantly traveling the road. Friendships are made that last a lifetime. Since these clubs plan trips lasting a day or a weekend, one or two weeks, or up to two months—for extended tours throughout the United States and foreign countries—you have a selection of many trips, many events, at all seasons of the year in almost any section of the world.

BICYCLE MANUFACTURERS' ASSOCIATION

This organization is over half a century old, yet it is more virile now than at any time since its organization. It is basically a trade association composed of the American bicycle and bicycle component manufacturers, but its staff promotes the good of the sport throughout the country, develops standards for higher bicycle quality, publishes service manuals for bicycles, and helps in the development of bicycle paths and legislation favorable to the cyclist. It publishes many booklets to aid the cyclist which can be obtained simply by writing for them. Included among the many available, free booklets are: *Directory of Bicycle Riding Clubs in the USA, Bicycle Movie Catalog, Bicycle Safety and Operation Courses* (several booklets), *Bicycle Regulations in the Community, Bicycle Racing on Campus, Boom in Bikeways* and *Bike Safety News* (periodical publications). It also offers motion pictures, and the assistance of field service representatives. The address is:

Bicycle Manufacturers' Association
1101 15th Street, N.W.
Washington, D.C. 20005

In addition to those listed the BMA has a storehouse of information on details of work being done in municipalities all over the country, as well as plans for car bike carriers and material on cycle camping. If you need information, they have the sources at their fingertips and will help you.

LEAGUE OF AMERICAN WHEELMEN

The League of American Wheelmen was originally founded in 1880. By 1898 it had grown into a nationwide organization of over 100,000 members which fought for roads for cyclists and had a nationwide touring service with maps and guidebooks similar to those of the AAA which followed it. In the low period of cycling which occurred during the rise of the automobile, the League diminished to the vanishing point and was only revived in the 1960s by a group of members in the Chicago area. Since that time it has grown to become the nation's leading bicycle organization and a clearinghouse for news about bicycling clubs and noncompetitive events. Its monthly bulletin is a storehouse of information on what's going on in cycling circles throughout the country, and its annual membership directory enables a member to find cycling friends wherever he goes.

The League sponsors regional rallies and interclub events throughout the country. Several annual events that are combined with tours draw participants nationwide.

Individual LAW clubs also sponsor tours in conjunction with cycling organizations in other lands, such as the Cyclists' Touring Club of England. Transportation and lodging are all arranged beforehand.

The League is active in promoting bikeways and mapping routes for bicycling throughout the United

States and Canada. It establishes and cooperates with other organizations in running bicycle safety and proficiency training courses through state and regional directors who coordinate these activities in their areas.

Their increased membership and vast resources make the LAW a source of help in almost every phase of cycling except licensed competition.

The League's address nationally is:

League of American Wheelmen
19 South Bothwell
Palatine, Illinois 60067

AMERICAN YOUTH HOSTELS, INC.

Youth hostels encourage outdoor activities and inexpensive travel. Started in Germany, they have grown worldwide, and the American Youth Hostel movement is affiliated with other organizations throughout the free world—including Japan.

AYH members may stay overnight in any of the 4,200 hostels located in 47 countries. These are generally simple accommodations—although many, being old ships, castles, and schools, are of considerable size. Generally, the hostel consists of separate dormitory facilities for males and females, a common room for socializing with other participants, and cooking facilities which allow you to prepare your own food. Many European hostels provide supper and breakfast at a very nominal cost. Hostelers must carry a prescribed "sleeping sack," but beds and blankets are provided. Hostel rules require leaving the hostel as clean as when you arrived.

The hostel network in Europe is extensive, and many are close enough together that you can cycle from one to the other in a day. In the United States and Canada, the network is not as great, but it is growing. Most American hostels are in the Northeast, Central, and Western United States. The Youth Hostel Manual lists hostels and their costs; International Youth Hostel manuals cover foreign hostels. When going to a particular country, obtain the manual for that country for greater detail.

AYH has councils in many major United States cities from coast to coast. The local councils have large-scale activity programs for their members, including bicycling, skiing, sailing, and canoeing. While primarily youth oriented, there is no age limit, and most councils have extensive adult and family programs.

The National Council and many local councils sponsor extended tours lasting as long as eight weeks within the United States and to many foreign countries. Information on all activities and on camping and cycling supplies for sale can be obtained from:

National Headquarters
American Youth Hostels, Inc.
Delaplane, Virginia 22025

INTERNATIONAL BICYCLE TOURING SOCIETY

The International Bicycle Touring Society was formed in 1964 by a group of cycle tourists from the United States, England, and France, all of whom were friends and acquaintances of a San Diego surgeon, Dr. Clifford Graves.

As an Army Medical Officer in World War II, Dr. Graves had the unique experience of escaping from enemy encirclement during the Battle of the Bulge on his bicycle. After the war, Dr. Graves, a multilinguist, traveled much of Europe on his bicycle and for years led highly successful European and domestic bicycle tours for the San Diego Council of American Youth Hostels.

The first internationally attended tour of New England in 1964 was so enthusiastically received by the 40 participants, that they decided to continue the association. Members lay out and lead tours in increasing numbers each year; the tour leader donates his time for the love of the sport. Dr. Graves handles most of the correspondence and gets out the annual bulletin which contains a list of tours requested and members who have volunteered to be tour leaders.

Minimum age for membership is 21. Members come from many countries in Europe and from Canada, the United States, and Japan. Communication is kept open with bicycle touring organizations in many countries—Alliance Internationale de Cyclotourisme, Federation Francaise de Cyclotourisme, Cyclists' Touring Club, and others—who often help in the planning and leadership of foreign tours.

Tours vary in challenge and in length—from one to four weeks, two to three weeks being most common. You don't have to participate in the full tour. The cyclist must have demonstrated his ability to ride at least 50 miles a day, but many of the members in their 60s and up to 70 have taken part in the most grueling trips through 10,000-foot-high Pyrenean and Alpine passes. (Most of the trips are through more interesting hilly terrain.)

Tours are not regimented. The only requirement is that you get to the day's destination by suppertime. Excellent lodgings are selected in advance where the group can socialize and discuss the next day's routing and destination.

This is "gentleman touring." A "sag-wagon" is provided to carry luggage and to rescue those incapacitated by a mechanical breakdown or illness. Its rental cost and the responsibility for driving it each day are divided among the group. You pay for your own meals and lodging and share the costs of scouting the tour. People from all walks of life take part—the Governor of Indiana scouted, led, and rode the entire tour in his state with his first lady. Annual membership dues are $5.00. Information can be obtained from:

Dr. Clifford Graves
846 Prospect Street
La Jolla, California 92037

CYCLISTS' TOURING CLUB

The Cyclists' Touring Club of England is a pioneer touring group, similar to the American LAW. However, it provides insurance and a travel service which will lay out your route and obtain reservations and passage. Its handbook lists recommended places for lodging in the British Isles. They run bicycle tours to selected areas each year, and since they have excellent contacts with foreign touring clubs, they can supply information on travel and cycling conditions and routes in other countries. A bimonthly magazine is sent to all members. Dues are about $12.00 per year. Their address is:

Cyclists' Touring Club
69 Meadrow
Godalming, Surrey, England
Another British organization with a similar service is:
The British Cycling Federation
26 Park Crescent
London, England

FEDERATION FRANCAISE DE CYCLOTOURISME

This French organization will keep you in touch with French cycle touring events and with regional and nationwide rallies. They also have a directory service for lodging and suggested points of interest which compose a scheme of point-winning for cycle touring prowess. Dues are $9.00 per year. Their address:

Federation Francaise de Cyclotourisme
8 Rue Jean Marie Tego
75013 Paris, France

UNITED STATES CYCLING FEDERATION (USCF)

The United States Cycling Federation is the governing body of the sport of bicycle racing in the United States. Through its affiliation with the Unione Cycliste Internationale, headquartered in Paris, and its membership in the United States Olympic Association, its members are represented in the World Championships, the Pan-American Games, the Olympic Games, and the United States' championship competition.

Its membership includes all the bicycle racing clubs in the United States. All recognized races obtain USCF sanction, and all riders in these races must have USCF licenses (these are obtained through state representatives). Classes of license are: veterans, over age 40; seniors, 18 to 39; juniors, 15 to 17; intermediates, 12 to 14; midgets, 9 to 11; and women, over age 15. The USCF runs state and national championships and selects the Olympic Team and participants in the Pan-American and World Championships.

To learn more about bicycle competitive events, contact your state representative, or write to the USCF:

United States Cycling Federation
Box 669 Wall St. Station
New York, New York 10005

AUTOMOBILE CLUB OF MISSOURI, AAA

One pioneering development was the establishment in 1972 of an extensive program of cycle proficiency training and of local and distant bicycle tours by the very progressive Automobile Club of Missouri—which is interested in all types of road transportation. You may contact them at:

Auto Club Headquarters
201 Progress Parkway
Maryland Heights, Missouri 63043

CANADIAN CYCLING ASSOCIATION

For information on travel in Canada, contact:
The Canadian Cycling Association
333 River Road
Vanier, Ontario, Canada

ALLIANCE SPORTIVE DU QUEBEC, INC.

This group conducts cycling tours and events in Quebec Province and elsewhere and can provide contact with cycling clubs in the province. For information, contact:

11652 Alfred Laliberte
Montreal, Canada

DUTCH ORGANIZATIONS

The Dutch Touring Club (ANWB) assists in cycling events and helped in the AIT rallies in 1967, 1968, and later. They also have descriptive folders on cycling routes in Holland. For information, write to:

ANWB
Wassenaarseweg 220
Den Haag, Netherlands
The Dutch Cycle Touring Club (NRTU) conducts tours from spring to fall:
Nederlandse Rejwiel Toer Unie
Postbus 76
Zoetermeer, Netherlands
The Dutch cycling organization, Stichting Fiets, publishes cycling route maps and lists where bicycles can be hired. For information write to:
Stichting Fiets
Europaplein 2
Amsterdam, Netherlands

SCANDINAVIA

In Scandinavia a good source of information is:
Jørgen Beyerholm Jr.
Vestervang 35
3450 Blovstrod pr Allerød
Denmark
Include four international reply coupons (about 80¢) with your request.

Sources of Information

There are several bicycling magazines that can be consulted to obtain up-to-date information on new products and accessories. Contact the publisher or representative.

GENERAL INTEREST

Bicycling!
Rodale Press
33 East Minor Street
Emmaus, Pa. 18049
>Monthly, $9 per year
>(on newsstands)

Bike World
PO Box 366
Mountain View, Cal. 94040
>Monthly, $8.50 per year

Cycling
IPC Business Press Ltd.
205 East 42nd Street
New York, N.Y. 10017
>Weekly, $49.40 per year
>(published in England)

RACING MAGAZINES

Competitive Cycling
PO Box 2066
Carson City, Nev. 89701
>Monthly, $7 per year

International Cycle Sport
Kennedy Bros. Publishing Ltd.
Howden Hall
Silsden Nr. Keighley
Yorkshire, England
>Monthly, $14.50 per year
>(published in England)

Miroire Cyclisme
10 Rue des Pyramides
75001 Paris, France
>Monthly, 95 francs per year

VeloNews
Box 1257
Brattleboro, Vt. 05301
>18 issues yearly, $9 per year

TOURING MAGAZINES

CTC Journal
69 Meadrow
Godalming, Surrey
England
>Bimonthly, about $9 per year
>(free with CTC membership)

LAW Journal
19 South Bothwell
Palatine, Ill. 60067
>Monthly, $10 per year
>(free with League of American
>Wheelmen membership)

Cyclotourisme
8 Rue Jean Marie Trego
75013 Paris, France
>Bimonthly, about $12 per year

TRADE PUBLICATION

American Bicyclist and Motorcyclist
461 8th Avenue
New York, N.Y. 10001
>Monthly, $12 per year

CYCLING BOOKS ON ALL SUBJECTS

Rodale Press
33 East Minor Street
Emmaus, Pa. 18049
Bike World and *International Cycle Sport* both market a full line of cycling books.

Sources of Supply

EQUIPMENT AND SUPPLIES

Better bicycle stores in bicycling-oriented cities have a large stock of bicycling accessories. These can include spare parts for a wide range of equipment, material to upgrade your present bicycle, carriers and packs, car-carriers, cycling shoes and clothing, and books and magazines.

To get an idea of what parts and equipment are available and what they cost, there are several information-filled catalogs that are excellent for reference.

Raleigh Industries Catalog. Available from Raleigh dealers.

The *Schwinn Consumer Catalog.* Pictures bicycles and accessories, with prices. Available from any Schwinn dealer.

AMF and Huffman Manufacturing Co. and Columbia Manufacturing Co. are also expanding their dealers' line of accessories, and catalogs available.

More complete parts catalogs may be had from:

Cyclo-pedia (Gene Portuesi). 311 N. Mitchell, Cadillac, Michigan 49601. Cost, $2

Bikecology Bike Shops. 2910 Nebraska, P.O. Box 1880, Santa Monica, Cal. 90406

Bike Warehouse. 8063 Southern Blvd., Youngstown, Ohio 44512

Lickton's Cycle City. 310 Lake Street, Oak Park, Ill. 60302

Palo Alto Bicycle. 171 University Avenue, Palo Alto, Cal. 94302

Ron Kitching's Handbook. A two volume catalog and information manual, English. Available from Ron Kitching, Anglo-Continental Cycles and Accessories, Hookstone Park, England. Cost, about $3.00

Bike Riders' Aids. Holdworthy Co., London SE-20. Cost, about $1.50

Other available catalogs will be advertised from time to time in the cycling magazines listed above.

SOURCES OF SUPPLY

Literally hundreds of trade names are used, particularly on imported models, that do not give a clue to the manufacturer or importer. Some importers apply a single trade name to bicycles obtained from far-spread sources and vary these names from year to year. There are ever-increasing numbers of suppliers, so the following list (reprinted, with additions, from the January, 1978 Schwinn *Reporter* by permission of the Schwinn Bicycle Company) can only be used as a guide.

AMERICAN-MADE BICYCLES

Note that many American bicycle manufacturers utilize foreign components extensively. Many have complete frames or complete bicycle. made abroad under their own or foreign trade names. American bicycles are widely distributed through the manufacturers' franchises, department stores, and other retail outlets.

Maker	Location	Bicycle Brand	American Distributor
AMF Wheel Goods Division	Olney, Ill. and Little Rock, Ark.	AMF	
Chain Bike Corporation	Rockaway Beach, N.Y. and Allentown, Pa.	Ross	
Columbia Mfg Company	Westfield, Mass.	Columbia, Vista	
Huffy Corporation	Dayton, Ohio and Celina, Cal.	Huffy	
Murray Ohio Mfg Company	Nashville, Tenn.	Murray (and private brands)	
BMX Products	Chatsworth, Cal.		
Ret-bar Cycle Mfg Company	Peoria, Ariz.	Ret-bar Tricycle	
Schwinn Bicycle Company	Chicago, Ill.	Schwinn	
Romic Cycle Company	Houston, Texas	Romic	
Graftek/Exxon	South Plainfield, N.J.	Graftek Carbon Fiber	
Gobby Mfg Company	Glendale, Ariz.	Gobby	
Sentinel Bicycle Mfg Company	Chatsworth, Cal.	Sentinel	
Mathews	California		

Specialty Builders (There are over 60 specialty builders of high repute in the USA.)

F.M. Assenmacher	104 E. May, Mount Pleasant, Mich.	Assenmacher	
Advance Bicycle Engineering	75 Glenville Ave., Allston, Mass.	Mitch Kneller	
William Boston	505 Lakeview Drive, Swedesboro, N.J.	Bill Boston	
Albert Eisentraut	980 81st Ave., Oakland, Calif.	Eisentraut	
Colin Laing	3454 N. 1st Ave., Tucson, Ala.	Colin Laing	
Jim Redcay	George St., Lambertville, N.J.	Jim Redcay	

CANADA

Canada Cycle and Motor Company	Weston, Ontario and Cheektowaga, N.Y.	CCM	
Sekine Cycle	Rivers, Manitoba	Sekine	

MEXICO

Acer-Mex	San Battala, Maucalpan and West Coast Cycle Supply, Carson, Cal.		Linder Euro Imports and West Coast Cycle Supply
Bicicleta Condor	Guadalajara, Jal.		
Bicicletas de Mexico	Mexico #4 Districto Federal		

ARGENTINA

Bier Company	Buenos Aires	Botechia, Viscontea	
Cafici & Cia	Buenos Aires	Legnano	

BRAZIL

Monark	Sao Paulo	Monark	

COLOMBIA

Fabrica de Bicicleta Monark	Cali	Monark	

URUGUAY

Nelson Jorge Loffredo	Montevideo		

AUSTRIA

Steyr-Daimler-Puch	Wien, Graz	Steyr-Puch	Steyr-Daimler-Puch America Atlanta, Ga.

BELGIUM

A. Claeys, Flandria	Zedelgem	Flandria	Flandria U.S.A., N.Y., N.Y.
R. Claeys, Superia	Zedelgem	Superia	
Kessels N.V.	Oostende	Kessels, Eddy Mercks	

DENMARK

Schroeder Cykler	Hallerup	Schroeder	Victor Sports Ridgefield Park, N.J.
Smith and Company	Odense		
O.F. Olsens Cyklefabrik	Copenhagen		

FRANCE

Andre Bertin	62 St. Laurent-Blangy	Bertin	
Cizeron	42 St. Etienne	Raphael Geminiani	Benoto Inc, Chicago, Ill.
Societe Dangre	59 Valenciennes	Paris Sport	Victor Sports Ridgefield Park, N.J.
		Starnord	Beacon Cycle Supply Milwaukee, Wis.
A. Jeunet	Dole, Jura	Jeunet	
Societe Le Jeune	75020 Paris	Le Jeune	Franklin Imports Ridgefield Park, N.J. United Imports Sales Gardena, Cal.
Peugeot	25 Beaulieu-Valentigney	Peugeot	Cycles Peugeot Gardena, Cal.
Gaston La Pierre	21 Dijon	La Pierre	
Manufrance	42 St. Etienne		
Mercier	42 St. Etienne	Mercier	Beacon Cycle Supply Milwaukee, Wis.
Societe Micmo-Gitane	44 Machecoule	Gitane	Gitane Corp. Hawthorne, Cal.
Starnord	55 Valenciennes	Starnord	Victor Sports Ridgefield Pk., N.J.
Stella	44 Nantes	Stella	
Motobecane	93 Pantin, St. Quentin	Motobecane, Astra	Motobecane America Long Beach & Tustin, Cal.
		Motoconfort	D.P. Harris, New York, N.Y.
Follis	Lyon	Follis	Linder Euro Imports Culver, City, Cal.
Meral Cycles	72 Aubigne-Raeau	Meral	
Cazenave-S.A.M.	33 Belin	Cazanave	Benoto Inc, Chicago, Ill.
Liberia	Grenoble	Liberia	G. Joannu, Miami, Fla.

Specialty Builders

René Herse	92 Levallois-Perret	René Herse	
Alex Singer	92 Levallois-Perret	Alex Singer	
Rene Andre	75 Paris	Rene Andre	
Jo Routens	Grenoble	Jo Routens	
R. Ducheron	75011 Paris	Ducheron	

FINLAND

Helkama Oy	Helsinki 20

HOLLAND

Gazelle Rijwielfabrik	Dieren	Gazelle	
Batavus Rijwielfabrik	Heerenveen	Batavus	Batavus America, Atlanta, Ga.
N.V. Magneet Rijwielen	Weesp	Magneet	B.M. Lawrence San Francisco, Cal.
Rijwielen EROBA	Echt, Limburg	Eroba	

ITALY

Bennotto, Walter	Torino	Bennotto	Satellite Industries
Emilio, Bozzi	Milano	Legnano, Frejus	Tom Avenia, New York, N.Y. Merry Sales San Francisco, Calif.
Carnielli SpA	Vittorio Veneto	Bottecchia, Grazellia	Stuyvesant Bicycle New York, N.Y.
Chiorda Trapletti	Vigano S. Martino	Chiorda	Stuyvesant Bicycle New York, N.Y.
Chiorda Sud	Rome	Chiorda	
Cinelli, Cino	Milano	Cinelli	Kopps Cycle, Princeton, N.J.
F.I.V. Edorado Bianchi	Mandello de Lario, Treviglio	Bianchi, Gimondi	Stuyvesant Bicycle New York, N.Y.
Rizatto, Cesare & Co.	Padova	Atala	Stuyvesant Bicycle New York, N.Y.
Ernesto Colnago	Milano (Cambiago)	Colnago, E. Merckx	Rolls, Rolls Cycles Whitestone, N.Y.

Gios Biciclette	Torino	Gios	
Fabo di Ing. Falconi	Padova	Fabo, Alan	
Olmo, Giuseppe, SpA	Celle Ligure	Olmo, Oldino	Stuyvesant Bicycle New York, N.Y.
Motovelo-Fiorelli	Novi Ligure	Fiorelli, Coppi	Italmet Industrial Huntington, N.Y.
Maserati		Maserati	Elsco Corp. Jacksonville, Fla.

WEST GERMANY

Kalkhoff Werke	4950 Cloppenburg	Kalkhoff	
Rixe	4805 Bielefeld	Rixe	Victoria Distributors, Lancaster, Pa.
Otto Kynast	4570 Quackenbruck	Kynast	
Hans Schauff	5480 Remagen	Hans Schauff	Beacon Cycle Supply Milwaukee, Wis.
Nürnberger Hercules Werke	8500 Nürnberg	Hercules	
Staiger KG	7000 Stuttgart		

NORWAY

Jonas Oglaend	Sandnes	Oglaend

SPAIN

Orbea S.C.I.	Eibar, Guipozcoa	Orbea	
Torrot		Torrot	Pegasu Imports Flushing, N.Y.
Zeus Industrial S.A.	Abadinado, Viscaya	Zeus	Zeus-USA, New York, N.Y.

SWEDEN

Monark Crescent AB	Varberg	Monark, Crescent	International Motorcycles Lancaster, Pa;
		MCB	Peden Equipment Houston, Tex.

SWITZERLAND

Alpa-Werke	Sirnach		
ETS Cycles Allegro	Neuchatel	Allegro	Ochsner & Ochsner
Jeker Haefeli Company	4710 Balsthal	Mondia	
Neue Tour de Suisse Rad	Kreuzlingen		

POLAND

Zaklady Rozerowe "Romet"	Warsaw	Romet

HUNGARY

Pannonia Cycle	Budapest	Pannonia
Konsumex	Budapest	

CZECHOSLOVAKIA

Eska	Cheb	Eska	Motokon Foreign
Favorit	Rokycany	Favorit	Trade Corp., Praha

INDIA

Sen-Raleigh	Calcutta, W. Bengal	
Atlas, Cycle Industries	Hariyana (Delhi)	Atlas
Everest, Cycles Ltd.	Assam, Ludhiana	Atlas
Hero Cycle Industries	Punjab	
T.I. Cycles of India	Madras	Raleigh
Matchless Industries	Calcutta	

TURKEY

Bisan	Istanbul	Bisan, Peugeot

JAPAN

Bridgestone Bicycle	Tokyo	Bridgestone, Kabuki	C. Itoh & Co., Bridgestone Div. New York, N.Y.
Marubeni Yamaguchi	Tokyo	Marubeni	Marubeni America Los Angeles, Cal.
Maruishi Bicycle Co.	Tokyo	Maruishi	Maruishi America Los Angeles, Cal.
Miyata Cycle	Chigasaki	Miyata	Toyoda-America Inc. Skokie, Ill.
Kawamura Cycle	Kobe	Nishiki, Azuki	West Coast Cycle Supply Carson, Cal.
Katakura Bicycle Co.	Fussa City, Tokyo	Katakura	Louisville Cycle, Louisville, Ky.
National Bicycle	Osaka	Panasonic	Panasonic Co., Secaucus, N.J.
Nissan Bicycle	Osaka		
Sekine	Tokyo		
Nichibei Fuji	Tokyo	Fuji	Toshoku-America, Fuji America Div. New York, N.Y. Toshuko Ltd. San Francisco, Cal.
Zebra Kenko Bicycle Co.	Bunkgo Ku, Tokyo	Soma	Soma Sports New York, N.Y.

TAIWAN

Ace International	Taipei
Jyochii	Taipei
Maruberi-Hodaka	Tainan
Taiwan Bicycle	Takao
Wulen	Taipei

UNITED KINGDOM (GREAT BRITAIN)

Raleigh Industries	Nottingham	Raleigh	Raleigh Industries of America Boston, Mass.
Carlton Cycle Company	Worksop	Carlton	Raleigh Industries of America Boston, Mass.
Dawes Cycles Ltd.	Tyseley, Birmingham	Dawes	Service Cycle Farmingdale, N.Y.
Holdsworthy Company Ltd.	London SE 20	Holdsworth	
Falcon Cycles	Barton on Humber	Falcon, Eddy Merckx	Omega Import Export Norfolk, Va.
Trusty Mfg. Company	North Birmingham	Viscount	Roger Young & Assoc. Chatsworth, Cal.
Jack Taylor	Stockton on Tees	Jack Taylor	
Bob Jackson	Leeds	Bob Jackson	Mel Pinto Falls Church, Va.
Condor Cycles	London	Condor	Park Cycles Ridgefield Park, N.J.
Speedwell Gear Case Co., Ltd.	Birmingham	Titan	CDI Industries, Dallas, Tex.
S.M. Woodrupp		Woodrupp }	Park Cycle Ridgefield Park, N.J.
Mercian Cycles Ltd.		Mercian }	
W.R. Pashley, Ltd.	Stratford on Avon	Pashley	

SOUTH AFRICA

Raleigh Cycles (S.A.), Ltd.	Nuffield Springs, Transvaal	Raleigh

AUSTRALIA

Guthrie Bicycles Pty. Ltd.	Brisbane	
Jack Walsh	Sydney	Walsh

NEW ZEALAND

Morrison Industries, Ltd.	Hastings

Index